OXFORD MONOGRAPH
INTERNATIONAL LA

General Editors

PROFESSOR VAUGHAN LOWE
*Chichele Professor of Public International Law in the University of Oxford and
Fellow of All Souls College, Oxford*

PROFESSOR DAN SAROOSHI
*Professor of Public International Law in the University of Oxford and
Fellow of The Queen's College, Oxford*

PROFESSOR STEFAN TALMON
*Professor of Public International Law in the University of Oxford and
Fellow of St. Anne's College, Oxford*

Extraterritorial Use of Force
Against Non-State Actors

feb. 2006
better than
RCATI copy (or Rahn '04)
for comparison.

OXFORD MONOGRAPHS IN INTERNATIONAL LAW

The aim of this series is to publish important and original pieces of research on all aspects of international law. Topics that are given particular prominence are those which, while of interest to the academic lawyer, also have important bearing on issues which touch the actual conduct of international relations. Nonetheless, the series is wide in scope and includes monographs on the history and philosophical foundations of international law.

Extraterritorial Use of Force Against Non-State Actors

NOAM LUBELL

Lecturer, Irish Centre for Human Rights, School of Law
National University of Ireland, Galway

OXFORD
UNIVERSITY PRESS

OXFORD

UNIVERSITY PRESS

Great Clarendon Street, Oxford OX2 6DP

Oxford University Press is a department of the University of Oxford.
It furthers the University's objective of excellence in research, scholarship,
and education by publishing worldwide in

Oxford New York

Auckland Cape Town Dar es Salaam Hong Kong Karachi
Kuala Lumpur Madrid Melbourne Mexico City Nairobi
New Delhi Shanghai Taipei Toronto

With offices in

Argentina Austria Brazil Chile Czech Republic France Greece
Guatemala Hungary Italy Japan Poland Portugal Singapore
South Korea Switzerland Thailand Turkey Ukraine Vietnam

Oxford is a registered trade mark of Oxford University Press
in the UK and in certain other countries

Published in the United States
by Oxford University Press Inc., New York

© Noam Lubell 2010

The moral rights of the author have been asserted

Crown copyright material is reproduced under Class Licence
Number C01P0000148 with the permission of OPSI
and the Queen's Printer for Scotland

Database right Oxford University Press (maker)

First published 2010
First published in paperback 2011

All rights reserved. No part of this publication may be reproduced,
stored in a retrieval system, or transmitted, in any form or by any means,
without the prior permission in writing of Oxford University Press,
or as expressly permitted by law, or under terms agreed with the appropriate
reprographics rights organization. Enquiries concerning reproduction
outside the scope of the above should be sent to the Rights Department,
Oxford University Press, at the address above

You must not circulate this book in any other binding or cover
and you must impose the same condition on any acquirer

British Library Cataloguing in Publication Data

Data available

Library of Congress Cataloging-in-Publication Data

Lubell, Noam.
Extraterritorial use of force against non-state actors / Noam Lubell.
p. cm.—(Oxford monographs in international law)
ISBN 978–0–19–958484–0
1. Non-state actors (International relations) 2. War (International law)
3. Terrorism—Prevention—Law and Legislation. I. Title.
KZ6405.N66L83 2010
341.6—dc22   2010010918

Typeset by Newgen Imaging Systems (P) Ltd., Chennai, India
Printed in Great Britain
on acid-free paper by
CPI Antony Rowe, Chippenham, Wiltshire

ISBN 978–0–19–958484–0
ISBN 978–0–19–964122–2(pbk.)

1 3 5 7 9 10 8 6 4 2

To my grandparents, Mimi, Sam, Rita, and Aubrey

General Editors' Preface

The regulation of the use of force by states is one of the most controversial and important areas of public international law. The general prohibition on the use of force by states contained in Article 2(4) of the United Nations Charter represents the culmination of efforts over a number of centuries to try and impose constraints on the right of monarchs and rulers to wage war. And yet since the adoption of the United Nations Charter this prohibition has often been the subject of serious breach. The content of this prohibition must evolve if it is to retain its relevance and normative force, and yet if the exceptions to this prohibition are interpreted too broadly then its continued existence becomes problematic.

Due to the nature of threats faced by states, a persistent feature of the use of force has seen states take military action against non-state actors who are not located in their territory, often in recent years as part of the 'war on terror'. Dr Lubell's study represents a serious and significant contribution to the modern debates on what are, and what should be, the limits on the extraterritorial use of force by states against non-state actors, and in so doing the work should be commended for making a contribution to the corpus of international law governing both *ius ad bellum* and *ius in bello*.

AVL
DS
ST

Preface

This book addresses a challenging, important, and surprisingly neglected area of international legal concern. Most writing in the field of the use of force by states focuses on the use of armed force by states against other states; or by parties to an armed conflict within individual states; or by the deployment of power by states against those within their jurisdiction. Increasingly, attention is also given to the depredations of transnational terrorism, that is, the activities of non-state actors operating across frontiers.

Very little attention is given to the use of force by states acting beyond their frontiers against non-state actors located in other jurisdictions, yet there are frequent instances of the problem. High profile examples from the last decade would be Israel's use of force against Hezbollah in South Lebanon, Colombia's attacks against FARC rebels in Ecuador, and American drones targeting suspected Al-Qaeda terrorists in Pakistan. In fact, examples from the early period of modern international law can be traced back at least to the 1837 *Caroline* incident, when the British fired on and sent over Niagara Falls an American-owned ship used by Canadians rebelling against (British rule in) Canada.

Indeed, this is the incident that gave international law the classic definition of the concept of self-defence. More recently self-defence was invoked by the United Nations Security Council and NATO as justifying a forcible response to the atrocities of 11 September 2001 perpetrated by Al-Qaeda on the United States. On the other hand, in the *Wall* case,[1] the International Court of Justice opined that self-defence could only be invoked by one state in respect of an attack by another state. The issue is the subject matter of a key chapter of the present book that looks at the *ius ad bellum* (the law regarding the legality of resort to armed force).

However, the bulk of this book deals with the law relevant, not to the 'whether' of the use of force, but to the 'how' of its deployment. In so far as we are dealing with the law applicable to armed conflict (*ius in bello*) the book examines the relevant rules of that body of law. This includes examination of the obligations of states vis-à-vis formal parties to an armed conflict, as well as with regard to civilians involved in the conflict, and the controversial notion of unlawful combatants. Whether the conflict is to be considered international or non-international is also studied.

The applicability of international human rights law is the other major focus of the book's concern. This also invokes the (contested) dimension of how far

---

[1] *Legal Consequences of the Construction of a Wall in the Occupied Palestinian Territory, Advisor Opinion* [2004] ICJ Rep 36.

human rights treaties can apply extraterritorially and how far international human rights law generally can be applicable in armed conflict. Throughout, we are guided as to whether and how the three examined legal frameworks may interact and influence each other.

This book is based on the author's dissertation for his University of Essex Ph.D. We had the pleasure of being his co-supervisors, one of those tasks that we were sorry to see come to an end. The trilateral discussions were thoroughly rewarding. The product, this book, is one in which we can only take vicarious responsibility. It is Noam Lubell's achievement and a worthy addition to the prestigious list of Oxford Monographs in International Law.

Professor Sir Nigel Rodley KBE
Professor Francoise Hampson OBE

School of Law
University of Essex
Wivenhoe Park
Colchester

Acknowledgements

Throughout all stages of working on this book, I have had the good fortune to be supported by numerous individuals and institutions to whom I am extremely grateful. Overall, including the doctoral study years and the adaptation into the current book, this project spanned over six years. As is common in work of this type, it occupied a central position in its author's life, both professionally and personally, and this list of acknowledgments reflects both the professional and personal gratitude to those who accompanied it.

The book began as a doctoral thesis undertaken at the University of Essex, UK, where my thesis supervisors were Professors Francoise Hampson and Sir Nigel Rodley. One could not wish for better supervisors. Their advice and comments were immensely important, and our joint discussions and debates throughout the years were something I always looked forward to, and for which I am grateful. During the past ten years before and after the thesis I have had occasion to study with them, collaborate in projects and joint teaching, and to continuously engage in a variety of settings. It has been a true privilege to have been granted access to two of the finest minds in the field. Each in their own way they have, and continue to be, a source of inspiration and a model to aspire towards. I am forever indebted to them, and am proud to have each of them as a mentor and friend.

While researching and writing, a number of institutions provided a warm home and occasionally employment. My thanks for this go to everyone at Essex University's Law Department and the Human Rights Centre, in particular to Anne Slowgrove; to The Harry S Truman Research Institute for the Advancement of Peace at the Hebrew University, Jerusalem, and Professor Eyal Ben-Ari; The School of Law at The College of Management Academic Studies, Israel, and Professor Frances Raday. I have also been kindly assisted by scholarships and grants for which I am extremely grateful, and wish to thank the following: The Law Department at Essex University; The Karten Scholarship through The Anglo-Jewish Association; Mrs Muriel Beck of the Ferdinand Beck Fund.

For over two years now I have been based at the Irish Centre for Human Rights, National University of Ireland, Galway. It is here that the doctoral thesis developed into the current book. It is the best working environment I could have wished for, and I am grateful to the Director Professor William Schabas, and all my past and present colleagues at the Centre: Nadia Bernaz, Kathleen Cavanaugh, Shane Darcy, Vinodh Jaichand, Ray Murphy, Louise Burke, Fiona Gardiner, Louise McDermott, and all the PhD and LLM students who form an integral part of this environment.

The development of the book was enabled through the generous support of the Millennium Research Fund at the National University of Ireland, Galway.

Eadaoin O'Brien provided valuable research assistance during the updating of the work.

In addition to Francoise Hampson and Nigel Rodley, a number of individuals read through the whole manuscript at different stages, and I am grateful to them for taking the time and providing constructive comments. The examiners of the doctoral thesis, Professors Geoff Gilbert and Judge Sir Christopher Greenwood; the anonymous reviewers at Oxford University Press; and the personal proof-reading assistance kindly provided by Jonathan Lubell. The process of bringing the book to publication could not have been smoother, and I am most grateful to all those at Oxford University Press who have been involved, including Merel Alstein, Ela Kotkowska, John Louth, Susan Rabel, and all others.

During the years of my research I have benefited at various stages from discussions with many people working on related issues. In the course of conversations, sharing panels at conferences, and other joint events, more people than can possibly be mentioned have provided food for thought. I am thankful to them all, even if on occasion they motivated me to disprove their opinions rather than agree. Special mention must be made of David Kretzmer, who gave me my first encouragement 15 years ago to enter the world of international human rights law, and has always been a person with whom I was glad to be able to engage.

Many friends and family throughout these years also deserve heartfelt thanks for the support they gave, accompanied by food, drink, and friendship to sustain the body and soul. They are, in no particular order: Shamma Boyarin, Shlomo Goldman, Maayan Blum, Ohev Shechter, Yael Stein, Oren Kakun, Sheila Varadan, Jamil Addou, Elizabeth Griffin, Clive Sinclair, Haidee Kenedy, Andrew Fagan, Judith Mesquita, Mandie Winston, Francoise Hampson, Caroline Cohen, Karen Kochan, Jeremy Swimer, Pierre Gentile, Matt Pollard, Jonathan Horowitz, Judith Posner, Stephanie Segal, and especially Lulu and Laurie Cohen for providing a true home away from home.

Finally, I wish to thank my immediate family, who also happen to be amongst my closest friends. Their love and friendship provides a constant source of support and has directly influenced the work process and, ultimately, the outcome. Although as the eldest I take great care to avoid showing it, I constantly learn from my remarkable siblings, Yoel and Ma'ayan. Any achievement, including this book, is owed to my parents, Pamela and Jonathan. It is customary in publications to thank others for assistance while retaining responsibility for any faults in the final product. My gratitude to my parents for all that turned out well while taking responsibility myself for the faults, extends far beyond the sole confines of this particular endeavour. Above all, I wish to thank my wife, Nancie. The work on this book proceeded thanks to her encouragement, advice and support. I am grateful every day anew to be working and living alongside someone who is such an incredible source of wisdom and inspiration.

Galway, January 2010

Table of Contents

PART III: INTERNATIONAL HUMAN RIGHTS LAW

application.

Table of Cases

List of Abbreviations

ACHR	American Convention on Human Rights
ADF	Allied Democratic Forces
ALC	Congo Liberation Army
AQAM	Al Qa'ida Associated Movement
AQN	Al Qa'ida Network
AU	African Union
CAT	Convention against Torture and Other Cruel, Inhuman or Degrading Treatment or Punishment
CIA	Central Intelligence Agency
DRC	Democratic Republic of the Congo
ECHR	European Convention on Human Rights
FBI	Federal Bureau of Investigation
FRY	Federal Republic of Yugoslavia
GWOT	Global War on Terror
ICCPR	International Covenant on Civil and Political Rights
ICJ	International Court of Justice
ICRC	International Committee of the Red Cross
ICTY	International Criminal Tribunal for the former Yugoslavia
IHL	International Humanitarian Law
IRA	Irish Republican Army
KLA	Kosovo Liberation Army
LRA	Lord's Resistance Army
MLC	Congo Liberation Movement
NATO	North Atlantic Treaty Organization
PKK	Kurdistan Workers' Party
PLO	Palestine Liberation Organization
POW	Prisoner of War
TRNC	Turkish Republic of Northern Cyprus
UDHR	Universal Declaration of Human Rights
UN	United Nations
WMD	Weapons of Mass Destruction

INTRODUCTION

Introduction

1. Background

Recent times have provided numerous cases of states using force against individuals and groups outside their territory. The United States has carried out airstrikes targeting and killing individuals in Pakistan and Somalia;[1] European states have engaged in force against pirates in the Horn of Africa;[2] Colombia bombed a guerrilla rebel base in Ecuador;[3] and Turkey was engaged in heavy military operations against Kurdish fighters in Iraq.[4] Extraterritorial use of force against non-state actors is clearly not a rare phenomenon. In fact, it is not even new. The oft-cited *Caroline Case* from 1837,[5] involved the British taking forcible measures against Canadian rebels in US territory. Extraterritorial forcible action has taken many forms, ranging from killings to kidnapping, and large-scale military operations. Certain states seem to have had more frequent involvement in actions of this kind, whether as a result of policy or of geo-political circumstance. In 1916, the United States sent troops into Mexico following an attack in the US by Francisco Villa and his men, whom the Mexican government were apparently unable to control,[6] while in more recent times the US has used an unmanned aircraft to target and kill alleged Al-Qaeda members driving through the desert of Yemen, as well as targeted strikes in Pakistan and Somalia.[7] Israel has sent agents into other countries to kidnap individuals, including Nazi leader Adolph Eichmann, abducted from Argentina in 1960,[8] and Israeli citizen Mordechai Vanunu, who was accused of publicizing secret information on Israel's nuclear capability and was abducted from Rome in 1986.[9] The Israeli military was

---

[1] 'Uzbek rebel "killed" in Pakistan' *BBC News*, 2 October 2009; ' "Drone attack" kills Taliban wife' *BBC News*, 5 August 2009; 'US bombs Islamist town in Somalia' *BBC News*, 3 March 2008.

[2] S Otterman and M Mcdonald, '11 Pirates Seized by French Navy' *New York Times*, 15 April 2009.

[3] 'Farc aura of invincibility shattered' *BBC News*, 1 March 2008.

[4] 'Turkish Incursions into Northern Iraq' *Reuters*, 22 February 2008.

[5] R Jennings, 'The Caroline and McLeod Cases' 32 *AJIL* 82 (1938).

[6] J Scott, 'The American Punitive Expedition into Mexico' 10 *AJIL* 337 (1916); G Finch, 'Mexico and the United States' 11 *AJIL* 399 (1917).

[7] W Pincus, 'U.S. Strike Kills Six in Al Qaeda' *Washington Post*, 5 November 2002; F Bokhari, 'Pakistan tries to ease tension after US attack' *Financial Times*, 16 January 2006; n 1, *supra*.

[8] Resolution Adopted by the Security Council at its 868th Meeting on 23 June 1960 (On Questions Relating to the Case of Adolf Eichmann), UN Doc S/4349.

[9] Y Melman, 'Capturing nuclear whistle-blower was "a lucky stroke" agents recall' *Haaretz*, 21 April 2004.

deployed extraterritorially in 1976 to rescue hostages from a hijacked airplane in a Ugandan airport.[10] In late 2003 Israeli aircraft struck at alleged non-state actor militant camps in Syrian territory,[11] and in the summer of 2006, Israel was engaged in an armed conflict with Hezbollah in Lebanon.[12]

In 1999 Turkish security forces arrested Kurdistan Workers' Party ('PKK') leader Ocalan in Kenya and transferred him to Turkey.[13] North Korea has been accused of using force against individuals abroad in circumstances as bizarre as the abduction of a South Korean film director and actress in order to make films for the North Korean leader.[14] There have been numerous incidents involving the Democratic Republic of Congo ('DRC') and many of its bordering countries which sent state forces to conduct cross-border operations against (both state and) non-state actors.[15] Uruguayan agents were involved in the abduction of a Uruguayan trade union leader residing in Argentina.[16] All these are but a sample of cases in which states have taken extraterritorial forcible actions against non-state actors.

The issue of these types of operations has gained increased significance ever since 11 September 2001. Following the attacks on that day, the US and other states have described many of their actions as part of a new 'war on terror', linking this to everything from full-scale armed conflict in Afghanistan, to the targeted killings mentioned above.[17] The non-state actors against whom the measures are taken are not only the familiar local rebel groups operating on a sub-national level, but also transnational groups, with members, support and an agenda that go beyond any national border. The huge advances of recent decades, particularly in communications technology, financial transfers, access to weapons and travel, have facilitated the ease with which groups and individuals can plan and conduct their actions. These advances, as well as the disarray and even complete break-down of political and government structures such as the former Soviet Union, the former Yugoslavia, Somalia and Afghanistan, have provided a fertile breeding ground in which individuals and groups with criminal and/or political agendas can develop, train and gain possession of weaponry and other capabilities to further their aims.

Many extraterritorial forcible measures against non-state actors are nowadays referred to as part of a 'war on terror'.[18] Not only does terrorism itself have no

---

[10] Security Council Official Records, 31st Year, 1939th Meeting, 9 July 1976, New York, UN Doc S/PV.1939 (1976).

[11] Statement by Ambassador Dan Gillerman, Permanent Representative, Emergency Session, Security Council, New York, 5 October 2003.

[12] See discussion in the Concluding Chapter, *infra*.

[13] *Öcalan v. Turkey*, App no 46221/99, 12 May 2005.

[14] 'Kidnapped by North Korea' *BBC News*, 5 March 2003.

[15] See discussion of Rwanda, Burundi, and Uganda, amongst others, in 'Scramble for the Congo: Anatomy of an Ugly War' Africa Report no 26, International Crisis Group, 20 December 2000.

[16] *Delia Saldias de Lopez v. Uruguay*, Comm no 52/1979, UN Doc CCPR/C/OP/1 (1984).

[17] See Ch 5, *infra*, on non-traditional models of conflict.

[18] See Ch 5, *infra*, on non-traditional models of conflict.

unanimously agreed definition,[19] but this 'war' is the subject of much controversy, not just with regard to actions taking place under its headings, but also as
to whether such a 'war' exists and, if it does, then what is its legal and practical
meaning.[20] Consequently, using the context of terrorism as a frame of reference
for the current analysis is perhaps not a useful approach, since it builds on unsta-
ble foundations. Individuals, groups, their own actions and the actions taken
against them, could fall within and outside the scope of such a study, depending on differing definitions of terrorism and a 'war on terror', thus allowing for
easy manipulation of the conclusions.[21] Instead, the approach taken here is based
not on the rhetoric of terrorism, but on the factual and visible phenomenon of
extraterritorial use of force against non-state actors. While this is likely to cover
many extraterritorial operations taken under the heading of counter-terrorism,
the question of whether states or commentators agree upon its name is then
not the crucial question. Nevertheless, terrorism and the 'war on terror' remain
relevant in certain aspects, as will be evident in the section on the relationship
between the non-state actor and the territorial state, and especially in the chapter
on non-traditional models of conflict, in which the possibility of a 'war on terror'
as armed conflict will be examined. In general however, the discussion of extraterritorial forcible measures against non-state actors casts a more definable net
than extraterritorial counter-terrorism, and includes most of the latter within it,
as well as other situations (such as the abductions of Eichmann and Vanunu).

As noted above, states have not been shy in the past of using extraterritorial
force against non-state actors and, perhaps even with added vigour, are continuing to do so today. Whatever objections may be raised, it is unlikely that actions
of this kind will completely cease in the near future. The framework for addressing these actions is, however, not always clear. Force against non-state actors is
sometimes justified by the acting state as being a matter of straightforward self
defence.[22] In other types of extraterritorial forcible measures, self-defence might
not be mentioned, and on occasion the state allegedly responsible will not admit
its involvement in the incident.[23] Can extraterritorial forcible measures against
non-state actors be considered legitimate self-defence under international law?
Are those measures that do not conform to the parameters of self-defence necessarily unlawful, or could there be other legal justifications for them? And when
these operations do take place, where are the rules to be found against which
the manner of the use of force can be assessed—is it the laws of armed conflict
or of law enforcement or both? These are some of the questions to be examined. The analysis here was carried out in the period from 2003 to 2007, and

---

[19] See n 65, *infra*, and accompanying text.
[20] See Ch 5, *infra*, on non-traditional models of conflict.
[21] Similar reasoning underpins other examinations. eg, see H Duffy, *The 'War on Terror' and the Framework of International Law* (CUP: Cambridge, 2005) 46.
[22] See Ch 1, *infra*, on self-defence against non-state actors.
[23] *Issa and ors v. Turkey*, App no 31821/96, 16 November 2004.

the arguments and conclusions have remained unaffected since. Nonetheless, a number of sources since 2008 have been referred to as necessary during the subsequent adaption, though there are endless further pertinent sources from this period as well as new ones being produced every minute, many of which could not be mentioned here.

2. The legal frameworks

There are three primary areas of international law that are directly relevant to answering these questions: The UN Charter and framework of international law regulating the resort to force in the territory of other states;[24] the law of armed conflict, often referred to as international humanitarian law ('IHL');[25] and the law enforcement framework found in international human rights law.[26] Whilst it is possible to take one of these frameworks in isolation, and for instance look at the applicability of international humanitarian law to the 'war on terror', such an approach risks missing the bigger picture, and only providing a partial answer to the legality of the operations under examination. The starting point is, therefore, a set of factual circumstances as encompassed in the notion of extraterritorial forcible measures against non-state actors, and sets out to examine all the primary potentially applicable laws and how these might assist in the determination of lawfulness of these operations. Not all three frameworks will always be applicable, and indeed in some cases the greatest difficulty revolves around the debate over the applicability of a particular set of laws and the question of which rules and principles should regulate the action (eg, is the situation an armed conflict to which the rules of armed conflict apply?).[27] This only heightens the need to cover all three frameworks in the same place, so as to strengthen the chance that if appropriate rules are not found in one set of laws, then a solution might be found in another.

Navigating between the different frameworks is, however, not a simple matter, and the relationships between them are anything but clear. The international law system consists of many different branches, and the risk of fragmentation is well recognized.[28] The debates are often concerned with the search for a solution when faced with different—even conflicting—rules stemming from two branches of

---

[24] See Part I, *infra*.

[25] See Part II, *infra*. While the 'law of armed conflict' may be a more accurate term insofar as it provides a better literal description of the framework, 'international humanitarian law' has become the term more commonly used in writings and by international bodies, and will therefore be the term employed in this work.

[26] See Part III, *infra*.

[27] See the discussion of the Yemen incident in the Concluding Chapter, *infra*.

[28] 'Fragmentation of International Law: Difficulties Arising from the Diversification and Expansion of International Law', Report of the Study Group of the International Law Commission, finalized by Martti Koskenniemi, UN Doc A/CN.4/L.682, 13 April 2006.

international law which could both apply simultaneously to the situation at hand. In the context of our current scope this type of question is most apparent in the relationship between international humanitarian law and international human rights law. The obvious example is that of a case of armed conflict during which a combatant deliberately takes aim and fires across a valley at an opposing combatant, despite the latter not having presented an immediate threat at that point (indeed, perhaps not even holding a weapon). Under international humanitarian law this would generally be considered a lawful—and indeed common—act of war.[29] Under international human rights law, however, intentionally taking the life of an individual who does not at that moment pose a direct serious threat would not accord with the obligation to use lethal force only as the very last option. This and other similar circumstances are addressed in the context of the debates on parallel applicability of the two branches of law. The solutions on offer revolve around principles such as *lex specialis* and the concept of complementarity. These can be mechanisms for resolving apparent clashes between competing rules by asserting the primacy of one rule over another. Alternatively, they can serve to highlight the potential of either reinforcing each other; serving as interpretative guidelines for each other; or filling in gaps that might appear when using just one of the rules. While the precise methods for implementing the theories of parallel applicability are still in the process of clarification, it does appear that the issue is receiving significant attention.[30]

The obstacles to safe navigation between the frameworks do not, however, end with the problems of parallel applicability. Significant challenges can arise from situations in which the different frameworks initially appear to operate in isolation of each other. Indeed, in theory, certain separations are meant to exist between the frameworks, in particular between the rules on the resort to force and the rules regulating the use of force. In the context of armed conflict, this is known as the distinction between the *ius ad bellum*—the laws regulating the resort to armed force and issues such as self-defence, and the *ius in bello*—the laws regulating the conduct of the parties to an armed conflict. This means that whether or not the resort to force had support in law, once force is in fact being used, there is a need to turn to the laws regulating its conduct regardless of the decision as to the legality of the operation. There are a number of solid reasons for maintaining this separation between the frameworks. The *ius in bello*, at least in the context of international armed conflict, is predicated upon an equality of belligerents and the accompanying expectation of reciprocity. Thus, for example, opposing parties to the conflict are obliged to adhere to rules on treatment of prisoners of war, and expect that their own combatants taken captive by the other party will receive the same protection. Were the rules to apply differently to the

---

[29] See section 1.1 of Ch 6, *infra*, on combatants.
[30] For further examination of the parallel applicability of international humanitarian law and international human rights law see Ch 9, *infra*.

two parties as a result of one side's unlawful action under the *ius ad bellum*, this equality and reciprocity would be undermined. Were a state to receive reduced protections and benefits of the *ius in bello* due to its initial violation of the *ius ad bellum*, there is a danger of it seeing no advantage to adhering to the laws on conduct, and consequently acting outside the law altogether. Furthermore, the idea that the way in which the *ius in bello* is to be applied might depend on the actions of the parties under the *ius ad bellum* will, in many cases, be unworkable. Any party to a conflict is likely to claim that it is the opposing state that has violated the *ius ad bellum*, and the determination of legality on the resort to force is notoriously fraught with both legal debates and political minefields.[31]

Notwithstanding the above, this separation is not necessarily always maintainable. In particular, it may be the case that even after an armed conflict has begun and the *ius in bello* has become applicable, the *ius ad bellum* may continue to be relevant. An example of this would be the expansion of the conflict to a new geographical area, which would give rise to a claim that this violates the principle of proportionality as encompassed in the *ius ad bellum* rules of self-defence.[32] Indeed, the proportionality of self-defence under the *ius ad bellum* is measured in part by the scale of the operations undertaken by the defending state, and whether this is proportionate to its legitimate need to defend itself. In most circumstances this assessment will inevitably be possible only once these military operations have started and the scale is apparent. Consequently, the *ius ad bellum* assessment will be taking place at a time in which military operations—to which the *ius in bello* applies—have already begun. This is, however, a very narrow opening in the separating wall, which allows for the *ius ad bellum* rules to remain relevant after the conflict started. It does not, therefore, stand in contradiction to the earlier stated concept of separation, according to which the application of the *ius in bello* remains unaffected by the outcome of the *ius ad bellum* determination.

The relationship between these frameworks does not apply in the same manner outside of the arena of classic international armed conflicts. In non-international armed conflicts taking place within the territory of a state, the *ius ad bellum* framework loses its relevance. Whilst there are international laws which can potentially curb and regulate internal use of force—eg international human rights law and the laws of non-international armed conflict—the nature of statehood implies a certain authority to use force within the state's own territory. The *ius ad bellum* framework is designed to restrict the use of force between states, rather than any

---

[31] Indeed, this has been apparent in the debates over defining the crime of aggression in the statute of the International Criminal Court. There is, however, a chance for progress in the coming year. See *Press Conference on Special Working Group on Crime of Aggression*, UN Department of Public Information, News and Media Division, New York, 13 February 2009; Report of the Special Working Group on the Crime of Aggression, UN Doc ICC-ASP/ 7/20/ Add.1.

[32] See Ch 2, n 129, *infra*, and accompanying text.

internal exercise of force. Were this examination, therefore focusing on internal situations, the primary frameworks of relevance would therefore be just two out of the three, international human rights law and international humanitarian law (the *ius in bello*) applicable in non-international conflicts. However, our scope addresses a different set of circumstances, one which is neither covered by the inter-state model of international armed conflict, nor by the notion of internal conflicts. As will be seen in Part II, in those cases where the extraterritorial force against non-state actors is said to rise above the threshold of armed conflict, there is a strong argument to be made that the applicable rules of international humanitarian law should be those designed for non-international armed conflict, since the force is between a state and a non-state actor, and not an international conflict between opposing states.[33] At the same time, unless the forcible measures are taking place on the high seas (eg against pirates) we are nevertheless faced with cases in which one state is using force on the territory of another state. Consequently, as will be explored in the next three chapters, the rules of the *ius ad bellum* are of crucial concern and do indeed serve to assess the legality of the resort to force. Accordingly, we are faced with situations in which the *ius ad bellum* might be applicable to the resort to force, whilst the actual regulation of the force would be in the context of the rules on non-international conflict. This might, prima facie, appear to contradict the earlier assertion that the *ius ad bellum* is relevant to international armed conflict rather than non-international conflict. However, the key to untangling this knot is in the understanding that there are two simultaneous relationships occurring. This can be seen in the distinction between the inter-state sphere, as opposed to the regulation of force against the non-state actor. In other words, when state A resorts to force against an individual or group located in state B, there is both a question of whether state A has violated the sovereignty of state B (or acted in any unlawful manner insofar as the inter-state relationship is concerned) and the separate question of the rules regulating the actual use of force against the non-state actor, be they human rights law, IHL (or both). The latter question will necessitate a determination of the existence of an armed conflict based on the accepted threshold tests, which are based on identifying the parties and the nature of the violence, rather than on questions of the *ius ad bellum*.[34] Here too, therefore, there is an element of separation between the legal frameworks.

An added complexity to this type of situation occurs when a single forcible operation against the non-state actor might be considered to involve a level of violence below the threshold for non-international armed conflict, but is argued to be part of a wider ongoing armed conflict occurring in other territories. There are two stages to approaching this argument. First, there is the question of whether this operation can indeed be considered part of a wider conflict. This is primarily dependant on factual assessments of matters such as the connections between

---

[33] See detailed arguments in Ch 4, *infra*.
[34] See section on threshold and identifying the parties in Ch 4, *infra*.

the targeted non-state actor and the other operations said to be part of this conflict. As will be seen in the case of the 'war on terror', the reality is often far from the rhetoric and in many cases claiming the existence of a single armed conflict encompassing many distanced operations has little support in the facts.[35] Secondly, if, nonetheless, this incident might be part of an existing conflict, and therefore one to which the *ius in bello* is applicable, the *ius ad bellum* will still be of relevance in cases where this operation is taking place in the territory of a new state. In such a case, the rules of the *ius ad bellum* would serve to assess the legality of the resort to a forcible operation on the soil of another state, and would be the primary framework for the inter-state relationship. The *ius in bello* laws, on the other hand, would serve as a source of rules for regulating the actual use of force against the non-state actor.[36]

Assessing the actual use of force against the non-state actor will also give rise to the question of applicability of international human rights law and how this legal framework relates to the other frameworks. The relationship between human rights law and international humanitarian law has already been mentioned earlier and will be further explored in a later chapter. However, the connection between international human rights law and the *ius ad bellum* is a relationship which has received comparatively less attention than the issues dealt with above.[37] At first glance, there would appear to be little connection. Whether the resort to a forcible operation on the territory of another state has amounted to a violation of the *ius ad bellum* is a matter that belongs to the sphere of the inter-state relationship, and would need to be examined in the context of that set of rules. The human rights framework would, conversely, belong to the sphere of the state-individual, and would provide rules to assist in examining the way in which the state acted towards the individual.[38] There is, however, at least one point in which the two sets of rules could cross paths. The assessment of whether a violation of human rights has occurred will in many cases take into account the obligation that the state will have acted in accordance with the law.[39] This could be seen, for example, when a state sends its agents into another state—with no approval by the latter—in order to forcibly detain an individual and return him/her to stand trial, as in the *Eichmann* abduction case.[40] In this situation there are a number of

[35] See discussion in Ch 5, *infra*.

[36] See discussion in context of Afghanistan, Pakistan and Yemen, in Concluding Chapter, *infra*.

[37] One example in recent years can be found in questioning the link between a human right to peace and the *ius ad bellum*. See W Schabas, 'Lex specialis? Belt and suspenders? The Parallel Operation of Human Rights Law and the Law of Armed Conflict, and the Conundrum of Jus ad Bellum', 40 *Israel Law Review* 592 (2007).

[38] There would of course be a preliminary question of whether international human rights obligations can apply to actions taken extraterritorially. This is dealt with in depth in Chs 7 and 8, *infra*.

[39] Eg, 'No one shall be deprived of his liberty except on such grounds and in accordance with such procedure as are established by law', International Covenant on Civil and Political Rights (16 December 1966) 999 UNTS 3, entered into force 23 March 1976, Article 9.

[40] See n 8, *supra*.

different human rights concerns including how this impacts upon the subsequent trial, and possible ill-treatment in the process of abduction. However, there is also a question of whether the inter-state aspect permeates the human rights sphere and the state-individual relationship. If the action is deemed unlawful with respect to the inter-state sphere, in that the forcible operation on foreign territory does not accord with the appropriate rules of international law, then it could be argued that, regardless of other human rights aspects, this illegality means that the operation as a whole was not in accordance with the law, as required by the human rights obligations. Conversely, if one were to maintain the separation between the two frameworks of law, it could be argued that adherence to the law required by the human rights obligations refers to domestic matters such as issuing an arrest warrant, and not to international rules on use of force and state sovereignty. This potential link between the laws and how it might impact upon determination of human rights violations will be returned to in the chapters on international human rights law.

3. Structure

As can be seen by the examples cited at the start of this section, the scope of operations covered is wider than the struggle between the US and its allies against those referred to under the name of Al-Qaeda. Taking forcible measures against non-state actors located outside the state's borders can include a wide array of situations. There will therefore be an analysis and clarification of how to assess whether the use of force was lawful, and how to identify the applicable legal framework and rules according to which they are to be assessed and, hopefully, regulated. Following this introductory section explaining the rationale and scope of the work, there will be three main parts, each comprised of three chapters, containing an examination of the legal frameworks and applicable rules.

Part I focuses upon the inter-state aspects, and on the questions surrounding the legality of resorting to force against a non-state actor located in the territory of another state. The chapters in Part I will look at the notion of self-defence against non-state actors and how this fits within the traditional inter-state rules governing resort to force; the parameters of self-defence against non-state actors; and the possibility of resort to extraterritorial force outside the framework of self-defence.

Part II deals with the framework of international humanitarian law and how this branch of law addresses issues related to extraterritorial forcible measures against non-state actors. The traditional models of armed conflict will be introduced in the first chapter of Part II, together with the possibility of these being applicable to extraterritorial use of force against non-state actors. The next chapter in this part will address the debates surrounding the 'war on terror' as an armed conflict, and the claims that this is a new model of conflict which demands new

legitimate targets

rules. The final chapter will address the primary relevant rules of IHL relating to status of individuals and members of armed groups, and some of the rules relating to use of force against them, if the circumstances are defined as armed conflict, highlighting problems that arise in the context of hostilities involving non-state actors.

Part III covers the framework of international human rights law. The first chapter in this part will address some of the primarily affected rights in the context of operations involving killings and abductions; the second chapter will provide an extensive examination of the possibility of international human rights law being applicable to extraterritorial operations. Additionally, should the operations be occurring in the context of armed conflict, the final chapter of this part will present the issue of parallel applicability of human rights law and IHL.

The concluding chapter of this work will provide a brief recapitulation of the main issues raised throughout the preceding chapters, and draw them together by demonstrating their applicability and interaction in the context of specific cases.

This examination of the applicable laws will inevitably bring up some of the most contentious areas in each of the legal frameworks, including the question of self-defence against non-state actors;[41] attacks against civilians directly participating in hostilities;[42] and extraterritorial applicability of human rights law.[43] Some of these areas are themselves at the heart of this analysis, and as such will receive extensive attention. Other matters are directly relevant, but the debate surrounding them goes far beyond the scope here, and it would be impossible to cover them all in the manner of works devoted to each issue alone. Perhaps the most challenging task here is the need to address such a wide variety of legal issues across a number of legal fields, encountering numerous legal controversies along the way, in the knowledge that one single work cannot provide all the answers to all these long-standing debates. In that respect, in some controversial areas, such as the right of self-defence against non-state actors, the classification of certain complex types of conflicts, and extraterritorial applicability of human rights obligations, specific positions and approaches to the law are advocated; other issues, such as the status of members of armed groups in non-international conflicts and the modalities of parallel application of human rights law and international humanitarian law, are all analysed but not always with definitive solutions. The decision to nonetheless proceed with a project encompassing all these areas was based on the need to address factual circumstances in a manner that includes all the primary aspects of international law which must be engaged when assessing the situations at hand. Without such an approach, the types of operations and conflicts covered would be examined each time from a different angle and in the context of specific legal rules, but with a risk of missing the larger

---

[41] See Ch 1, *infra*, on self-defence.   [42] See Ch 6, *infra*, on individual status.
[43] See Ch 8, *infra*, on extraterritorial applicability.

picture and the way these different approaches may impact upon each other. On all matters raised, therefore, the focus here will be to provide a clear overview of the terrain in which the debate takes place; the fundamental issues at hand; and to see how the different interpretations and positions in the debates can affect the question of extraterritorial force against non-state actors. Along the way, certain positions and views will be favoured, and this will be explained but, recognizing that in many of these areas there are ongoing controversies, opposing opinions and potential alternative approaches will also be presented. Many of these are clearly contentious issues, especially when referring to matters surrounding the question of a 'war on terror'. Anyone familiar with some of the debates covered is likely to recognize that certain views advocated might be seen as supporting one side of a debate, while the position preferred in other matters would be more in line with the opposing side. There will be an engagement in an objective analysis of the legal frameworks and applicable rules.

A number of the issues analysed also raise questions about the adequacy of the law in certain areas, and the claim of a need for development. These will be examined, and in some of the cases these calls might be supported by opinions raised. Overall however, this is neither a call for new laws, nor a proposal for changes; rather, it is an examination of the issues at hand in light of existing international law, and of how international law as it stands can assist in regulating the matters under discussion. Insofar as any legal inadequacies might be unearthed by the foray into these issues, elaborate proposals for development and possible changes will have to be the subject of a separate work. Moreover, while in some cases past developments are relevant this is not an historical exposé on the development of rules on the use of force. It is international law as it currently stands which is the foundation of this analysis.

4. Definitions

The use of language is crucial to understanding the debate, and many controversies exist regarding the terms and definitions used in connection with this issue. There is a constant danger of getting caught up in the rhetoric. It is therefore impossible to continue without a brief excursion into the realm of semantics. Additionally, explaining the terms of reference used will set out the scope of the issues to be covered within this work.

4.1 Extraterritorial

The actions scrutinized will be those taking place outside the recognized borders of the state. Situations in which a state exercises effective control of a territory that is not its own, such as an occupied territory, will not be examined. While much of the analysis with regard to extraterritoriality is directly relevant to occupied territories, and occupation situations will be mentioned in certain contexts, the exercise of effective control can create fundamental practical and legal differences.[44] The examples mentioned above took place outside both the borders and effective control of territory by the state, and it is these types of cases which will be focused upon. While these measures could also be taking place in neutral areas such as on the high seas, as can be seen in the case of force against pirates,[45] a presumption is made that the vast majority of extraterritorial forcible measures occur in the territory of another state.[46] Throughout, the state taking the extraterritorial measures will be referred to as the 'outside state' and the state on whose territory such measures are taking place will be the 'territorial state'.

4.2 Forcible measures

The focus here is on measures involving the use of force by the outside state. Extradition requests (which may also lead to use of force by the territorial state), financial steps (such as freezing of assets), and other non-forcible measures are not included. Forcible measures can range from full-scale military operations to undercover agents sent to kill an individual or to capture by force an individual (in many cases amounting to what appear to be forced abductions intended to remove the individual from his/her current location and place them in detention elsewhere). Furthermore, while the possibility of consent by the territorial state might on occasion be mentioned in a specific context, the focus is on forcible measures taken without the consent of the territorial state. Finally, the analysis is of unilateral state action, and not of UN sanctioned or multi-national peace support operations.[47]

4.3 Non-state actors

Individuals or groups who are not acting on behalf of a state, are non-state actors. The key to the distinction made here is that the non-state actor is not acting under control and on behalf of a state, and is not a part (*de facto* or *de jure*) of any state

---

[44] In particular, the existence of occupation impacts upon the potential of full applicability of human rights obligations, as will be mentioned in Ch 8, *infra*, on extraterritorial applicability.

[45] See discussion of piracy in section 4 of Ch 3, *infra*; Ch 4, nn 122–7 and accompanying text, *infra*; Ch 8, nn 153–162 and accompanying text, *infra*; see also *United States v. Yunis* 924 F. 2d 1086 (DC Cir 1991); *Alejandre Jr and ors v. Republica de Cuba ('Brothers to the Rescue')*, Case 11.589, Report no 86/99, OEA/Ser.L/V/II.106 Doc. 3 rev at 586 (1999) (in international airspace).

[46] Although, as will be seen, there may be cases which involve the use of force in international air space or the high seas.

[47] For an example of problems raised in such circumstances, see *Behrami and Behrami v. France*, App no 71412/01 and *Saramati v. France, Germany and Norway*, Decision on Admissibility, App no 78166/01, 2 May 2007.

apparatus, thus maintaining an identity and existence independent of the state. It is, however, recognized that in many cases there may be links between the non-state actor and a state, including the sharing of ideology or receipt of forms of support. However, unless the non-state actor is under the control of a state, or its actions can be attributed to a state,[48] then for the purposes of the issues raised it will be considered to be a non-state actor.

While in many cases the individuals might belong to groups controversially branded as terrorists, other types of groups might also be subjected to these measures, for instance extraterritorial forcible measures have been contemplated by the US in dealing with groups involved in the supply and trafficking of narcotics.[49] It should also be noted that individual persons can be at the receiving end of extraterritorial forcible measures not on account of the activities of any group to which they might belong, as in the case of Mordechai Vanunu's abduction in Rome by Israeli agents and subsequent transportation to Israel to stand trial for revealing secret information on Israel's nuclear capabilities.[50]

The non-state actor may be one which operates within the state as well as extraterritorially; one which is based only in a neighbouring state; or a transnational group not limited to one state. The deciding factor for inclusion within the current scope, is not the geographical nature of the non-state actor (which is not always easily defined), but the nature of the operations taken against it—the focus is on operations that take place outside the state's borders.

The role of non-state actors in the international legal system is a subject of continuing and growing discussion. It encompasses numerous areas of international law and presents considerable challenges therein. Some of these challenges will be

---

[48] For an elaboration of the standards and tests for determining whether individuals and groups are state agents, and whether their actions can be attributed to the state, see 'Draft Articles on Responsibility of States for Internationally Wrongful Acts', International Law Commission, 53rd session (2001) arts 4–11 (extract from 'Report of the International Law Commission on the Work of its Fifty-third Session', Official Records of the General Assembly, 56th session, Supp no 10 (A/56/10), chap IV.E.1, November 2001); 'Commentaries to the Draft Articles on Responsibility of States for Internationally Wrongful Acts', International Law Commission, 53rd session, 2001 (extract from the 'Report of the International Law Commission on the Work of its Fifty-third Session', Official Records of the General Assembly, 56th session, Supp no 10 (A/56/10), chap IV.E.2, November 2001, pp 80–122); *Case Concerning Military and Paramilitary Activities in and Against Nicaragua*, [1986] ICJ Rep 14, paras 93–116; *Prosecutor v. Dusko Tadic*, Case no IT-94-1-A, ICTY App Ch, 15 July 1999, paras 146–62; *Application of the Convention on the Prevention and Punishment of the Crime of Genocide, Bosnia and Herzegovina v. Serbia*, Judgment on Merits, General List No 91; ICGJ 70 (ICJ 2007) 26 February 2007, paras 379–415. There may also be links in the form of post-facto endorsement, see *Case Concerning United States Diplomatic and Consular Staff in Tehran (US v. Iran)*, 1980 ICJ Rep 3.

[49] M Healy, 'Navy May Send Ships to Fight Colombia Drugs' *LA Times*, 23 November 1989; see also abductions of Alvarez-Machain and others in relation to a Drug Enforcement Administration ('DEA') incident following the murder of a DEA agent. See discussion in A Abramovsky, 'Extraterritorial Abductions: America's "Catch And Snatch" Policy Run Amok' 31 *Virginia Journal of International Law* 151 (1991).

[50] See n 9, *supra*.

dealt with in this work and, as will be apparent from the first chapter, are in fact at the heart of certain questions under examination.

Significant concern is raised by the considerable effect non-state actors have over the enjoyment of human rights by individuals all over the world.[51] This control is evident in many shapes and forms including the practice of multi-national corporations; rebel groups during armed conflict; the policies of international financial bodies; domestic violence; private education institutions; privatization of penal and security functions; and more. In this respect, the primary concern and subsequent area of debate is the need to ensure that with power comes responsibility, and that the private actors behave in such a way so as not to impede human rights. Within this, there are questions over whether it is best achieved by directly imposing human rights obligations and accountability on the non-state actors themselves, or by ensuring effective mechanisms by which states will have oversight and accountability for the conduct of non-state actors. The traditional approach within human rights law indicates a preference for the latter. This is based on the language of human rights treaties, and the fact that international human rights law was initially developed to regulate—and restrict where necessary—the power that states have over the rights of individuals. This debate over the human rights obligations of non-state actors demonstrates the concern over the ability of international law to contend with the rising prominence of non-state actors in the domestic and international spheres. However, these particular questions are not the ones of greatest concern in the context of the scope of this work. The present focus is not on the actions *of* the non-state actor but rather on the regulation and applicable rules to the actions of states in their conduct *against* non-state actors. Moreover, although the questions surrounding the human rights obligations of non-state actors may not have been firmly settled, it is clear there are ongoing debates and attempts to find solutions, and that possible avenues to resolving the issues are being put forward.[52] In other areas which are of direct relevance, and will receive detailed attention in the following chapters, there is however greater ambiguity and less apparent solutions are on offer.

The greatest challenge to emerge in the context of extraterritorial force against non-state actors is in the area of the rules of the *ius ad bellum*. The laws on the resort to armed force outside of states' own borders are premised—at least at first sight—on the notion that such actions are taken by states and against states. Even when non-state actors enter the debate, this usually occurs in the context

---

[51] In general, see A Clapham, *Human Rights Obligations of Non-State Actors* (OUP: Oxford, 2006); see also Report of the Special Representative of the Secretary-General on the Issue of Human Rights and Transnational Corporations and other Business Enterprises, Addendum, Corporations and Human Rights: a Survey of the Scope and Patterns of Alleged Corporate-Related Human Rights Abuse, UN Doc A/HRC/8/5/Add.2, 23 May 2008.

[52] See, eg Clapham, *ibid*, and 'Protect, Respect and Remedy: a Framework for Business and Human Rights, Report of the Special Representative of the Secretary-General on the issue of Human Rights and Transnational Corporations and other Business Enterprises, John Ruggie', UN Doc A/HRC/8/5, 7 April 2008.

of resolving disputes between states, and discussion revolves around state responsibility for the conduct of the non-state actors. In the case of *Nicaragua*,[53] for example, the International Court of Justice ('ICJ') was faced with a situation in which non-state actors played a prominent role, but ultimately focused on the attribution of their actions to states, and the repercussions of attribution and responsibility in the context of self-defence and use of force between states.[54] The case of *Democratic Republic of the Congo v. Uganda* presented additional examination of how non-state actors might affect use of force between states.[55] The situations examined here raise, however, another set of questions and challenges not adequately answered in the existing case law. In essence, the problem before us is not how to respond to states that are responsible for the conduct of non-state actors, but rather the issue of taking forcible measures against independent non-state actors whose conduct cannot necessarily be attributed to a particular state. Forcible action of this type is hardly new,[56] but it is nevertheless not explicitly or adequately addressed in international law. Moreover, the growing ability of non-state actors to operate outside of state control, whether due to breakdown of state structures (eg 'failed states') or the capability to wreak havoc with nothing but small clandestine cells, is presenting further obstacles and challenges to the international legal framework.

Attempts to counter threats and, on occasion, to respond to actual attacks by non-state actors, raise vexing questions in the context of the laws on the resort to force: does the right to self-defence under international law include the right to use extraterritorial force in response to attacks by an independent non-state actor? Can this right be exercised on the territory of another state if that state cannot be held responsible for the attack by the non-state actor? What if the non-state actor has bases of operations in more than one state? Finally, could there be rules other than those of self-defence, which might permit extraterritorial force against non-state actors? These questions will be examined in the following chapters. Whilst possible solutions will be raised, it will be evident that the rules of international law are not always formulated in a manner that can provide perfect answers. To a certain extent this is not a flaw in the law itself, but rather a result of a legal system predicated on a world in which states are the primary actors. Moreover, the international rules regulating the resort to force were formulated with the stated objective of limiting resort to force and maintaining international stability.[57] However, some of the approaches to allowing and regulating states' resort to force against non-state actors risk destabilizing the very foundations

---

[53] See n 48, *supra*.   [54] *Nicaragua*, n 48, *supra*, paras 131, 195, 229, 230.

[55] *Case Concerning Armed Activities on the Territory of the Congo (Democratic Republic of the Congo v. Uganda)*, paras 146,147.

[56] See examples of the *Caroline* in 1837 and the US Mexican border early last century, *ibid*, nn 5 and 6.

[57] Charter of the United Nations (26 June 1945) 59 Stat 1031; TS 993; 3 Bevans 1153, entered into force 24 October 1945, Preamble, Arts 1 and 2.

of this desired stability. As will be posited, certain situations can be covered by acceptable interpretations of the rules of self-defence, but when the paradigm of self-defence and armed attacks is not clearly applicable, problems will remain. Some of the current practices of states may, with time, contribute to the development of new rules but, as of now, such rules have not emerged, and it is difficult to see what form they could take without opening the door to a potential flood of forcible interventions in the territory of other states.

The field of international humanitarian law has challenges of its own raised by the role of non-state actors, although arguably these do not risk destabilizing foundational principles as in the other two branches of law raised above. Considering that so many of the armed conflicts since World War II have been ones in which a non-state actor was one of the main parties involved in the fighting, the relevant law has had to develop in such a way that this reality cannot be ignored. Common Article 3 of the 1949 Geneva Conventions binds all parties to non-international armed conflicts, which would include non-state actors. Additional Protocol II of 1977, aimed at regulating non-international armed conflicts, explicitly mentions 'organized armed groups'.[58] The applicability of IHL to non-state actors is also apparent in customary international law, and through international criminal law for violations of these rules. Indeed, the first trial to come before the International Criminal Court related to the alleged crimes of a leader of a militia group.[59] IHL therefore clearly recognizes that the role of non-state actors in armed conflict cannot be ignored, and strives to include them in the body of applicable rules. Nonetheless, it should also be stressed that whilst IHL developed so as to encompass the conduct of non-state actors, states did their utmost to ensure that these laws maintain the separation between them and the non-state actors, and do not elevate the latter to the status or position of the former. This is readily apparent in two areas. First, both Common Article 3 and the 1977 Protocol contain provisions clarifying that they do not amount to any change in the legal status of the parties of the conflict.[60] Secondly, whilst the treaty rules of non-international conflict apply equally to states and non-state actors, a comparison of these rules to those in the treaties applicable to international armed conflict reveals the desire of states to avoid enhancing the status of the non-state groups. The clearest indication of this is the lack of any provision on prisoner of war ('POW') status in the context of non-international conflicts. Under the rules of international armed conflict, individuals who qualify for the status of POW will receive immunity from prosecution for

---

[58] Protocol Additional to the Geneva Conventions of 12 August 1949, and relating to the Protection of Victims of Non-International Armed Conflicts (Protocol II) (8 June 1977) 1125 UNTS 609, entered into force 7 December 1978, art 1.

[59] *Prosecutor v. Thomas Lubanga Dyilo* ICC-01/04-01/06.

[60] Common Article 3 states that 'The application of the preceding provisions shall not affect the legal status of the Parties to the conflict.'; according to Art 3 of Protocol II, 'Nothing in this Protocol shall be invoked for the purpose of affecting the sovereignty of a State or the responsibility of the government, by all legitimate means, to maintain or re-establish law and order in the State or to defend the national unity and territorial integrity of the State.'

acts that were in accordance with IHL such as confining their attacks to military objectives and carrying them out in a lawful manner (although they can be prosecuted for violations of IHL).[61] There are no similar provisions in the laws applicable to non-international conflicts, as can be expected upon consideration of the interests of states. In the context of international conflicts, soldiers of the enemy are not in fact committing any crime by virtue of their participation in the conflict, and taking them prisoner merely reflects the need to keep them off the battlefield for the duration of the war. In a non-international conflict, individuals who take up arms against the state are, by contrast, likely to be committing some of the most serious crimes the state can envisage, eg treason. Including a POW status in these conflicts would amount to requiring states to grant immunity from prosecution to rebels who—so long as they only attack soldiers and military targets—are fighting against the state. Consequently, it can be said that IHL recognizes the central role of non-state actors in modern armed conflict and the ensuing need for the law to take account of their existence, whilst simultaneously allowing the preservation of the Westphalian system of states by not providing non-state actors the status or legitimacy to undermine states' authority.

The question of the status given to non-state actors also affected the classification of conflicts. The 1977 Additional Protocols followed the division into international and non-international armed conflicts. However, the final versions of the Protocols reflected a desire to recognize certain struggles as something other than an internal conflict with rebels, as can be seen in the inclusion of paragraph 4 of Article 1 in Protocol I, on international conflicts. According to this provision, 'armed conflicts in which peoples are fighting against colonial domination and alien occupation and against racist regimes in the exercise of their right of self-determination' are to be considered international armed conflicts.[62] By falling into the category of international conflicts, armed groups would escape the lack of status clauses in the non-international rules, and their members would have the possibility of benefiting from rules designed for those fighting on behalf of states, including receiving prisoner of war status and immunities.[63] Armed groups involved in such struggles would consequently be able to argue that IHL recognizes that they have a status higher than that of a group of criminal rebels. As will be seen in later chapters, this nexus between the status of parties and conflict classification, has various implications in the context of extraterritorial force against non-state actors.

As in the cases of human rights law and the international laws on resort to force, the increasing necessity of addressing the role of non-state actors operating

---

[61] See section 1.1 of Ch 6, *infra*, on combatants.

[62] Protocol Additional to the Geneva Conventions of 12 August 1949, and relating to the Protection of Victims of International Armed Conflicts (Protocol I) (8 June 1977) 1125 UNTS 3, entered into force 7 December 1978, Art 1.

[63] They would nevertheless have to fulfil certain criteria, as required in the rules of international armed conflict. See section 1.1 of Ch 6, *infra*, on combatants.

across borders, can present challenges to the traditional understanding of the rules of international law. As will be seen in the chapters on IHL, when extraterritorial force against non-state actors amounts to armed conflict, a debate exists over whether it should be classified as international or non-international.[64] One of the difficulties that would be faced if these situations were classified as international would be whether this raises questions over recognition of status for the non-state actors, and how to reconcile the conflict type with matters such as granting prisoner of war immunities. The preferred approach, as will be substantiated in later chapters, is to view these situations—if they do indeed amount to armed conflict—as non-international. Accordingly, in those situations in which IHL is applicable, it would not serve as grounds for claiming any elevated or state-like status for the non-state actors concerned.

4.4 Terrorism

As noted earlier, for reasons of scope and clarity, terrorism is not used as the foundation point for the analysis. However, the theme of terrorism runs through many of the arguments put forth by governments and commentators, and the term as used will, therefore, be repeated. The definition of 'terrorism' is open to multiple interpretations, and the only clear consensus is that it is a term reserved for actions of which the speaker disapproves. Primary areas of contention have included the question of whether terrorism is limited to acts against states or whether states can also be guilty of terrorism, and over the use of the term in the context of groups struggling for self-determination and/or against occupation.[65] Although use of words with the 'terror' root have become politically loaded, it would be practically impossible to avoid their use altogether. The terms have become embedded into the debates ranging over a multitude of issues dealing with non-state groups, and are included in the language of international law and its institutions.[66]

Nevertheless, for our purpose, there is in fact no need to elaborate or agree upon a particular definition of terrorism. Where the term terrorism in its various forms is used, it will be in the context of reference to it by states and commentators.

---

[64] The detailed analysis of this can be found in Ch 4, *infra*.

[65] For a description of the attempts to reach a definition, see B Saul, 'Attempts to Define "Terrorism" in International Law' 52 *Netherlands International Law Review* 57 (2005); Duffy n 21, *supra*, pp 17–46; For an earlier review of the issues, see T Franck and B Lockwood, 'Preliminary Thoughts towards an International Convention on Terrorism' 68 *Amsterdam Journal of International Law* 69 (1974).

[66] For example, International Convention for the Suppression of the Financing of Terrorism, GA Res 109, UN GAOR, 54th session, Supp no 49; UN Doc A/54/49 (vol I) (1999); S Treaty Doc no 106–49 (2000); 39 ILM 270 (2000), adopted 9 December 1999, entered into force 10 April 2002; International Convention for the Suppression of Terrorist Bombing, GA Res 164; UN GAOR, 52nd session, Supp no 49, at 389; UN Doc A/52/49 (1998), entered into force 23 May 23 2001; see also the work of the UN Security Council Counter-Terrorism Committee at <http://www.un.org/sc/ctc/>.

At the heart of this analysis, however, are the rules that apply to all forms of extraterritorial forcible operations against non-state actors, whether or not they are defined as counter-terrorism, and regardless of what definition of terrorism is used. The 'war on terror' is presented in inverted commas due to the controversies surrounding the very use of the term. A substantial part of chapter 5 will be devoted to analyzing the question of whether or not a 'war on terror' can denote a real war or armed conflict, as defined by international law.

Following the above explanation of the rationale and scope of this work, and the structure and definitions employed throughout, Part I will now begin the substantive analysis, by focusing on the international laws governing the resort to force in the context of extraterritorial forcible measures against non-state actors.

PART I

THE INTER-STATE RELATIONSHIP: EXTRATERRITORIAL USE OF FORCE AND SELF-DEFENCE AGAINST NON-STATE ACTORS

1

The Possibility of Self-Defence Against Non-State Actors

1. Introduction

Extraterritorial measures, unless taking place in areas such as the high seas, take place within the territory of another state. This raises a question concerning the legality of using force within another state, even if directed at a non-state actor and not at the state itself, and whether this violates the UN Charter prohibition on use of force. The focus of this Part is on situations in which the extraterritorial forcible measures are conducted without the consent of the territorial state. Should such consent exist, questions may remain—some of which are addressed in other chapters—but there would be less need to question whether the use of force by the acting state had violated the sovereignty or transgressed rules of interstate relations.

Many of the issues examined in this Part, such as anticipatory self-defence, are amongst the most contested topics in the field of international law on resort to force and self-defence. It is not the purpose, nor indeed is it possible within the scope of this book, for this chapter to provide an extensive analysis of each and every one of the topics. Rather, the aim is to provide an understanding of the main elements of the debate, and then reflect upon how these debates are affected when the force in question is directed against non-state actors located in other states.

2. The prohibition on use of force

The fundamental principles regulating inter-state use of force, are to be found in the UN Charter.[1] According to Article 2(4), 'All Members shall refrain in their international relations from the threat or use of force against the territorial

---

[1] Charter of the United Nations (26 June 1945) 59 Stat 1031; TS 993; 3 Bevans 1153, entered into force 24 October 1945.

integrity or political independence of any State, or in any other manner inconsistent with the Purposes of the United Nations'.

This Article is one of the bedrocks of modern day international order, which has prevention of war as a primary goal.[2] Although it reflects the strong post-World Wars desire to put an end to the scourge of war, the Charter does recognize that an absolute ban on force cannot stand the test of reality, and allows for self-defence in Article 51:

Nothing in the present Charter shall impair the inherent right of individual or collective self-defence if an armed attack occurs against a Member of the United Nations, until the Security Council has taken measures necessary to maintain international peace and security. Measures taken by Members in the exercise of this right of self-defence shall be immediately reported to the Security Council and shall not in any way affect the authority and responsibility of the Security Council under the present Charter to take at any time such action as it deems necessary in order to maintain or restore international peace and security.

The Charter also allows for the UN Security Council to decide upon measures involving the use of military force in order to maintain or restore international peace and security and put an end to a threat to the peace, breach of the peace, or act of aggression.[3]

Two questions must be asked: (i) are the extraterritorial forcible measures described in violation of Article 2(4); and if so then (ii) are they nevertheless allowed by Article 51, or by other recognized rules.[4]

At the early stage of this chapter, it should once again be made absolutely clear, that we are concerned with forcible actions taken against *non-state* actors. Accordingly, if the individual or group against whom measures are taken is in fact operating as a state agent, this would be outside the purview of this current analysis. Non-state actors, for the purpose here, are only those whose actions cannot be attributed to the state.[5] The implications of the possible relationships between the territorial state and the non-state actor will be examined in a later section below.[6]

The taking of forcible measures unsanctioned by the Security Council on the territory of another state would seem prima facie to be in violation of Article 2(4), unless the use of unilateral force is in self-defence. Prima facie assessments, however, must be examined more closely before being accepted as correct. There are,

---

[2] A Randelzhofer, 'Article 2(4)' in B Simma (ed.), *The Charter of the United Nations, A Commentary* (OUP: Oxford, 1994) 108–9; L Henkin, 'The Reports of the Death of Article 2(4) are Greatly Exaggerated' 65 *AJIL* 544 (1971) 544.

[3] UN Charter, n 1, *supra*, Arts 39–42.

[4] The primary focus in this chapter is on self-defence, while Ch 3, *infra*, examines the possibility of justification through the concepts of counter-measures, necessity, and law enforcement.

[5] See discussion and sources in section 4.3 of the Introduction, *supra*, on non-state actors. See also further discussion in section 5, *infra*, on the territorial state.

[6] See section 5, *infra*, on the territorial state.

in fact, at least three possibilities as to the lawfulness of unilateral and unsanctioned extraterritorial forcible measures in light of Article 2(4):

(i)   The measures do not contradict the terms of Article 2(4);
(ii) the measures do contradict the general terms of Article 2(4), but are lawful under self-defence;[7]
(iii) the measures are a violation of Article 2(4), not justified by any other rule.

The first option might seem improbable at first sight, if force is clearly being used without consent on the territory of another state. However, it should be noted that a literal reading of Article 2(4) does not include language prohibiting every use of force, but rather that '[a]ll Members shall refrain in their international relations from the threat or use of *force against the territorial integrity or political independence of any State, or in any other manner inconsistent with the Purposes of the United Nations*'.[8]

It might be tempting to posit the argument that forcible measures taken against non-state actors, particularly if these are short swift operations not involving prolonged presence in the territorial state, do not interfere with the territorial integrity or political independence of the territorial state. It has, in fact, been said that there is a certain ambiguity in Article 2(4).[9] An example of this claim can be found in the context of the Entebbe raid of 1976, in which Israel claimed that the use of force was only for a temporary rescue mission and not directed at Uganda.[10] There was no agreement at the Security Council on the formulation of a resolution, but the debates show that the majority of countries—even some that displayed an element of understanding for Israel's operation—did not wish to reduce the scope of the Article 2(4) prohibition.[11]

Interpreting Article 2(4) so as to allow 'minor' or 'temporary' invasions, is, in the words of Franck, 'utterly incongruent, however, with the evident intent of the sponsors of this amendment', and the more widely accepted interpretation

---

[7]   Self-defence as the major recognized exception is the focus of the analysis at this stage. Chapter 3, *infra*, contains further exploration into the possibility of additional exceptions outside of self-defence.

[8]   Emphasis added.

[9]   D Bowett *Self-Defence in International Law* (Manchester University Press: Manchester, 1958) 12–13, 150–2.

[10]   Israel conducted a raid upon the Ugandan airport, in order to rescue hostages held by pro-Palestinian hijackers. The hijackers were killed, as were a number of Ugandan soldiers, hostages and an Israeli soldier. At the UN Security Council meeting, the Israeli representative raised the argument that the operation was not against the territorial integrity or political independence of Uganda. See Security Council Official Records, 31st Year, 1939th Meeting, 9 July 1976, New York, UN Doc S/PV.1939 (1976).

[11]   See for example the view of Sweden; Security Council Official Records, 31st Year, 1940th Meeting, 12 July 1976, New York, UN Doc S/PV.1940(OR); *ibid*; Gray points out that the claim of a narrow interpretation of 2(4) was not crucial to Israel's argument. C Gray *International Law and the Use of Force* (OUP: Oxford, 2004) 30–1; for the possibility of making similar arguments in the context of a direct military attack on another state's nuclear facility, see A D'Amato, 'Editorial Comment: Israel's Air Strike upon the Iraqi Nuclear Reactor' 77 *AJIL* 584 (1983) 584–5.

is that all uses of force are unlawful, other than the recognized exceptions in the Charter.[12] Even temporary and limited incursions described as 'in-and-out operations' are said to be an infringement of the principle contained in Article 2(4).[13]

The difficulty of upholding such a claim can be further deduced from the debate over a different topic, that of humanitarian intervention, in which analogous claims can be made in seeking to exempt certain uses of force from the Charter prohibition. This debate centres upon the question of whether it might be lawful for states to forcibly intervene in another state in order to avert a humanitarian catastrophe and protect fundamental human rights. One of the arguments made in support of humanitarian intervention is that it is not aimed against the territorial integrity or political independence of the state and, therefore, is not in violation of Article 2(4) of the UN Charter.[14] The debate over humanitarian intervention is ongoing and complex,[15] and the only certainty within it is that as of yet it remains unsettled.[16] Indeed, even among some supporters of the idea that states can and, perhaps, even have a duty, to intervene and protect in humanitarian catastrophes, it nevertheless appears recognized that the current state of the law does not support unilateral forcible intervention. This is evident in recent examinations of this question which, while recognizing that there may be an emerging 'duty to protect', see this duty, nevertheless, as needing Security

---

[12] T Franck *Recourse to Force: State Action Against Threats and Armed Attacks* (CUP: Cambridge, 2002) 12; See also Y Dinstein, *War, Aggression, and Self-Defence* (CUP: Cambridge, 2005) 86–8; H Waldock, 'The Regulation of the Use of Force by Individual States in International Law', 81 *Recueil des Cours* 455, 493 (1952); M Shaw, *International Law* (5th edn) (CUP: Cambridge, 2004) 1021; Brownlie notes that it is 'not intended to be restrictive, but, on the contrary, to give more specific guarantees to small states and that it cannot be interpreted as having a qualifying effect'. I Brownlie, *International Law and the Use of Force by States* (OUP: Oxford, 1963) 267; The International Court of Justice did not accept a restrictive approach to the ban on force with regard to UK actions in Albanian waters *Corfu Channel Case (UK v. Alb.)* 1949 ICJ 4, 34.

[13] Randelzhofer, n 2, *supra*, 117–18; see discussion of views in Gray, n 11, *supra*, 29–31.

[14] See the position of Belgium in relation to the intervention in Kosovo: 'the Kingdom of Belgium takes the view that this is an armed humanitarian intervention, compatible with Article 2, paragraph 4, of the Charter, which covers only intervention against the territorial integrity or political independence of a State' (*Legality of Use of Force (Serbia and Montenegro v. Belgium)*, Oral Proceedings, CR 1999/15, Public sitting held on 10 May 1999); See also the discussion of debate in Randelzhofer, *ibid*, 123–4; M Reisman, 'Criteria for the Lawful Use of Force in International Law' 10 *Yale Journal of International Law* 279 (1985) 282.

[15] For further detailed examination of the debate, see R Lillich (ed), *Humanitarian Intervention and the United Nations* 167, (1973); A Roberts, 'The So-Called "Right" of Humanitarian Intervention' in *Yearbook of International Humanitarian Law* (2000) 3–52; 'The Responsibility to Protect: Report of the International Commission on Intervention and State Sovereignty', International Development Research Centre, 2001; Gray, n 11 *supra*, 31–52; N Rodley and B Cali, 'Kosovo Revisted: Humanitarian Intervention on the Fault Lines of International Law' 7 *Human Rights Law Review* 275 (2007); APV Rogers, 'Humanitarian Intervention and International Law' 27 *Harvard Journal of Law and Public Policy* 725 (2004).

[16] The UK Foreign Office described it as not 'unambiguously illegal', Foreign and Commonwealth Office Paper, 'Is intervention ever justified', Foreign Policy Document no 148, 1986 (reprinted in part in 57 *British Yearbook of International Law* 614). The Foreign Office appeared a few years later to have taken a more positive approach towards the possibility of lawful humanitarian intervention, albeit in 'exceptional circumstances' see Baroness Symons written answer to Lord Kennet, *Hansard*, Col WA140, 16 November 1998.

Council authorization,[17] and the relevant reports do not claim that unilateral intervention does not violate Article 2(4).[18] In light of all this, while there are ongoing attempts to find interpretations to legitimize humanitarian intervention, the prevalent view does not seem currently to support interpreting Article 2(4) of the Charter in such a way that unilateral (without Security Council authorization) humanitarian intervention would be a legitimate exception to the ban on use of force. If it does not seem possible, at least at this time, to claim that unilateral forcible intervention on humanitarian grounds is in keeping with Article 2(4) it is, therefore, at least similarly problematic to maintain that non-humanitarian related extraterritorial forcible measures against non-state actors, could nevertheless benefit from that claim.

Accordingly, if extraterritorial forcible measures of this kind do contradict the terms of Article 2(4), it is now necessary to examine whether they might be allowed as a form of legitimate self-defence. Additional related arguments and possibilities will be examined in Chapter 3.[19]

3. Self-defence against non-state actors

Perhaps the most obvious claim to justify using extraterritorial force against a non-state actor, is that it is a case of self-defence.[20] Indeed, this has been the position taken by states on a number of occasions in which force was launched against non-state actors located in other states, including:

- The US invoked self-defence to support military operations against Al-Qaeda in Afghanistan, declaring that: 'In response to these attacks, and in accordance with the inherent right of individual and collective self-defence, United States armed forces have initiated actions designed to prevent and deter further attacks on the United States. These actions include measures against al-Qaeda terrorist training camps [...].'[21]

---

[17] Roberts also examines the question of authorization by other bodies such as the General Assembly or Regional Organizations. Roberts, n 15, *supra*, 37–40; See also *The Responsibility to Protect*, n 15, *supra*, ch 6 'The question of Authority'.

[18] 'A More Secure World: Our Shared Responsibility', Report of the Secretary-General's High-Level Panel on Threats, Challenges and Change, UN Doc A/59/565 (2004); Whilst clarifying that this is not the preferred outcome and has risks for the maintenance of international order, the reality of unilateral intervention being resorted to if the Security Council fails to act, is however raised. *The Responsibility to Protect*, n 15, *supra*.

[19] On measures taken outside the self-defence frameworks, and the possibilities of alternative paradigms.

[20] Another possibility is the claim that the action is taken within the context of an already ongoing armed conflict. For instance, the US justified attacking individuals in Yemen by claiming this was part of a 'war on terror'. This type of claim, including this particular example, will be examined in Parts II, III and the Concluding Chapter, *infra*.

[21] Letter, dated 7 October 2001, from the Permanent Representative of the United States of America, to the United Nations addressed to the President of the Security Council, UN SCOR, 56th session at 1; UN Doc S/2001/946 (2001). This clam also addressed the use of force against

- Iran invoked self-defence after a 1993 attack against Kurdish groups in Iraq: 'During the past few weeks, bands of armed and organized terrorist merce-naries have engaged in trans-border military attacks against and sabotage in Iranian border provinces [...] In response to these armed attacks from inside Iraq and in accordance with Article 51 of the Charter of the United Nations, today, 25 May 1993, the fighter jets of the Islamic Republic Air Force carried out a brief, necessary and proportionate operation against the military bases of the terrorist group [...].'[22]
- Ethiopia's claim to use force against non-state actors in Somalia, was based upon a perceived need to defend itself, as is apparent from the fact that 'the AU said Ethiopia had the right to intervene militarily in Somalia as it felt threatened by the Islamic militia operating there.'[23]
- Israel justified its attacks in Lebanon in summer 2006, as acts of self-defence against the Hezbollah, stating that 'Israel, like any State, has done, and will continue to do, whatever is necessary to protect the lives of its citizens. It has the right and the duty to act in self-defense.'[24]
- Israel justified attacking an Islamic Jihad training camp in Syria, invoking self-defence on grounds of the Jihad having carried out suicide bombings in Israel, and declaring that 'Israel's measured defensive response to the horrific suicide bombings, against a terrorist training facility in Syria, are a clear act of self-defense in accordance with Article 51 of the Charter.'[25]
- Turkey asserted a right to attack Kurdish rebels in Iraq, following the death of 13 Turkish soldiers. According to the Turkish Prime Minister: 'Turkey needed to be able to respond to a recent rise in bomb attacks blamed on PKK rebels from Iraq.'[26]

4. Can non-state actors be responsible for an 'armed attack'?

According to Article 51 of the Charter, self-defence can only be invoked if an armed attack occurs. Therefore, if the state claims to be taking action in

the Taliban regime. See section below on relationship between non-state actors and the terri-torial state. It is important to note that self-defence was already invoked at an early stage only in relation to Al-Qaeda prior to alleging Taliban responsibilities. See nn 40 and 41, *infra*, and accompanying text.

[22] Letter, dated 25 May 1993, from the Permanent Representative of the Islamic Republic of Iran to the United Nations Addresses to the Secretary General, UN Doc S/25843.

[23] 'Ethiopia urged to leave Somalia' *BBC News*, 27 December 2006, available at <http://news.bbc.co.uk/1/hi/world/africa/6212807.stm>.

[24] Statement by Ambassador Dan Gillerman, Permanent Representative, During the open debate on 'The Situation in the Middle East' United Nations, New York, 8 August 2006.

[25] Statement by Ambassador Dan Gillerman, Permanent Representative, Emergency Session, Security Council, New York, 5 October 2003.

[26] 'Turkish MPs back attacks in Iraq' *BBC News*, 18 October 2007, available at <http://news.bbc.co.uk/2/hi/europe/7049348.stm>.

self-defence, we must first inquire into the occurrence of an armed attack. The first issue in need of examination is whether the actions of a non-state actor can be deemed an armed attack which would, potentially, give rise to the subsequent right of self-defence.

There exist views that an armed attack must denote state involvement, or that self-defence can only be taken in response to an attack by a state or groups acting on behalf of one. This appears to be the position the International Court of Justice ('ICJ') took in its *Advisory Opinion on the Legal Consequences of the Construction of a Wall in the Occupied Palestinian Territory.*[27] This is also the position of certain commentators. Whilst, as will be seen below with regard to the ICJ, this claim is at times simply asserted without providing detailed reasoning, in other cases it is presented in the context of examining whether the non-state actor had support from the territorial state, and/or that the international laws relating to use of force are aimed only at actions of states.[28]

The relationship between the territorial state and the non-state actor can have a variety of implications,[29] but it is a separate question from the possibility of an armed attack by a non-state actor without other state involvement. There is in fact plentiful evidence to provide solid support for the contention that non-state actors can be responsible for armed attacks which give rise to self-defence. As is seen below, this evidence rests on both a reading of the texts, and on state practice in the interpretation of the rule, and is supported by leading commentators.[30]

Unlike other articles in the UN Charter (such as Article 2(4) on the prohibition on the use of force) which *do* mention specifically that they refer to states, Article 51 *does not* mention the nature of the party responsible for the attack, but

---

[27] *Legal Consequences of the Construction of a Wall in the Occupied Palestinian Territory*, Advisory Opinion, 9 July 2004, [2004] ICJ Rep, para 139.

[28] J Kunz, 'Individual and collective Self-Defense in Article 51 of the charter of the United Nations' *AJIL Editorial Comment* 872 (1947) 878; M Bothe, 'Terrorism and the Legality of Pre-emptive Force' 14 *European Journal of International Law* 227 (2003) 233; A McDonald, 'Terrorism, Counter-terrorism and the *Jus in Bello'* in M Schmitt and G Beruto (eds) *Terrorism and International Law: Challenges and Responses* (International Institute of Humanitarian Law, 2002); S Alexandrov, *Self-Defense Against the Use of Force in International Law* (Kluwer Law International: The Hague, 1996) 182–3; E Myjer and N White, 'The Twin Towers Attack: An Unlimited Right to Self-Defence?' 7 *Journal of Conflict and Security Law* 5 (2002) 7 (although Myjer and White acknowledge that the US position of viewing 11 September 2001 as an armed attack did find broad support, at 8–9); G Simpson in E Wilmshurst (ed) 'Principles of International Law on the Use of Force by States in Self-Defence' The Royal Institute of International Affairs, Chatham House, October 2005, 27–8.

[29] See section 5, *infra*.

[30] See Dinstein, Franck, Greenwood, Schmitt, and Paust, all n 49, *infra*; See also O Schachter, 'The Extraterritorial Use of Force Against Terrorist Bases' 11 *Houston Journal of International Law* 309 (1988–9) 311; F Berman in *Principles of International Law*, n 28, *supra*, 20; D Bethlehem in *Principles of International Law*, n 28, *supra*, 21; C Greenwood in *Principles of International Law*, n 28, *supra*, 21; V Lowe in *Principles of International Law*, n 28, *supra*, 22; A Roberts in *Principles of International Law*, n 28 *supra*, 23; P Sands in *Principles of International Law*, n 28, *supra*, 26; M Shaw in *Principles of International Law*, n 27, *supra*, 26. S Murphy, 'Self-Defense and the Israeli Wall Advisory Opinion: An Ipse Dixit from the ICJ?' 99 *AJIL* 62 (2005) 64, 67–70.

only that of the entity which has the right of response. Self-defence can be exercised by a member of the UN, ie states, but there is no mention or qualification concerning the nature of the body behind the armed attack.

According to the International Court of Justice's reading of Article 51, 'Article 51 of the Charter thus recognizes the existence of an inherent right of self-defence in the case of armed attack by one State against another State'.[31]

It is unclear how and why the Court interpreted Article 51 as having anything to say about the identity of the attacker.[32] Judge Higgins, in her Separate Opinion, mentions that although the UN Charter does not appear to limit armed attacks to actions of state, this limitation can be understood from the International Court of Justice decision in *Nicaragua v. USA*.[33] However, Higgins also notes her reservations to the *Nicaragua* proposition.[34] Indeed, it is not clear that one can rely on the *Nicaragua* decision for asserting the existence of a limitation. In the context of self-defence, *Nicaragua* dealt (amongst other issues) with the support of the Nicaraguan government to rebels fighting in El-Salvador, and whether the type of alleged support could amount to an armed attack by Nicaragua, thus possibly giving rise to self-defence action against Nicaragua.[35] The Court was assessing the question of attribution to a state and its consequences, and was not analyzing the separate question of whether in other circumstances a stand-alone action of a non-state actor with no state support could itself constitute an armed attack. It does not necessarily corroborate or negate the contention that non-state actors can be responsible for armed attacks as understood by Article 51 of the UN Charter.

Judge Kooijmans and Judge Buergenthal in their respective Opinions in the *Advisory Opinion on the Wall*, both expressed dissatisfaction with the Court's apparent lack of acceptance that armed attacks can be perpetrated by non-state actors, a sentiment echoed by commentators.[36]

The International Court of Justice had later occasion to again review the issue of self-defence against non-state actors, in its judgement on *Democratic Republic*

---

[31] *Advisory Opinion on the Wall*, n 27, *supra*, para 139.

[32] The Court recognized that Israel may wish to justify the construction as self-defence, *ibid*. The Palestinian submission, in relation to self-defence, focused the argument on the factual aspect of whether there was the required gravity of attack to claim self-defence by Israel, whether this was a form of unlawful preventive self-defence, disproportionate, and whether the rule applied in the context of occupation, but did not directly raise the claim that armed attacks can only be committed by states. *Advisory Opinion on the Wall*, n 27, *supra*, written statement submitted by Palestine, 30 January 2004, paras 529–34.

[33] *Case Concerning Military and Paramilitary Activities in and Against Nicaragua*, [1986] ICJ Rep 14.

[34] To be found in R Higgins, *Problems and Process: International Law and How We Use It* (Clarendon Press: Oxford, 1994) 250–51. These reservations appear, however, to focus on a separate aspect of the question, namely on whether the scale of activity demanded for reaching the threshold of an armed attack is different for attacks perpetrated by regular forces or by armed bands supported by a state.

[35] *Nicaragua*, n 33, *supra*, paras 131,195, 229, 230.

[36] Separate Opinion of Judge Kooijmans, n 27, *supra*, para 35, Declaration by Judge Buergenthal, n 27, *supra*, para 6; see also Greenwood, n 30 *supra*, 21; Roberts, n 30, *supra*, 23; Sands, n 30, *supra*, 26; A Cassese, *International Law* (OUP: Oxford, 2005) 354–5.

of the Congo v. Uganda.[37] However, the Court's position in this case is less than clear:

It is further to be noted that, while Uganda claimed to have acted in self-defence, it did not ever claim that it had been subjected to an armed attack by the armed forces of the DRC. The armed attacks to which reference was made came rather from the ADF. The Court has found above (paragraphs 131–135) that there is no satisfactory proof of the involvement in these attacks, direct or indirect, of the Government of the DRC. The attacks did not emanate from armed bands or irregulars sent by the DRC or on behalf of the DRC, within the sense of Article 3 (g) of General Assembly resolution 3314 (XXIX) on the definition of aggression, adopted on 14 December 1974. The Court is of the view that, on the evidence before it, even if this series of deplorable attacks could be regarded as cumulative in character, they still remained non-attributable to the DRC.

For all these reasons, the Court finds that the legal and factual circumstances for the exercise of a right of self-defence by Uganda against the DRC were not present. Accordingly, the Court has no need to respond to the contentions of the Parties as to whether and under what conditions contemporary international law provides for a right of self-defence against large-scale attacks by irregular forces.[38]

The Court appears to be interested primarily in whether the armed attacks could be attributed to the Democratic Republic of Congo, and once a negative answer was reached, the Court dropped further aspirations to enquire into a potential claim of self-defence against non-state actors. Indeed, the final sentence in the above quotation indicates that the Court did not see itself as answering this question. If the Court had felt that the issue was satisfactorily addressed and decided in the *Advisory Opinion on the Wall*, then one might assume it would have repeated its earlier stated position. In fact, the expressed lack of will to determine the question of self-defence against non-state actors indicates that the Court, perhaps slightly backtracking on itself, deemed this to be a question still open for debate.

In his separate opinion, Judge Kooijmans observes that the Court appears to be repeating its position that claims of self-defence need only be examined if the armed attack can be attributed (directly or indirectly) to a state. This, according to Judge Kooijmans, is not the desired approach, since:

[…] if the attacks by the irregulars would, because of their scale and effects, have had to be classified as an armed attack had they been carried out by regular armed forces, there is nothing in the language of Article 51 of the Charter that prevents the victim state from exercising its inherent right of self-defence.

[…] If armed attacks are carried out by irregular bands from such territory against a neighbouring State, they are still armed attacks even if they cannot be attributed to the territorial State. It would be unreasonable to deny the attacked State the right to self-defence merely because there is no attacker State, and the Charter does not so require.[39]

---

[37] *Case Concerning Armed Activities on the Territory of the Congo (Democratic Republic of the Congo v. Uganda)* paras 146–7.
[38] For further discussion on scale of armed attacks, see section 2 of Ch 2, *infra*.
[39] *DRC v. Uganda*, n 37, *supra*; separate opinion of Judge Kooijmans, n 27, *supra*, paras 29–30.

Indeed, state practice appears to support the position that non-state actors might be behind armed attacks which give rise to self-defence. This is particularly true when observing the response to the attacks of 11 September 2001. This is evidenced by the reference to the right to self-defence in Security Council Resolutions 1368 and 1373,[40] and by the North Atlantic Treaty Organisation (NATO) recognition of the acts as an armed attack.[41] Security Council Resolution 1368 was adopted prior to the negotiations with the Taliban over possible extradition of the attackers and the subsequent apportioning of blame to the Taliban, a fact which indicates that at the time of adoption it was not based on an assumption attributing the attacks to Afghanistan, but rather to Al-Qaeda, a non-state actor.[42] The view of the US is that this was a case of armed attack and self-defence,[43] and the response of the Security Council and NATO appears to confirm that states accepted this position. Whilst this may be described as a relatively new understanding of the rules on self-defence,[44] support for this position can be found prior to 2001,[45] including reference to an earlier case, that of the *Caroline*.[46]

[40] Security Council Res no 1368 (2001), adopted by the Security Council at its 4370th meeting, 12 September 2001; Security Council Res no 1373 (2001), adopted by the Security Council at its 4385th meeting, 28 September 2001. But see Myjer and White for a view questioning whether the Security Council resolutions formally determined this to be a case of armed attack and self-defence. See n 28, *supra*, 9–13.

[41] Exceptionally invoking the NATO commitment to collective self-defence. See NATO Press Release 124, 12 September 2001, available at <http://www.nato.int/docu/pr/2001/p01-124e .htm>. See also the Statement of the Organization of American States, 'Support for the Measures of Individual and Collective Self-Defense Established in Resolution Rc.24/Res. 1/01', Oea/Ser.F/ Ii.24, Cs/Tiar/Res. 1/01, 16 October 2001, available at <http://www.oas.org/OASpage/crisis/ follow_e.htm>; See Franck, n 12, *supra*, 65.

[42] See n 40, *supra*; M Schmitt, 'Counter-Terrorism and the Use of Force in International Law' The Marshall Center Papers no 5, The George C. Marshall European Center for Security Studies, 26–7; But see Pellet's reference to the 'troubling' element of Security Council Res no 1368 which in his opinion is an 'extremely wide interpretation' of the meaning of Article 51 of the Charter. A Pellet, '"No, This is not War!": The Attack on the World Trade Center: Legal Responses' *EJIL Discussion Forum*, 3 October 2001, available at <http://www.ejil.org/forum_WTC/ny-pellet .html>

[43] See the position expressed by John B Bellinger III, Legal Adviser to the Secretary of State: J Bellinger, 'Legal Issues in the War on Terrorism' International Humanitarian Law Project Lecture Series, London School of Economics, October 31, 2006. Transcript available at <http://www.lse .ac.uk/collections/LSEPublicLecturesAndEvents/pdf/20061031_JohnBellinger.pdf>.

[44] As is concluded by Judge Kooijmans, n 36, *supra*; see also analysis in C Tams, 'The Use of Force against Terrorists' 20 *EJIL* 359 (2009) 378–81.

[45] T Gill, 'The Eleventh of September and the Right of Self-Defense' in WP Heere (ed.), *Terrorism and the Military: International Legal Implications* (Asser: The Hague, 2003) 23–37, 30; Dinstein, *supra* n 12, *supra*, 204–6 (this appears also at 222 of the 1988 edn written many years prior to 11 September 2001); Franck mentions a fair number of occasions in which states asserted self-defence in attacking territory from which non-state actors originated, and attacks against alleged terrorists, including action taken by Turkey, Iran, Senegal, and Thailand, as well as the acquiescence or support for the 1998 US attacks in Sudan and Afghanistan. Franck, n 12, *supra*, 64, 95.

[46] This refers to the 1837 *Caroline* incident, involving British action against a ship used by Canadian rebels, in US territory, and the ensuing written diplomatic exchange between Britain and the US. See JB Moore, 2 *Digest of International Law* 409, 412 (1906).

The *Caroline Case* is considered to be a formative case in the development of the rules of self-defence, and as can be seen throughout this Part, is often referred to as defining the parameters for the right of self-defence under customary international law. In fact, this case involved Britain engaging in an extraterritorial forcible measure, claiming the right to self-defence in response to the acts of a non-state actor. British forces stationed in Canada in 1837 wished to take action against the supplies and support Canadian rebels were receiving from private citizens in the US. British forces entered the US and boarded a ship (named the Caroline) with armed force, set it on fire and sent it over the Niagara Falls, with two US citizens killed in the process.[47]

As noted by Greenwood:

[...] the famous Caroline dispute, itself shows that an armed attack need not emanate from a State. The threat in the Caroline case came from a non-State group of the kind most would probably call terrorist today. The United States was not supporting the activities of that group and certainly could not be regarded as responsible for their acts. Yet, nowhere in the correspondence or in the subsequent reliance on the Webster formula on self-defense is it suggested that this fact might make a difference and that the Webster formula might not apply to armed attacks that did not emanate from a State.[48]

It is, therefore, apparent that even in historical terms, the concept of self-defence as a result of attacks by non-state actors has been recognized by states.

A number of additional commentators, including Dinstein, Franck, Schmitt and Paust, all support the view that states have a right of self-defence against non-state actors.[49] In light of all the above, it is therefore submitted here that self-defence may lawfully be invoked in response to attacks perpetrated by non-state actors. It should however be noted at this stage that forcible measures taken by a state might not always be in response to a prior specific attack by the non-state actor, and there are further questions over forcible actions initiated by states, as will be seen in the later section on anticipatory or preventive measures.

Acceptance of the proposition that there may be self-defence against non-state actors does not relieve the need to examine certain particular legal and practical difficulties raised in the context of these situations. For instance, how does the inclusion of non-state actors affect the debate over anticipatory self-defence, or the proportionality of the response? These questions and others will be covered in Chapter 2 of this book. Before delving into the details of these problems,

---

[47] For a description of the case, see R Jennings, 'The Caroline and McLeod Cases' 32 *AJIL* 82 (1938).

[48] C Greenwood, 'International Law and the Pre-emptive Use of Force: Afghanistan, Al-Qaida, and Iraq', 4 *San Diego International Law Journal* 7, 17 (2003).

[49] Greenwood, *ibid*; T Franck, 'Editorial Comments: Terrorism and the Right of Self-Defense', 95 *AJIL* 839, 840 (2001); Dinstein, n 12, *supra*, 204–8; J Paust, 'Use of Armed Force against Terrorists in Afghanistan, Iraq, and Beyond', 35 *Cornell International Law Journal* 533, 533–4 (2002); Schmitt, n 42, *supra*. See also the separate opinion of Judge Kooijmans, n 27, *supra*, para 35, and the Declaration by Judge Buergenthal, n 27, *supra*, para 6; See further support from commentators n 30, *supra*.

attention will first be turned to another major issue hovering over this chapter, which needs to be addressed: the existence of an armed attack gives rise to a right to self-defence, and consequently might lead to use of force extraterritorially against the non-state actor, but where in this equation does the territorial state fit in?

5. The territorial state

When state A launches a military operation on the soil of state B, the instinctive observation would be that the two states are now engaged in armed conflict. However, what if state A declares it is only engaging in operations against members of a non-state actor, for which state B denies responsibility? In July 2006, Hezbollah fighters based in Lebanon attacked an Israeli military patrol in the border area, killing eight soldiers and abducting two, as well as launching rockets into Israel. Together with Israel's large-scale response, this was the commencement of an armed conflict that continued until the middle of the following month. Whilst claiming that Lebanon bore responsibility for the actions of the Hezbollah,[50] the Israeli Government also took the position that its conflict was with the Hezbollah group, and not with Lebanon—'Prime Minister Olmert emphasized that Israel is not fighting Lebanon but the terrorist element there, led by Nasrallah and his cohorts, who have made Lebanon a hostage and created Syrian- and Iranian-sponsored terrorist enclaves of murder.'[51]

How this can affect the classification of armed conflicts (as international or non-international) is an issue dealt with in Part II of this work.[52] Nonetheless, this situation is mentioned at this stage in order to demonstrate that even if state A is using force on the territory of state B, the categorizations of the situation are not necessarily clear-cut, and there may be a distinction between using force *in* a state but not *against* that state.

Examining the role played by the territorial state (state B in the above example) revolves around three matters:

(i) what is the connection between the territorial state and the non-state actor which carried out the armed attack—this is both a factual question of formal connections, as well as a political question of the relationship and attitude of the state towards the non-state actor;

(ii) does the territorial state bear responsibility for the actions of the non-state actor either directly or for not preventing these acts; and

---

[50] 'Hizbullah attack' Special Cabinet Communique, Israeli Government, 12 July 2006, available at <http://www.mfa.gov.il/MFA/Government/Communiques/2006/Special+Cabinet +Communique+-+Hizbullah+attack+12-Jul-2006.htm>.

[51] Cabinet Communique, Israeli Government, 16 July 2006, available at <http://www.mfa.gov .il/MFA/Government/Communiques/2006/Cabinet+Communique+16-Jul-2006.htm>.

[52] See also discussion of this conflict in the Concluding Chapter, *infra*.

  (iii) how does this affect the legality of the measures taken by the outside state? As is seen below, these three issues are intertwined.

The relationship between the territorial state and the non-state actor which carried out the initial armed attack against the other state, can be divided into five possibilities:[53]

  (i) the non-state actor is in fact so intertwined within the state mechanisms that it might be considered a state organ;

  (ii) the non-state actor is receiving some form of instruction, material support or vital assistance from the state;

  (iii) the non-state actor is independent, but has the consent of the territorial state to operate from its territory;

  (iv) the state claims to have no ties nor to have given consent, but is unwilling to interfere or make any moves against the non-state actor;

  (v) the state is unable to prevent the non-state actor from operating in its territory, even if disapproving of its activities.

The above scenarios describe the main possibilities that might exist in terms of a factual description of the relationship. The actual determination of the factual situation can at times be challenging, as can be seen in the case of Hezbollah and Lebanon. On the one hand, in addition to being an armed militant group, Hezbollah is also a political party which was a member of the Lebanese government. On the other hand, the Lebanese government made formal announcements dissociating itself from the armed actions of the Hezbollah.[54] The analysis of such a situation will clearly be contentious.[55] Once the factual determinations have been made on a case-by-case basis, then for the purposes of a legal analysis of the questions at hand, these factual situations can be further distilled into the following three categories:

(a) Attacks by the non-state actor can be attributed to the territorial state.

(b) Attacks by the non-state actor cannot be attributed to the territorial state, however the state bears some form of responsibility on account of its relationship with the non-state actor.

---

[53] There are various ways to present the relationship, eg Cassese offers six categories, and Simpson offers four. See Cassese, n 36, *supra*, 470–2 and Simpson, n 28, *supra*, 27. Within the above categories one could also divide them further for instance to cases in which the state is unable to prevent the activities of the group despite wanting to do so, and cases in which the state is unable but would also not have prevented the group even if it did have the power to do so. The chosen categories above are those which afford an understanding based on the distinctions relevant for the purpose of the present analysis.

[54] 'The Lebanese government was not aware of the events that occurred and are occurring on the international Lebanese border. The Lebanese government is not responsible for these events and does not endorse them.' Identical letters, dated 13 July 2006, from the Chargé d'affaires a.i. of the Permanent Mission of Lebanon to the United Nations addressed to the Secretary-General and the President of the Security Council, UN Doc A/60/938–S/2006/518.

[55] For more on this particular situation, see discussions in Part II and the Concluding Chapter, *infra*.

(c) Although the territorial state has done no wrong, the non-state actor is none-theless operating from within its territory.

Scenario (i) clearly comes under (a). Scenario (ii) might or might not fall into (a), depending on the exact connection between the state and the non-state actor. The most commonly referred to test for this, would be the one set out by the International Court of Justice *Nicaragua Case*.[56] The court set a relatively high threshold for the attribution of action by an armed group to a state, ruling that even provision of weapons to an armed group operating in another country would not on its own be enough to establish such attribution.[57] This threshold for attribution has been subject to criticism,[58] and some would have it set so that significant material assistance would lead to a determination of attribution. For the purpose of the present analysis, what needs to be noted is that scenario (i) and possibly scenario (ii) could belong to category (a). This first category is in effect tantamount to one state having launched an attack on another, which may then have a right to respond in self-defence against state agents. It will therefore receive no further consideration in the present analysis, since it is outside the scope of a work focusing on forcible measures directed against non-state actors.

Scenario (ii), if failing the attribution threshold, would then belong to cat-egory (b), as would scenarios (iii) and (iv), as will be seen shortly. There is strong support for the contention that even without directly sending the armed groups on their mission, if they do not attempt to prevent the non-state actor, states can bear responsibility under international law for the actions of non-state actors operating from within their territory. Following the International Court of Justice's determination in *Nicaragua*, provision of weapons or logistical or other support 'may be regarded as a threat or use of force, or amount to interven-tion in the internal or external affairs of other States'.[59] Violation of obligations were also raised by the Court in *DRC v Uganda*: 'The Court would comment, however, that, even if the evidence does not suggest that the MLC's conduct is attributable to Uganda, the training and military support given by Uganda to the ALC, the military wing of the MLC, violates certain obligations of interna-tional law'.[60]

The Court cited the provisions, which it described as customary international law, of the Declaration on Principles of International Law Concerning Friendly

---

[56] *Nicaragua,* n 33, *supra.*

[57] *Nicaragua,* n 33, *supra,* paras 115,195. The question of attribution can depend on a number of factors, such as the type of control the State may have over the group, and if the level of instruc-tion that may exist is that of specific instructions for specific operations. See more on this in 'Commentaries to the draft articles on Responsibility of States for internationally wrongful acts', International Law Commission, 53rd session (2001), (extract from the 'Report of the International Law Commission on the work of its Fifty-third session', Official Records of the General Assembly, 56th session, supp no 10 (A/56/10), chp.IV.E.2) November 2001) art 8.

[58] See discussion in section 5 of Ch 3, *infra,* on alternative paradigms.

[59] See n 33, *supra,* para 195.   [60] *DRC v. Uganda,* n 37, *supra,* para 161.

Relations and Co-operation Among States in accordance with the Charter of the United Nations:[61]

Every State has the duty to refrain from organizing, instigating, assisting or participating in acts of civil strife or terrorist acts in another State or acquiescing in organized activities within its territory directed towards the commission of such acts, when the acts referred to in the present paragraph involve a threat or use of force....

and

No State shall organize, assist, foment, finance, incite or tolerate subversive, terrorist or armed activities directed towards the violent overthrow of the regime of another State, or interfere in civil strife in another State.

It is not only direct material assistance that can lead to state responsibility but also, in the event of non-state actors carrying out terrorism from within its territory, a failure to act against them. This is evident from two Security Council Resolutions adopted after 11 September 2001, nos 1368 and 1373.[62] In Resolution no 1373, adopted under Chapter VII of the UN Charter (and binding upon all UN members), the Security Council decides that all states shall:

(a) Refrain from providing any form of support, active or passive, to entities or persons involved in terrorist acts, including by suppressing recruitment of members of terrorist groups and eliminating the supply of weapons to terrorists;

(b) Take the necessary steps to prevent the commission of terrorist acts, including by provision of early warning to other States by exchange of information;

(c) Deny safe haven to those who finance, plan, support, or commit terrorist acts, or provide safe havens;

(d) Prevent those who finance, plan, facilitate or commit terrorist acts from using their respective territories for those purposes against other States or their citizens;

(e) Ensure that any person who participates in the financing, planning, preparation or perpetration of terrorist acts or in supporting terrorist acts is brought to justice and ensure that, in addition to any other measures against them, such terrorist acts are established as serious criminal offences in domestic laws and regulations and that the punishment duly reflects the seriousness of such terrorist acts.[63]

Accordingly, states that provide assistance or fail to attempt to prevent the non-state actors from carrying out their plans, will have violated international law,[64]

---

[61] *Ibid*, para 162; Declaration on Principles of International Law Concerning Friendly Relations and Co-operation among States in accordance with the Charter of the United Nations, GA res 2625, Annex, 25 UN GAOR, Supp (no 28); UN Doc A/5217 at 121 (1970).

[62] See n 40, *supra*.

[63] SC 1373 para. 2; See also R Jennings and A Watts (eds), *Oppenheim's International Law Ninth Edition, vol 1, Peace*, (Longman: London, 1992) 393–406.

[64] This may even be a rule of customary international law. See Schachter, *supra* n 30, *supra*, 311.

and therefore bear responsibility.[65] How does this affect the legality of the extra-territorial forcible measures *against the non-state actor*, taken by the state which suffered the attack of the non-state actor? In fact, the effect is not decisive.

If the territorial state is implicated in the armed attack, then the outside state may have the right to use force against the territorial state and its agents, in addition to using it against the non-state actor. If, however, the territorial state bears a form of responsibility as detailed immediately above, but the actual armed attack cannot be attributed to it, then the outside state would not have the right to self-defence against the territorial state. This at least is the position of the International Court of Justice, as stated in *Nicaragua*.[66] It should nonetheless be noted, that this relates to the possibility of forcible self-defence measures against the territorial state itself, and not to the notion of self-defence measures against the non-state actor.[67] If one is to accept that non-state actors might be responsible for armed attacks which give rise to a right of self-defence, then this is a separate matter from the question of state responsibility of the territorial state. The notion of self-defence in this context does not rest upon the question of a breach of law by the territorial state, but on the fact that there is a state which is the victim of an armed attack and is need of recourse to self-defence in order to avert the danger.[68]

To clarify, the territorial state might bear responsibility either for the armed attack itself (if the attribution threshold is passed) or for failing to take measures against the non-state actor. In case of the former, it may find itself the object of lawful self-defence by the sending state. In case of the latter, it might not itself be a legitimate target of lawful self-defence operations, despite it possibly being in violation of international law.

However, if the territorial state aligns itself with the non-state actor, for example by subsequently endorsing the armed attack,[69] and then using its own forces to oppose the self-defence operations against the non-state actor, then the outside state may have no alternative but to also use force against the territorial state.[70]

---

[65] Indeed, states can bear responsibility for failing to take preventative measures against actions for which they themselves might not be held responsible. *Application of the Convention on the Prevention and Punishment of the Crime of Genocide, Bosnia and Herzegovina v Serbia*, Judgment on Merits, General List no 91; ICGJ 70 (ICJ 2007) 26 February 2007, paras 425–38, 471.

[66] *Nicaragua*, n 33, *supra*, para 195. This is also one of the areas in which the *Nicaragua* judgment has been criticized, in that it might appear to create a gap in which a state might be involved in the use of force against another state, without the victim state having a right of self-defence. J Hargrove 'Appraisals of the ICJ's Decision: Nicaragua v. United States (Merits)' 81 *AJIL* 135 (1987). See also discussion in Ch 3, *infra*.

[67] See earlier discussion of *Nicaragua*, noting that the case did not focus upon attacks by stand-alone non-state actors, but upon the links between groups and states and consequences of attributing group's acts to a state. Text accompanying nn 33, 34, *supra*.

[68] Lowe, n 30, *supra*, 22; An alternative analysis is offered by Tams, linking the self-defence arguments to what appears to be a lower threshold for the test of attribution, Tams, n 44, *supra*, 384–7. The position argued above is however different, in that it is submitted that the right of self-defence does not depend on the attribution to the territorial state.

[69] For an example of post-facto endorsement, albeit in a different context, see *Case Concerning United States Diplomatic and Consular Staff in Tehran (US v. Iran)*, 1980 ICJ Rep 3.

[70] For discussion of this in this context of the US and the Taliban, see text accompanying nn 19–26, *infra*.

The operation against the non-state actor taken in self-defence by the outside state is a lawful use of force, and the territorial state cannot therefore mount a forcible resistance in the name of self-defence;[71] in fact it could be argued that the territorial state is obliged not to interfere with the exercise of self-defence by the sending state.[72] Notwithstanding these possibilities, whether or not the territorial state can itself be subjected to forcible self-defence, this does not alter the fact that there was an armed attack by a non-state actor operating within its territory, and that another state was a victim of this armed attack, and therefore has a right to self-defence against the non-state actor.

Following this approach, scenario (v) and category (c) above,[73] in which the territorial state is not complicit in any way in the activities of the non-state actor, but is unable to prevent these activities, leads to a similar conclusion that regardless of the legal responsibility of the territorial state, the outside state may have the right to self-defence against the non-state actor. Moreover, if the territorial state finds the non-state actor operations objectionable, but is unable to prevent them, it would avoid the need for unilateral force by the victim state were it to co-operate with that state and allow it, or others, to assist in countering the non-state actor.[74] By choosing not to do so it hovers on the borderline between 'unable' and 'unwilling'.[75]

The possibility of taking action on the territory of another state in order to curb attacks by a third party is not unique to the challenges of confronting non-state actors, and the debate here can find analogy in the context of the use of force as it relates to the laws of neutrality.[76] As noted by Randelzhofer:

> For the purpose of responding to an 'armed attack', the state acting in self-defence is allowed to trespass on foreign territory, even when the attack cannot be attributed to the state from whose territory it is proceeding. It does not follow from the fact that the right of self-defence pursuant to Art. 51 is restricted to the case of an 'armed attack' that

---

[71] Y Dinstein, 'Dinstein, Comment' at the conference exploring *Terrorism as a Challenge for National and International Law*, Max-Planck Institute for Comparative Public Law and International Law, Heidelberg, 24–5 January 2003, available at <http://edoc.mpil.de/conference-on-terrorism/index.cfm>; Dinstein quotes *The United States of America v. Ernst von Weizsäcker and ors ('The Ministries Trial')* Nuremberg 1949 'there can be no self-defense against self-defense' (based on a phrase from Wharton, *Criminal Law, vol I* (12th edn) (The Lawyers Co-operative Publishing Co: Rochester, NY, 1932) 180).

[72] R Mullerson, '*Jus Ad Bellum: Plus Ça Change (Le Monde) Plus C'est La Même Chose (Le Droit)?*' 7 *Journal of Conflict and Security Law* 149 (2002) 185; M Schmitt, 'Counter-Terrorism and the Use of Force in International Law' The Marshall Center Papers no 5, The George C Marshall European Center for Security Studies, 33–4.

[73] Text accompanying nn 53–56, *supra*.

[74] Berman, n 30, supra, 62; Lowe, n 30, *supra*, 63–4; Shaw, n 30, *supra*, 65; M Wood in *Principles of International Law*, n 30, *supra*, 66.

[75] Berman, n 30, *supra*, 62.

[76] This analogy has been noted by various commentators, such as Greenwood, n 30, *supra*, 63, and Berman, n 30, *supra*, 62; For discussion of approaching the laws of neutrality in light of the modern rules on self-defence, and the possibility of allowing for self-defence actions in this context when they are necessary and proportionate, see S Neff, *The Rights and Duties of Neutrals* (Manchester University Press: Manchester, 2000).

defensive measures may only affect the attacker. Thus it is compatible with Art. 51 and the laws of neutrality when a warring state fights hostile armed forces undertaking an armed attack from neutral territory on the territory of the neutral state, provided that the state concerned is either unwilling or unable to curb the ongoing violation of its neutrality.[77]

In light of all the above, if the territorial state will not or cannot prevent the attacks launched by the non-state actor operating from within its borders, the victim state may have the right to take self-defence measures against the non-state actor in the territorial state.[78]

Accepting that self-defence might be an option in the context of extraterritorial forcible measures against non-state actors is only the first stage in an examination of self-defence in this context. The next question raised is whether this right to self-defence can be exercised without further ado, or if certain steps must be taken before the outside state can turn to forcible measures.

---

[77] A Randelzhofer, 'Article 51' in B Simma (ed.), *The Charter of the United Nations, A Commentary* (OUP: Oxford, 1994) 661–78, 673; But see Brownlie for a detailed examination of past practice and the views regarding intervention in the territory of neutral states, whereby other than perhaps limited exceptional circumstances, the legality of interventions is generally doubtful. Brownlie, n 12, *supra*, 309–16; As noted by Randelzhofer, it is, however, submitted here that self-defence against armed attacks would constitute exceptional circumstances that warrant this action.

[78] Dinstein, n 12, *supra*, 245; Bethlehem, n 30, *supra*, 63; Lowe, n 30, *supra*, 63–4; Shaw, n 30, *supra*, 65; Wood, n 74, *supra*, 66. The potential implications for the classification of the conflict in the context of international humanitarian law, will be explored in Part II, *infra*.

2

The Parameters of Self-Defence

1. Necessity

Necessity and proportionality are the two primary principles relating to the use of force by states, and are often mentioned in tandem.[1] As noted by the International Court of Justice, '[t]he submission of the exercise of the right of self-defence to the conditions of necessity and proportionality is a rule of customary international law'.[2]

Necessity and proportionality encompass a number of separate requirements, and those of proportionality will be dealt with in a later section. As for necessity, when dealing with self-defence against states, then as long as the aggressor signals the intention to continue attacking, the necessity requirement may find itself swept aside fairly swiftly, since unless the Security Council has taken action to remove the need for self-defence, the victim state is likely to have some foundation for claiming forcible self-defence is its only option. The circumstances before us are, however, of a different kind and, as will be seen, the involvement of non-state actors gives added meaning to the principle of necessity.

Necessity in the context of self-defence appears in the *Caroline Case*:

It will be for it to show, also, that the local authorities of Canada,—even supposing the necessity of the moment authorized them to enter the territories of the United States at all,—did nothing unreasonable or excessive; *since the act justified by the necessity of self-defence, must be limited by that necessity, and kept clearly within it.*[3]

and:

Undoubtedly it is just, that while it is admitted that exceptions growing out of the great law of self-defence do exist, those exceptions should be confined to cases in which the

---

[1] 'The concepts of necessity and proportionality are at the heart of self-defence in international law', M Shaw, *International Law* (5th ed.) (CUP: Cambridge, 2003) 1031; J Gardam, *Necessity, Proportionality and the use of Force by States* (CUP: Cambridge, 2004); C Gray, *International Law and the Use of Force* (OUP: Oxford, 2004) 120–6.

[2] *Advisory Opinion on the Legality of the Threat or Use of Nuclear Weapons,* [1996] ICJ Rep, 8 July 1996, para 41.

[3] Letter, dated 27 July 1842, from Mr Webster to Lord Ashburton, Department of State, Washington, available at <http://www.yale.edu/lawweb/avalon/diplomacy/britain/br-1842d .htm>. Emphasis added.

'necessity of that self-defence is instant, overwhelming, and leaving no choice of means, and no moment for deliberation.'[4]

The need for both immediacy ('instant, overwhelming', 'no moment for deliberation') and for unavailability of other means ('leaving no choice of means') are both clearly present in the *Caroline* formula of self-defence. Necessity, proportionality and immediacy are considered yardsticks of self-defence.[5] How these concepts are to be understood and what their place is in the modern day UN Charter formulation of self-defence is, as will be seen below, not a matter of uniform agreement.

Immediacy is hereby understood as referring to the temporal relation between the armed attack and the self-defence response. Requirement of immediacy would mean that the victim of the armed attack needed to respond without delay in order for the self-defence to be legitimate. The *Caroline* standard of 'no moment for deliberation' is however too restrictive to be applied literally.[6] In fact, the *Caroline* standard would be more pertinent in an examination of the question of anticipatory self-defence, as opposed to reacting after the initial armed attack has occurred.[7] When taking a decision to act in self-defence, time may be needed precisely for deliberation if a state is expected to first explore available non-forcible avenues in order to fulfil the criteria of necessity. State practice also points to time requirements that may be necessary in order to engage in self-defence, such as in the case of the Falklands/Malvinas conflict between the UK and Argentina. While the UK asserted the right to self-defence, it was a few days before the commencement of military deployment, and a number of weeks before actual combat activities.[8] The UN Charter formulation appears to envisage the Security Council moving swiftly to dispel the need for forcible self-defence, and accordingly the only cases in which states would have to resort to forcible self-defence would be in the brief window of time before the Security Council takes action. As is often the case, reality evolved on a different track to the original design, and swift action by the Security Council to prevent escalation of armed conflict has not been a common occurrence.[9] So long as there has been an armed attack, and no effective

---

[4] Letter, dated 6 August 1842, from Mr Webster to Lord Ashburton, Department of State, Washington, available at <http://www.yale.edu/lawweb/avalon/diplomacy/britain/br-1842d.htm>.

[5] Y Dinstein, *War, Aggression, and Self-Defence* (CUP: Cambridge, 2005) 209.

[6] T Franck, 'Editorial Comments: Terrorism and the Right of Self-Defense', 95 *AJIL* 839, 840 (2001) 840; Roberts, Ch 1, n 30, *supra*, 43–4; Dinstein, *ibid*, 242–3.

[7] See section 2.3, *infra*, on anticipatory self-defence.

[8] R Higgins, 'The Attitude of Western states Towards Legal Aspects of the Use of Force' in A Cassese (ed), *The Current Legal Regulation of the Use of Force* (Martinus Nijhoff: Dordrecht, 1986) 435–52, 441; R Holmes, 'Falklands War (1982)' in *The Oxford Companion to Military History* (OUP: Oxford, 2004).

[9] 'Unfortunately, in almost six decades of operation, the Security Council has displayed time and again a reluctance or inability to adopt a decision identifying the aggressor in a specific armed conflict [. . .] Even when faced with an obvious case of an armed attack, political considerations may prevent the Council from taking a concerted stand'. See Dinstein, n 5, *supra*, 214.

action has been taken by the Security Council to prevent the continuation of the situation, states may need to exercise the right to self-defence for a significant period after the initial armed attack.[10] This period can be explained as a result of time needed for effective military deployment, as was the case with regard to the UK's exercise of self-defence in the Falklands/Malvinas,[11] or as time used to explore other options before resorting to force, as was mentioned in the context of the long period between the attacks of 11 September to the US military operations in Afghanistan.[12] Between 11 September 2001 and the launching of US operations in Afghanistan on 7 October, there were demands for co-operation from the Taliban government.[13] Exploring other options leads us to another component of necessity, that of 'leaving no choice of means'.[14]

After suffering an armed attack, does a state have to attempt all avenues of action before resorting to forcible self-defence? First, it should be noted that the position on this question can depend on which stage in the chain of events it is being asked, and more specifically on whether the initial armed attack is over and whether more are expected. If a state is responding to an ongoing armed attack, then it would appear that unless there has been intervention by the Security Council, the state does not have to attempt other measures before engaging in forcible self-defence. On the other hand, if the initial armed attack is over although the attacks are expected to continue, and there appears to be a window of opportunity for non-forcible responses, then the state must attempt other measures before it is entitled to exercise the forcible right of self-defence.[15] The principle of necessity requires that forcible response be taken only if there are no alternative means of effectively responding to the danger.[16]

This aspect of necessity reveals a potentially added complexity when dealing with circumstances in which the armed attack was carried out by a non-state actor. When the attack was carried out by a state, the primary alternative to forcible self-defence is diplomatic efforts—whether by the victim state or others in the international community—that are undertaken directly with the attacker, in an attempt to reach a solution without further violence. If a non-forcible approach with the attacker is not an option, or is tried and fails, then there is little else that can be expected from the victim state in the way of exhausting other options. However, if the initial armed attack was carried out by a non-state actor, then

---

[10] Franck, n 6, *supra*, 841–2.   [11] *Ibid.*

[12] See n 13, *infra*, and n 21, *infra*, and accompanying text.

[13] S Murphy, 'Contemporary Practice of the United States Relating to International Law, Legal Regulation of Use of Force: Terrorist Attacks on World Trade Center and Pentagon' 96 *AJIL* 237 (2002) 243–6. See n 21, *infra*, and accompanying text.

[14] Letter from Mr Webster, n 4, *supra*.

[15] *Case Concerning Military and Paramilitary Activities in and Against Nicaragua*, [1986] ICJ Rep 14, para 267.

[16] D Bethlehem in E Wilmshurst *Principles of International Law on the Use of Force by States in Self-Defence*, The Royal Institute of International Affairs, Chatham House, October 2005, 57–8; Lowe, *ibid*, 58; Roberts *ibid*, 59; Wood, *ibid*, 62.

even if diplomacy is attempted with the attacker—in this case the non-state actor—and then fails, there is an additional stage that can be explored before exercising self-defence. The initial attacker may be unwilling to stand down from its aggressor position, but it may be possible to end its threatening activities without the victim state sending in the troops, since there is a third role in this scenario which would not exist if the initial attack were by a state. Namely, the territorial state in which the non-state actor is located. The state which suffered the armed attack, can attempt turning to the territorial state requesting, or even demanding, that it exercise its jurisdiction and take measures to prevent the hostile activities by the non-state actor. This means that there is an additional tool in the box of available options, this being the possibility of seeking a solution via the territorial state. So long as this option exists and has not been tried, then it can be said that the requirement of necessity has not been fulfilled. In the words of Roberto Ago, Special Rapporteur of the International Law Commission:

The reason for stressing that action taken in self-defence must be *necessary* is that the State attacked (or threatened with imminent attack, if one admits preventive self-defence) must not, in the particular circumstances, have had any means of halting the attack other than recourse to armed force. In other words, had it been able to achieve the same result by measures not involving the use of armed force, it would have no justification for adopting conduct which contravened the general prohibition against the use of armed force. The point is self-evident and is generally recognized; hence it requires no further discussion.[17]

If the territorial state were to take effective action against the non-state actor, which thereby terminates the attacks and the continuing threat, then forcible action by the victim state would not be justifiable.[18]

Applying this view to the circumstances of an armed attack by a non-state actor means that in order for use of force in self-defence to be lawful, the victim of the armed attack should first attempt to have the territorial state take measures against the non-state actor. If it does not do so, it could find itself in violation of the UN Charter prohibition on the use of force. As noted in a previous section, the relationship between the territorial state and the non-state actor may be such that it will choose not to take the demanded measures—in which case it may be in violation of other international obligations—or it might claim an inability to act. In both these cases, the victim state could then claim to have no remaining option but to use force.

[17] R Ago, 'The internationally wrongful act of the State, source of international responsibility (part 1)' Addendum to the 8th report on state responsibility by the Special Rapporteur, 32nd session of the ILC (1980); UN Doc A/CN.4/318/Add.5-7 (extract from the *Yearbook of the International Law Commission, 1980, Vol II(1)*, para 120). See also R Jennings and A Watts (eds), *Oppenheim's International Law Ninth Edition, vol 1, Peace*, (Longman: London, 1992) 421.
[18] Lowe, n 16, *supra*, 22–3. One might also question how to define the effective termination of the threat, eg should it include trial and punishment of the non-state actor. At a minimum however, it would probably have to include any measure which appears to prevent the non-state actor from posing a threat of continuous attacks.

Seeking a solution through the territorial state has consequences on more than one level. First, the lawfulness of launching operations against the non-state actor can hinge upon whether this diplomatic approach was first tried. Secondly, should the territorial state not take action against the group, this may have implications as to whether the outside state might also direct force against targets belonging to the territorial state itself, and not only at the non-state actor. The case of the US attacks in Afghanistan serve to illustrate this issue.

The attacks of 11 September 2001 can, and have been, recognized as armed attacks, and it was swiftly accepted by the UN Security Council and others in the international community that the US would have a right to self-defence.[19] The attacks were attributed to Al-Qaeda, a non state actor operating from its bases in Afghanistan, and the right of self-defence was therefore in the context of responding to Al-Qaeda.[20] Before exercising the right of self-defence, the US requested the cooperation of the Taliban—the *de facto* government of Afghanistan—and while there are differing accounts interpreting the exchange between the governments,[21] for the sake of this analysis it will be assumed that the Taliban response did not satisfy the need for measures that would have curbed Al-Qaeda's hostile activities.[22] If that is the case, then the US would have satisfied the requirement of necessity, and would have been lawfully entitled to exercise the right of self-defence against Al-Qaeda. Directing attacks against the Taliban government will have been a different matter—whilst a variety of types of relationships between the Taliban and Al-Qaeda may involve a breach of international law, resorting to force in the name of self-defence can only arise in response to armed attacks.[23] Attacking the Taliban would therefore have been legitimate for one of two reasons:

(i) if the armed activities by Al-Qaeda can be attributed to the Taliban, or
(ii) if the Taliban subsequently aligned itself with Al-Qaeda and forcibly opposed the US self-defence operations against Al-Qaeda.[24]

---

[19] Ch 1, *supra*, nn 40, 41 and accompanying text.   [20] Ch 1, *supra*, n 42.

[21] ME O'Connell, 'War and Armed Conflict: Evidence of Terror' 7 *Journal of Conflict and Security Law* 19 (2002); M Schmitt, 'Counter-Terrorism and the Use of Force in International Law' The Marshall Center Papers no 5, The George C Marshall European Center for Security Studies, 39.

[22] It should also be noted that the Taliban had in the past been demanded by the Security Council to extradite Bin Laden and take measures against terrorist camps in their territory. Security Council Res no 1267 (1999), adopted by the Security Council at its 4051st meeting on 15 October 1999; Security Council Res no 1333 (2000), adopted by the Security Council at its 4251st meeting on 19 December 2000.

[23] The US position appears to be that it was justified in attacking the Taliban on account of the harbouring of Al-Qaeda and not preventing its activities; see J Bellinger, 'Legal Issues in the War on Terrorism' *International Humanitarian Law Project Lecture Series* London School of Economics, October 31, 2006, available at <http://www.lse.ac.uk/collections/LSEPublicLecturesAndEvents/pdf/20061031_JohnBellinger.pdf>. This however does not conform with the analysis as presented in section 5 of Ch 1, *supra*, on the territorial state. See also Schmitt, n 21, *supra*, 41.

[24] See section 5 of Ch 1, *supra*, on the territorial state.

Since it appears that the US strikes in Afghanistan combined Al-Qaeda and Taliban targets from the outset, justification for this would need to be sought in the former reasoning. There are divergent views on how to define the ties between Al-Qaeda and the Taliban, and whether the latter can be held accountable for the acts of the former.[25] Consequently, depending on the view one takes regarding the accountability of the Taliban, it is possible that the decision to target the Taliban itself may have lacked a lawful basis, unlike the wider agreement on the lawfulness of attacking Al-Qaeda in self-defence.[26]

This situation can be contrasted with other cases where to claim necessity for action appears implausible. For instance, Uganda's desire to act against rebels from the Lord's Resistance Army ('LRA') across the border in the Democratic Republic of Congo ('DRC'), would not have met the requirement of necessity because at the same time the UN was facilitating and assisting the movement of hundreds of DRC troops to the North-East of the country in order to deal with this rebel group.[27]

While it is clear that the debate is not settled, it is submitted that it can be supported from all the above that states may claim a right to self-defence as the result of an armed attack by a non-state actor. In certain circumstances, including the inability or unwillingness of the territorial state to take action—thereby contributing to the requirement of necessity—it would be lawful to exercise this right of self-defence against non-state actors located in the territory of other states.

2. The scale of the initial armed attack

When faced with armed attacks by states, there is the view that virtually any intentional use of armed force by one state against another could qualify as an armed attack, including a soldier firing a shot at a patrol on the other side of an international border.[28] On the other hand, there are those who would define this scenario as a 'minor border incident', which does not cross the threshold of an armed attack, since an armed attack involves 'massive armed aggression against the territorial integrity and political independence of a state that imperils its life or government [...]'.[29] The discussion of this topic has generally focused on

---

[25] See Gray, n 1, *supra*, 166; 'Responsibility for the Terrorist Atrocities in the United States, 11 September 2001—an Updated Account' UK Government press release, available at <http://www.pm.gov.uk/output/Page3682.asp>; O'Connell, n 21, *supra*, 19–20, 30–2.

[26] See detailed analysis of this in Schmitt, n 21, *supra*, 41–53.

[27] 'DR Congo Troops to Uganda Border' *BBC News*, 5 October 2005.

[28] 'If "armed attack" means illegal armed attack it means, on the other hand, any illegal armed attack, even a small border incident' in J Kunz, 'Individual and collective Self-Defense in Article 51 of the charter of the United Nations' *AJIL Editorial Comment* 872 (1947) 878; See also *Oil Platforms (Islamic Republic of Iran v. United States of America)* ICJ Rep 1993, 35, paras 71–2, on the possibility that mining of a single military vessel might allow for self-defence.

[29] A Cassese, *International Law* (OUP: Oxford, 2005) 354, 469; See also S Alexandrov, *Self-Defense Against the Use of Force in International Law* (Kluwer Law International: The Hague, 1996) citing G Schwarzenberger, 'The Fundamental Principles of International Law' 87 *Hague*

armed attacks by states. In *Nicaragua,* the International Court of Justice ('ICJ') had occasion to examine the question of a required scale of attack in the context of armed groups. The Court determined that:

the prohibition of armed attacks may apply to sending by a State of armed bands to the territory of another State, if such operation because of its scale and effects, would have been classified as an armed attack rather than a mere frontier incident had it been carried out by regular armed force.[30]

As noted previously, insofar as attacks by armed groups were examined, the ICJ *Nicaragua* decision was concerned with the attribution of their activities to states, and the effects such attribution may have on the rights and actions of states. In that respect, the above quotation does not actually give a direct answer to the threshold for determination of an *armed attack by an independent non-state actor*, but rather to the scale of attack necessary for it to be considered an *armed attack by the state that sent the armed groups*.[31] The last part of the quotation does however indicate that according to the Court, even if the operation was carried out directly by a state's armed forces, there is a threshold separating 'mere frontier incidents' from armed attacks. If this is the position on armed attacks by states, then *a fortiori* it is likely that armed attacks by non-state actors would need to pass at least a similar threshold, going beyond 'mere frontier incidents'. In the case of *DRC v. Uganda*, while clarifying that it was not going to grapple with the issue of self-defence against non-state actors operating on their own, the Court noted that '[a]ccordingly, the Court has no need to respond to the contentions of the Parties as to whether and under what conditions contemporary international law provides for a right of self-defence against large-scale attacks by irregular forces'.[32]

The Court's formulation of the question it was not going to answer, does appear to reveal a view that consideration of self-defence, would arise in the context of *large-scale* attacks.

The Court's apparent dismissal of frontier incidents has however been criticized by Dinstein:

The question of a frontier incident is particularly bothersome. It stands to reason that, if a rifle shot is fired by an Arcadian soldier across the border of Utopia and the bullet hits

---

Recueil 195, 333 (1955-I); J Mrazek, 'Prohibition of the Use and Threat of Force: Self-Defence and Self-help in International Law', 27 *Canadian Yearbook of International Law* 81, 109 (1989); Benst Broms, *The Definition of Aggression in the United Nations,* Turku (1968), 129; A Randelzhofer, 'Article 51' in B Simma (ed), *The Charter of the United Nations, A Commentary* (OUP: Oxford, 1994) 661–678, 669.

[30] *Nicaragua,* n 15, *supra,* para 195.

[31] It should also be noted that the Court's decision on this matter was not wholly subscribed to by all. See *Military and Paramilitary Activities in and Against Nicaragua (Nicaragua v. United States of America),* Merits, Judgment, ICJ Reports 1986, 68, dissenting opinion of Judge Jennings at 543. Gray also notes that considering the fact that the case dealt with collective self-defence, the Court may have presented this threshold so as to limit possibilities for third state intervention. Gray, n 1, *supra,* 148.

[32] *Case Concerning Armed Activities on the Territory of the Congo (Democratic Republic of the Congo v. Uganda),* Judgment, ICJ General List no 116, 19 December 2005, para 147.

a tree or a cow, no armed attack has been perpetrated. But it would be fallacious to dismiss automatically from consideration as an armed attack every frontier incident. [....] When elements of the armed forces of Arcadia ambush a border patrol (or some other isolated unit) of Utopia, the assault has to rank as an armed attack and some sort of self-defence must be warranted in response.[33]

Whilst accepting a threshold of force for an incident to be considered an armed attack, Dinstein maintains that below the threshold would be incidents such as breaking into a diplomatic bag or even detaining a ship, but that an 'armed attack presupposes a use of force producing (or liable to produce) serious consequences, epitomized by territorial intrusions, human casualties or considerable destruction of property'.[34]

The precise definition of 'armed attack' is not self-explanatory and,[35] as noted, there are differences of opinion on this matter. The International Court of Justice has spoken of a threshold, and the opinions of commentators appear to be divided, with support both for the notion of almost any consequential armed force, particularly if resulting in casualties, being considered an armed attack;[36] others would deem there to be a threshold for defining an armed attack which leaves certain instances of force such as relatively small border incidents, as below that threshold.[37] The possible required threshold is, therefore, an issue that is not settled with regard to the well-established concept of self-defence against states, and consequently the same question remains open with regard to armed attacks by non-state actors.

The question of whether there is a separate threshold for independent (as opposed to the *Nicaragua* context) armed attacks by non-state actors has not yet been sufficiently tested to warrant an answer, but it is perhaps significant that much of the discussion surrounding self-defence in response to independent armed attacks by non-state actors, has arisen in the context of the overwhelming impact and casualties of 11 September 2001.[38] Another instance in which the threshold of violence in the context of non-state actors has arisen, is with regard to non-international armed conflicts. In conflicts of this type, there is the question of the threshold of violence necessary for the actual determination that the circumstances at hand do indeed constitute an armed conflict.[39] This is an issue

---

[33] Dinstein, n 5, *supra*, 195.   [34] *Ibid*, 193. See also *Oil Platforms*, n 28, *supra*.

[35] Alexandrov, n 29, *supra*, 96–7; B Simma (ed), *The Charter of the United Nations, A Commentary* (OUP: Oxford, 1994) 111–12; Randelzhofer, 'Article 51', n 29, *supra*, at 668–9.

[36] See n 33, *supra*, 34; Bethlehem, n 16, *supra*, 15; Wood, n 16, *supra*, 20.

[37] Lowe, n 16, *supra*, 16; A Randelzhofer, 'Article 51', n 29, *supra*, 669. A growing area of interest and perhaps concern, is with relation to attacks by means not envisaged in the past, some of which might not necessitate overt use of cross-border force, for example computer network attacks. See M Schmitt, 'Computer Network Attack and the Use of Force in International Law: Thoughts on a Normative Framework' 37 *Columbia Journal of Transnational Law* 885 (1999).

[38] Ch 1, *supra*, nn 40, 41.

[39] This is primarily a factual determination based upon the scale and intensity of violence, which above a certain threshold can be considered a non-international armed conflict. The determination of the factual existence of an armed conflict does not alter the legal status of the parties

which reflects upon the existence of an armed conflict situation and the corollary issue of applying the laws of armed conflict. In that respect it is of considerable significance to extraterritorial forcible measures against non-state actors, and is dealt with in greater detail in the later chapter covering the applicability of the laws of armed conflict. It is, therefore, a separate issue from the one currently at hand, which is the definition of an 'armed attack'. It may, however, be possible to draw from the realm of thresholds for determination of armed conflict, that there does exist recognition of differing scales of violence for inter-state force as opposed to force between states and non-state actors. Accordingly, the idea that for an act of violence by an independent non-state actor to constitute an armed attack, it would have to be of a larger scale than an attack by a state, may have merit.[40] Such an approach would be further warranted by the balance that must be struck between the recognition of a state's need to defend itself against armed attacks, while not allowing for all low level violence by armed groups to trigger a right to enter the territory of other states. Regardless of the scale of attack which would make self-defence applicable, the exercise of self-defence will not be allowed if the test of necessity has not been satisfied.

A further matter is the 'accumulation of events' approach according to which, while one incident might not qualify as an armed attack, if it is shown to be part of a chain of incidents then these may in total have accumulated in such a way as to give rise to self-defence. This claim has been raised in the context of Arab-Israeli conflicts, with regard to Israeli operations in Jordan, Egypt and Syria, which were claimed at times to be legitimate self-defence against the accumulation of attacks emanating from within these territories. Israel's actions were reviewed by the UN Security Council, more often than not, with disapproval and even condemnation, and usually regarded as unlawful due to them being considered one or all of disproportionate, illegally pre-emptive, punitive and reprisals.[41] The UK was also condemned in the Security Council for use of an unlawful reprisal in relation to a military operation it took against the Harib Fort in Yemen in 1964, which it claimed was a defensive measure against a series of shootings and raids.[42]

to the conflict, ie it does not grant new legitimacy to the non-state actor. See discussion of non-international armed conflicts in Ch 4, *infra*.

[40] See also Part II, *infra*, in Ch 4, sections 2, 4, 5.1 and Ch 5, section 3, on armed attack and armed conflict, and discussion of threshold in section on new types of conflict.

[41] D Bowett, 'Reprisals Involving Recourse To Armed Force', 66 *AJIL* 1 (1972); Alexandrov, n 29, *supra*, 172–9; although Franck points out that on at least one occasion—the 1956 Israeli actions against the *fedayeen* in Sinai—there may be significance in that the General Assembly did not condemn Israel. T Franck, *Recourse to Force: State Action Against Threats and Armed Attacks* (CUP: Cambridge, 2002) 56.

[42] D Bethlehem, 'International law and the use of force: the law as it is and as it should be', written evidence submitted by Daniel Bethlehem QC, Director of Lauterpacht Research Centre for International Law, University of Cambridge Select Committee on Foreign Affairs, Minutes of Evidence, 8 June 2004, available at <http://www.publications.parliament.uk/pa/cm200304/cmselect/cmfaff/441/4060808.htm>.

The questions of proportionality and pre-emption will be dealt with in later sections of this chapter. As for reprisals, it should be noted that the following discussion is concerned with peacetime reprisals, or *ad bellum* reprisals, to be distinguished from *in bello* reprisals which occur during an armed conflict.[43]

The 1928 *Naulilaa* Tribunal described reprisals as:

a form of self-help by the injured state, an action of response—after an unsuccessful demand—to an act contrary to the law of nations by the offending state [...] It aims at imposing, on the offending state, the reparation for the offence or the return to legality, in avoiding new offences.[44]

Bowett notes that the difference between reprisals and self-defence 'lies essentially in their aim or purpose':

Self-defense is permissible for the purpose of protecting the security of the state and the essential rights—in particular the rights of territorial integrity and political independence—upon which that security depends. In contrast, reprisals are punitive in character: they seek to impose reparation for the harm done, or to compel a satisfactory settlement of the dispute created by the initial illegal act, or to compel the delinquent state to abide by the law in the future. But, coming after the event and when the harm has already been inflicted, reprisals cannot be characterized as a means of protection.[45]

In the past, reprisals were accepted as lawful provided they satisfied certain criteria: existence of a previous violation, unsuccessful demand for redress and that they were proportionate to injury.[46] Nowadays, the predominant view is that peacetime armed reprisals are not allowed,[47] although this is not without difficulties.[48] It should be noted however, that the attitude towards reprisals depends much on how the concept is defined, and that according to certain interpretations, not all reprisals would necessarily be unlawful. This refers, in particular, to the view that certain actions might be described as reprisals but do also fall within the parameters of legitimate self-defence.[49] Accordingly, any action that fits the requirements for permissible self-defence, even if some are also calling it

---

[43] For general discussion of *ius ad bellum* reprisals, see: Bowett, 'Reprisals', n 41, *supra*; W O'Brien, 'Reprisals, Deterrence and Self-Defense in Counterterror Operations', 30 *Virginia Journal of International Law* 421 (1990).

[44] Extract translated from the original French. '*The Naulilaa Case*', *Responsabilité de l'Allemagne à raison des dommages causés dans les colonies portugaises du sud de l'Afrique (sentence sur le principe de la responsabilité). Portugal contre Allemagne. Lausanne, 31 juillet 1928*, reprinted in 2 *Recueil des Sentences Arbitrales*, vol II, 1026.

[45] Bowett, 'Reprisals', n 41, *supra*, 3. However, Bowett also points out the difficulties in maintaining the distinction, primarily on account of ascertaining motive, and differentiating between protection and retribution.

[46] Higgins, n 8, *supra*, 444; M Shaw, *International Law* (5th ed.) (CUP: Cambridge, 2003) 1023.

[47] 'There is general agreement among the Western nations that peacetime reprisals are unlawful under the Charter'. And 'Most writers in the West have declared peacetime reprisals unlawful, and governments too have adopted this position' both in Higgins, n 8, *supra*, 444 and Bowett, Ch 1, n 9, *supra*, 14.

[48] Bowett, 'Reprisals', n 41, *supra*; O'Brien, n 43, *supra*; n 58 and accompanying text, *infra*.

[49] Dinstein, n 5, *supra*, 222; Shaw, n 46, *supra*, 1023–4.

a reprisal, could therefore be lawful under the rules of self-defence.[50] The legality of reprisals that do not conform to the requirements of self-defence is, however, doubtful.[51]

If forcible measures taken in response to an accumulation of small attacks by a non-state actor are, therefore, judged to fit the description of reprisals, they are likely to be deemed unlawful unless they can be presented as falling within the accepted parameters of self-defence. This proposition should not be rejected out of hand, and does find some support. According to Ago:

> If, for example, a State suffers a series of successive and different acts of armed attack from another State, the requirement of proportionality will certainly not mean that the victim State is not free to undertake a single armed action on a much larger scale in order to put an end to this escalating succession of attacks.[52]

Dinstein is of the opinion that if 'continuous pin-prick assaults form a distinctive pattern, a cogent argument can be made for appraising them in their totality as an armed attack'.[53]

The above two positions are not one and the same. The latter view appears to allow for a series of instances each of which might not have been an armed attack on its own, to be accumulated into a whole which would then be considered an armed attack. The former view however, speaks of a series of incidents, each of which on its own was already an armed attack, which might give rise to self-defence. In this case, the victim state may have had the right to respond in self-defence, regardless of the accumulation, but the effect of allowing the separate attacks to be considered together, would become relevant when assessing the proportionality of the response.[54]

Past events may play a role in determining the continuing character of the threat. However, the problem of presenting an accumulation of events as the basis for self-defence is two-fold. First, self-defence has at its conceptual core an armed attack which necessitates a forcible response in order to remove the serious continuing danger posed to the state. If the accumulation is described as a series of individual past events then, by definition, they are over and are not obvious candidates for the title of a specific current threat necessitating self-defence. Secondly, if the accumulated events may not have themselves individually passed the threshold for an armed attack, but are instead presented as evidence of a

---

[50] '[…] while reprisals involving armed force may be lawful if resorted to in conformity with the right of self-defence. Reprisals as such undertaken during peacetime are thus unlawful, unless they fall within the framework of the principle of self-defence' from Shaw, n 46, *supra*, 1023–4; O Schachter 'The Extraterritorial Use of Force Against Terrorist Bases' 11 *Houston Journal of International Law* 309 (1988–9) 312.

[51] See further examination in section 1 of Ch 3, *infra*, on countermeasures.

[52] Ago Report, n 17, *supra*, para 121.

[53] Dinstein, n 5, *supra*, 230–1. See also discussion of 'accumulation of events', or '*nadelstichtaktik*', in N Feder, 'Reading the U.N. Charter Connotatively: Toward a New Definition of Armed Attack' 19 *New York University Journal of International Law and Politics* 395 (1987) 414–18.

[54] See further discussion in section 4, *infra*, on proportionality.

likely future armed attack, then they enter the debatable arena of pre-emptive self-defence, although they might contribute to determining the magnitude of the threat.[55] The link between accumulation of events and anticipatory action is encapsulated in an observation by Schmitt:

> [U]nless one is willing to deny victim States a consequential right of self-defense against terrorists, it is reasonable to interpret self-defense as permitting the use of force against terrorists who intend, and have the capability, to conduct further attacks against the victim. By this interpretation, it is not the imminency of an isolated action that is relevant, but rather the relationship between a series of attacks. Once the first of the related attacks has been launched, the question becomes whether the victim State has sufficient reliable evidence to conclude that further attacks are likely, not whether those further attacks are themselves imminent.[56]

This approach would appear to mark a departure from the requirement of imminency with relation to anticipatory measures. As will be shown shortly, even if one were to accept that states are entitled to take forcible self-defence action to thwart future attacks, the commonly accepted interpretation of this would have to include an imminent and serious threat which cannot be avoided without forcible measures. If the threat is of such severe magnitude, then any possible claim for self-defence is in effect in relation to this imminent attack, and not to the past events. Either way, the 'accumulation of events' approach itself constitutes a problematic basis for claiming a right to self-defence, unless involving a current ongoing armed attack or imminent threat of one.[57] Notwithstanding this conclusion, it is also true that, as in the past debate on reprisals, non-acceptance of an accumulation approach does have its drawbacks, such as ignoring the wider set of circumstances in which an incident takes place, and preventing states from responding and perhaps preventing the next attacks.[58] In the context of self-defence against non-state actors, it also raises a question over how a state can respond to continuous small attacks if these are seen as not individually passing the threshold for armed attack, and if not allowing for accumulation. This matter will be examined in Chapter 3.

A question can also be raised about the ability to determine if and when the initial armed attack is over. For instance, if the attack consists of individuals taking over civilian aircraft, as it did on 11 September 2001, it becomes difficult to know how many other aircraft might be carrying members of the group about to act in a similar way. Moreover, the suspicion that there are additional cells of

---

[55] 'A critical determinant of the magnitude of the terrorist threat would often be the pattern of prior attacks. An attack that is part of a series of attacks adds to the "necessity" of forcible defense. It cannot be judged in isolation.' Schachter, n 50, *supra*, 313.

[56] Schmitt, n 21, *supra*, 25; on risk created by the link between accumulation of events to anticipatory self-defence see C Tams, 'The Use of Force against Terrorists' 20 *EJIL* 359 (2009) 390.

[57] See also discussion in Alexandrov, n 29, *supra*, 182–4.

[58] Bowett, 'Reprisals', n 41, *supra*; O'Brien, n 43, *supra*.

the same group who might be planning to carry out similar operations in the following days, might also provide support for the claim that the armed attack is still under way. Determining whether or not the attack is over can be crucial to the debate over immediacy in the context of the type of response taken by the state. Nevertheless, on this aspect of self-defence it would appear that it is not altogether different to armed attacks by states. In the latter situations, it might also not be possible to know whether the aggressor state is planning to launch another barrage of missiles or not. Whether the armed attack was by a state or non-state actor, one can only expect the victim state to act in accordance with the secure knowledge of past and present events, and reliable evidence of imminent future events where this is available. Moreover, when it comes to taking action to prevent future attacks, this is already a matter of substantial debate, as will be seen in the following section.

3. Pre-emptive or anticipatory self-defence

At the outset of the discussion of this topic, a moment of attention should be given to the semantics involved. It appears that in the context of self-defence, 'anticipatory' and 'pre-emptive' are often used interchangeably.[59] However, there is a difference between these terms. An anticipatory act is 'a prior action that takes into account or forestalls a later action',[60] whereas a pre-emptive act is 'marked by the seizing of the initiative: initiated by oneself.'[61] The former can be understood as being associated with a specific event that is known to be approaching, whilst the latter term might encompass action taken in the absence of information of a specific future event, but rather to forestall a more amorphous potential contingency, in which the imminence, and perhaps even the certainty, of a future attack ever occurring is questionable. Until recently the basis of opinions that allowed for some form of self-defence against a future attack, was in the context of the need to thwart a specific imminent attack.[62] In fact, there is also a suggestion that the term 'interceptive' self-defence be used, indicating in even stronger terms that the situation is one of a specific attack that is definitely about to strike the state.[63] So long as it was clear that the type of attack under discussion was of the imminent kind, it would not have seemed necessary to differentiate between 'anticipating' or 'pre-empting' it. However, in recent times the debate has included the discussion of a possible right of states to take action in order to prevent hypothetical future eventualities which cannot easily be described as specific imminent attacks. This

---

[59] Roberts speaks of another differentiation, between 'pre-emptive' and 'preventive'. Roberts, n 16, *supra*, 43; See also G Simpson in *Principles of International Law*, n 16 *supra*, 64.
[60] Merriam-Webster's Collegiate Dictionary (11th ed.) (Miriam-Webster, 2003) 54, n 60.
[61] Merriam-Webster's Collegiate Dictionary (11th ed.) (Miriam-Webster, 2003) 978, n 61.
[62] See nn 68, 109 and accompanying text, *infra*, 109.
[63] See n 80 and accompanying text, *infra*.

is most clearly evidenced in the US doctrine of pre-emption, according to which 'pre-emptive' appears to denote the widening of the net to capture situations that in the past were not raised as potential, legitimate forms of self-defence.[64] This interpretation of 'pre-emptive' differs from the understanding of this term as may have been used in the past interchangeably with 'anticipatory'.[65] In the current context it is useful to bear in mind the distinction between 'anticipatory' and 'pre-emptive'. Notwithstanding, since the majority of writings on this issue (including most of those cited in this section), have used the two terms interchangeably, it will nevertheless have to appear as such when quoting writings and other sources.[66]

Anticipatory self-defence is at the heart of the founding formulation of self-defence in international law, as it appears in the case of the *Caroline*.[67] The circumstances of that case involved action taken to thwart an impending attack. The *Caroline* formula speaks of a necessity of self-defence which is 'instant, overwhelming, and leaving no choice of means, and no moment for deliberation.'[68] It is clear that this formulation envisages the possible need to act in anticipation of an impending attack. On the other hand, it is equally evident that this formulation does not entertain the wider notion of pre-emptive action against possible future attacks which are not specific and imminent.

Article 51 of the UN Charter is however not a replica of the *Caroline* formula. In fact, by allowing for a right of self-defence if 'an armed attack occurs', it appears to be more limited than the *Caroline*, and, prima facie, to rule out the possibility of self-defence against future attacks, however imminent they may be. Indeed, from the discussions at the San-Francisco Conference preceding the adopting of the Charter, it was clear that the drafters intended to limit self-defence so as to preclude anticipatory action. Governor Stassen (a leader of the US team), speaking of Article 51 limiting self-defence, said:

this was intentional and sound. We did not want exercised the right of self-defense before an armed attack had occurred.[69]

---

[64] See quotations at nn 90, 91, *infra*.

[65] Gray notes an occasion on which the UK government may have purposely chosen to use 'anticipatory' in distinction from the wider 'pre-emptive' of the US. Gray, n 1, *supra*, 179.

[66] Greenwood notes the difficulty in attempting terminological precision. See C Greenwood, 'International Law and the Pre-emptive Use of Force: Afghanistan, Al-Qaida, and Iraq', 4 *San Diego International Law Journal* 7 (2003) 9.

[67] See discussion of the case in Ch 1, n 46 and accompanying text, *supra*; According to Dinstein, the *Caroline* is not the best example for anticipatory self-defence, Dinstein, n 5, *supra*, 184–5; However, as can be seen throughout this section, this case is accepted as a centre-point for discussion on the topic.

[68] Letter from Mr Webster, n 4, *supra*.

[69] Minutes of 48th meeting of US delegation, SF (20 May 1945) 1 Foreign Relations of the US (1945) 813, 818, quoted in Franck, n 41, *supra*, 50. Franck also quotes the following from the meetings of the US delegation: A member of the delegation 'posed a question as to our freedom under this provision in case a fleet had started from abroad against an American republic but had not yet attacked' Stassen's response was 'we could not under this provision attack the fleet but we could send a fleet of our own and be ready in case an attack came.' 38th meeting (14 May 1945) 707, 709, quoted in Franck, n 41, *supra*, 50.

This was interpreted accordingly by Kunz in 1947, stating that 'The "imminent" armed attack does not suffice under Art. 51'.[70] According to Brownlie it 'can only be concluded that the view that Article 51 does not permit anticipatory action is correct and that the arguments to the contrary are either unconvincing or based on inconclusive pieces of evidence'.[71]

There has been ongoing support for this view,[72] but with the modern warfare of long-range missiles and capabilities unknown at the time of the drafting, it may be difficult to sustain it at an absolute level.[73] Indeed, the limiting approach of Article 51 is not deemed acceptable by many commentators. As noted by Bowett:

> It is not believed, therefore, that Art.51 restricts the traditional right of self-defence so as to exclude action taken against an imminent danger but before 'an armed attack occurs'. In our view such a restriction is both unnecessary and inconsistent with Art.2(4) which forbids not only force but the threat of force, and, furthermore, it is a restriction which bears no relation to the realities of a situation which may arise prior to an actual attack and call for self-defence immediately if it is to be of any avail at all. No state can be expected to await an initial attack which, in the present state of armaments, may well destroy the state's capacity for further resistance and so jeopardize its very existence.[74]

Support for some form of anticipatory self-defence comes from many additional commentators,[75] and states seem to have refrained from criticizing (even if not outspokenly endorsing) what appeared as a classic form of anticipatory self-defence by Israel in 1967.[76] According to the UK Attorney General, it 'has been the consistent position of successive United Kingdom Governments over many

---

[70] Kunz, n 28, *supra*, 878.

[71] I Brownlie, *International Law and the Use of Force by States* (OUP: Oxford, 1963) 278 and 275–8.

[72] Randelzhofer, 'Article 51', n 29, *supra*, 675–6; Dinstein, n 5, *supra*, 183–7.

[73] Franck, n 41, *supra*, 50. Brownlie himself notes that 'The whole problem is rendered incredibly delicate by the existence of long-range missiles ready for use: the difference between attack and imminent attack may now be negligible' n 71, *supra*, 368.

[74] D Bowett, *Self-Defence in International Law* (Manchester University Press: Manchester, 1958) 191–2.

[75] Jennings and Watts, n 17, *supra*, 421–2; Higgins, n 8, *supra*, 442; WK Lietzau, 'Combating Terrorism: Law Enforcement or War?' in *Terrorism and International Law: Challenges and Responses* 75-84, 78; Bethlehem, n 16, *supra*, 34; Greenwood in *Principles of International Law*, n 16, *supra*, 35; Lowe, n 16, *supra*, 35; Roberts, n 16, *supra*, 35–6; Sands in *Principles of International Law*, n 16, *supra*, 36; Wood, n 16, *supra*, 39. Indeed, recognition for the need of anticipatory self-defence can be found in the foundations of international law. See H Grotius, *The Law of War and Peace* (*De Jure Belli ac Pacis*) originally published in 1625, English translation by John W Parker (Cambridge, 1853); 'A Nation has the right to resist the injury another seeks to inflict upon it, and to use force [...] against the aggressor. It may even anticipate the other's design, being careful, however, not to act upon vague and doubtful suspicions, lest it should run the risk of becoming itself the aggressor.' E de Vattel, *The Law of Nations, Applied to the Conduct and Affairs of Nations and Sovereigns*, Vol IV (7th edn) (J Chitty translation, 1849) 3.

[76] Higgins, n 8, *supra*, 442–4; Franck, n 41, *supra*, 104–5.

years that the right of self-defence under international law includes the right to use force where an armed attack is imminent'.[77]

How then to reconcile acceptance of anticipatory self-defence with Article 51 of the Charter? One possibility is based on the fact that Article 51 speaks of self-defence being an 'inherent' right. Accordingly, some have taken this as evidence that it does not impair the pre-existing anticipatory component of this 'inherent' right. As noted by Higgins, it 'is also contended that the continued validity of this pre-charter law on anticipatory self-defence is consistent with the reference in Art. 51 to the right of self-defence being "inherent" '.[78]

There are, however, strong reasons to dismiss the possibility that customary international law continues to contain a right of self-defence that is different to, and wider than, the UN Charter, including the fact that this would render the efforts and restrictions placed into Article 51 almost meaningless, by containing clear constraints (eg referencing the role of the Security Council) for self-defence to actual armed attacks, while allowing anticipatory self-defence outside the sphere of these parameters.[79]

An additional approach would be to make use of the concept of 'interceptive' self-defence. Whilst preferring the restrictive interpretation of self-defence, Dinstein supports the notion of 'interceptive' self-defence, according to which the anticipatory action is taken only when the other side has taken such steps as to indicate that it has unequivocally committed itself to carrying out the armed attack, eg deployed its troops in the direction of the border, even if they have not yet crossed it:[80]

The crux of the issue, therefore, is not who fired the first shot but who embarked upon an apparently irreversible course of action, thereby crossing the legal Rubicon....Whereas a preventative strike anticipates a latent armed attack that is merely 'foreseeable' (or even just 'conceivable'), an interceptive strike counters an armed attack which is in progress, even if it is still incipient: the blow is 'imminent' and practically 'unavoidable'.

It follows that in some cases, one might be able to interpret the commencement of certain activity as a situation falling within the Article 51 requirement of an armed attack that has 'begun to occur', and thus as part of 'classic' self-defence, rather than anticipatory.[81]

---

[77] Lord Goldsmith, Attorney General of the UK, House of Lords, Hansard, col 370, 21 April 2004.

[78] Higgins, n 8, *supra*, 442.

[79] See Dinstein's strong refute of such claims, Dinstein, n 5, *supra*, 185; See also Brownlie, Ch 1, n 12, *supra*, 272–5; see discussion of the question of a separate customary right to self-defence, in Randelzhofer, 'Article 51', n 29, *supra* at 666–7, 675–8; see also Myjers and White, on the concept of wider customary rights in the context of collective security: E Myjer and N White, 'The Twin Towers Attack: An Unlimited Right to Self-Defence?' 7 *Journal of Conflict and Security Law* 5 (2002) 17.

[80] Dinstein, n 5, *supra*, 191; See also discussion of possibility of intercepting rockets in flight, in Brownlie, n 11, *supra*, 367–8.

[81] H Waldock, 'The Regulation of the Use of Force by Individual States in International Law', 81 *Recueil des Cours* 455 (1952) 498, also cited *ibid*, See Simpson, Ch 1, n 28, *supra*, 38.

An additional view of the anticipatory self-defence dilemma is that while self-defence against a threat of attack that has not yet occurred is proscribed by law, it might in limited circumstances be tolerated by the international community.[82] State practice appears to support the view that, while there may not have been amassed strong evidence of numerous actual invocations of a legal right to anticipatory self defence,[83] states, including those acting as UN Security Council members, will tolerate anticipatory self-defence (or at least refrain from harsh rebuke) provided it does not appear to have stepped outside the strict *Caroline* requirements of necessity and immediacy.[84]

In summary, once again it is apt to quote Jennings and Watts:

> The better view is probably that while anticipatory action in self-defence is normally unlawful, it is not necessarily unlawful in all circumstances, the matter depending on the facts of the situation including in particular the seriousness of the threat and the degree to which pre-emptive action is really necessary and is the only way of avoiding that serious threat; the requirements of necessity and proportionality are probably even more pressing in relation to anticipatory self-defence than they are in other circumstances.[85]

When examining the question of anticipatory self-defence against non-state actors, it would appear that there is not a markedly different answer. First, as noted earlier in this Chapter, the *Caroline Case* itself dealt with self-defence against a non-state actor. Coupled with the fact that the *Caroline* formula is also still today seen as legitimizing a limited form of anticipatory self-defence, it would be hard to argue that the *Caroline* formula is not proof that there exists a limited possibility of anticipatory self-defence against non-state actors. It is interesting to note in this context that in the course of examining the question of necessity for anticipatory self-defence, Jennings and Watts use the following example:

> When, to give an example, a State is informed that a body of armed men is being organized on neighbouring territory for the purpose of a raid into its territory, and then the danger can be removed through an appeal to the authorities of the neighbouring country or to an appropriate international organization, no case of necessity has arisen. But if such an appeal is fruitless or not possible, or if there is danger in delay, a case of necessity arises, and the threatened State is justified in invading the neighbouring country for the purpose of disarming the intending raiders.[86]

If, therefore, one accepts the proposition that, in certain circumstances, a state might have little choice but to resort to anticipatory self-defence against another state, the same can be said when there is a necessity to do so in the face of an

---

[82] Cassese, n 29, *supra*, 362.   [83] Gray, n 1, *supra*, 130.
[84] As has been commented was the case in the Israeli-Arab war of 1967; Franck, n 41, *supra*, 97–107.
[85] Jennings and Watts, n 17, *supra*, 421–2.   [86] *Ibid.*

imminent attack emanating from a non-state actor.[87] As in the earlier examined question of the scale of the attack,[88] it might be the case that the notion of anticipatory self-defence against non-state actors will find greater acceptance in circumstances involving dangers of large magnitude.

A particular challenge that might be raised in the context of measures against non-state actors, is that it can be extremely difficult to have advance knowledge of an impending non-state actor attack as non-state groups are more likely to be operating in clandestine cells, and are less vulnerable to being on satellite imagery than large militaries of other states. Furthermore the fear that non-state actors could, in modern times, lay their hands upon potent weapons, including chemical, biological and even nuclear materials, could further compound the challenge.[89] This could prompt the introduction of a wider concept of pre-emption, which does not require strict knowledge of a specific impending attack. Indeed, these considerations appear in the US Department of Defense, and military reports: 'Terrorists have demonstrated that they can conduct devastating surprise attacks. Allowing opponents to strike first—particularly in an era of proliferation is unacceptable. Therefore, the United States must defeat the most dangerous challenges early and at a safe distance, before they are allowed to mature'.[90]

These concerns presumably constitute part of the reasoning underlying the adoption of an approach advocating pre-emptive measures to counter these threats, as has been evident for a number of years in the US doctrine:

The United States has long maintained the option of preemptive actions to counter a sufficient threat to our national security. The greater the threat, the greater is the risk of inaction and the more compelling the case for taking anticipatory action to defend ourselves, even if uncertainty remains as to the time and place of the enemy's attack. To forestall or prevent such hostile acts by our adversaries, the United States will, if necessary, act preemptively. The United States will not use force in all cases to preempt emerging threats, nor should nations use preemption as a pretext for aggression. Yet in an age where the enemies of civilization openly and actively seek the world's most destructive technologies, the United States cannot remain idle while dangers gather.[91]

---

[87] Schachter, n 50, *supra*, 312; P Sands, 'International Law and the Use of Force', 1 June 2004, written evidence submitted by Professor Philippe Sands QC, to Select Committee on Foreign Affairs, available at <http://www.publications.parliament.uk/pa/cm200304/cmselect/cmfaff/441/4060801.htm>, paras 9, 35.

[88] See section 2, *supra*, on scale of armed attack.

[89] Greenwood n 66, *supra*, 16. On the possibilities of such groups acquiring nuclear weapons, see R Chesney, 'National Insecurity: Nuclear Material Availability and the Threat Of Nuclear Terrorism' 20 *Loyola of Los Angeles International and Comparative Law Review* 29 (1997). On the dangers of biological weapons, see D Koplow, 'That Wonderful Year: Smallpox, Genetic Engineering, and Bio-Terrorism' 62 *Maryland Law Review* 417 (2003).

[90] 'The National Defense Strategy of the United States of America', US Department of Defense, March 2005, 9.

[91] 'The National Security Strategy of the United States of America', The White House, September 2002, 15.

A similar view has been voiced by the former US Secretary of Defense,[92] whilst the UK Secretary of State for Defence has also suggested rethinking pre-emption in light of terrorist threats.[93]

The position of the US in favour of what appears to be a wide interpretation of pre-emption is not to be taken for granted, considering the fact that in the past the Security Council passed a resolution strongly condemning Israel for carrying out a pre-emptive strike against the Osiraq nuclear reactor in Iraq.[94] The seemingly different position in that case can be the result of a number of factors, including a perception that the circumstances of that particular case may not have warranted an attack due to a lack of exhaustion of viable alternatives as well as no imminent need.[95] Another difference between the case of Osiraq and the US position quoted above, with regard to terrorism, is that the threat from terrorism may be perceived to be of a different nature and requiring a different approach. Political and other pressures can also play a role in the perception and attitude towards potential threats. An additional concern, which has been voiced with regard to the need for anticipatory self-defence against non-state actors, is that terrorist attacks are often aimed at civilian 'soft targets', which would be likely to be destroyed and cannot be defended in the same way as defended military targets. Preventive actions therefore take on added importance.[96]

The primary question raised is whether the types of threats posed by non-state actors, justify widening the, arguably, existing, but narrow, allowance for anticipatory self-defence, into a wider form of pre-emption forgoing the requirement of a known imminent attack. It would appear that there is currently very little legal support for redrawing the boundaries of self-defence in such a manner.[97]

One should recall the primary and fundamental concern that lies at the heart of the objection to pre-emptive self-defence, and the reason that even those who support a right to anticipatory action are in most cases wary of the need to keep

---

[92] '[...] defending the U.S. requires prevention, self-defense and sometimes preemption. It is not possible to defend against every conceivable kind of attack in every conceivable location at every minute of the day or night. Defending against terrorism and other emerging 21st century threats may well require that we take the war to the enemy. The best, and in some cases, the only defense, is a good offense.' See 'Secretary Rumsfeld Speaks on "21st Century Transformation" of US Armed Forces', remarks as delivered by Secretary of Defense Donald Rumsfeld, National Defense University, Fort McNair, Washington, DC, 31 January 2002. Available at <http://www.defense.gov/speeches/speeches.aspx?speechid=183>.

[93] 'Another specific area of international law we perhaps need to think more about is whether the concept of imminence—ie the circumstances when a State can act in self-defence without waiting for an attack—is sufficiently well developed to take account of the new threats faced'. See J Reid, 'Twenty-First Century Warfare—Twentieth Century Rules', *The RUSI Journal* 151: 3 (2006) 14–16.

[94] Security Council Res no 487 (1981), 19 June 1981.

[95] Higgin, n 8, *supra*, 442–4; see also Gray, n 1, *supra*, 133.

[96] R Mullerson, '*Jus Ad Bellum: Plus Ça Change (Le Monde) Plus C'est La Même Chose (Le Droit)?*' 7 *Journal of Conflict and Security Law* 149 (2002) 180.

[97] Berman in *Principles of International Law*, n 16, *supra*, 40.

it within strict limitations. Succinctly put, this is the fear that pre-emption will become 'a pretext for unprovoked aggression.'[98]

The *Caroline* test required not only that the threat be imminent, but also that there be no alternative means to counter it ('leaving no choice of means'[99]), other than forcible self-defence. The two requirements are inextricably linked: the less imminent the attack, the more likely it is that non-forcible alternatives can be tried before resorting to forcible self-defence. This was at the centre of the differing reactions to the Israeli strike against the Iraqi nuclear installation, as opposed to the 1967 war. In the latter, there appeared to be widespread acceptance that Israel faced little choice but to launch military operations in the face of an imminent attack. In the former case, however, it might be said that with the lack of an imminent attack, Israel had other avenues of action it could have pursued instead of resorting to a military strike.[100] The need to establish necessity becomes even greater when contemplating anticipatory self-defence.[101] The link between imminence and the possibility of other means, as can be seen, is one more reason for requiring that self-defence be limited to imminent attacks.

Allowing for pre-emptive self-defence in the absence of a known imminent attack which cannot be thwarted by other means (ie outside the *Caroline* formula), leaves the system on a perilous slippery slope, at the bottom of which is an international order in which states would freely disregard the foundational prohibition on the use of force, by alleging that they were pre-empting obscure future dangers or threats.[102] As noted by McGoldrick, 'under a pre-emption doctrine, conflicts will almost certainly escalate.'[103] There is, therefore, sound reason behind the view that if anticipatory self-defence is to be allowed at all, it must be limited to the strict confines of imminent attacks, and not to vague future threats of attack.[104] It should be noted however, that the concept of imminence might also need to be interpreted to take into account the nature and gravity of the threat, and the capabilities, means and technologies of delivery.[105]

Indeed, despite the above mention of positions within the US and UK, it appears that both these governments do recognize that anticipatory action must be limited:

Under the most dangerous and compelling circumstances, prevention might require the use of force to disable or destroy WMD in the possession of terrorists or others or to strike targets (e.g., terrorists) that directly threaten the United States or U.S. friends or other interests.[106]

---

[98] Higgins, n 8, *supra*, 442. This is what leads some to maintain support for a ban on anticipatory self-defence: 'It may thus be contended that, however *unrealistic* the ban on pre-emptive self-defence deriving from Article 51 may be in the present circumstances of warfare, States prefer to avoid *risks of abuse*' Cassese, n 29, *supra*, 361.

[99] See n 4, *supra*.   [100] See nn 76, 94, 95, *supra*, and accompanying text.

[101] Gardam, n 1, *supra*, 153–4.

[102] 'A More Secure World: Our Shared Responsibility' Report of the Secretary General's High-level Panel on Threats, Challenges and Change, UN Doc, A/59/565, 2004, paras 188–92.

[103] D McGoldrick, *From '9-11' to the 'Iraq War 2003'* (Hart: Oxford, 2004) 76.

[104] Greenwood, n 75, *supra*, 35; Shaw in *Principles of International Law*, n 16, *supra*, 48; Wood, n 16, *supra*, 52.

[105] Shaw, *ibid*; Sands, n 75, *supra*, 44; Greenwood, n 75, *supra*, 42.

[106] 'The National Defense Strategy of the United States of America', n 90, *supra*, 10. Emphasis added.

And according to the UK Attorney General 'international law permits the use of force in self-defence against an imminent attack, but does not authorise the use of force to mount a pre-emptive strike against a threat that is more remote'.[107]

The acceptance of anticipatory self-defence, coupled with a warning of restricting it to imminent attacks, finds significant support in the 2004 'Report of the Secretary General's High-level Panel on Threats, Challenges and Change', in which the discussion of self-defence refers also to the context of terrorism threats. The Report declares that:

> a threatened State, according to long established international law, can take military action as long as the threatened attack is *imminent*, no other means would deflect it and the action is proportionate. The problem arises where the threat in question is not imminent but still claimed to be real.[108]

Indeed, whilst accepting that allowance for some form of anticipatory action against imminent attacks has strong support, the cautionary words of Higgins must be borne in mind:

> Even so far as conventional military action is concerned there must be circumstances (notwithstanding the wording of Art. 2(4)) which allow a State to take preemptive action in self-defence, without waiting to be struck first. But it is equally important that this possibility is not abused, and is not used as a pretext for unprovoked aggression. The test enunciated in *The Caroline* help strike that balance: for the State considering an anticipatory use of self-defence, the necessity must be instant, overwhelming, and leaving no choice of means, and no moment for deliberation.[109]

To summarize this section, it appears that international law has developed in such a way as to recognize the threats posed by non-state actors, as was evident in the earlier chapter examining whether self-defence can be used against these groups. There is not, however, any substantial support for the claim that international law has now stretched the boundaries of self-defence so as to allow for pre-emptive action against anything other than an imminent attack which cannot be prevented without recourse to force. This is as true with regard to non-state actors as it is in the context of attacks by states.

4. Proportionality of the action taken in self-defence

Once forcible action is taken in self-defence, there remain questions over the precise form it takes. Proportionality is a crucial requirement of lawful self-defence,[110] and would be demanded of any measure taken against non-state actors. Whilst it is a fundamental principle of international law, particularly in the context

---

[107] Lord Goldsmith, n 77, *supra*.
[108] See n 102, *supra*, para 188. The given example of not imminent is 'for example the acquisition, with allegedly hostile intent, of nuclear weapons-making capability'.
[109] Higgins, n 8, *supra*, 442.   [110] See nn 1, 2, *supra*.

of self-defence,[111] it should be noted that the principle of proportionality comes in a number of different guises and forms, and one should be aware of which form is being used, in order to avoid confusion. Proportionality is in essence a formula balancing two (or more) variables, but these variables can change depending on the context within which the principle is being employed.[112] Thus:

(i) In the context of law enforcement, under international human rights law the proportionality principle requires that the force being used be proportionate to the sought objective (eg not to fire a lethal weapon to prevent someone evading a parking ticket).[113]

(ii) Under the *ius in bello*—the laws of armed conflict regulating the means and methods of warfare—the proportionality principle accepts that lethal force may be used as a first resort (unlike human rights law) against lawful targets, but requires a balancing that would ensure no excessive harm is done to civilians and civilian objects ('collateral damage').[114]

(iii) In the context of self-defence, and the rules of the *ius ad bellum*, with which we are currently concerned, the principle of proportionality is used in order to gauge the lawfulness of the measures of self-defence. On one side of the formula we therefore have the actions taken by the state in self-defence, but against what are we measuring this? There are essentially two possibilities here:

(a) That self-defence actions are measured in proportion to the events preceding them, with particular reference to the armed attack that gave rise to the self-defence;

(b) That the proportionality of self-defence is measured in relation to the threat that is being faced and the means necessary to end the attack.

The former calculation has been employed in various cases, such as Israeli cross border operations into neighbouring countries during the 1950s and 1960s, although these past cases were sometimes characterized as reprisals which, as noted earlier, are distinct from self-defence.[115] Indeed, according to past rules

---

[111] *Advisory Opinion on Nuclear Weapons*, n 2, *supra*, para 41; J Delbruck, 'Proportionality' in *Encyclopaedia of Public International Law, vol 7* (Elsevier Science Publishers, 1984) 398.

[112] N Lubell, 'Challenges in Applying Human Rights Law to Armed Conflict' 859 *International Review of the Red Cross* 737 (December 2005) 745–6.

[113] UN Basic Principles on the Use of Force and Firearms by Law Enforcement Officials, UN Doc. A/CONF.144/28/Rev.1 at 112 (1990); UN Code of Conduct for Law Enforcement Officials, GA res 34/169, annex, 34 UN GAOR Supp (no 46) at 186; UN Doc. A/34/46 (1979); *McCann and ors v. United Kingdom*, 21 EHRR 97, paras 147–9; N Rodley, *The Treatment of Prisoners under International Law* (OUP: Oxford, 1999) 185–8; CK Boyle, 'The concept of arbitrary deprivation of life' in BG Ramcharan (ed), *The Right to Life in International Law* (Nijhoff: Dordrecht, 1985) 221–44. See detailed discussion in Ch 7, *infra*.

[114] Protocol Additional to the Geneva Conventions of 12 August 1949, and relating to the Protection of Victims of International Armed Conflicts (Protocol I) 1125 UNTS 3, entered into force 7 December 1978, Art 51.5(b). See detailed discussion in Ch 6, *infra*.

[115] See nn 41–57, *supra*, and accompanying text.

governing reprisals, in order to be lawful they would need to have been proportionate to the preceding harm.[116] In self-defence, however, the proportionality requirement is cognisant of there being an ongoing danger which the self-defence is aimed at ending, and the proportionality and limitations placed upon actions taken in self-defence must therefore be measured in relation to the achievement of this legitimate aim, as is the position of many commentators,[117] and explained by Ago:

It would be mistaken, however, to think that there must be proportionality between the conduct constituting the armed attack and the opposing conduct. The action needed to halt and repulse the attack may well have to assume dimensions disproportionate to those of the attack suffered. What matters in this respect is the result to be achieved by the 'defensive' action, and not the forms, substance and strength of the action itself.[118]

Some views take this even further, so as to allow for the counter-force to continue until complete victory. Self-defence, in the words of Kunz:

…serves primarily to repel an illegal armed attack. But, contrary to municipal law, it may not stop here: it seems to give the state or states exercising the right of individual or collective self-defense the right to resort to a justified war, to carry this war to victory, to impose a peace treaty upon the vanquished aggressor, always presupposing that the Security Council has failed and continues to fail of taking the measures necessary to maintain international peace and security. The right of self-defense is, in such cases, a right to resort to war. But as the action is war, even if illegal on the side of the aggressor, the state or states acting in self-defense are bound by the laws of war.[119]

Along these lines, Dinstein differentiates between 'on-the-spot' reactions, in which there must be proportionality between the scale and effects of force and counter-force, to actual war, which does not have the same concept of proportionality, and can be fought to the finish.[120]

Whilst the principle of proportionality is considered a fundamental principle of international law, when faced with the need to implement it in practice its precise content becomes infamously elusive.[121] The underlying difficulty is that the principle can require one to place on the two sides of the balancing scales different elements, which seemingly have little in common and cannot easily be measured against each other. For instance, in the laws of armed conflict principle of proportionality, one is required to measure direct and concrete military

---

[116] *Ibid.*

[117] Bowett, n 74, *supra*, 269; Berman, n 97, *supra*, 33, 52; Greenwood, n 75, *supra*, 53; Shaw, n 104, *supra*, 55; Wood, n 16, *supra*, 57; Schmitt, n 21, *supra*, 20. However, see Simpson, Ch 1, n 28, *supra*, 56.

[118] Ago Report, n 17, *supra*, para 121.   [119] Kunz, n 28, *supra*, 876–7.

[120] Dinstein, n 5, *supra*, 221, 237–9.

[121] Dinstein refers to an element of elasticity as a characteristic of proportionality. Dinstein, n 5, *supra*, 231. 'Very different conclusions may be reached as to what is proportionate action depending on how the equation is defined and applied.' Gardam, n 1, *supra*, 155.

advantage (itself not a concept with clear defining criteria), against the expected harm to civilians and civilian objects.[122]

Whilst perhaps not as confounding a task in the context of self-defence, measurement of the legitimate force against the threat posed by the attacker is not completely free of uncertainty.[123] If the proportionality of the response is to be measured against the danger faced by the state, a primary challenge must be the ability to measure this danger.[124]

When faced with non-state actors, the same basic line of thought would be appropriate, in that proportionality cannot be confined to an exact measurement against the original attack, and must include a balancing of the means necessary to achieve an end to the danger.[125] However, adherence to the proportionality requirement may be even harder to assess, since the activities and capabilities of the non-state actor are likely to be less apparent than that of a state. This makes it difficult to gauge the existence of an ongoing situation which needs to be countered by the self-defence, and by which the proportionality is to be measured.

Of particular concern with regard to assessing the scope of response to attacks by non-state actors, is the matter of dealing with splintered groups that have operational cells in a number of countries. Groups such as Al-Qaeda are said to have cells operating in many territories,[126] and even groups with a localized agenda can operate in and from other countries, for example the Palestinian Hamas and Lebanese Hezbollah, which have been reported to maintain a presence in South America.[127] There are in fact two separate issues at hand:

(i) in the context of self-defence, the question is whether a state's response to an armed attack by a non-state actor located in a second state, can legitimize a self-defence response against cells of the non-state actor located in a third state; and

(ii) if one is to accept the possibility of the existence of a cross-border armed conflict between a non-state actor and a state, there is a question as to whether such an ongoing conflict could encompass numerous military operations in various countries, as all being part and parcel of the same armed conflict.

---

[122] Protocol 1, n 114, *supra*. See discussion of proportionality in the context of terrorism in D Kretzmer, 'Targeted Killing of Suspected Terrorists: Extra-Judicial Executions or Legitimate Means of Defence?' 16 *EJIL* 171, 201; see further discussion in Ch 6, *infra*.

[123] See discussion of proportionality in Gardam, n 1, *supra*, 155–87.

[124] Berman, n 97, *supra*, 52.   [125] Schachter, n 50, *supra*, 315.

[126] 'Terror cells regroup—and now their target is Europe' *The Observer*, 11 January 2004; but see also discussion of characteristics of Al-Qaeda as well as the further difficulties raised by the possibility of loosely connected networks of groups, in Ch 5, *infra*.

[127] 'Security Authorities: Hezbollah and Hamas Networks are being Established in South America' *Haaretz*, 10 February 2004 (translated from Hebrew).

The latter matter will be dealt with in the context of the 'war on terror' in Chapter 5 and in the final Chapter of this work. As for the first question, the US has asserted that its right to self-defence can go beyond one single territory, as noted by Bellinger:

We would all be better off if al Qaida limited itself to the territory of Afghanistan, but unfortunately, that is not the reality that we face. There is no principle of international law that limits a state's ability to act in self-defense to a single territory, when the threat comes from areas outside that territory as well.[128]

The laws of self-defence do not contain an in-built geographical limitation. However, the proportionality requirement of self-defence might limit the response in such a fashion. This possibility has been raised by questioning whether it would have been proportionate, in the example of the Falklands/Malvinas conflict, for the UK to attack Argentinean targets in geographical areas removed from the primary area of conflict.[129] This observation notwithstanding, if a state suffers an armed attack from a group with multiple bases in different territories, and if the only means to repel ongoing attacks must involve tackling the non-state actor in more than one territory, then this possibility cannot be completely ruled out. Two major considerations must be taken into account however, before embarking on this course of action. First, the necessity test must be applied separately for each of the territories concerned. For example, whilst there may have been the necessity of carrying out self-defence operations against Al-Qaeda bases in Afghanistan, this would not have been the case with regard to cells operating from many other territories—whether it is cells in Hamburg or Tashkent—in which the territorial state would readily take action itself. As raised earlier,[130] in the context of self-defence against non-state actors, the requirement of necessity dictates the need to first establish that the territorial state itself is unwilling or unable to put an end to the armed attacks. The second consideration with regard to responding to a splintered group, is that care must be taken to differentiate between a situation in which self-defence against more than one territorial area is necessary in the context of the armed attack that the state is repelling, as opposed to a claim that this splintered group presents a threat for potential future armed attacks emanating from its cells in multiple countries. The latter is perhaps closer to the claims that are in fact sounded, and if that is the case then it is necessary to deal with these claims while bearing in mind the elements of the debate on pre-emptive self-defence.[131] The real

---

[128] Bellinger, n 23, *supra*.

[129] R Higgins, *Problems and Process: International Law and How We Use It* (Clarendon Press: Oxford, 1994) 232; See discussion in C Greenwood, 'The Relationship between *Ius ad Bellum* and *Ius in Bello*' 9 *Review of International Studies* 221 (1983). See also discussion in the legal frameworks section in the Introduction, *supra*.

[130] See nn 15–27, *supra* and accompanying text.

[131] See section 3, *supra*, on pre-emptive or anticipatory self-defence.

risk in this situation is that the state acting in self-defence will move from the legitimate action of countering the armed attack and current danger it is facing, towards an amorphous pre-emptive mode of acting, possibly unlawfully, in order to eradicate potential future threats. This differentiation and risk of abuse must therefore be kept firmly in mind when attempting to assess the necessity and proportionality of the state's measures.

3

Measures Taken Outside the Self-Defence Framework

As noted at the start of this Part, unilateral use of force on the territory of another state, including forcible measures taken by military troops, police forces or clandestine agents, would be a breach of international law unless falling under self-defence.[1] Nonetheless, while the past notion of forcible self-help appears to have been restricted by the modern international legal order,[2] international law does recognize circumstances which may preclude wrongfulness. There is, therefore, a need to examine whether extraterritorial use of force against non-state actors might, in certain conditions, not be a breach of international law, even if taken outside the framework of self-defence. These will be looked at below, followed by the possibility of alternative paradigms or interpretations that would allow for use of force other than in self-defence, which will be examined in the final section of this chapter.

The Draft Articles on Responsibility of States for Internationally Wrongful Acts, recognize:

...six circumstances precluding the wrongfulness of conduct that would otherwise not be in conformity with the international obligations of the State concerned. The existence in a given case of a circumstance precluding wrongfulness in accordance with this chapter provides a shield against an otherwise well-founded claim for the breach of an international obligation. The six circumstances are: consent (article 20), self-defence (article 21), countermeasures (article 22), force majeure (article 23), distress (article 24) and necessity (article 25).[3]

---

[1] R Jennings and A Watts (eds), *Oppenheim's International Law Ninth Edition, vol. 1, Peace,* (Longman: London, 1992) 385–8.

[2] 'In an advanced legal order self-help is excluded... Only where self-help is forbidden does self-defense become meaningful', in J Kunz 'Individual and collective Self-Defense in Article 51 of the charter of the United Nations' *AJIL Editorial Comment* (1947) 872, 875–6; According to Dinstein, forcible measures must meet self-defence requirements, and '[...] self-defence is a permissible form of "armed self-help".' Y Dinstein, *War, Aggression, and Self-Defence* (CUP: Cambridge, 2005) 176; D Bowett, *Self-Defence in International Law* (Manchester University Press: Manchester, 1958) 19.

[3] Commentaries to the draft articles on Responsibility of States for internationally wrongful acts, adopted by the International Law Commission at its 53rd session (2001) (extract from

Other than self-defence, the categories that demand closer inspection, in the context of the issue at hand, are those on countermeasures and necessity.

1. Countermeasures

The question of armed reprisals was examined earlier in the context of reprisals being considered an exercise of the right to self-defence. There is, however, an additional question of whether armed reprisals may be taken outside the self-defence framework. In the past, the term countermeasures was at times seen as including reprisals involving the use of force.[4] However, as noted earlier, use of force in the form of *ad bellum* reprisals is now viewed as contrary to the prohibition on the use of force, and the support that is still sometimes given to maintaining the validity of reprisals of this kind is usually given only when use of force would in fact be justified by the rules of self-defence.[5] Article 50 of the Draft Articles clearly states that:

1. Countermeasures shall not affect:
    (a) The obligation to refrain from the threat or use of force as embodied in the Charter of the United Nations.

Indeed, the countermeasures described by the International Law Commission do not include armed reprisals, or any other use of force. According to the official commentary on the Draft Articles, '[i]n certain circumstances, the commission by one State of an internationally wrongful act may justify another State injured by that act in taking *non-forcible* countermeasures in order to procure its cessation and to achieve reparation for the injury.'[6]

It would seem, therefore, that forcible countermeasures are not allowed, unless it is possible to show that the circumstances at hand fulfil the requirements for self-defence.[7]

the 'Report of the International Law Commission on the work of its Fifty-third session', Official Records of the General Assembly, 56th session, supp no 10 (A/56/10), chp.IV.E.2) November 2001, 169.

    [4] M Shaw, *International Law* (5th edn) (CUP: Cambridge, 2003) 708; '*The Naulilaa Case*', *Responsabilité de l'Allemagne à raison des dommages causés dans les colonies portugaises du sud de l'Afrique (sentence sur le principe de la responsabilité). Portugal contre Allemagne. Lausanne, 31 juillet 1928*, reprinted in 2 *Recueil des Sentences Arbitrales, vol II*, 1026.
    [5] See earlier discussion of reprisals in Ch 2, section 2, *supra*.
    [6] ILC Commentary, n 3, *supra*, 180. Emphasis added.
    [7] Dinstein, n 2, *supra*, 226; Franck presents the possibility that differing interpretations of the UN Charter articles on use of force and evolving state practice may nevertheless leave some latitude with regard to countermeasures. See T Franck *Recourse to Force: State Action Against Threats and Armed Attacks* (CUP: Cambridge, 2002) 54, 131–3. See also related discussion on the interpretations and difficulties with the *Nicaragua Case* in section 5, *infra*, on alternative paradigms.

2. Necessity

As for a plea of necessity to exclude wrongfulness, Article 25 lays out strict restrictions:

1. Necessity may not be invoked by a State as a ground for precluding the wrongfulness of an act not in conformity with an international obligation of that State unless the act:
   (a) Is the only way for the State to safeguard an essential interest against a grave and imminent peril; and
   (b) Does not seriously impair an essential interest of the State or States towards which the obligation exists, or of the international community as a whole.
2. In any case, necessity may not be invoked by a State as a ground for precluding wrongfulness if:
   (a) The international obligation in question excludes the possibility of invoking necessity; or
   (b) The State has contributed to the situation of necessity.[8]

Without straying outside the scope of the current work, it should briefly be noted that insofar as use of force directly against another state is concerned, it appears that paragraph 1(b) would prevent the plea of necessity being invoked. While in the context of extraterritorial forcible measures against non-state actors, it might be said that the use of force against the non-state actor does not inherently have to involve impairing the essential interest of the territorial state, this would be a problematic contention in light of the interpretation of Article 2(4) of the UN Charter discussed above.[9] In fact, the ILC Commentary gives a number of examples in its examination of necessity, including two cases which involved the use of force and amounted to extraterritorial forcible measures against non-state actors. In the *Rainbow Warrior* incident,[10] the ILC notes the Arbitral Tribunal's reluctance to accept the excuse of necessity,[11] and indeed it was widely accepted that the French government had not acted in accordance with the law.[12] The ILC also mentions the *Caroline Case* as an example of necessity, rather than as one of

---

[8] Draft Articles on Responsibility of States for internationally wrongful acts, adopted by the International Law Commission at its 53rd session (2001) (extract from the 'Report of the International Law Commission on the work of its 53rd session, Official Records of the General Assembly, 56th session, supp no 10 (A/56/10), chp.IV.E.1), November 2001, Art 25.

[9] Ch 1, *supra*, n 8–18, and accompanying text.

[10] This incident in 1985 concerned the sinking in Auckland Harbour of a Greenpeace vessel which was engaged in protest of nuclear testing, by agents of the French government. For further details see n 12, *infra*.

[11] ILC Commentary, n 3, *supra*, 199.

[12] For a legal analysis see M Pugh, 'Legal Aspects of the *Rainbow Warrior* Affair' 36 *International and Comparative Law Quarterly* 655 (1987).

self-defence, as it is often presented.[13] A reason given for defining this as a case of necessity is that the rules on use of force had a different basis in that period (the year 1837).[14] Whether or not the *Caroline Case* exemplified the principle of necessity—as opposed to self-defence—in the first half of the 19th century,[15] it has clearly since become a standard bearer for the rules on self-defence.[16] Insofar as the ILC's example of use of force as a plea of necessity does in fact coincide with the rules of self-defence, it is submitted that, in the context of extraterritorial use of force, for a valid excuse of necessity there would have to be circumstances which in fact allow for lawful self-defence. This position is supported by the stringent qualifications of the necessity claim, in particular 1(a), which demand that there be a 'grave and imminent peril' from which the state needs to protect itself. In other words, for a state taking extraterritorial forcible measures against non-state actors to have a valid plea of necessity it would have to claim this on the basis of a grave and imminent peril posed by the non-state actor which, if accepting the notion of self-defence against imminent armed attacks, would have been likely to allow the state to operate under the rules of self-defence.

3. Hot pursuit

A further possible allowance to be raised for use of force other than in self-defence, is the doctrine of hot pursuit, whereby the state continues to pursue individuals, even after they have exited its national boundaries. Whilst this may at first seem to be a doctrine pertinent to the types of situations examined, it is in fact of minimal relevance. Hot pursuit is a doctrine belonging to the law of the sea.[17] Although it was also raised in a land-based context of states pursuing armed groups across borders—primarily by South Africa and the then Rhodesia—but this use of the doctrine was not accepted.[18] Moreover, as is apparent from the following definition of hot pursuit, even if it were transferable to land-based operations, it would not provide a sound basis for the unilateral forcible operations currently contemplated. A primary source for this doctrine, is to be found in Article 111 of the 1982 UN Convention on the Law of the Sea.[19] After setting out the conditions for engaging in hot pursuit, including that:

Such pursuit must be commenced when the foreign ship or one of its boats is within the internal waters, the archipelagic waters, the territorial sea or the contiguous zone of the

---

[13] See discussion in Ch 2, section 1 on necessity of self-defence, *infra*.

[14] ILC Commentary, n 3, *supra*, 196.

[15] See Dinstein, n 2, *supra*, 246–7 for criticism of the ILC's approach to the *Caroline Case*.

[16] See discussion in Ch 2, sections 1 and 3 on necessity and anticipatory self-defence.

[17] For detailed discussion of the doctrine of hot pursuit, see N Poulantzas, *The Right of Hot Pursuit in International Law* (Kluwer Law International: The Hague, 2002).

[18] C Gray, *International Law and the Use of Force* (OUP: Oxford, 2004) 112.

[19] United Nations Convention on the Law of the Sea (10 December 1982) 1833 UNTS 3, entered into force 16 November 1994.

pursuing State, and may only be continued outside the territorial sea or the contiguous zone if the pursuit has not been interrupted.

Paragraph 3 of the Article then makes clear that the 'right of hot pursuit ceases as soon as the ship pursued enters the territorial sea of its own State or of a third State'.

The right of hot pursuit would not therefore allow for unilateral use of force on the territory of another state, unless accompanied by treaty concessions or agreements allowing such incursions.[20]

This doctrine cannot be relied upon as legitimizing use of force on the territory of another state without its consent. Indeed, commentators who have examined the possibility of applying the doctrine of hot pursuit in these circumstances have found that it does not provide the required support.[21] A state pursuing individuals into the territory of another state and using force in the other state, even if this appears to be analogous to a situation of hot pursuit, will be acting lawfully only if its actions conform to the requirements of self-defence. Bowett acknowledges that the 'right of hot pursuit, whatever its conditions in the past, must under present-day international law be subject to those limitations and conditions which govern any exercise of the right of self-defence.'[22]

4. Piracy

Piracy presents a rare example in which states are authorized to take enforcement measures outside their own territory. According to the UN Convention on the Law of the Sea:

On the high seas, or in any other place outside the jurisdiction of any State, every State may seize a pirate ship or aircraft, or a ship or aircraft taken by piracy and under the control of pirates, and arrest the persons and seize the property on board. The courts of the State which carried out the seizure may decide upon the penalties to be imposed, and may also determine the action to be taken with regard to the ships, aircraft or property, subject to the rights of third parties acting in good faith.[23]

The above provision does not cover situations in which the ship is in the territorial waters of a state. Neither can the doctrine of hot pursuit allow for pursuing a ship

---

[20] Bowett, n 2, *supra*, 40–1; S Cayci, 'Countering Terrorism and International Law: the Turkish Experience' in M Schmitt and G Beruto (eds) *Terrorism and International Law: Challenges and Responses* (International Institute of Humanitarian Law, 2002) 137–46, 142; Poulantzas, n 17, *supra*, 11–13, 35. Poulantzas also provides numerous examples of such agreements at 12–35, and fn 7.

[21] Jennings and Watts, n 1, *supra*, 386–7; Dinstein, n 2, *supra*, 246; Bowett, *ibid*; Poulantzas, n 17, *supra*, 11–13, 35.

[22] *Ibid*. See also: Jennings and Watts, *ibid* and Cayci, n 20, *supra*.

[23] United Nations Convention on the Law of the Sea, n 19, *supra*, Art 105. For detailed discussion of Piracy as reflected in modern international law and practice, see D Guilfoyle, *Shipping Interdiction and the Law of the Sea* (CUP: Cambridge, 2009) 26–74. See also T Treves, 'Piracy, Law of the Sea, and Use of Force: Developments off the Coast of Somalia' 20 *EJIL* 399 (2009).

into the territorial waters of another state.[24] The increasing concern over the cases of piracy in the Horn of Africa, occurring in the context of the ongoing instability in Somalia, created a need for counter-piracy operations that are not limited to the high seas, and take place also within the area of Somali jurisdiction. Following this, the UN Security Council authorized states conducting counter-piracy operations to enter Somalia's territorial waters.[25] This authorization does not point to a significant departure from the respect for state sovereignty recognized in the existing law on piracy, since the Security Council explicitly points to the prior agreement by the Transitional Federal Government of Somalia.[26] Accordingly, action against pirate ships is permitted on the high seas, but forcible measures against pirates cannot take place in the territorial waters of a state without its consent.

5. An alternative paradigm and its difficulties

This Chapter thus far leads to the conclusion that the doctrine of self-defence is the sole avenue for legitimizing unilateral forcible action by states against non-state actors in the territory of other states. Indeed, in the absence or demise of alternative doctrines, states clearly having realized that self-defence remains the only legitimate justification for use of force, invoke self-defence frequently and in such a variety of circumstances as to raise the concern that they are stretching the notion beyond its intent.[27] These tendencies are opposed by the views taking a narrower approach to the concept.[28] Bethlehem notes that:

The reliance by States on self-defence in virtually every conceivable circumstance has led, on the one hand, to normative drift, as attempts have been made to stretch the concept, and, on the other hand, to a propensity towards doctrinal purity in the restatement of the concept by courts and commentators. The result has been the crystallisation of a law on self-defence today which is materially out of step with the reality of contemporary international life.[29]

Criticism of the perceived state of modern laws governing the use of force has been fairly common, particularly following the ICJ *Nicaragua* judgment.[30] The *Nicaragua Case* did involve armed groups, but the questions at the heart

[24] *Ibid*, Art 111, and discussion above.
[25] Security Council Res no 1846 adopted by the Security Council at its 6026th meeting on 2 December 2008, UN Doc S/RES/1846 (2008).   [26] *Ibid*.
[27] Gray, n 18, *supra*, 99; D Bethlehem, 'International law and the use of force: the law as it is and as it should be', written evidence submitted by Daniel Bethlehem QC, Director of Lauterpacht Research Centre for International Law, University of Cambridge Select Committee on Foreign Affairs, Minutes of Evidence, 8 June 2004, available at <http://www.publications.parliament.uk/pa/cm200304/cmselect/cmfaff/441/4060808.htm> paras 19, 21.
[28] Such as those raised earlier that argue against anticipatory self-defence.
[29] Bethlehem, n 27, *supra*, para 21.
[30] See n 35, *infra*, and accompanying text. See also dissenting opinion of Judge Jennings, 543–4.

of the case and most of the debates surrounding it arise in the context of inter-state disputes and uses of force. As such, it is not dealing with the question of extraterritorial force against independent non-state actors but, as will be seen, some of the problems raised in this case are relevant to the question currently under examination. For the purpose of the issue at hand, a major problem which surfaced from the court's judgment was as follows: in the context of collective self-defence by state C aiding state B against state A, although state A might be responsible for violating the prohibition on the use of force against state B, it is nevertheless possible that this violation would not be sufficient to qualify as an armed attack, and there would therefore be no right for state C to use force against state A in the name of collective self-defence.[31] In other words, this could be read to say that, according to the rules on the use of force, the notion of an armed attack that gives rise to self-defence under Article 51, is not equivalent to the force prohibited in Article 2(4).[32] This interpretation of the rules appears to be firmly rooted in the UN Charter, despite not always being easy to digest, as noted by Randelzhofer:

> If Art. 51 is thus read in connection with Art. 2(4), the stunning conclusion is to be reached that any state affected by another state's unlawful use of force not reaching the threshold of an 'armed attack', is bound, if not exactly to endure the violation, then at least to respond only by means falling short of the use or threat of force, which are thus often totally ineffective. This at first sight unacceptable result is undoubtedly intended by the Charter, since the unilateral use of force is meant to be excluded as far as possible.[33]

In *Nicaragua*, the Court was considering the question in the context of collective self-defence, and made a point of clarifying that it was not answering the question of the legality of possible direct measures taken by the state which itself suffered from the use of force.[34] This has led commentators to question whether there is a gap according to which a state might be the victim of force but not have a right to respond with force, or whether the court was in fact leaving open the possibility that when a state suffers from force which is below the level of an armed attack, it can respond with force which is less than self-defence.[35] Neither of these conclusions is particularly satisfactory—the latter appears to negate the current state of the law,[36] while the former appears to leave states vulnerable to force without

---

[31] *Case Concerning Military and Paramilitary Activities in and Against Nicaragua* [1986] ICJ Rep 14, paras 195, 210–11.

[32] Bethlehem, n 27, *supra*, para 16; A Randelzhofer, 'Article 51' in B Simma (ed), *The Charter of the United Nations, A Commentary* (OUP: Oxford, 1994) 661–78, 663.

[33] Randelzhofer, *ibid*, 663–4.　　[34] *Nicaragua*, n 31, *supra*, para 210.

[35] R Higgins, *Problems and Process: International Law and How We Use It* (1994) 248–51; Randelzhofer, 'Article 51', n 32, *supra*, 664–7; J Hargrove 'Appraisals of the ICJ's Decision: *Nicaragua v. United States* (Merits)' 81 *AJIL* 135 (1987) 138.

[36] As seen throughout this chapter, self-defence appears to be the only exception to the ban on unilateral force.

a right to forcible response.[37] In the past, the doctrine of reprisals may have provided room for lesser scale forcible responses, but assuming the current state of the law prohibits forcible reprisals outside the parameters of self-defence,[38] there does not seem to be a possibility for force other than self-defence. The originally envisaged system of collective security, with a formidable United Nations acting through an effective Security Council, would have lessened the concerns of states.[39] The criticism of the actual functioning of the UN system, combined with the 'gap' interpretation of *Nicaragua*, has led some to consider reviving pre-Charter rules and to act outside the framework perceived in Article 51 of the Charter.[40] Viewing these debates from the perspective of extraterritorial measures against non-state actors, it is clear there are common difficulties.

The obvious analogy is of the question of a right to respond when the non-state actor has carried out violent activities which do not amount to an armed attack. As noted earlier, some interpretations posit a threshold of scale for an armed attack that would mean there could be violent incidents that do not cross this threshold, and that this could also include recurrent incidents of violence perpetrated by armed groups that cannot be accumulated in order to give a combined result which crosses the threshold.[41] The problem of responding to force less than an armed attack would consequently be even more acute when confronted by a non-state actor. Granted, there is always the possibility of turning to the territorial state and demanding that it put an end to the activities by the non-state actor operating from its territory, and in fact this was shown to be a requirement of necessity before self-defence action can be taken;[42] but if the territorial state is unwilling, or unable, to take action and there is no right of self-defence since the threshold of armed attack wasn't crossed, then what can the victim state do?

Had the state needed to respond to violence by a non-state actor located within its territory, it could have done so with the tools of law enforcement. Dinstein mentions the notion of extraterritorial law enforcement, which raises the possibility that his approach may contain our answer. His description of it is as follows:

[...] to use the idiom 'extra-territorial law enforcement' to describe the phenomenon of recourse to cross-border counter-force against terrorists and armed bands. The present

---

[37] Randelzhofer, 'Article 51', n 32, *supra*, 664. Randelzhofer examines possible solutions and their objections.

[38] Ch 2, *supra*, nn 43–50, and accompanying text.

[39] M Reisman, 'Criteria for the Lawful Use of Force in International Law' 10 *Yale Journal of International Law* 279 (1985) 279–80; Randelzhofer, 'Article 51', n 32, *supra*, 663. See also dissenting opinion of Judge Jennings in *Nicaragua Case*, 543–4.

[40] R Delahunty, 'Paper Charter: Self-Defense and the Failure of the United Nations Collective Security System' 56 *Catholic University Law Review* 871 (2007) 881, 904–5; The possibility is even considered of denouncing the Charter and turning to unilateral determination of the right to use force in self-defence. W Bradford, '"The Duty to Defend Them": A Natural Law Justification for the Bush Doctrine of Preventive War' 79 *Notre Dame Law Review* 1365 (2004) 1481–2.

[41] See Ch 2, section 2, *supra*, on scale of the initial armed attack.

[42] See Ch 2, section 1, *supra*, on necessity.

writer believes that this idiom properly telescopes the notion of measures enforcing international law, taken by one State within the territory of another without the latter's consent. Extra-territorial law enforcement is a form of self-defence, and it can be undertaken by Utopia against terrorists and armed bands inside Arcadian territory only in response to an armed attack unleashed by them from that territory. Utopia is entitled to enforce international law extra-territorially if and when Arcadia is unable or unwilling to prevent repetition of that armed attack.[43]

It appears that despite the use of the term law-enforcement, Dinstein envisages actions taken under this heading as being legitimate only in response to an armed attack. In that case, we are back to the starting line with our problem of responding to force when the armed attack threshold has not been reached. An alternative approach would be to develop the extraterritorial law enforcement concept into a wider notion, allowing for lower scales of force, both in terms of the trigger for its employment, and the type of action taken under its heading. In the context of alleged terrorist groups it could, on the one hand, be argued that, in the absence of the territorial state taking measures against the non-state actor (despite being obligated to do so[44]), the outside state is merely carrying out law enforcement measures that the territorial state should have been doing itself and furthermore that this would not violate Article 2(4) of the Charter, since it is not aimed against the territorial integrity or political independence of the territorial state. On the other hand, the narrow approach to Article 2(4) is strongly disputed, and the more persuasive opinion is that Article 2(4) prohibits any use of force on foreign territory, other than in accordance with the exceptions in the Charter.[45]

Furthermore, while a state's competence to legislate with regard to extraterritorial actions is recognized in certain contexts, its jurisdiction to enforce its laws is essentially territorial.[46] The term extraterritorial law-enforcement could therefore be perceived as calling into question accepted limitations over the powers granted to states. Abduction of an individual from a foreign country is an example that is given for unlawful exercise of enforcement jurisdiction.[47] One might counter this criticism by observing that this would not be a case of states attempting to enforce their own domestic laws extraterritorially, but in fact a case of a state acting against individuals in a manner that sets out to enforce international laws, such as the prevention of terrorism or the arrest of war criminals. Paust combines two of the above arguments:

It is also of interest that the use of force to capture and abduct an international criminal located within foreign territory would certainly not be directed against the territorial

---

[43] Dinstein, n 211, *supra*, 247.   [44] Chapter 1, nn 60–3 and accompanying text, *supra*.

[45] Exceptions being self-defence and Security Council authorization. See section 2, *supra*, on 'the prohibition on the use of force'.

[46] Higgins, n 35, *supra*, 70; See discussion on this in section on different types of jurisdiction in Pt III, *infra*, on human rights and law enforcement.

[47] Shaw, n 4, *supra*, 577. See further on Eichmann, *infra*; see also Pt III, *infra,* on abduction in the context of human rights and law enforcement.

integrity or political independence of such foreign state. If it were otherwise serving of the overall purposes of the Charter, and absent the specific expectation of impropriety in the case of transnational kidnapping, such a limited use of force to enforce international law might arguably be permissible.[48]

This observation notwithstanding, it would appear to fail to overcome certain critical obstacles. First, the preferred approach to Article 2(4) is that it be understood to prohibit all force, and not be narrowly restricted to force used against territorial integrity and political independence.[49] Secondly, whilst international law does sanction, and even demand, state action against certain individuals or groups, it does so in a way that does not endorse extraterritorial force used in another state without consent. The starting point of the requirement to act against terrorist groups is the assumption that states are operating within their territories and lawful competence, as can be seen in the preamble of Security Council Resolution no 1373 which recognizes 'the need for States to complement international cooperation by taking additional measures to prevent and suppress, *in their territories through all lawful means,* the financing and preparation of any acts of terrorism'.[50]

As for acting against individuals alleged to have committed crimes under international law, the concept of universal jurisdiction denotes the competence of states to conduct trials in their territory in order to hold to account individuals guilty of committing international crimes such as war crimes and torture.[51] These formulations of the notion of universal jurisdiction do not profess to grant states enforcement jurisdiction and the right to send troops into other states.

A second problem with a notion of extraterritorial law enforcement mirroring domestic law enforcement is that, even if one is to hold that the self-defence paradigm is too narrow to deal with certain threats, extraterritorial law enforcement risks stretching the grounds for taking action far beyond what might be deemed necessary. For example, one can note the ease with which this alternative notion lends itself to moving from dealing with stemming current violent activities of an armed group over to hunting for war criminals, as envisaged in the preceding paragraphs. The key to the acceptance and inviolability of the concept of self-defence is that it is limited to encountering current severe danger, which in modern international law is conceptualized in the notion of an armed attack. A wide interpretation of extraterritorial law enforcement would challenge the fundamental premise of respect for state sovereignty, even in the absence of such

---

[48] J Paust, 'Responding Lawfully to International Terrorism: The Use of Force Abroad', 8 Whittier Law Review 711 (1986) 726.

[49] See Chapter 1, section 2 on the prohibition on the use of force, *supra.*

[50] Chapter 1, n 39, *supra.* Emphasis added.

[51] Convention against Torture and Other Cruel, Inhuman or Degrading Treatment or Punishment, (10 December 1984) 1465 UNTS 85, entered into force 26 June 1987) Art 5; Geneva Convention (I) for the Amelioration of the Condition of the Wounded and Sick in Armed Forces in the Field (12 August 1949) 75 UNTS 31, entered into force 21 October 1950, Art 49.

threats, for the purpose of capturing and punishing individuals guilty of past crimes. Granted that, in some cases such as Israel's capture and abduction of the Nazi official Adolf Eichmann in Argentina, one might argue that it serves the interests of the international community in combating impunity for the worst of crimes.[52] However, while international law does envisage universal jurisdiction, it does not go as far as authorizing abductions,[53] and while many may have been understanding of the Israeli operation to capture Eichmann, the Security Council found it to be a violation of international law.[54] Moreover, why stop at Nazi war criminals? There are doubtless tens of thousands of other war criminals freely walking the streets of many countries, and allowing for extraterritorial law enforcement of this nature is a recipe for permitting endless incursions and abductions on a chaotic level. An additional risk of allowing extraterritorial measures outside the response to armed attacks is the widening of the scope of grounds for action, to include anything from abduction of individuals claimed to be possessing and publicizing valuable state secrets[55] to extraterritorial force in a 'war on drugs'.[56] The prospect of opening the door to allow states the relative freedom of defining what is a threat that justifies sending forces to operate in the territory of another state, is one that does not bode well for international order.[57]

If, nevertheless, there are to be attempts to develop a concept of extraterritorial law enforcement, it would have to contain clear restrictions such as limiting the notion to measures in which the state is reacting to an international crime. However, in all probability, controversies will arise over questions such as whether 'terrorism' is an international crime of this type and how it is defined; and more importantly, whether it would depend on the individual's prior conviction in an international forum, or a domestic conviction, or even on the basis of unproven domestic charges for an action of which the state claims the individual is guilty. It is, therefore, unlikely that restrictions of this type will suffice to prevent the above mentioned risks of abuse.

The above critique of the notion of extraterritorial law enforcement which is wider than self-defence, is not intended to trivialize the challenges presented at the start of this section. There clearly are difficulties within the current strict interpretations of the laws on the use of force, and this becomes increasingly

---

[52] See discussion in Paust, n 48, *supra*.   [53] See n 47, *supra*.

[54] Resolution adopted by the Security Council at its 868th Meeting on 23 June 1960 on questions relating to the case of Adolf Eichmann, UN Doc S/4349; Franck, n 7, *supra*, 114; for an analysis of the case, see M Lippmann, 'The Trial Of Adolf Eichmann and the Protection of Universal Human Rights under International Law', 5 Houston Journal of International Law 1 (1982).

[55] As was the case of the abduction by Israel of Mordechai Vanunu. See discussion in Part III, *infra*.

[56] The US engaged and colluded in the abduction of individuals, including Alvarez-Machain, in relation to a Drug Enforcement Administration (DEA) incident, following the murder of a DEA agent. See discussion in A Abramovsky, 'Extraterritorial Abductions: America's "Catch And Snatch" Policy Run Amok' 31 Virginia Journal of International Law 151 (1991).

[57] See for example, *ibid*, in the opening hypothetical scenario.

apparent when viewed in the context of measures against non-state actors.[58] The various cases that are currently seen as unlawful might, with time, be evidence of a change in state practice that contributes to new understandings. It has been noted that whilst restrictive Charter rules would render certain actions unlawful, it might be possible to identify an 'aura of legitimacy'[59] in the response of the international community, and an element of toleration or acquiescence to a more flexible approach to the rules.[60] As noted by Higgins:

My own position is that, if it is felt that the erstwhile articulation of norms no longer serves community interests, then those norms can properly be subjected to processes for change. The normal processes for change will include non-compliance. New, or refined, norms often emerge from a process of widespread non-compliance with old norms. But there is a distinction between non-compliance, on the one hand, and interpretation *infra legem* to achieve certain outcomes, on the other. And we should not pretend that they are the same. We should, moreover, be very sure that the norms as presently articulated are so irredeemably inappropriate to the factual realities that we do indeed wish to undermine them. I believe that the application of Article 2(4) and Article 51 has been very unsatisfactory. But I am not yet convinced that they have no useful purpose to perform or that unilateral outcome-directed action without reference to common norms is not dangerous.[61]

This comment was made over a decade ago, primarily with respect to the problems of indirect use of force (eg one state supporting armed groups against another state) and humanitarian intervention. The debate over responding to the activities of independent non-state actors, as has come to the fore in the current 'war on terror' and been raised in this Chapter, has only exacerbated the problems in recent years.[62] Perhaps indeed there is a process of change, but as for the law as it stands and the possibility of future changes, Higgins' words still ring true.

As of now, the current state of the law does not appear to have room for lawful use of unilateral extraterritorial forcible measures against non-state actors, other than through the framework of self-defence.

---

[58] Bethlehem, n 27, *supra*, paras 18, 32.   [59] Franck, n 7, *supra*, 131–2.

[60] R Mullerson, '*Jus Ad Bellum: Plus Ça Change (Le Monde) Plus C'est La Même Chose (Le Droit)?*' 7 *Journal of Conflict and Security Law* 149 (2002) 185; Franck, n 7, *supra*, 131–9.

[61] Higgins, n 35, *supra*, 252–3.   [62] Bethlehem, n 27, *supra*, para 32.

Part I—Conclusion

Part I analysed the legal questions surrounding extraterritorial forcible measures against non-state actors within the framework of inter-state rules on the use of force. If there is one certain conclusion from these chapters, it is that almost every element of the matters which were examined is a subject of debate and disagreement. It is nonetheless possible to arrive at a conclusion, which may not be shared by everyone, but finds strong support as evidenced throughout the chapters. It is therefore submitted that:

- The concept of 'armed attack' as it appears in Article 51 of the UN Charter, includes attacks by non-state actors operating from the territory of other states. To qualify as an armed attack, it must pass a certain threshold of intensity, which at the least would be expected to cause casualties and significant harm, and may require a higher threshold than attacks by states.

- An armed attack by non-state actors can give rise to the right of self-defence by the attacked state.

- Exercise of self-defence against non-state actors must conform to all the accepted parameters, in particular to necessity and proportionality. Necessity dictates that all other alternative effective means be first attempted, if they can put an end to the ongoing danger. In the context of attacks by non-state actors, this must include the option of the territorial state preventing the non-state actor from carrying out any attacks.

- Assuming that the other requirements of self-defence are met, then only if the territorial state is not taking effective measures against the non-state actor, either due to a lack of willingness or ability, can forcible measures be taken on that state's territory.

- Anticipatory self-defence must be limited to specific imminent attacks, and pre-emptive self-defence against general vague threats is not permitted. In any event, once again the principle of necessity requires a situation in which it is clearly not possible to rely upon the territorial state to prevent the attack.

- The only legitimate justification for using force on the territory of another state without its consent is that of self-defence, and examination of other doctrines leads back in a full circle to the self-defence requirements. Whilst in the past forcible measures may have been permitted in the form of reprisals, counter-measures or necessity, these concepts no longer allow for unilateral extraterritorial use of force. It may be possible to interpret these

concepts, and also that of hot pursuit, as in certain circumstances allowing lawful forcible measures, but this would only be the case if the circumstances in fact fulfil the requirements allowing the state to engage in lawful
self-defence. Other concepts and alternative paradigms present numerous
obstacles, and while there may be room for development, as of now there is
no accepted framework for unilateral forcible measures other than that of
self-defence.

In summary, extraterritorial forcible measures against non-state actors, could be
lawful, even if taken without the consent of the territorial state, but only if they
meet the above requirements. Outside of lawful self-defence as defined above, it
is likely that unilateral use of force on the territory of another state, would be in
violation of the fundamental principle banning the use of force.

PART II

INTERNATIONAL HUMANITARIAN LAW

4

Force Against Non-State Actors as Armed Conflict

Part II of this work deals with extraterritorial forcible measures through the lens of international humanitarian law ('IHL'). The issues that will need examining include the question of whether IHL is an appropriate legal framework that can be applied to such measures. If it is found to be applicable only in certain circumstances, then these must be defined. Furthermore, as will be seen, within IHL there are a number of categories and classifications which affect the precise rules to be used for particular situations. These too will need explanation, as will the content of the relevant rules and the obstacles encountered when coming to apply them to extraterritorial forcible measures against non-state actors.

IHL is the body of international law designed to regulate the conduct of armed conflict, thus the applicability of IHL to any given situation is dependent on it being defined as an armed conflict. For IHL to be relevant to an extraterritorial forcible measure against a non-state actor, one must accordingly first inquire whether the measure is taken as part of an armed conflict. From the examples given in the Introductory Chapter, the fighting between the US and Al-Qaeda in Afghanistan is a potential candidate for classification as belonging to the realm of armed conflict,[1] as is the conflict between Israel and the Hezbollah in the summer of 2006.[2] In a number of other cases of extraterritorial forcible measures, it would be far-fetched to claim an existence of armed conflict between the state and the group or individual involved. For example, at the time of his abduction by Israel, Mordechai Vanunu was not taking part in an armed conflict, and his abduction from Italy for the purpose of trial in Israel does not belong to the realm of the laws regulating armed conflict.[3] Before continuing with this section it is, therefore, important to keep in mind that direct applicability of IHL

---

[1] Classification of the situation between the US and Al-Qaeda needs to be divided into separate possible headings: US operations in Afghanistan prior to the new Afghan government; US operations in Afghanistan alongside the Afghan government; various US operations against Al-Qaeda during the last few years, wherever they may take place (eg Yemen). Questions can be raised over the classification as international or non-international and the status of Al-Qaeda members. This will be further explored in section 3, 4, and 5 of this chapter, *infra*, and in further general discussion throughout Chs 5 and 6, *infra*.

[2] See discussion in Concluding Chapter.   [3] See discussion of his case in Ch 7, *infra*.

to extraterritorial forcible measures is only an option in those cases in which an armed conflict could be said to exist. As will be explored in greater detail later,[4] a significant element of the debate over the relevance of IHL to the use of extraterritorial force against non-state groups revolves around the very use of this framework of rules in order to govern these measures. This debate can in fact be divided into two different questions:

(i) is the framework of IHL *applicable* to certain situations;
(ii) is the IHL framework *suitable* for handling these situations.

The former centres upon the possibility of categorizing a particular situation as armed conflict; for without an armed conflict IHL simply does not apply. The latter question should be deemed irrelevant unless a positive answer is given to the first question.[5] If, however, the situation is an armed conflict, then the suitability debate is one which concerns itself with questions of whether the IHL rules are formulated in a manner which allows for them to adequately regulate the conduct of parties, taking into account the modern factual circumstances.[6] In addition, a third, and more problematic, question—as will be seen later—is sometimes raised when, despite concluding that a situation does not amount to armed conflict, some might wish to question whether nevertheless IHL should come into play, perhaps by redrawing the boundaries of the armed conflict definition.[7] The examination in the following chapters will begin with the recognized models of international and non-international armed conflicts, and whether extraterritorial operations against non-state actors could be classified as one of these types of conflicts. The discussion will then turn to the possibility of other models of armed conflict, including the regulation of these through customary international law. This will be followed with a presentation of the types of rules that would apply, and the problems surrounding them.

1. The definition of armed conflict

According to the Appeals Chamber of the International Criminal Tribunal for the former Yugoslavia ('ICTY'):

[...] an armed conflict exists whenever there is a resort to armed force between States or protracted armed violence between governmental authorities and organized armed groups or between such groups within a State. International humanitarian law applies

---

    [4] See Ch 5, *infra*.
    [5] See Ch 5, *infra*. M Sassoli, 'Transnational Armed Groups and International Humanitarian Law' Program on Humanitarian Policy and Conflict Research, Harvard University, Occasional Paper Series no 6 (Winter 2006) 22; G Rona, 'Interesting Times for International Humanitarian Law: Challenges From the "War on Terror"' *Fletcher Forum of World Affairs*, 27:2 (2003) 58.
    [6] This concept will be developed in the following chapters.   [7] See Ch 5, *infra*.

from the initiation of such armed conflicts and extends beyond the cessation of hostilities until a general conclusion of peace is reached; or, in the case of internal conflicts, a peaceful settlement is achieved.[8]

Indeed, it would be difficult to think of any event we would instinctively label an armed conflict as not fitting within the above description. However, the lack of certain details in this definition perhaps put it at risk of becoming over-inclusive. In particular, what is needed in order to make the ICTY definition more precise is an understanding of the threshold of violence that might be necessary before one can determine the existence of an armed conflict. The terms 'protracted' and 'organized' will also need elaboration. The key question of how to define the factual threshold which must be crossed in order for a situation to qualify as an armed conflict is of direct significance to some of the cases at hand—for instance in the dispute as to whether one can identify a global war on terror that fulfils the necessary threshold of organized violence. In general, it appears that the threshold can be different for international armed conflict and non-international armed conflict. Indeed, one of the reasons the ICTY definition may appear a little vague is that it is all-inclusive, covering both international and non-international armed conflicts, even though—as will be seen in the following two sections—different criteria might be used to determine the existence of armed conflict in these two separate contexts. The differing criteria are also evident from the part of the ICTY definition which speaks of 'resort to armed force' in the context of inter-state violence, but raises the threshold to 'protracted armed violence' in the context of armed conflicts involving non-state actors. These issues will therefore be dealt with separately in the following sections on the different types of armed conflict.

While many might use the terms interchangeably, war and armed conflict are not one and the same. In the past, war was the common term used to describe inter-state hostilities, often following an official declaration of war marking the commencement of the conflict. However, the modern evolution of conflict included a conceptual change, making the applicability of IHL dependant on the factual existence of a state of armed conflict, regardless of any declarations.[9] This has not, however, ended the relevance of war as a legal term. For example,

---

[8] *Prosecutor v. Dusko Tadic,* Decision on the Defence Motion for Interlocutory Appeal on Jurisdiction, ICTY, 2 October 1995, para 70.

[9] Art 2 of the Geneva Conventions states that 'the present Convention shall apply to all cases of declared war or of any other armed conflict which may arise between two or more of the High Contracting Parties, even if the state of war is not recognized by one of them.' See *Geneva Convention for the Amelioration of the Condition of the Wounded and Sick in Armed Forces in the Field* (12 August 1949) 75 UNTS 31, entered into force 21 October 1950; *Geneva Convention for the Amelioration of the Condition of Wounded, Sick and Shipwrecked Members of Armed Forces at Sea* (12 August 1949) 75 UNTS 85, entered into force 21 October 1950; *Geneva Convention relative to the Treatment of Prisoners of War* (12 August 1949) 75 UNTS 135, entered into force 21 October 1950 *Geneva Convention relative to the Protection of Civilian Persons in Time of War* (12 August 1949) 75 UNTS 287, entered into force 21 October 1950; see also J Pictet (ed), *Commentary on the Geneva Convention of 12 August 1949 for the Amelioration of the Condition of the Wounded and Sick in Armed Forces in the Field* (International Committee of the Red Cross: Geneva,

Dinstein asserts that war applies only to comprehensive use of force.[10] There has also been use of the term 'armed conflict short of war' to denote use of force under IHL in a situation that does not amount to war,[11] and the occurrence of limited armed conflicts such as the Falklands/Malvinas conflict, might be making war and armed conflict more and more similar.[12] Whilst declarations of war between states are now of less importance insofar as the application of IHL is concerned, such a declaration can still have far-reaching domestic implications, for instance automatically activating emergency laws on a variety of issues such as detention powers or insurance claims. As far as international law is concerned however, the relevance of 'war' as a legal term has declined, and the primary focus is on the international rules designed to regulate situations of factual armed conflict.[13]

Furthermore, some might say that since war is predominantly described as an appropriate term for inter-state conflict, certain operations covered such as US actions against Al-Qaeda operatives, might theoretically be part of a US versus Al-Qaeda armed conflict but not a war.[14] If however the US was in armed conflict with a state supporting a non-state actor, as may have been the case in Afghanistan, then this could be labelled as actual war.[15]

In light of the above, notwithstanding certain ramifications of whether or not the term *war* can be used, the main concern currently at hand is whether certain extraterritorial forcible measures should be analysed in the context of IHL, which is triggered by armed conflict. Therefore, despite the 'war' rhetoric, the crucial issue in our context is the question of whether there exists a situation of armed conflict between the state and the non-state actor.

2. The link between armed conflict and armed attack

The issue of armed attacks was dealt with in detail in Chapter 1, mostly surrounding the question of whether a state claiming to have been attacked by

---

1958). For a general overview on 'war' in the modern era, see C Greenwood, 'The Concept of War in Modern International Law' 36 *International and Comparative Law Quarterly* 283 (1987).

[10] Y Dinstein, *War, Aggression, and Self-Defence* (CUP: Cambridge, 2005) 11–13. This refers to war in the *material* sense, as opposed to war in the *technical* sense, which is a result of declaration.

[11] See position of the Advocate General of the Israeli Military, in M Finkelstein, 'Legal Perspectives in the Fight Against Terror—The Israeli Experience' 1 *IDF Law Review* 341 (2003) 343–4.

[12] C Garraway, 'Discussion' in WP Heere (ed.), *Terrorism and the Military: International Legal Implications* (Asser: The Hague, 2003) 41.

[13] Greenwood, n 9, *supra*, 305. See also C Greenwood, 'Scope of Application of Humanitarian Law' in D Fleck (ed.) *The Handbook of Humanitarian Law in Armed Conflicts* (OUP: Oxford, 1995) 39–63, 39–43.

[14] C Bassiouni, 'Legal Control of International Terrorism: A Policy-Oriented Assessment' 43 *Harvard International Law Journal* 83 (2002) 99; Ch 5, *infra*.

[15] Y Dinstein, 'Ius Ad Bellum Aspects of the "War on Terrorism"' in Heere, n 12, *supra*, 13–22, 19; Ch 5, *infra*.

a non-state actor would have an ensuing right to respond by way of extraterritorial forcible measures. The connection between armed attacks by non-state actors and the applicability of IHL raises two matters that need addressing. First, there is the question of whether the existence of an armed attack leads to a qualification of the ensuing forcible measures against the non-state actor as necessarily being armed conflict. Secondly, there is the question of whether the initial attack is itself a situation to which the laws of armed conflict apply. This latter question has been given differing answers. For example, the attacks of 11 September 2001 have been viewed through the lens of IHL,[16] and therefore as war crimes,[17] with not everyone agreeing to this categorization.[18] The focus of the current chapter in the context of our scope, is on the applicability of IHL to the measures taken by the state, and not on the possible prior act of the non-state actor. The categorization of the initial act is, however, of relevance when dealing with a single extraterritorial forcible measure by the state itself, whether in response to earlier acts of a non-state actor, or to single strikes initiated by the state. Whether or not single extraterritorial forcible measures against a non-state actor can, on their own, be defined as acts of armed conflict to which IHL applies is an issue relating to the examination of thresholds and definitions of armed conflict, to be addressed in the coming sections. As will be seen, the threshold for determining the existence of an armed conflict and the applicability of IHL differs between international and non-international armed conflict. In the former, the low threshold could lead to the applicability of IHL for the very first strike, even if it is at a relatively low scale and has no continuation. In non-international armed conflicts there is a higher threshold for determining the existence of armed conflict. That being the case, a single forcible act by a state against a non-state actor would not automatically trigger the applicability of IHL; if the threshold of intensity has not been crossed, then there is no armed conflict. This would not leave the use of force unregulated, since the framework of international human rights law and its regulation of force can be found applicable.[19] Although the single act might not qualify as crossing the required threshold, it might be argued to be taking place in the context of an already existing armed conflict. Whilst this could mean that IHL would apply, any such

---

[16] Remarks by Alberto R. Gonzales Counsel to the President Before the American Bar Association Standing Committee on Law and National Security Washington, DC, 24 February 2004, available at <http://www.justicescholars.org/pegc/archive/White_House/gonzales_remarks_to_ABA_20040224.pdf>. See also US Department of Defense *Military Commission Instruction no 2: Crimes and Elements for Trials by Military Commission*, 30 April 2003, s 5C, available at <http://www.defenselink.mil/releases/release.aspx?releaseid=3801>.

[17] Bassiouni, n 14, *supra,* 100.

[18] 'Since the September 11 attacks were not carried out during an armed conflict, they cannot be considered war crimes' A McDonald, 'Terrorism, Counter-terrorism and the *Jus in Bello*' in M Schmitt and G Beruto (eds) *Terrorism and International Law: Challenges and Responses* (International Institute of Humanitarian Law, 2002).

[19] See Ch 8, *infra.*

claim would have to be carefully scrutinized and, as in the case of the alleged 'war on terror', raises numerous questionable aspects.[20]

There now remains the first question raised above, concerning the link between an armed attack by non-state actors and the classification of the response as armed conflict. Many have determined that the 11 September 2001 attacks were 'armed attacks' as defined by international law.[21] The arguments making that case tend to go hand in hand with the claim that the US is engaged in an armed conflict with Al-Qaeda. In other words, it was an armed attack therefore we have an armed conflict, as can be seen in the following view of Alberto Gonzales, then Counsel to the US President:

As a practical matter, this state of war is not in dispute—not by the United Nations Security Council, which passed a resolution in response to the September 11th attacks recognizing the right of states to act in self-defense; not by members of NATO, or the Rio or ANZUS treaties, all of which unanimously invoked their treaty clauses regarding collective defense from armed attack; and not by the United States Congress, which acted to support the President's use of all necessary and appropriate military force against al Qaeda.[22]

This position appears to identify the recognition of the right of self-defence following armed attack as equivalent to recognition of an existing armed conflict (referred to in this and the next quotation as 'war'[23]). On the other hand, the view has been expressed that even if attacks such as 11 September 2001 could be armed attacks as defined in international law, the concept of armed conflict would be inappropriate.[24] It has also been posited that the determination of an existing armed conflict, rests not upon the armed attack, but upon the response, as argued by O'Connell:

Some try to argue that a war began on September 11 because the attacks were an 'act of war,' or those attacks plus others by Al Qaeda during the previous ten years. Wars, however, do not begin with an attack. They begin with a counter-attack. States may have the right to engage in a war of self-defense following an attack. If they chose not to do so, there is no war. War, as discussed above requires exchange, intensity and duration.[25]

Kenya, the United Kingdom, Indonesia and Spain have all been attacked by al Qaeda. They have all responded, but not with a military counter-attack. They have turned to their law enforcement agencies. None of these countries declared they were in a war.[26]

With regard to the second assertion, the different response by these countries might also be explained by the difference in scale of attack when compared

---

[20] See discussion in Ch 5, *infra*.   [21] See discussion of self-defence in Part I, *infra*.
[22] Gonzales, n 16, *supra*.   [23] See nn 9–13, *supra*, and accompanying text.
[24] 'International Humanitarian Law and the Challenges of Contemporary Armed Conflicts' Report Prepared by the International Committee of the Red Cross (Geneva, 2003) 31.
[25] ME O'Connell, 'When Is a War Not a War? The Myth of the Global War on Terror', *ILSA Journal of International and Comparative Law* 12 (2006) 4.
[26] *Ibid.*

to 11 September 2001 and the fact that, unlike the attacks in the US, the attacks on these countries might or might not have been viewed as armed attacks that give rise to self-defence under the UN Charter.[27] Consequently, the question currently before us remains whether the categorization of an attack by a non-state actor as armed attack (a possibility recognized in the previous chapter) is, in and of itself, a sufficient foundation for determining the existence of armed conflict between the state and the non-state actor. Prima facie, it might be assumed that an armed attack would be expected to lead to an armed conflict. Nevertheless, neither the law nor the actual responses of states always unfold according to this design.

Not every case of an armed attack will inevitably lead to a forcible response—the clearest example is contained in Article 51 of the UN Charter, which qualifies the right of self-defence subject to the Security Council taking appropriate measures to remedy the situation.[28] Theoretically, according to the Charter, an armed attack may occur and quickly be over, after which the Security Council takes effective measures to remove any further threat and imposes penalties (eg sanctions) on the aggressor—in which case a right to self-defence may no longer exist and an armed conflict might not ensue. Conversely, IHL can be applicable to situations where there was no clear armed attack. For instance, while it might seem that international armed conflicts would usually be triggered by an armed attack, the evolution of non-international armed conflicts is more likely to follow a path of escalation of internal strife and violence, leading to the applicability of IHL regardless of any one specific armed attack. Therefore, as a matter of law, on the one hand an armed attack is not automatically followed by an armed conflict, while on the other hand, it is possible to have an armed conflict without a prior determination of a specific armed attack. The two concepts can exist independently of each other, with or without a link between them.[29]

As noted earlier, there are strong grounds for maintaining the separation between the *ius ad bellum* and the *ius in bello*.[30] Here too, while the determination of an armed attack could in some circumstances be linked to the determination of armed conflict, the two are not necessarily dependent upon each other, and the independence of the frameworks is maintained. The examination of a situation under IHL as a result of determining the factual existence of an armed

---

[27] See discussion of self-defence, armed attacks by non-state actors, and the necessary scale for definition of armed attack, all in Part I, *supra*.

[28] 'Nothing in the present Charter shall impair the inherent right of individual or collective self-defense if an armed attack occurs against a Member of the United Nations, until the Security Council has taken measures necessary to maintain international peace and security.' See also discussion of self-defence in Part I, *supra*.

[29] Jinks points out the different policy objectives of these concepts, and the lack of a clear relation between the definitional requirements and thresholds of the two. See D Jinks, 'The Applicability of the Geneva Conventions to the "Global War on Terrorism"' 46 *Virginia Journal of International Law* 165 (2005) 171–2.

[30] See discussion of legal frameworks in section 2 of the Introduction, *supra*.

conflict, rather than as a result of armed attack, does not make the *ius ad bellum* redundant; it simply means that when assessing the legality of the use of force, there are two separate questions that must be asked. The first is with concern to the legality of the resort to force and whether applicable rules of *ius ad bellum* have been adhered to. The separate second question is whether there factually exists an armed conflict and, if so, whether the rules of IHL are adhered to while the force is being used. They are separate concerns, but both must be addressed.

In summary of this section, it is apparent that applicability of IHL is not dependent on the condition of an armed attack having occurred, but rather on the determination that an armed conflict is currently in existence. Armed attacks may, or may not, be a precursor or act of armed conflict, whilst armed conflicts can also occur regardless of the determination of an initial armed attack. When assessing the level of violence and force being used, the initial armed attack may well be one of the incidents taken into account, but it is not the sole, or even necessary, determinant. Ultimately, the determination of whether IHL can apply to extraterritorial forcible measures rests therefore less on whether or not there has been an earlier armed attack, but primarily on whether one can identify factually if this measure is taken in the context of an occurring armed conflict. As mentioned earlier:

An armed conflict exists whenever there is resort to armed force between states or protracted armed violence between governmental authorities and organized armed groups or between such groups within a state.[31]

This description needs further elaboration. The next question to be examined is, therefore, whether extraterritorial forcible measures against non-state actors can fit within the scope and definition of an armed conflict.

3. The division into international and non-international armed conflict

The laws of armed conflict have traditionally been divided into two categories—those of international armed conflict, and those of non-international armed conflict. This is reflected in the existence of two separate Protocols of 1977 to the Geneva Conventions,[32] and more recently in the separate categories of war crimes in the statute of the International Criminal Court.[33] In reality the

---

[31] *Tadic*, n 8, *supra*.

[32] Protocol Additional to the Geneva Conventions of 12 August 1949, and Relating to the Protection of Victims of International Armed Conflicts (Protocol I) (8 June 1977) 1125 UNTS 3, entered into force 7 December 1978; Protocol Additional to the Geneva Conventions of 12 August 1949, and Relating to the Protection of Victims of Non-International Armed Conflicts (Protocol II), (8 June 1977), 1125 UNTS 609, entered into force 7 December 1978.

[33] Rome Statute of the International Criminal Court, UN Doc 2187 UNTS 90, entered into force 1 July 2002, Art 8.

distinction is not as clear as on paper. There has long been debate over the classification of so-called internationalized internal armed conflicts, such as armed conflicts involving a third state as well as internal violence between the government and non-state actors.[34] It is in fact feasible that, within one area of fighting, there may be three or more parties fighting side by side and with each other—each combination of two parties fighting under a different set of rules.[35] Which set of laws to apply at which time can, of course, cause much practical and legal confusion. To a certain extent, this has been eased by the ICTY stating that under customary international law, much of the essence of the laws regulating international armed conflict is applicable also to non-international armed conflict.[36] There has also been a call to examine the possibility of creating a unified set of rules which might aid the application of a clear framework of laws that is less likely to suffer from subjective manipulation of categories, or from just plain confusion in defining situations at hand, although it is clear that a number of issues would have to be resolved for this to be feasible.[37] The comprehensive study by the International Committee of the Red Cross ('ICRC') on Customary International Humanitarian Law,[38] takes the position that a vast majority of the IHL rules apply equally to both international and non-international armed conflicts. However, as will be seen later in this part, it is precisely those minority areas in which the rules are not the same—such as the combatant/civilian status of individuals—which are of prime importance to the issue currently at hand.

Furthermore, a cross border conflict between a state and an armed group, such as the 2006 conflict between Israel and the Hezbollah,[39] appears to defy the neat separation between international and non-international. Additionally, the depiction of a 'global war on terror' also provides new challenges to the separation between international and non-international armed conflicts.[40] A conflict between a state and a transnational network operating in and from numerous other states, but not necessarily with their support, is anything but an exact match for the traditional concepts of international and non-international armed conflicts. Not being a conflict between states creates difficulties in defining it as

---

[34] HP Gasser, 'Internationalized Non-international Armed Conflicts: Case Studies of Afghanistan, Kampuchea, and Lebanon', 33 *American University Law Review* 145 (1983); D Schindler, 'International Humanitarian Law and Internationalized Internal Armed Conflicts', 22 *International Review of the Red Cross* 255 (1982); D Schindler, 'The Different Types of Armed Conflicts According to the Geneva Conventions and Protocols', 163 *Recueil Des Cours* 117 (1979).

[35] *Ibid*; Y Dinstein, *The Conduct of Hostilities Under the Law of International Armed Conflict* (CUP: Cambridge, 2004) 14–15; Sassoli, n 5, *supra*, 4–5.

[36] Tadic, n 8, *supra*, paras 96–127.

[37] J Stewart, 'Towards a Single Definition of Armed Conflict in International Humanitarian Law: A Critique of Internationalized Armed Conflict', 850 *International Review of the Red Cross* 313 (2003).

[38] J Henckaerts and L Doswald-Beck, *Customary International Humanitarian Law, vol 1: Rules* (CUP: Cambridge, 2005).

[39] See discussion of this conflict in the Concluding Chapter.

[40] A Roberts, 'The Laws of War in the War on Terror' *Israel Yearbook on Human Rights 2003*, vol 32, 193–245, 196, 201–03.

international, while the fact that borders are crossed raises questions of whether it is non-international.[41] For example, the US military actions against Al-Qaeda in Afghanistan occurred both in the context of simultaneous hostilities against the Taliban at a time it was governing the country and later side by side with a new Afghan government. The situation in Afghanistan has, therefore, been described as containing a number of different categories of conflict (some of them occurring simultaneously including non-international, international and internationalized non-international armed conflict,[42]) as well as being a 'new' type of conflict.[43] Categorizing the US hostilities against Al-Qaeda—a non-state actor—as international armed conflict is a problematic contention, while the extraterritorial nature of the hostilities raises questions about it being non-international armed conflict.[44] These issues will be further analysed in this chapter and Chapter 5 of this work. Finally, it should be noted that the following sections on international and non-international armed conflicts are primarily concerned with the potential *applicability* of these frameworks of rules to the contexts under examination. There is, however, an additional question which must be borne in mind—and that is whether a particular framework is suitable and can adequately provide the needed regulation. Whilst the latter will arise in the next two sections, it will be returned to in greater detail in Chapter 5 of this work.

4. International armed conflict

The primary treaty rules governing the conduct of international armed conflicts are to be found in the 1907 Hague Regulations, the 1949 Geneva Conventions and the 1977 First Protocol to the Geneva Conventions. International armed conflicts are generally considered to be armed conflicts involving two or more opposing states.[45] The threshold that must be crossed in order to determine the existence of an armed conflict is not necessarily a high one. In fact, as seen in the definition of armed conflict of the ICTY, all it might take is 'a resort to armed

---

[41] International Humanitarian Law and the Challenges of Contemporary Armed, n 24, *supra*, 18; Roberts, *ibid*, 196, 201–03); W Lietzau, 'Combating Terrorism: Law Enforcement or War?' in *Terrorism and International Law*, n 18, *supra*, 75–84, 78–9.

[42] S Murphy, 'Evolving Geneva Convention Paradigms in the "War on Terrorism": Applying the Core Rules to the Release of Persons Deemed "Unprivileged Combatants"' The George Washington University Law School Public Law and Legal Theory Working Paper no 239 (2007) 14–32; D Pokempner, 'The "New" Non-State Actors in International Humanitarian Law' 38 *George Washington International Law Review* 551 (2006) 553–4.

[43] See discussion in Ch 5, *infra*.

[44] D Jinks, 'September 11 and the Laws of War' 28 *Yale Journal of International Law* 1 (2003) 20; Murphy, n 42, *supra*, 13.

[45] Pictet, n 9, *supra*; Dinstein, *supra*, n 35, 14–16; M Sassoli, 'Use and Abuse of the Laws of War in the "War on Terrorism"' *Law and Inequality: A Journal of Theory and Practice* 22 (2004) 199–200; Rona, n 5, *supra*, 58, 64.

force between States'.[46] The commentary to the 1949 Geneva Conventions supports this notion:

It remains to ascertain what is meant by 'armed conflict'. The substitution of this much more general expression for the word 'war' was deliberate. One may argue almost endlessly about the legal definition of 'war'. A State can always pretend, when it commits a hostile act against another State, that it is not making war, but merely engaging in a police action, or acting in legitimate self-defence. The expression 'armed conflict' makes such arguments less easy. Any difference arising between two States and leading to the intervention of armed forces is an armed conflict within the meaning of Article 2, even if one of the Parties denies the existence of a state of war. It makes no difference how long the conflict lasts, or how much slaughter takes place. The respect due to human personality is not measured by the number of victims.[47]

It has, however, been pointed out that such a definition is a wide one, seeing as states do not always view isolated clashes as being armed conflict,[48] and also that the threshold for international armed conflict is undefined and can vary according to circumstance.[49] Notwithstanding these comments, in a recent Opinion Paper, the ICRC supports a straightforward definition which asserts that 'International armed conflicts exist whenever there is resort to armed force between two or more States.'[50] In fact, when considering that the Geneva Conventions declare that: 'The Convention shall also apply to all cases of partial or total occupation of the territory of a High Contracting Party, even if the said occupation meets with no armed resistance',[51] it seems possible that the laws of international armed conflict could come into play in a situation in which there is very little actual fighting, if any. It would appear, therefore, that the existence of an international armed conflict between states does not necessarily require as high a threshold or protracted hostilities as in the case of the threshold for non-international armed conflicts.[52]

The main question currently before us is whether extraterritorial operations taken against non-state actors could perhaps be considered part of an international armed conflict. According to Article 2 of the Hague Regulations[53] and Article 2 common to the 1949 Geneva Conventions, the conventions shall apply to armed conflicts between contracting parties.[54] Since non-state actors cannot be contracting parties to these treaties,[55] it follows that these treaty rules will

---

[46] Tadic, n 8, *supra*.   [47] Pictet, n 9, *supra*, 32.
[48] Greenwood, 'Scope of Application', n 13, *supra*, 42.
[49] UK Ministry of Defence, *The Manual of the Law of Armed Conflict* (OUP: Oxford, 2004) 29.
[50] 'How is the Term "Armed Conflict" Defined in International Humanitarian Law?' International Committee of the Red Cross (ICRC), Opinion Paper, March 2008, 5.
[51] Geneva Conventions 1949, Art 2.
[52] See section 5, *infra*, on non-international armed conflict.
[53] Regulations Annexed to the Hague Convention (IV) Respecting the Laws and Customs of War on Land, 1907.
[54] Unlike the Geneva Conventions, the 1907 Hague treaties only apply if all the parties to the conflict are parties to the treaties.
[55] Although they can declare an intent to abide by treaties, or enter into specific agreements with states on adherence to rules of IHL, see the discussion of the possibilities in Sassoli, n 5, *supra*, 28–30.

not apply to armed conflicts between a state and a non-state actor.[56] Many of the rules are also recognized as customary international law,[57] and by definition, since it does not involve being a signatory to a treaty, in customary international law there is no notion of a high contracting party, which would automatically exclude the possibility of a non-state actor coming under the purview of these rules. However, the determination of custom tends to focus on the substantive elements of the rules rather than on the conditions for applicability; the relevance of the applicability clauses in the context of customary law is therefore unclear.[58] This curiosity can be circumvented by observing that the substantive elements of the rules of international armed conflict are obviously predicated on inter-state conflicts, as noted by Murphy, 'the Conventions' several hundred articles are built around the paradigm of two opposing states, operating normally through the use of their regular armies, though perhaps assisted by militias or volunteer corps.'[59]

This is most clear in the many detailed rules on prisoners of war, and in the rules of the Fourth Convention on Civilians which rely heavily on the notions of countries operating in sovereign territories (or occupying each other's territory).[60] Moreover, state practice does not lend support to there being any agreement on widening the concept of international armed conflict beyond that recognised in the treaties, and which is based upon conflicts between states.[61]

Article 1(4) of the First Additional Protocol to the Geneva Conventions, extends the application of the rules of international armed conflict, to 'include armed conflicts in which peoples are fighting against colonial domination and alien occupation and against racist regimes in the exercise of their right of self-determination'. This article could be relevant to cases of conflict between a state and a non-state actor, but it is unlikely to be applicable to the situations examined. Although the situations described in Protocol I do indeed open the door for consideration of international armed conflict involving a non-state actor, this is a narrow doorway, clearly defined so as to include only those non-state actors who, by and large, are engaging in a struggle for self-determination and fighting against an oppressor within national boundaries, or under a regime of occupation. The current focus is on forcible measures taken extraterritorially, excluding occupied territories, which are not, therefore, within the general design of Protocol I. A possibility should, however, be mentioned in which a state engaged in a type of conflict described in Article 1(4),

---

[56] With the exception of Common Article 3 to the Geneva Conventions, which will be dealt with in section 5, *infra*.

[57] On the Hague Regulations see *Judgment of the International Military Tribunal of Nuremberg*, 30 September and 1 October 1946, 65; *Legality of the Threat or Use of Nuclear Weapons,* Adv. Op 1996, ICJ Rep (I), 256, para 75; *Legal Consequences of the Construction of a Wall in the Occupied Palestinian Territory*, Adv. Op. 2004, ICJ Rep, para 89. The ICRC has recognized a significant proportion of the laws of international armed conflict, as customary international law. See ICRC Study, n 38, *supra*.

[58] See Ch 5, nn 86–95, *infra*, and accompanying text.   [59] Murphy, n 42, *supra*, 8.

[60] *Ibid*.   [61] Sassoli, 'Transnational', n 5, *supra*, 4.

and in which the main staging area for hostilities is within the state or territory it is occupying, sends its agents to conduct an operation against members of the armed group who are in hiding or operating from another territory. For example, Israel's failed attempt on the life of Hamas leader Khaled Mashal in Jordan or the killing of Islamic Jihad leader Fathi Shkaki in Malta,[62] could both be seen as extraterritorial forcible measures occurring in the context of the conflict over the Occupied Territories of the West Bank and Gaza.[63] However, although many rules of the Protocol are said to be part of customary international law, the same cannot be said with assurance about Article 1(4), which has been the subject of controversy.[64] Consequently, since Israel, and likewise the US, Turkey and others mentioned in this chapter, are not a party to Protocol I, this instrument would not apply to their operations. Similarly, for the reasons mentioned above, the fighting between the US and Al-Qaeda in Afghanistan is not a situation to which Article 1(4) of Protocol I applies.[65]

In general it, therefore, appears that other than those limited exceptions mentioned in Protocol I, the rules of international armed conflict can only apply to situations in which two (or more) states are engaged in armed conflict against each other. This conclusion notwithstanding, certain situations evolving from extraterritorial force against non-state actors could still lead to the classification of an international armed conflict. First, the 'non-stateness' of the non-state actor may change or become sufficiently ambiguous so as to raise the possibility that the non-state actor is acting as an agent of, or within, the structure of another state. If, from the start, it was clear that the individual/group was part of the state structure, then we would not be dealing with a non-state actor, and the issue would thus be outside the scope, which is concerned only with measures against non-state actors.[66] However, the situation is not always straightforward

---

[62] B Gellman, 'For Many Israelis, Assassination Is Only as Bad as Its Execution' *Washington Post*, 12 October 1997.

[63] Although Israel is not party to Protocol I, so it would not apply to this situation.

[64] Although it may in effect be influencing practice. See Greenwood, 'Scope of Application' n 13, *supra*, 43.

[65] Murphy, n 42, *supra*, 13.

[66] See discussion in Introduction, *supra*; for elaboration of standards and tests for determining whether individuals and groups are state agents, and whether their actions can be attributed to the state, see Draft Articles on Responsibility of States for internationally wrongful acts, adopted by the International Law Commission at its 53rd session (2001) (extract from the 'Report of the International Law Commission on the work of its 53rd session', Official Records of the General Assembly, 56th session, supp no 10 (A/56/10), chp.IV.E.1), November 2001, Arts 4–11; Commentaries to the draft articles on Responsibility of States for internationally wrongful acts, adopted by the International Law Commission at its 53rd session (2001) (extract from the 'Report of the International Law Commission on the work of its 53rd session, Official Records of the General Assembly, 56th session, supp no 10 (A/56/10), chp.IV.E.2) November 2001, 80–122; *Case Concerning Military and Paramilitary Activities in and Against Nicaragua* [1986] ICJ Rep 14, paras 93–116; *Prosecutor v. Dusko Tadic*, Case no IT-94-1-A, ICTY App Ch, 15 July 1999, paras 146–62; Application of the Convention on the Prevention and Punishment of the Crime of Genocide; *Bosnia and Herzegovina v. Serbia*, Judgment, Merits, General List No 91; ICGJ 70 (ICJ 2007) 26 February 2007, paras 379–415.

and fixed in time. For instance, it is certainly plausible to argue that initially Al-Qaeda was a non-state actor, and may have remained as such at the time the US began its military operations in Afghanistan, but that at some point during the hostilities, when it appeared that some of the Al-Qaeda members were fighting within the structure and chain of command of the Taliban—the then *de facto* government—those individuals and any hostilities they were involved in at that time and place, would have been part of an international armed conflict. Certainly, once it was clear that the US was engaged in armed conflict with the Taliban then the fighting between the US and the Taliban was an international armed conflict. If, following the US invasion and the commencement of battle, Al-Qaeda fighters became integrated within the organizational structure of the Taliban forces, it could be argued that they too were then part of an international armed conflict.[67] To clarify, the criterion for determining if this could be classified as an international armed conflict is not whether the non-state actor was acting as a state agent at an earlier stage, for instance when committing an attack against the state and provoking a response (eg 11 September 2001). Rather, the defining point is whether it is acting within a state structure at the time of the extraterritorial forcible measure we are classifying as part of an armed conflict. The categorizations are not always clear, as can be seen from the case of the conflict between Israel and the Lebanese Hezbollah in 2006, in which the status of the Hezbollah was not easily ascertained.[68]

Secondly, if the non-state actor is not acting within a state structure, or if there is no official connection whatsoever between the two, but there develops some form of violent altercation between agents of the state exercising the measures and agents of the territorial state then, depending on the type of altercation, this could also evolve into an international armed conflict.[69] There may also be a possibility of the state aligning itself with the non-state actor and thus becoming part of the conflict.[70] Finally, if the measures taken by the outside state were to constitute a situation of occupation of the territory of another state, this would fall within the realm of international armed conflict.[71] Notwithstanding, in these scenarios the rules of international armed conflict would be applicable to the fighting between the agents of the two states, and not necessarily by default also to the situation between the outside state and the non-state actor.[72]

In essence it would, therefore, appear that the only way extraterritorial forcible measures against non-state actors could be governed by the laws of international

---

[67] Bearing in mind the fact that one conflict can in fact be separated into fighting between different parties, with some categorized as international armed conflict, and some as non-international. See Dinstein, n 35, *supra*, and Sassoli, n 35, *supra*, and accompanying text.

[68] See discussion in Part I, *supra*, and the examination of this conflict in the Concluding Chapter, *infra*.

[69] See related discussion in Part I, *supra*, on the inter-state relationship and self-defence.

[70] Dinstein, n 10, *supra*, 236.

[71] Hague Regulations, n 53, *supra*, Art 42; Geneva Convention IV, n 9, *supra*, Art 2.

[72] See n 35, *supra*.

armed conflict would be in cases where the apparent non-state actor was in fact a state agent or assimilated into the forces of another state, thereby bringing into question its 'non-stateness'. Prima facie, it seems that extraterritorial forcible measures against non-state actors are not prime candidates for being declared international armed conflict. Nevertheless, since the possibility has been raised with regard to specific situations, the analysis presented in this section will be mentioned again in later sections and chapters examining the 'war on terror' and the Israel-Hezbollah hostilities of 2006.[73]

5. Non-international armed conflict

The alternative recognized model is non-international armed conflict. The examination now turns to consider whether extraterritorial forcible measures against non-state actors might be governed by IHL, through categorization as non-international armed conflicts. The focus in this section will be on the potential applicability of these laws to the circumstances at hand, rather than on whether the content of the laws is suitable for regulation of the situation.[74] The laws of non-international armed conflict, which at least in treaty form are far less detailed than the ones applying to international armed conflict, are found in Common Article 3 to the 1949 Geneva Conventions and in the 1977 Second Protocol to the Conventions. Further rules have been accepted as customary international law.[75] To what situations would these laws apply? Common Article 3 speaks of 'conflict not of an international character occurring in the territory of one of the High Contracting Parties'. The Second Protocol has additional requirements: that the conflict should be between the armed forces of the state and 'dissident armed forces or other organized armed groups which, under responsible command, exercise such control over a part of its territory as to enable them to carry out sustained and concerted military operations and to implement this Protocol'.[76] Two questions immediately arise when examining the potential applicability of these rules to extraterritorial forcible measures against non-state actors. First, whether the notion of non-international armed conflict can include actions taking place outside the territory of the state. Secondly, what is the threshold of violence that must be crossed for these measures to be considered part of such an armed conflict?

As will be seen, it has been suggested that the rules of non-international armed conflict could indeed apply to extraterritorial operations taken against non-state

---

[73] Ch 5, *infra*, and Concluding Chapter, *infra*.

[74] The question of suitability will be examined in the context of the next chapter.

[75] *Tadic*, n 8 *supra*; ICRC Study, n 38, *supra*. See also Y Dinstein, C Garraway, and M Schmitt, *The Manual on the Law of Non-International Armed Conflict: with Commentary* (San Remo: International Institute of Humanitarian Law, 2006).

[76] Protocol II, Art 1.

actors, such as of the US against Al-Qaeda.[77] When dealing with fighting occurring within a state's own territory, applying the laws of non-international armed conflict to operations against non-state actors is clearly acceptable, and even required (provided the threshold for armed conflict is crossed[78]). But can this cover fighting that takes place extraterritorially? The following analysis suggests that this is precisely the case.

Protocol II contains the requirement, that the non-state actor 'exercise such control over a part of its territory...'—it is clear from the Article that the word 'its' refers to the state. In other words the non-state actor must be controlling part of the territory of the state with which it is engaged in conflict. This would seem to rule out the Protocol's applicability to extraterritorial measures of the type currently under examination.[79] Unlike the Protocol, Common Article 3 does not contain this requirement for control over territory of the state but it does, nevertheless, contain a reference to territory, by speaking of conflict that is occurring 'in the territory of one of the High Contracting Parties'. Prima facie, it would seem that this refers to conflicts occurring within the territory of the state engaged in the fighting. Indeed, as noted by Wippman, Common Article 3 has 'language which at least suggests that ordinarily non-international armed conflicts must be internal to one state'.[80] The assumption that non-international conflicts are those which take place within the engaged state's territory can also be found in writings that describe such conflicts as 'internal'.[81] This assumption is not out of place since, as Murphy says:

A fair reading of the negotiating history suggests that this 'common Article 3' paradigm was principally designed to address the situation of an armed conflict internal to a single state. One of the parties to that armed conflict would normally be the government of the state; the other party would be a major insurgent group seeking to obtain control of the country. Thus, common Article 3 contemplates an armed conflict between a state and non-state actor, but does so largely in the context of the classic civil war.[82]

Extraterritorial operations, by definition, do not occur within the territory of the state taking these measures, and as such cannot be described as internal. Indeed,

---

[77] Ch 5, *infra*; S Cayci, 'Countering Terrorism and International Law: the Turkish Experience' in *Terrorism and International Law*, 137-146, n 18, *supra*, 142.

[78] See section 5.1, *infra*, on threshold.

[79] It might be applicable to situations in which a state is acting extraterritorially in assistance of another state in an existing conflict between the non-state actor and the territorial state. However, such situations are outside the defined scope of this work.

[80] D Wippman, 'Do New Wars Call for New Laws?' in D Wippman and M Evangelista (eds), *New Wars, New Laws?* (Transnational Publishers, New York, 2005) 1–28, 16.

[81] See the chs on Internal Armed Conflicts, in APV Rogers, *Law on the Battlefield* (Manchester University Press: Manchester, 2004) 215–238 and in UK Ministry of Defence *The Manual of the Law of Armed Conflict* (OUP: Oxford, 2004) 383–410; L Moir, *The Law of Internal Armed Conflict* (CUP: Cambridge, 2008); *Manual on the Law of Non-International Armed Conflict, supra*, n 75, 2; Greenwood speaks of non-international armed conflict as occurring in national territory. See Greenwood, 'Scope of Application, n 13, *supra*, 47.

[82] Murphy, n 42, *supra*, 10. See Jinks, 'Applicability', n 29, *supra*, 188.

a reading of Common Article 3 as applying to *internal* armed conflicts has been voiced in the context of US operations in the 'war on terror' both from within the US administration, in support of US actions,[83] and as part of arguments critical of US positions.[84]

Notwithstanding all the above, there are arguments supporting the possibility of Common Article 3 applying to extraterritorial operations, based on a textual reading and on a contextual approach that considers the reasoning and objective of the article. It has been said about Common Article 3 that 'This very vague formulation leaves ample room for interpretation, particularly of the terms "armed" conflict and "non-international" character', and that 'it does not formally exclude a broad interpretation.'[85] Whilst this opinion was not expressed in the context of extraterritorial operations against non-state actors,[86] the implications of a vague formulation open to interpretation can certainly have bearing on the viability of the current analysis. The requirement of being within the territory of a high contracting party does not necessarily need to be interpreted to cover only situations when a state is engaged in internal hostilities.

As noted earlier, the concept of internationalized non-international armed conflicts demonstrates that the categorization of applicable rules is not always straightforward.[87] For example, in cases when a state is engaged in a non-international armed conflict and another state intervenes by request to assist the government in fighting the non-state actor, this other state would then be acting extraterritorially, but could nevertheless be viewed as party to a non-international armed conflict. Whilst the question of the lawfulness of intervention by invitation is not within the scope of the current work,[88] it does provide support for the possibility that a state can effectively be engaged in extraterritorial forcible measures against a non-state actor, which would be part of and governed by the rules of non-international armed conflict. This example does not in fact negate the description of the situation in Common Article 3 so long as the territorial state which required the assistance is itself a party to the Geneva Conventions— the conflict would then be taking place 'in the territory of one of the High Contracting Parties', regardless of whether or not another state had joined in the

---

[83] 'Memorandum, dated 22 January 2002, from Jay S Bybee, Assistant Attorney General, to Alberto R Gonzales, Counsel to the President, and William J Haynes II, General Counsel of the Department of Defense' in K Dratel and J Greenberg (eds), *The Torture Papers: The Road to Abu Ghraib* (CUP: New York, 2005) 81–117, 86.

[84] McDonald, n 18, *supra,* 61–2.

[85] R Abi-Saab, 'Humanitarian Law and Internal Conflicts: The Evolution of Legal Concern' in A Delissen and G Tanja (eds), *Humanitarian Law of Armed Conflict Challenges Ahead: Essays in Honour of Frits Kalshoven* (Martinus Nijhoff: Dordrecht, 1991) 209–23, 215–6. Abi-Saab notes that in the past this was seen as a 'major defect', but can now be seen as an advantage.

[86] *Ibid.* The questions raised by Abi-Saab include the nature of hostilities and of the parties, and foreign intervention.

[87] See nn 34–5, *supra,* and accompanying text.

[88] For an analysis see L Doswald-Beck, 'The Legal Validity of Military Intervention by Invitation of the Government' 56 *British Yearbook of International Law* 189 (1985).

hostilities alongside the territorial state. Adapting this scenario to the types of measures examined one can point out that, to be absolutely precise, the Common Article 3 requirement does not actually require that the state in which it occurs should be involved in the conflict. Theoretically, one could read it to mean that state A could be involved in an armed conflict not of an international character, occurring in the territory of state B, which is a high contracting party to the Conventions, without state B having a part in the conflict. Insofar as the Geneva Conventions have achieved global recognition with 194 state parties,[89] virtually any territory would be that of a high contracting party.[90] Indeed, it is not altogether preposterous to advance an interpretation of this type, and it in fact appears to nest comfortably with the original intention of Common Article 3, as explained by Sassoli:

> Does this imply that conflicts between a High Contracting Party and an armed group, which do not occur on the territory of that High Contracting Party, but on the territory of another State, are not non-international armed conflicts? Or, does it simply recall that according to the principle of the relative force of treaties, those treaty rules apply only on the territories of States that have accepted them? From the perspective of the aim and purpose of IHL, the latter interpretation must be correct, as there would otherwise be a gap in protection, which could not be explained by States' concerns about their sovereignty.[91]

Certainly, situations of internal hostilities are likely to have been the primary concern for states,[92] but interpreting Common Article 3 so as to include the possibility of cross-border non-international armed conflicts, is entirely plausible when considering the context in which the rules were formulated. Moreover, it is equally the case that extraterritorial force against a non-state actor was not at the heart of the rules for international armed conflicts, which were designed for conflicts between states. The question, then, is which of these sets of rules would appear both more suitable and potentially applicable to the situation before us. As will be seen later,[93] one of the primary differences between the rules of international and non-international armed conflict is the possibility of being recognized as a prisoner of war during international conflicts, as opposed to non-international armed conflict which do not contain a grant of the same status to individuals, thereby leaving it open to a state to domestically prosecute

---

[89] See ICRC database at <http://www.cicr.org/ihl.nsf/Pays?ReadForm>. See also the view of the ICRC that 'As the four Geneva Conventions have universally been ratified now, the requirement that the armed conflict must occur "in the territory of one of the High Contracting Parties" has lost its importance in practice. Indeed, any armed conflict between governmental armed forces and armed groups or between such groups cannot but take place on the territory of one of the Parties to the Convention.' ICRC Opinion Paper, n 50, *supra*.

[90] Exceptions might be conflicts taking place on the high seas, or in a new state which did not become party to the Conventions. These would not be unregulated conflicts—see discussion of rules applying to all conflicts, in Ch 5, *infra*.

[91] Sassoli, 'Use and Abuse', n 45, *supra*, 200–01.

[92] Jinks, 'Applicability' n 29, *supra*, 188.   [93] See Ch 6, *infra*.

individuals who took up arms against it. A primary reason for states creating and maintaining two separate categories of conflict has been to avoid giving any recognized status or right to fight to rebels and insurgents.[94] Armed conflicts that begin as internal can lead to some of the fighting spilling over borders, and it cannot be the case that by stepping across the border a rebel would suddenly be entitled to claim elevation to prisoner of war status and subsequent immunity for attacks against state forces.[95] Bearing in mind the primary intention of states to refrain from granting such status to insurgents, the trans-border element of a situation does not change the fact that the appropriate legal status is the one that conforms to the framework of rules for non-international conflicts. Indeed, according to Bassiouni, the 'fact that, historically, such conflicts were confined to the territory of a given state does not alter the legal status of the participants in that conflict and the international humanitarian law applicable to them. The laws of armed conflict are not geographically bound'.[96]

A similar approach is taken by Jinks, who when speaking of the possibility of Common Article 3 referring only to conflicts occurring within the territory of the state that is party to the conflict, says that:

Despite its textual plausibility, this reading of the provision is problematic. First, this interpretation would create an inexplicable regulatory gap in the Geneva Conventions. On this reading, the Conventions would cover international armed conflicts proper and wholly internal armed conflicts, but would not cover armed conflicts between a state and a foreign-based (or transnational) armed group or an internal armed conflict that spills over an international border into the territory of another state. There is no principled (or pragmatic) rationale for this regulatory gap.[97]

Notably, this approach is not advanced solely by the concern over a regulatory gap, but is strongly supported by the fact that any such gap 'could not be explained by states' concerns about their sovereignty'.[98] This approach was recently adopted in practice by the US Supreme Court, determining that the rules of Common Article 3 applied to an alleged Al-Qaeda member captured in foreign land.[99] The Court reasoned that 'The term "conflict not of an international character" is used here in contradistinction to a conflict between nations.'[100] Accordingly,

---

[94] Pictet, n 9, *supra.*

[95] Although if the neighbouring state became a party to the conflict against the first state then the inter-state aspect would be an international armed conflict.

[96] Bassiouni, n 14, *supra,* 99. See also E Gillard, 'The Complementary Nature of Human Rights Law, International Humanitarian Law and Refugee Law' in *Terrorism and International Law*, n 18, *supra,* 50–6, 55; A Paulus and M Vashakmadze, 'Asymmetrical War and the Notion of Armed Conflict—A Tentative Conceptualization' 873 *International Review of the Red Cross* 95 (2009) 112.

[97] Jinks, 'September', n 44, *supra,* 40–1. See also Sassoli, 'Transnational', n 5, *supra,* 9.

[98] Sassoli, 'Transnational', n 5, *supra,* 9.

[99] US Supreme Court *Hamdan v. Rumsfeld* (no 05-184) 29 June 2006, 65–9.

[100] *Ibid,* 67.

Common Article 3 is not limited only to classic civil wars occurring within the state and, as supported by the commentaries, 'the Article should be applied as widely as possible'.[101]

A further concern that merits attention is the link between the applicable rules and the likelihood of their implementation in practice. In addition to the above matters of recognition and status, the rules of non-international conflict are better suited for conflicts involving non-state parties, due to the practical feasibility of implementation. Applying the rules of international conflicts would place, in most cases, impossible burdens on the non-state actor to comply with a myriad of detailed provisions such as those of the Third Geneva Convention. The inability to comply with rules of this type, would mean that the non-state actor would inevitably be considered to be in breach of the law and, as an assured outlaw, have very little incentive to comply with any rules at all. Rather, it is the rules of non-international conflict that are better suited to regulating the actions of non-state actors, and raising the chances that they abide by international law.[102]

The notion that extraterritorial hostilities between a state and a non-state actor can be regulated by the rules of non-international armed conflict finds support in the views of numerous commentators.[103] The essence of this claim rests primarily on viewing the category of non-international armed conflict as *non-international*, ie a conflict that is not between states, whether or not it is purely *internal*.

Common Article 3 can, thereby, provide minimal rules for those armed conflicts not falling within the requirements of Article 2.[104] This approach has been demonstrated to have support from the wording of the treaties which use the term non-international and by commentators examining the rationale behind the categorization. However, the potential applicability of the non-international armed conflict rules to any given situation will, as noted earlier, only come into play if, on the basis of a factual determination, the circumstances can be described as constituting an armed conflict. Without a determination of this kind we do not enter the domain of IHL applicability. This brings us to the question of threshold for determination.

---

[101] Pictet, n 9, *supra*, 50. See also, in the commentary, 'In the end the draft text submitted by the International Committee of the Red Cross was approved with the exception of the words "especially cases of civil war, colonial conflicts, or wars of religion" which were omitted. The omission of these words, far from weakening the text, enlarged its scope,' at 43.

[102] For discussion of the challenges in gaining compliance with IHL from non-state actors, see *Exploring Criteria & Conditions for Engaging Armed Non-State Actors to Respect Humanitarian Law & Human Rights Law*, Geneva, 4–5 June 2007, conference report available at <http://www.genevacall.org/resources/conference-reports/conference-reports.php>.

[103] Sassoli, 'Transnational', n 5, *supra*, 8–9; Murphy, n 42, *supra*; Bassiouni, n 14, *supra*; Jinks, 'Applicability', n 29, *supra*, 189; Human Rights First, 'Submission to HRC, 18 January 2006, Re: Follow-Up to Human Rights First's Memorandum to the Human Rights Committee', 18 October 2005, 2005 Memorandum to the Human Rights Committee 3, fn 7.

[104] Which required armed conflict between parties to the Convention (states). See section 4, *supra*, on international armed conflict.

5.1 The threshold for determination of non-international armed conflict

Classifying a situation as non-international armed conflict can be a contentious matter, and the difficulties of determining whether the threshold of an armed conflict has been reached are often raised.[105] The ICTY description of armed conflict speaks of 'protracted armed violence between governmental authorities and organized armed groups'.[106] According to this, the primary elements that must be present are a certain level of violence and the existence of parties to the conflict. These will be addressed in turn below.

While Common Article 3 does not contain a description of the necessary level of hostilities, it has been noted that an armed conflict would involve 'protracted armed violence',[107] of a certain intensity,[108] and exclude 'situations of internal disturbances and tensions, such as riots, isolated and sporadic acts of violence' as later set out in Protocol II.[109]

This could cover prolonged ongoing military hostilities, such as the battle-ground fighting in Afghanistan between the US and Al-Qaeda, or the fighting between Israel and the Hezbollah.[110] Outside of this level of military opera-tions, the threshold requirement might, however, prove an obstacle for trying to claim that short-term and one-time extraterritorial operations would qual-ify. Nevertheless, this does not have to rule out the applicability of Common Article 3 to situations of a lesser duration than the fighting in Afghanistan. The Inter-American Commission on Human Rights, in the *Abella Case*, found that the clashes between government forces and individuals who had attacked the La Tablada military base constituted a non-international armed conflict, despite the fact that the events occurred over a period of roughly 30 hours. This was due to the nature and level of violence, involvement of armed forces and military style operations against a military object.[111] The criterion of 'protracted' may not have been fulfilled in such a short period of time, but the demand of a lengthy time-period is problematic, since IHL must be applied from the very start of a conflict situation, and at the moment of outbreak of hostilities it is not always possible to

---

[105] UK Manual, n 81, *supra*, 386–7; K Watkin, 'Controlling the Use of Force: A Role for Human Rights Norms in Contemporary Armed Conflict' 98 *AJIL* 1 (2004) 25–6; Sassoli, 'Use and Abuse', n 45, *supra*, 201–02; J Klabbers, 'Rebel with a Cause? Terrorists and Humanitarian Law' 14 *EJIL* 299 (2003) 304–05; Moir, n 81, *supra*, 67–88; Jinks, 'September', n 44, *supra*, 21–9; H Spieker, 'Twenty-five years after the adoption of Additional Protocol II: Breakthrough or failure of humani-tarian legal protection?', *Yearbook of International Humanitarian Law, vol 4*, (TMC Asser Press: The Hague, 2001) 134–43.

[106] *Tadic*, n 8 *supra*.   [107] *Ibid.*

[108] *Prosecutor v. Akayesu*, Case ICTR-94-4-T, 2 September 1998, para 619.

[109] Protocol II, Art 1.

[110] Under certain interpretations these might be regarded as non-international armed conflicts. See above on extraterritorial interpretation of non-international conflicts, and Ch 5, *infra*.

[111] *Juan Carlos Abella v. Argentina*, Case 11.137, Report no 55/97, IACHR, OEA/Ser.L/V/II.95 Doc. 7 rev. at 271.

know how long they will last.[112] Indeed, the ICTY has accepted that the term 'protracted' be interpreted 'as referring more to the intensity of the armed violence than to its duration'.[113] A separate question with regard to 'protracted', is whether this could also be covered by numerous events which do not occur continuously in the same place.[114] As noted by the ICTY:

> Trial Chambers have relied on indicative factors relevant for assessing the 'intensity' criterion, none of which are, in themselves, essential to establish that the criterion is satisfied. These indicative factors include the number, duration and intensity of individual confrontations; the type of weapons and other military equipment used; the number and calibre of munitions fired; the number of persons and type of forces partaking in the fighting; the number of casualties; the extent of material destruction; and the number of civilians fleeing combat zones. The involvement of the UN Security Council may also be a reflection of the intensity of a conflict.[115]

In summary thus far, the key to identifying the conflict lies in the nature and intensity of violence, in addition to the identification of the parties.[116]

The Inter-American Commission case did recognize, nonetheless, that there is difficulty in defining the threshold of application. Could it be taken any lower than the *Abella Case*? The Israeli military conducted a raid on a Ugandan airport in 1976, and engaged in a shoot-out with the hijackers of an Air France airliner. Could this operation, involving the Israeli Air Force and military commandos with a high level of violence against a group of hijackers belonging to an organized group, also qualify as an armed conflict? The hijackers were a non-state actor, and according to the *Abella* interpretation of Common Article 3, perhaps this too could be a short-term non-international armed conflict.[117] The operations are sometimes of an even smaller scale, such as the targeted killing of alleged Al-Qaeda members in Yemen, which involved the use of an unmanned drone and no sending of special forces for a ground shoot-out. Could an incident of this kind, if isolated, qualify as a situation of armed conflict? There are difficulties with such an assertion on at least two grounds: first, unlike the *Abella Case*, there was no bilateral fighting involved, other than the quick strike by the drone; secondly, one would have to show that these individuals were, at the time of the strike, part of an organized group involved in a conflict.[118] An argument that might be raised in order to circumvent these issues would be the assertion that a specific measure is a part of a wider ongoing conflict (calling it for

---

[112] Sassoli, 'Transnational', n 5, *supra*, 6–7.

[113] *Prosecutor v. Haradinaj and ors*, Judgment, ICTY, Case no IT-04-84-T, 3 April 2008, para 49.

[114] See discussion on the Yemen incident and Ch 5, *infra*.

[115] *Haradinaj*, n 113, *supra*.   [116] See section 5.2, *infra* on organized groups.

[117] Collusion between the hijackers and the Ugandan authorities, depending on the type of links and support that may have been given by Uganda, might raise the possibility that this incident also involve rules of international armed conflict.

[118] See further discussion in Ch 5, *infra* on the 'war on terror', Ch 6 on individual status, and the discussion of this case in the Concluding Chapter.

instance, a 'war on terror') that already exists between the state carrying out the strike, and the group to which the individuals belong. This assertion would, however, require the questionable linking of a series of events to be attributed to one ongoing conflict,[119] and the claim that these events have passed the threshold with regard to intensity of violence. This will be examined further in Chapter 5 of this work.[120]

5.2 Identifying the parties to the conflict

The involvement of the state's military in any armed action will naturally raise questions about whether the situation should be classified as armed conflict. Indeed, when determining the existence of a conflict, the use of military forces will be one of the elements that may be looked to when seeking to classify the situation.[121] However, military involvement alone is not evidence that the threshold into armed conflict has been crossed, and the military might be used in non-conflict operations such as search and rescue missions or assisting in the aftermath of natural disasters. A situation involving military forces which has arisen frequently in recent times is the use of naval forces in the case of piracy. Piracy is, at its essence, a criminal act rather than a situation of armed conflict. According to the UN Convention on the Law of the Sea:

Piracy consists of any of the following acts:

(a) any illegal acts of violence or detention, or any act of depredation, committed for private ends by the crew or the passengers of a private ship or a private aircraft, and directed:
   (i) on the high seas, against another ship or aircraft, or against persons or property on board such ship or aircraft;
   (ii) against a ship, aircraft, persons or property in a place outside the jurisdiction of any State;
(b) any act of voluntary participation in the operation of a ship or of an aircraft with knowledge of facts making it a pirate ship or aircraft;
(c) any act of inciting or of intentionally facilitating an act described in subparagraph (a) or (b).[122]

This definition excludes acts within the territorial waters or jurisdiction of a state. These cases which would not meet the definition of piracy, could be

---

[119] For the question of linking a series of events in the context of self-defence, see the section on accumulation of events in Part I.

[120] The Concluding Chapter will then also raise the possibility of this operation being considered part of the conflict occurring in Afghanistan.

[121] J Pictet (ed), *Commentary on the Geneva Convention of 12 August 1949 for the Amelioration of the Condition of the Wounded and Sick in Armed Forces in the Field* (International Committee of the Red Cross: Geneva, 1958) Art 3.

[122] United Nations Convention on the Law of the Sea (10 December 1982) 1833 UNTS 3, entered into force 16 November 1994, Art 101.

considered as armed robbery against ships.[123] Indeed, other than the jurisdictional concern, piracy and armed robbery against ships are similar crimes, and are often debated and tackled in unison.[124] The force envisaged in international treaties is a form of law enforcement at sea. The fact that it is conducted by the navy can be attributed to the navy being the most clearly available and able body to carry out enforcement of this kind. Indeed, enforcement by military units seizing the pirate ship is the method envisaged in the Convention on the Law of the Sea.[125] Accordingly, the measures against piracy, similarly to the measures against armed robbery against ships, belong in the realm of law enforcement rather than armed conflict.

Moreover, piracy would also fail to meet the basic requirements to be classified as an armed conflict. Such sporadic acts with a relatively low level of casualties and damage are unlikely to meet the threshold discussed earlier. Crucially, the clearest obstacle would be the inability to identify parties to any such conflict. First, the pirates themselves would have to meet the basic criteria of an organized group, which includes elements of hierarchy, disciplinary measures and further characteristics which are not necessarily to be assumed solely on the basis of the ability of a group of criminals to organise a raid on a cruise ship.[126] Secondly, even if the pirates were to be defined as possessing the organizational capabilities, there is no identifiable party with whom they could be said to be engaged in an armed conflict. Their choice of victims for their raids ranges from tourist cruise ships, to ships carrying food and aid.[127] It is a random selection targeted for any chance of individual gain, rather than a strategic selection based on the identity of an opposing party. Whilst it is conceivable that an organized armed group would embark on sustained high level violent pirate attacks against a particular state, such a scenario is not a

---

[123] For a definition see 'Code of Practice for the Investigation of the Crimes of Piracy and Armed Robbery Against Ships 2001', International Maritime Organization Resolution A.922(22), para 2.2.

[124] For examples, see Code of Practice, *ibid*; Security Council Res no 1846 adopted by the Security Council at its 6026th meeting, on 2 December 2008, UN Doc S/RES/1846 (2008); Security Council Res no 1851 adopted by the Security Council at its 6046th meeting, on 16 December 2008, UN Doc S/RES/1851 (2008). See also the reports regularly published by the International Maritime Organization, 'Reports on Piracy and armed robbery against ships', available at <https://www.imo.org/Circulars/mainframe.asp?topic_id=334&offset=21>. See also statement by US Secretary of State Hillary Clinton: 'These pirates are criminals, [...] They are armed gangs on the sea, and those plotting attacks must be stopped and those carrying them out must be brought to justice.' In 'France detains Somali pirates, U.S. to boost fight' *Reuters*, 15 April 2009.

[125] 'A seizure on account of piracy may be carried out only by warships or military aircraft, or other ships or aircraft clearly marked and identifiable as being on government service and authorized to that effect.' United Nations Convention on the Law of the Sea, n 122, *supra*, Art 107.

[126] See discussion below on required level of organization.

[127] 'Italian cruise ship foils pirates' *BBC News*, 26 April 2009; 'Pirates halt Somali aid shipments' *BBC News*, 21 May 2007.

reflection of the piracy currently occurring. Therefore, and in light of all the above, the existing cases of piracy would not qualify as instances of armed conflict, and the rules of IHL are not applicable to them. The regulation of force against pirates will, therefore, be in accordance with the law enforcement model.[128]

A key element exemplified in the above discussion of pirates, is the need to identify the parties to a conflict. The existence of an armed conflict implies (at least) two opposing parties. Common Article 3 does not give criteria as to the definition of a party to a conflict, although it would appear to envisage a clear level of organization.[129] According to the ICRC, 'non-governmental groups involved in the conflict must be considered as "parties to the conflict", meaning that they possess organized armed forces. This means for example that these forces have to be under a certain command structure and have the capacity to sustain military operations.'[130]

The ICTY, when faced with the need to determine whether a particular group (the Kosovo Liberation Army ('KLA')) 'possessed the characteristics of an organised armed group, able to engage in an internal armed conflict',[131] relied on the following findings—'zone commanders acted in accordance with directions from the General Staff',[132] and 'zone commanders of the KLA issued orders to the commanders of units within their zone';[133] 'Zone commanders also authorized the movement of soldiers';[134] 'the capacity of the KLA units to coordinate their actions';[135] the General staff played a key role in supply of weapons and in issuing political statements;[136] the existence of group regulations which were distributed to the soldiers,[137] and that 'The Regulations provided that the first duty of a unit commander was, inter alia, to supervise obedience to and enforcement of the KLA's programme and regulations';[138] 'the establishment of a military police, which, generally, were responsible for the discipline of the soldiers and for controlling the movements of KLA servicemen';[139] and the participation in political negotiation meetings.[140] These findings point to a high level of organization and, undoubtedly, any hostilities

---

[128] See further discussion in section 2.2 of Ch 8, *infra*, on authority or control outside formally acknowledged detention facilities.

[129] The commentary speaks of 'distinguishing a genuine armed conflict from a mere act of banditry or an unorganized and short-lived insurrection.' See also UK Manual, n 81, *supra*, 386–7; J Pejic 'Terrorist Acts and Groups: a Role for International Law?' 75 *British Year Book of International Law* 71 (2004) 86; Moir, n 81, *supra*, 36–8.

[130] ICRC Opinion Paper, n 50, *supra*, 3.

[131] *Limaj and ors*, Judgment, ICTY, IT-03-66-T, 30 November 2005, para 134. Examinations of this were conducted by the court in further cases, such as *Prosecutor v. Boskoski and Tarculovski*, Judgment (Trial Chamber), ICTY, IT-04-82-T, 10 July 2008, paras 194–206.

[132] *Ibid* para 98. This was found to be 'not necessarily without fail', but 'generally' correct.

[133] *Ibid*, para 105. [134] *Ibid*, para 107. [135] *Ibid*, para 108.
[136] *Ibid*, paras 100, 101. [137] *Ibid*, paras 110–11. [138] *Ibid*, para 112.
[139] *Ibid*, para 113. [140] *Ibid*, paras 125–9.

involving groups possessing these characteristics could be distinguished from mere banditry. However, it should be borne in mind that while the finding of these characteristics in this specific case can indicate that this combination of attributes is sufficient to determine the requisite level of organization, it does not rule out the possibility that less comprehensive organizational capacity might also have sufficed. In other words, the finding that a certain set of characteristics combines to a total which is above a certain organizational threshold does not give us a definitive answer of where the threshold is exactly located on the scale below this combination. Nonetheless, it appears unquestionable that a minimum level of organization must exist,[141] and that it should include the ability to command and control members of the group, and carry out the group's operations. Accordingly, the findings of the ICTY are of assistance in deciding what type of questions can be asked when looking to determine the level of organization.

When examining the possibility of extraterritorial forcible measures against members of a group which is purportedly part of an armed conflict, a further matter arises in connection to membership of an organized group. When dealing with groups exhibiting armed militia characteristics, including clear command and control structures and even uniforms, there is less difficulty. However, many groups defy easy recognition, and once the existence of an armed conflict has been accepted, there are likely to remain a number of challenges involved in defining which individuals are actually members of the opposing party to the extent that they might be legitimately targeted under the rules of armed conflict. Moreover, even if it is found that an armed conflict exists between a state and a group, questions will remain as to the definition of the status of the individual members, and when they might be subjected to lawful targeting. This will be dealt with in greater detail in the later sections on combatants, civilians and direct participation.

Following the above it seems that extraterritorial forcible measures against non-state actors can satisfy the requirements to come under the scrutiny of laws applicable in non-international armed conflict. If the territorial state itself becomes a party to the conflict, then the rules of international armed conflict would apply between the states. The involvement of the territorial state could take the form of forcibly resisting the measures by the outside state or through alignment with, and attribution to it, of the activities of the non-state actor. This determination can be challenging on a factual basis, as is apparent in the case of the Hezbollah in Lebanon.[142] However, so long as the non-state actor remains independent of the territorial state, the armed conflict between it and the outside state should be considered a non-international armed conflict for all the reasons outlined above. This position can be supported by corresponding interpretation of the relevant rules of IHL. While the applicability rules of Protocol II appear

---

[141] See n 129, *supra*.   [142] See discussion in the Concluding Chapter.

to exclude extraterritorial situations, Common Article 3 can be interpreted so as to include them. Finally, should there be disagreement over this interpretation of Common Article 3, there nevertheless is room for arguing that the rules of non-international armed conflict can and should extend to certain extraterritorial operations through customary international law. This latter possibility will be further explored in Chapter 5 of this work.

5

Non-Traditional Models of Armed Conflict

Chapter 4 of this work examined whether extraterritorial forcible measures, that are considered to be part of armed conflict, could be either international or non-international armed conflicts. There is, however, the need to explore a third possibility—that although these measures might fall into the realm of international humanitarian law ('IHL') they fit neither of these two recognized categories of armed conflict. As will be seen in the first part of this chapter, such opinions have been voiced within the context of the suggestion that there is a 'war on terror'. While the focus is not solely upon counter-terror operations, it is precisely the extraterritorial dimensions of the alleged 'war' that lie at the heart of the problem, and the debate over the existence and categorization of a 'war on terror' provides an ideal template to delve further into many of the questions under examination. The next two sections will first address the question of whether the reference to a transnational 'war on terror' is merely rhetoric or in fact covers a situation which can be defined as armed conflict (and consequently to which IHL might be applicable). This will be followed by an analysis of whether the existing situations demonstrate the need to consider new categories of armed conflict and, if so, what would be the applicable rules.

1. The global 'war on terror' as an armed conflict

The first question to be addressed, is the very use of the phrase 'war on terror'. As a form of rhetoric, indicating the need to struggle with a grave phenomenon which plagues society, it might be a perfectly acceptable term, in the same way as 'war on poverty'. However, when used in order to define a situation as an armed conflict to which the laws of war apply it is an entirely different matter. Just as declaring a 'war on poverty' is not enough to justify engaging in unilateral military operations against those considered responsible for the problem, simply announcing a global 'war on terror' is as nonsensically inadequate a foundation to determine the existence of an armed conflict. This is not to say that it is impossible for an armed conflict to be linked to the notion of a 'war on terror', but that use of the phrase alone is not a sufficient determinant. An armed conflict must involve at least two parties and 'terror' or 'terrorism' would not qualify as such, since these are descriptions of a method, rather than of a distinct entity capable of being a party to a conflict.[1] Moreover, not only is 'terror'/'terrorism' a method rather than an entity, it is also one which is notorious for lacking any agreed definition.[2] Furthermore, terrorism was in the past seen as a phenomenon to which states reacted through criminal and law enforcement means rather than by war.[3] Its mere invocation cannot, therefore, be grounds for automatic categorization as war. One approach might be that this is not a war, and we should not be treating it as such,[4] but considering the extent to which the 'war on terror' has become a cornerstone foundation for extensive military operations, the categorization of it as an armed conflict must be subjected to closer examination.

At the outset it should be clarified that whilst the rhetoric is one of war the application of IHL, as noted earlier, depends on the determination of an armed conflict and it is the criteria for the latter that must be applied in the following assessment. Seeing as 'terror' itself is not a party to a conflict the first stage will be to reveal precisely who is the designated enemy and how the proponents of the war define them. Following this there will be a need to see whether this might fit within one of the recognized models of armed conflict in accordance with the criteria that defines these and, in a later section, to examine the need and possibility of alternative models of conflict.

The US Administration under President Obama has sought to distance itself from the previous administration's rhetoric of a 'war on terror', and some of the more controversial policies that accompanied it,[5] though certain practices linked

---

[1] For a general critique of a variety of aspects relating to the 'war on terror' see J Record, 'Bounding The Global War On Terrorism' US Strategic Studies Institute, December 2003, available at <http://www.strategicstudiesinstitute.army.mil/Pubs/Display.Cfm?pubID=207>; G Rona, 'Interesting Times for International Humanitarian Law: Challenges From the "War on Terror"', *Fletcher Forum of World Affairs*, 27:2 (2003); D Jinks, 'The Applicability of the Geneva Conventions to the "Global War on Terrorism"' 46 *Virginia Journal of International Law* 165 (2005); R Brooks, 'War Everywhere: Rights, National Security Law, and the Law of Armed Conflict in the Age of Terror' 153 *University of Pennsylvania Law Review* 675 (2004).

[2] See discussion of this term in the Introduction, *supra*.

[3] A Roberts, 'The Laws of War in the War on Terror' *Israel Yearbook on Human Rights, Vol 32* (2003) 193–245, 202–03; RJ Sievert, 'War on Terrorism or Global Law Enforcement Operation?' 78 *Notre Dame Law Review* 307 (2003) 310; W Lietzau, 'Combating Terrorism: Law Enforcement or War?' in M Schmitt and G Beruto (eds) *Terrorism and International Law: Challenges and Responses* (International Institute of Humanitarian Law, 2002); R Wedgwood, 'Military Commissions: Al Qaeda, Terrorism, and Military Commissions' 96 *AJIL* 328 (2002) 329–30; see also the reservation of the UK to Art 1 of the First Protocol Additional to the Geneva Conventions: 'It is the understanding of the United Kingdom that the term "armed conflict" of itself and in its context denotes a situation of a kind which is not constituted by the commission of ordinary crimes including acts of terrorism whether concerted or in isolation.'

[4] Keijzer discusses the possibility that this is not a war one can win, and of boarding up the windows and waiting for the hurricane to die out. See N Keijzer, 'Terrorism as a Crime' in WP Heere (ed.), *Terrorism and the Military: International Legal Implications* (Asser: The Hague, 2003) 115–32, 116.

[5] 'Under Obama, "War on Terror" Phrase Fading' *Associated Press*, 1 February 2009; 'Obama Administration Says Goodbye to "War On Terror": US Defence Department Seems to Confirm

to it that are examined have continued and possibly even intensified.[6] Regardless of any change in use of the phrase its presence both in legal arguments and in practice over the past decade has been all pervasive and merits detailed examination. If there has been a 'war on terror' then one party would certainly be the United States. There have been varying statements from different officials over the years in relation to a 'war on terror' including the following descriptions of an enemy:

- The nation is at war with terrorist organizations that pose a threat to its security and that of other societies that cherish the principle of self-government.[7]
- The United States has been at war with al Qaeda.[8]
- The enemy includes Al-Qaeda and other international terrorists around the world, and those who support such terrorists [. . .] and certainly terrorists who can strike not only within the United States but who can threaten our forces abroad and our friends and allies.[9]

Al-Qaeda appears to be deemed an opposing party to the conflict, but so do a number of other unnamed entities. The difficulties of determining whether Al-Qaeda can satisfy the basic prerequisites defining a party to a conflict, and the even greater question mark hovering over the possibility of an armed conflict against 'other international terrorists around the world' will be explored later but for now the starting point is the possibility of the US being engaged in an extraterritorial armed conflict with Al-Qaeda. It is evident from the content and timing of the statements, that this 'war on terror' is perceived to exist as a global war not limited to the battlefield context of Afghanistan and/or Iraq. In these latter situations it is clear that an armed conflict has existed and the current chapter is focused not upon these, but on the wider possibility of other extraterritorial forcible measures against non-state actors in the context of the perceived global 'war on terror'. The time-frame of this global armed conflict is, however, unclear and this creates a problem since one needs to identify a timeline for a conflict in order to know when the IHL framework is applicable.[10] Whilst some may 'benchmark the war on terrorism as beginning in March 1973 when Yassir Arafat ordered

---

use of the Bureaucratic Phrase "Overseas Contingency Operations" ' *Guardian*, 25 March 2009; see also changes mentioned in section 2 of Ch 7, *infra* on torture.

[6] See discussion of drone strikes in Pakistan in section 2 of the Concluding Chapter, *infra*.

[7] Secretary of Defense Donald Rumsfeld, 'US National Military Strategic Plan for the War on Terrorism', Chairman of the Joint Chiefs of Staff, Washington DC 20318, 1 February 2006.

[8] Remarks by Alberto R Gonzales, Counsel to the President, before the American Bar Association Standing Committee on Law and National Security, Washington DC, 24 February 24 2004, available at <http://www.pegc.us/archive/White_House/gonzales_remarks_to_ABA_20040224.pdf>.

[9] Excerpts from interview with Charles Allen, Deputy General Counsel for International Affairs, US Department of Defense by Anthony Dworkin, December 16, 2002, available at <http://www.crimesofwar.org/onnews/news–pentagon–trans.html>.

[10] Rona, n 1, *supra*, 62.

the murder of two United States diplomats in Khartoum',[11] US administration officials have taken a position which appears to be more restrictive, if not altogether unambiguous, noting that the war with Al-Qaeda is 'Since at least that day'—referring to 11 September 2001.[12] Accepting the assumption that this was the starting date, determining a potential end-point is far more difficult, as will be seen in a later section.[13]

Continuing now, for the sake of argument, with the assumption that the US is engaged in armed conflict with Al-Qaeda, the next task is to identify what type of conflict this might be. The fact that hostilities take place extraterritorially does not transform the non-state actor into a state and, as noted earlier,[14] international armed conflicts are those which involve states as parties. The only exception to this conclusion would be in the case of Al-Qaeda members who may have been fighting within the structure of the Taliban forces in Afghanistan and in this case the laws of international armed conflict could apply.[15] Other than this, it appears generally accepted that the 'war on terror' cannot be of the international type.[16]

As for non-international armed conflict, it has been asserted by a number of commentators that this is a potentially applicable framework for some of the hostilities between the US and Al-Qaeda.[17] The primary obstacle to this is the question of whether the notion of non-international armed conflict can include extraterritorial hostilities, and Chapter 4 of this work has suggested that this is possible. The fact that the US does not recognize Al-Qaeda members as entitled to combatant status[18] has been mentioned as an additional impediment[19] but, since the laws of non-international armed conflict do not contain rules on granting of combatant status,[20] the non-recognition of status does not prevent the

---

[11] AN Pratt, '9/11 and Future Terrorism: Same Nature, Different Face' in *Terrorism and International Law*, n 3, *supra*, 155–62, 156.

[12] Gonzales, n 8, *supra*, 3. See also discussion below on threshold of violence.

[13] See n 99, and accompanying text, *infra*.

[14] Section 4 of Ch 4, *supra*, on international armed conflict.

[15] Y Dinstein, 'Ius Ad Bellum Aspects of the "War on Terrorism"' in Heere, n 4, *supra*, 13–22, 22; R Goldman and B Tittemore, 'Unprivileged Combatants and the Hostilities in Afghanistan: Their Status and Rights Under International Humanitarian and Human Rights Law' American Society of International Law, Task Force on Terrorism, Task Force Papers (December 2002) 29–30.

[16] Goldman and Tittemore, *ibid*, 29; Rona, n 1, *supra*, 64; A Dworkin, 'Military Necessity and Due Process: The Place of Human Rights in the War on Terror' in D Wippman and M Evangelista (eds), *New Wars, New Laws?* (Transnational Publishers: New York, 2005) 53–73, 54; D Jinks, 'September 11 and the Laws of War' 28 *Yale Journal of International Law* 1 (2003) 12; A McDonald, 'Terrorism, Counter-terrorism and the Jus in Bello' in *Terrorism and International Law*, n 3, *supra*, 57–74, 65; M Sassoli, 'Transnational Armed Groups and International Humanitarian Law, Program on Humanitarian Policy and Conflict Research, Harvard University, Occasional Paper Series, no 6, Winter 2006, 4.

[17] Jinks, 'September' *ibid*, 12; S Cayci, 'Countering Terrorism and International Law: the Turkish Experience' in *Terrorism and International Law*, 137–46, n 3, *supra*, 142; Human Rights First submission to HRC, 18 January 2006, RE: Follow-Up to Human Rights First's Memorandum to the Human Rights Committee, 18 October 2005. See also the discussion in section 5 of Ch 4, *supra*, on non-international armed conflict.

[18] See Ch 6, *infra*, on individual status.   [19] McDonald, n 16, p 65.

[20] See Ch 6, *infra*, on individual status.

categorization as non-international. Moreover, the problems of individual status are a question of application of particular rules, rather than a general question of the applicability of the IHL framework.

For a potentially applicable framework to apply in practice to this situation one must first examine whether the case at hand satisfies the necessary criteria. As noted in Chapter 4, for extraterritorial hostilities against a non-state actor to be categorized as non-international armed conflict it is necessary to determine whether the situation has crossed a certain threshold of violence and whether the non-state actor has the necessary characteristics to be considered a party to a conflict. As will be seen below, both these issues are debatable.

Beyond the inherent problem in the lack of an agreed and objective definition for the requisite threshold of violence,[21] there is an additional difficulty in reaching agreement on which acts can be attributed to this perceived conflict. The widest inclusive approach is demonstrated in the position taken by Wedgwood:

Al Qaeda's campaign throughout the 1990s against American targets amounted to a war. In recitation, this may seem more obvious now. The cumulative chain of events is quite striking—the 1992 attempt to kill American troops in Aden on the way to Somalia; the 1993 ambush of American army rangers in Mogadishu; the 1993 truck bombing of the World Trade Center by conspirators who later announced that they had intended to topple the towers; the 1995 bombing of the Riyadh training center in Saudi Arabia; the 1996 bombing of the Khobar Towers American barracks in Saudi Arabia (five weeks after bin Laden was permitted to leave Sudan); the 1998 destruction of two American embassies in East Africa; and the 2000 bombing of the U.S.S. Cole, in a Yemeni harbor. The innumerable other threats against American embassies and offices around the world; the plot to down ten American airliners over the Pacific and to bomb the Lincoln and Holland Tunnels in New York, as well as the United Nations; the smuggling of explosive materials across the Canadian border for a planned millennium attack at Los Angeles Airport; and finally, the attacks on the Pentagon and the World Trade Center—were taken to constitute a coherent campaign rather than the isolated acts of individuals. Al Qaeda's open ambition to acquire a nuclear device has made the metaphor of war even more compelling.[22]

The first problem with this position is that it reaches into past years to draw on events that took place prior to 2001, whereas some claims of a 'war' largely focus upon 11 September 2001 as the starting point.[23] Even taking into account that the US had engaged in military action against Al-Qaeda in previous years,[24] and if one were to accept that a conflict may have begun earlier, the determination of

---

[21] See Ch 4, n 107–19, and accompanying text, *supra*.

[22] Wedgwood, n 3, 18, *supra*, 330. It is interesting to note that Wedgwood refers to the 'metaphor' of war. See also Sievert, n 3, *supra*, 312; J Dalton, 'What is War?: Terrorism as War after 9/11' 12 *ILSA Journal of International and Comparative Law* 523 (2006) 524–5.

[23] See n 12, *supra*.

[24] The 1998 attacks in Afghanistan and Sudan. See Letter, dated 20 August 1998, from the Permanent Representative of the United States of America, to the United Nations, Addressed to the President of the Security Council, UN SCOR, 53rd sess. at 1, UN Doc S/1998/780.

whether an armed conflict exists currently must nevertheless rest upon current events and the level of hostilities that exists in the present. The second problem with the above position is the reliance upon 'threats', 'plots', and 'ambition', which would seem to be questionable sources of proof of actual violence.[25] Looking at recent years, Dalton notes that:

Since September 11th, 2001, there have been further brutal terrorist attacks in Bali (twice), Madrid, London, and Jordan. It is quite clear that the conflict with al Qaeda is not an internal disturbance, nor is it isolated or sporadic.[26]

To others, however, six or so attacks in the same number of years is precisely what might be termed as 'sporadic'.[27] A further, and significant, query that arises in relation to the aforementioned incidents, is whether they can all in fact be attributed to a single organization. This will be examined further below, but for now it should be noted that if the said violence cannot in fact be attributed to Al-Qaeda, it raises serious questions over whether these incidents can be construed as evidence of an existing high level of violence between the group and the US.[28]

The fact that there had not been a high number of incidents did not prevent administration officials from maintaining their position on the existence of an ongoing conflict and everyone from the Secretary of Homeland Security, to the Federal Bureau of Investigation ('FBI') and Central Intelligence Agency ('CIA') Directors, to the Attorney General had warned of impending attacks,[29] thus contributing to the argument that there was an existing conflict. The fact that these attacks tended to fail to materialize could mean that either the warnings were unfounded, or that security and intelligence services have succeeded in thwarting them. Either way, for the application of IHL there has to be an existing armed conflict, not just a warning of one. The factual level of violence in the 'war on terror' was difficult to qualify as anything other than sporadic and below the threshold of armed conflict although arguably, as some of the above views present, the totality of all acts said to be linked to Al-Qaeda could perhaps be perceived by some as having crossed the threshold. This argument rests on grouping all these acts of violence into one conflict involving a distinct enemy. The next matter to be examined is, therefore, the nature of the non-state actor and whether it can be described as a party to the conflict.

As quoted earlier, the opposing party to the conflict is described as Al-Qaeda, but also 'other international terrorists around the world, and those who support such terrorists'.[30] The latter phrase hardly corresponds to the meaning of a party

---

[25] See n 29 and accompanying text, *infra*.   [26] Dalton, n 22, *supra*, 527–28.

[27] ME O'Connell, 'When Is a War Not a War? The Myth of the Global War on Terror,' *ILSA Journal of International and Comparative Law* 12 (2006) 538.

[28] See further discussion at n 32–46, *infra*, and accompanying text.

[29] All quoted in J Mueller, 'Terrorphobia: Our False Sense of Insecurity' *The American Interest*, vol 3, no 5, May–June 2008.

[30] Interview, n 9, *supra*.

to a conflict as understood in international law, which requires the identification of a specific entity possessing a recognizable organizational structure.[31] Moreover, even if other organizations engage in violence, this would still not mean that they are in conflict with the US. An attack on Spanish soil is not an armed conflict involving the US unless, arguably, the target was associated with the US (eg an embassy) or if the Spanish government considered itself at war with the perpetrators and asked the US to assist. Should additional groups engage in hostilities with the US at an intensity to qualify as armed conflict then such a conflict might be said to exist with them as parties, possibly even a few separate conflicts, but unless these hostilities are actually taking place one cannot speak of them as being a party to the conflict.

As for Al-Qaeda it is hard to conclude that it currently possesses the characteristics of a party to a conflict. Most notable is the fact that its description ranges from being a distinct group, to a network of groups, or even a network of networks, and in some cases an ideology rather than an entity.[32] Al-Qaeda has been described as an organized entity with 'central direction, training, and financing'[33] and up until 2001 it appears that it could be identified as an organized group with a clear leadership and even a fixed location, including training camps and headquarters.[34] The US invasion of Afghanistan precipitated the physical dispersal of the group and the transition towards a decentralized network of many groups and individuals operating on the basis of a shared ideology and, in some cases, past training in the Afghan camps,[35] although there may still be loose connections to the leadership of a 'mother Al-Qaeda (*Al Qaeda al Oum*)'.[36] The shift away from describing Al-Qaeda as a distinct group and towards a depiction of networks and ideology was most apparent in the view of the US government itself:

In the GWOT,[37] the primary enemy is a transnational movement of extremist organizations, networks, and individuals—and their state and non-state supporters—which have in common that they exploit Islam and use terrorism for ideological ends. The Al Qa'ida Associated Movement (AQAM), comprised of al Qa'ida and affiliated extremists, is the most dangerous present manifestation of such extremism. Certain other violent extremist groups also pose a serious and continuing threat. Networks provide survivability via a combination of redundant systems, secrecy, and a cellular structure. They can be highly adaptable, and the al Qa'ida Network (AQN) is an example of such adaptation. Following the elimination of the AQN base of operations in Afghanistan, the remaining leadership and key operational elements dispersed around the globe, effectively franchising

---

[31] Ch 4, *supra,* on non-international armed conflict.

[32] See nn 38, 39, *infra*; For a detailed study of Al-Qaida see J Burke, *Al-Qaeda: Casting a Shadow of Terror* (IB Tauris: London, 2003).

[33] Gonzales, n 8, *supra,* 3. See also Jinks, 'September', n 16, *supra,* 38.

[34] M Mohamedou, 'Non-Linearity of Engagement: Transnational Armed Groups, International Law, and the Conflict between Al Qaeda and the United States' *Program on Humanitarian Policy and Conflict Research*, Harvard University, July 2005, 13.

[35] It is said that the number of people trained in the camps ranges between 10 to 20,000, *ibid.*

[36] *Ibid,* 14.	[37] Global War on Terror.

Islamist extremism and terrorist methodology to regional extremist organizations. The AQN's adaptation or evolution resulted in the creation of an extremist 'movement,' referred to by intelligence analysts as AQAM, extending extremism and terrorist tactics well beyond the original organization. This adaptation has resulted in decentralizing control in the network and franchising its extremist efforts within the movement. Other extremist networks have proven to be equally adaptive.[38]

The Australian government, which at times has been supportive of the US position in the 'war on terror', sets forth a similar assessment going so far as to point out that 'for many Muslim extremists, Al Qaida has become more an idea or ideology than a physical entity.[39] At best, it appears that if Al-Qaeda is to be described as a distinct entity, perhaps the most appropriate depiction that has been offered is of a structure that is 'murky' with a loosely organized but highly focused network.[40] The bomb attacks on public transport in Madrid in 2004[41] and London in 2005[42] underscore the difficulty in connecting the dots to reveal any clear image of a single group behind all the attacks. In these, and other cases, although the perpetrators appear to have been inspired by and share the Al-Qaeda ideology questions were raised over the existence of sufficient concrete evidence to directly attribute the attacks to the same Al-Qaeda group responsible for the September 2001 attacks.[43] Indeed, even the Director of the FBI spoke of a three-tiered threat with the core Al-Qaeda organization as the first tier, a second tier of 'small groups who have some ties to an established terrorist organization, but are largely self-directed. Think of them as al Qaeda franchises—hybrids of homegrown radicals and more sophisticated operatives', and a third tier of 'homegrown extremists. They are self-radicalizing, self-financing, and self-executing. They meet up on the Internet instead of in foreign training camps. They have no formal affiliation with al Qaeda, but they are inspired by its message of violence.'[44]

There is, therefore, great difficulty in credibly claiming that all incidents are part of a single armed conflict with Al-Qaeda unless being inspired by the

[38] 'US National Military Strategic Plan for the War on Terrorism', Chairman of the Joint Chiefs of Staff, Washington DC 20318, 1 February 2006, 13.

[39] 'Transnational Terrorism: The Threat to Australia', Government of Australia, 2004, 31, available at <http://www.dfat.gov.au/publications/terrorism>.

[40] 'Transnationality, War and the Law: A Report on a Roundtable on the Transformation of Warfare, International Law, and the Role of Transnational Armed Groups', Program on Humanitarian Policy and Conflict Research, Harvard University, April 2006, 9.

[41] 'Scores die in Madrid bomb carnage' *BBC News*, 11 March 2004, available at <http://news.bbc.co.uk/2/hi/europe/3500452.stm>.

[42] 'In depth—London attacks' *BBC News*, 8 July 2005, available at <http://news.bbc.co.uk/2/hi/in_depth/uk/2005/london_explosions/default.stm>.

[43] J Bennetto and I Herbert, 'London bombings: the truth emerges' *The Independent,* 13 August 2005; P Hamilos, 'The worst Islamist attack in European history' *The Guardian,* 31 October 2007. See also Sassoli, 'Transnational' n 16, *supra*, 9–11; J Pejic, 'Terrorist Acts and Groups: a Role for International Law?' 75 *British Year Book of International Law* 71 (2004), 86–7.

[44] R Mueller, 'From 9/11 to 7/7: Global Terrorism Today and the Challenges of Tomorrow' *Transcript* of Chatham House Event, 7 April 2008, available at <http://www.chathamhouse.org.uk/files/11301_070408mueller.pdf>.

same ideology would suffice. Accumulating all acts described as terrorism, and its supporters, into a single conflict on the basis of a shared ideology is akin to claiming that not only could the Korean war, the Vietnam war and the Cuban Missile Crisis in the 1950s–1970s all be considered part of a single armed conflict (as indeed they might be according to the rhetoric of the Cold War) but that anyone, or any group, suspected of holding Communist opinions, anywhere around the globe, would also be seen as a party to the conflict.[45] The threshold of violence and the identity of the party to the conflict are thereby linked. If numerous incidents round the world classified as terrorism could be attributed to the same entity then one could argue that the threshold for conflict has been crossed. If, however, these incidents are perpetrated by separate groups with no unified and organized command and control structure it becomes difficult to add them all up together as evidence of an existing conflict.

Undoubtedly the US and many other countries are faced with a threat from groups ready to use violence against civilians and methods which might be described as terrorism. Indeed, many of these groups might share similar ideologies and have members that at some stage in the previous two decades underwent the same training. The many acts described earlier in this section perpetrated by such groups clearly demonstrate that the threat is real—but not every threat, or indeed every act of violence, can appropriately be categorized as an armed conflict in accordance with international law. The application of the rules of IHL are preserved for those situations which answer the definition of armed conflict and were created and meticulously designed for specific types of circumstances. Situations that fall outside the definitions of armed conflict must be addressed through other frameworks, such as law enforcement and, if need be, international co-operation in investigation, intelligence sharing, extraditions and judicial cooperation. This is not to say that the armed conflict model and the rules of IHL can never apply to extraterritorial operations in the context of terrorism and, as noted earlier in this section, the battlefields of Afghanistan serve as an example of this possibility but their invocation cannot depend on the rhetoric of war, or even the potential threat of armed groups, but rather by the finding that the circumstances at hand amount to an armed conflict as defined by international law. The 'war on terror' may be a useful phrase for various other purposes but it should not be understood as referring to war or armed conflict as defined in international law. If it is to be used then it should be understood as encompassing a variety of situations and methods[46] and while some of them might be armed conflicts, others are not.

---

[45] S Murphy, 'Evolving Geneva Convention Paradigms in the "War on Terrorism": Applying the Core Rules to the Release of Persons Deemed "Unprivileged Combatants"' The George Washington University Law School Public Law and Legal Theory Working Paper no 239 (2007) 40.

[46] Dalton, n 22, *supra*, 533; Roberts, n 3, *supra*, 194.

To conclude thus far, there is a fair amount of support for the possibility that certain components of the 'war on terror' may fall within the parameters of an armed conflict and be regulated by the framework of IHL.[47] This would be the case with regard to the hostilities between the US and Al-Qaeda in Afghanistan. Theoretically, the same could apply to other situations, should there be the requisite level of hostilities and an identifiable opposing party which satisfies the requirements of a minimal organizational structure and capabilities. A wider form of a conflict between the US and loosely connected networks of unnamed groups around the world does not, however, answer the definition of an armed conflict as examined in Chapter 4 of this work.[48] Whether or not this necessitates contemplating new models of armed conflict is the focus of the following section.

2. The need for a new category of conflict?

From the preceding sections it appears clear that extraterritorial forcible measures that fulfil the threshold requirements could qualify as armed conflicts to which IHL would consequently be applicable. Let us also, for the sake of argument, accept that some of these operations, especially those taking place in the context of a 'war on terror', form part of an armed conflict which displays characteristics different from the traditional international armed conflict or non-international armed conflict, in that it is not between states and one of the parties is a transnational non-state actor not operating within the confines of one country. It has been said, most notably by senior figures within the US administration, that the current circumstances are a 'new kind of war'[49] and even that in this new war certain aspects of the Geneva Conventions are rendered obsolete and quaint.[50] There are two propositions found at the heart of the claim that we are faced with a different type of conflict:

(i) This is a new phenomenon, which is an armed conflict falling outside the accepted categories as defined in international law.
(ii) There is a need to develop new laws in order to regulate this conflict.

---

[47] C Bassiouni, 'Legal Control of International Terrorism: A Policy-Oriented Assessment' 43 *Harvard International Law Journal* 83 (2002) 99.

[48] 'International Humanitarian Law and the Challenges of Contemporary Armed Conflicts' Report Prepared by the International Committee of the Red Cross, Geneva, 2003, 18–19; Sassoli, 'Transnational', n 16, *supra*; M Sassoli, 'Use and Abuse of the Laws of War in the "War on Terrorism"' *Law and Inequality: A Journal of Theory and Practice* 22 (2004) 200; Jinks, 'Applicability', n 1, *supra*, 187.

[49] Condoleezza Rice *on Fox News Sunday*, 10 November 2002, available at <http://www.foxnews.com/story/0,2933,69783,00.html>.

[50] Memorandum, dated 25 January 2002, from Alberto R Gonzales, Counsel to the President, to President Bush in K Dratel and J Greenberg (eds), *The Torture Papers: The Road to Abu Ghraib* (CUP: New York, 2005) 118–21, 119.

2.1 A new phenomenon

Are extraterritorial operations against non-state actors a new phenomenon? The list of examples noted in the Introduction Chapter of this work clearly indicates otherwise. States have engaged in cross-border forcible operations against non-state actors for many years, with examples stretching back over a century.[51] Nevertheless, the insistence that there is now a 'new kind of war'[52] is often founded upon the claims that it involves a new type of non-state actor, and that '[t]he "new terrorists" in contrast, are driven by an apocalyptic and millenarian religiously-based worldview which posits that the world must be destroyed in order to cleanse the globe of paganism and impurity.'[53] This conception is however open to argument and an analysis of Al-Qaeda, for example, has concluded that the group has clear political goals (primarily aimed at changing/removing US policy/presence in the Middle-East), and that it 'would conceivably cease hostilities against the United States [...] in return for some degree of satisfaction regarding its grievances.'[54] Numerous other elements are cited as being new, including the blurring of the combatant-civilian divide; the means and methods used for attacks; the divergence from traditional state-centred models of conflict; and the multi- and extraterritorial scope.[55] Other than the latter, however, these elements have actually presented themselves time and again in the context of traditional non-international armed conflicts. In fact, even the claims of inadequacy of the law are not new in the context of fighting non-state groups with situations half a century ago leading to the following remarks by Thompson in a 1966 publication:

There is a very strong temptation in dealing with both terrorism and with guerrilla actions for government forces to act outside the law, the excuses being that the processes of law are too cumbersome, that the normal safeguards in the law for the individual are not designed for an insurgency and that a terrorist deserves to be treated as an outlaw anyway.[56]

As for the spatial dimension, a significant question with regard to a conflict spanning a multiplicity of territories is in fact whether these multiple situations are part of the same conflict with the same opposing party—a conclusion which, as noted in the previous section, is far from obvious.[57] Moreover, groups carrying out attacks in multiple countries are not a new phenomenon. Throughout

---

[51] See, eg, discussion of the *Caroline Case*, in Part I, *supra*.   [52] See nn 49, 50, *supra*.

[53] M Lippman, 'The New Terrorism and International Law' 10 *Tulsa Journal of Comparative and International Law* 297 (2003) 302–33, citing B Hoffman, 'Terrorism Trends and Prospects' in I Lesser and ors, *Countering the New Terrorism* (RAND: Santa Monica, 1999).

[54] Mohamedou, n 34, *supra*, 7, 18–22, 25.

[55] Mohamedou, n 34, *supra*, 2, 5; R Schondorf, 'Extra-State Armed Conflicts: Is There a Need for a New Legal Regime?' 37 *New York University Journal of International Law and Politics* 1 (2004) 8–9; Transnationality Roundtable, n 40, *supra*, 8.

[56] R Thompson, *Defeating Communist Insurgency: Experiences from Malaysia and Vietnam: Studies in International Security No 10* (Chatto and Windus: 1966) 52.

[57] See nn 36–46, *supra*, and accompanying text.

the 1980s, the Abu Nidal group was alleged to have been responsible for attacks in Rome and Vienna Airports, as well as being linked to further incidents in France and the UK and aircraft hijacking and bombing.[58] As for the extraterritorial dimension, states have in the past engaged in hostilities with non-state actors in extraterritorial contexts, whether in assistance of the territorial state, or acting unilaterally.[59] The primary novelty, if it is to be found, is not that these operations take place but rather in the insistence that it is happening in the context of a large-scale *bona fide* armed conflict or war. There are at least two reasons why states might choose to label these operations as armed conflict. First, on the socio-political level, governments of states engaged in conflict might employ the language of war to rally further support for their regime and the existence of war can be used to justify actions, including domestic legal measures, that their public might not have otherwise accepted. There may well be good reason for this language and the actions, although it could equally be cynically exploited. Secondly, claiming the existence of armed conflict is likely to be a precursor to the subsequent suggestion that IHL is applicable and that it is the rules of IHL that should be governing state conduct. These rules allow for a higher level of force and a looser finger on the trigger than if IHL were not applicable.[60] Whether or not situations should be classified as armed conflict in the first place was considered in previous sections and will be returned to later in the context of new types of conflict, but this stage of the examination will continue accepting for argument's sake that some of the situations claimed as new do indeed merit the qualification as armed conflict.

A further problem that is posited in the context of these new types of conflict is based on the perception that the existing armed conflict paradigm automatically entitles the non-state group to belligerent rights and combatant status for its members. On the one hand, allowing states to attack group members anywhere, while denying group members the right to use force against the state, is said to be 'extreme and unconvincing'[61] and 'hard to accept'.[62] On the other hand, providing the full benefits to members of these groups is said by others to be equally problematic.[63] This debate becomes misplaced, if one is to accept the paradigm of non-international armed conflict, since this type of conflict doesn't provide an entitlement to combatant status in the first place.[64] If the call for a new model of

---

[58] 'Abu Nidal' in J Thackrah *Dictionary of Terrorism* (Routledge: London, 2004) 1–3.

[59] See examples in Introduction, *supra*.   [60] See Ch 9, *infra*.

[61] A Dworkin, 'Revising the Laws of War to Account for Terrorism: The Case Against Updating the Geneva Conventions, On the Ground That Changes Are Likely Only to Damage Human Rights' *FindLaw's Legal Commentary*, 4 February 2003, available at <http://writ.findlaw.com/commentary/20030204_dworkin.html>. See also McDonald, n 16, supra, 65.

[62] S Ratner, 'Revising the Geneva Conventions to Regulate Force by and Against Terrorists: Four Fallacies' 1 *IDF Law Review* 7 (2003) 16.

[63] Dalton, n 22, *supra*, 528–9.

[64] 'Non-international armed conflict rules are, in fact, well suited to governing this type of conflict because they are not based upon a concept of "combatant" status and of the legal consequences

conflict is based upon a concern that the current armed conflict framework forces states to recognize that groups—whether Al-Qaeda or others—would have the right to attack state forces with impunity, then these worries can be alleviated by applying the non-international model. The rules of non-international armed conflict do not give any legal status to groups[65] and do not contain any provisions allowing for individual combatant status, while at the same time—depending on certain interpretations—they may allow state forces to target active members of armed groups.[66] Moreover, since the rules of non-international armed conflict do not grant combatant status an individual who attacks state soldiers does not have immunity from prosecution by that state. On the last point it should however be noted that when dealing with extra-territorial situations prosecution in domestic courts will also necessitate that domestic laws allow for jurisdiction over crimes committed against nationals abroad.[67] Indeed, this all appears to place the members of the groups at a dis-tinct disadvantage as opposed to the state; gives them little incentive to abide by any rules;[68] and perhaps offers too free a license to states to target mem-bers of the groups.[69] A partial answer for incentives may be found in noting that although they can still be prosecuted by the state they are fighting against, through abiding by international law, members of groups might nevertheless spare themselves from the fear of prosecution by international tribunals or exer-cise of universal jurisdiction by other states. Whilst the state they are fight-ing against might not favour this it does at least provide an incentive of some kind to refrain from attacking civilians. These concerns, as well as the potential risk of abuse by allowing states to target group members, had already existed with relation to non-international armed conflict and are not unique to these new extraterritorial conflicts with groups. In both these contexts questions have been raised about the possibility of requiring state forces to attempt a detention of group members prior to lethal targeting.[70]

Chapter 4 of this work concluded that it was possible for extraterritorial for-cible measures against non-state actors to fall within the existing recognized

---

that arise from it in international armed conflicts.' Pejic, n 43, *supra*, 85; See later chapter on indi-vidual status.

[65] Common Article 3 ends with the phrase 'The application of the preceding provisions shall not affect the legal status of the Parties to the conflict'.

[66] There are a number of differing opinions on the status of fighters in non-international armed conflict. See discussion in Ch 6, *infra*, on individual status.

[67] I Brownlie, *Principles of Public International Law* (OUP: Oxford, 2003) 301–05; M Shaw *International Law* (CUP: Cambridge, 2003) 584–97.

[68] 'Transnationality', *supra*, 40, 15. On the links between equality, reciprocity, and violations of IHL, see R Geiss, 'Asymmetric Conflict Structures' 864 *International Review of the Red Cross* 757 (2006).

[69] D Kretzmer, 'Targeted Killing of Suspected Terrorists: Extra-Judicial Executions or Legitimate Means of Defence?', 16 *EJIL* 171 (2005) 202; See Ch 6, *infra*, further discussion.

[70] See discussion in section 2.2 of Ch 6 on small-scale operations; Schondorf, *supra*, n 55 at 58.

models of armed conflict, and that the non-international armed conflict framework was in most cases the appropriate one. Crucially, the rules of applicability could be interpreted to allow for extraterritorial situations to be classified as non-international armed conflicts. These were arguments that focused upon applicability as opposed to suitability. As for the latter, the points then raised in the section above further indicate that this framework of rules appears to contain an approach that is generally suitable, and can address the concerns raised over the new situations,[71] although also sharing some of the inherent problems of non-international armed conflicts. However, it is clear that not everyone has been ready to accept the extraterritorial interpretation of Common Article 3 or the appropriateness of the non-international rules to extraterritorial hostilities.[72] There are, in fact, separate but intertwined issues at stake, relating both to the problem of classification of the conflicts as well as the existence of suitable substantive rules and, as seen in this chapter, concerns over the former tend to go hand in hand with calls for review of the latter. This analysis favours the approach that relies upon the notion of non-international armed conflict as an applicable and suitable framework for these perceived new situations, including but not limited to the 'war on terror'—if and when they are considered to be armed conflicts at all. However, the different opinions that have been encountered throughout this analysis cannot be ignored. This recognition of opposition to categorizing extraterritorial operations as non-international, together with states' claims of a new type of conflict, therefore necessitate an examination of the possible case for new rules and what these might be.

2.2 The need for new rules?

The first point, that must be stressed, is that taking the position that there exist situations which IHL does not appear to adequately regulate is by no means sufficient a foundation for demanding development and changes of IHL. It may also be the case that IHL does not have appropriate rules since these circumstances are not armed conflicts and the reason we might not find answers to the situation therein is that we are looking in the wrong place.[73] Perhaps we should be casting our gaze in other directions, to the realms of the rules of law enforcement, extradition, human rights law, and criminal law—as has been done in the past in not dissimilar situations.[74] The following paragraphs should not, therefore, be

---

[71] Though not completely free of obstacles: see n 114–117, *infra*, and accompanying paragraphs.

[72] Memorandum, dated 22 January 2002, from Jay S Bybee, Assistant Attorney General, to Alberto R Gonzales, Counsel to the President, and William J Haynes II, General Counsel of the Department of Defense in K Dratel and J Greenberg (eds), *The Torture Papers: The Road to Abu Ghraib* (CUP: New York, 2005) 81–117, 86–8; D Wippman, 'Do New Wars Call for New Laws?' in Wippman, n 16, *supra*, 1–28, 19; Schondorf, n 55, *supra*, 40–1.

[73] Rona n 1, *supra*, 58; Sassoli, 'Transnational', n 16, *supra*, 22. [74] See n 3, *supra*.

misconstrued as advocating the extension of the laws of armed conflict to situations which should not be defined as such. That being said, earlier chapters have pointed to certain cases of extraterritorial use of force between states and groups which do appear to merit the categorization as armed conflict, be it in the context of the US and Al-Qaeda in Afghanistan, or Israel and the Hezbollah. If these are perceived as new types of wars then do they require new rules? This is by no means a foregone conclusion.

A new factual situation does not automatically call for new laws to regulate it—the question that must first be answered is whether existing laws can adequately handle a new situation. The distinction between maintaining that a factual situation is new, and calling for new laws to regulate it, is an important one. It might well be appropriate to analyse and examine the novelty of a new set of circumstances and perhaps even to come up with new theoretical models and names designed to categorize and describe this situation.[75] These new names and categories should relate, however, to differing approaches to describing a *factual* situation and not automatically become new *legal* categories which would then call for new substantive rules applying to them. The existing legal categories may well be able to withstand and encompass a host of new factual circumstances without the need for new laws.

For example, it is certainly possible to imagine a new factual category of armed conflicts describing armed conflicts in which the majority of operations, and indeed the outcome of the war, rely primarily on computer network attacks (eg remotely disabling various critical military infrastructure). It would be perfectly acceptable to describe this as a new form of warfare not envisaged by the drafters of the 1907, 1949 and other IHL treaties said to apply to modern warfare. This would not, however, mean that the existing IHL treaties do not contain rules which can be used to regulate this new type of warfare.[76] Formulation of laws may be such that they are designed to adapt to a degree of changing circumstances[77] and can be understood and interpreted in a manner appropriate to new situations without the need each time to renegotiate them anew. Extraterritorial forcible measures against non-state actors occurring within the 'war on terror' might similarly be occurring in the context of a new set of circumstances, but that does not necessarily imply that the existing rules are inadequate.

Calling for new laws should also be differentiated from talking of a need 'to construe international humanitarian law in a realistic and flexible manner, so that it adapts itself to changing realities and to new challenges.'[78] Whether one

---

[75] See, eg, 'Extra-State Armed Conflicts' in Schondorf, n 55, *supra*.

[76] Schmitt discusses the notion of computer network attacks and the ways in which existing IHL would cover them. See M Schmitt, 'Targeting and Humanitarian Law: Current Issues' 34 *Israel Yearbook on Human Rights* 59 (2004) 100–04. The issue of cyber operations raises numerous questions also for the *ius ad bellum*, international cooperation in law enforcement, and much more. In some areas there may be need for new approaches, and significant attention is being given to this issue in current times.

[77] Murphy, n 45, *supra*, 1, 34.

[78] Y Shany, 'Israeli Counter-Terrorism Measures: Are they "Kosher" under International Law?' in *Terrorism and International Law*, n 3, *supra*, 96–118, 114.

agrees or not with certain 'flexible' interpretations there is a fundamental difference between claiming that laws do not apply and demanding different laws to an
approach that, whilst proposing various interpretations, does accept the applicability of the current legal framework. It should also be noted that the idea of considering new laws—which often comes from politicians and their legal advisors
(be it a UK Secretary of State for Defence,[79] or Counsel to the US President,[80]) is
not shared by all, even within the same administrations:

I don't think there is a need for revision of the Geneva Conventions [...] We believe that
the existing law provides an entirely satisfactory legal framework for warfare as it occurs
in the modern world, and specifically a framework for the war on terrorism. And the
United States will continue to reaffirm the existing principles. What we need is better
compliance with the existing laws, not new laws.[81]

The possibility should also be noted that claims of a need for new rules might be
designed to make the existing ones appear unreasonable in order to evade restrictions and allow states a freer hand in their actions. Notwithstanding, if new laws
nevertheless are contemplated the proposals would need to go beyond claims that
current laws are inadequate and actually clarify why and what it is specifically that
the proposers would like to change, and what new form it would take.[82] The viability of any treaty changes is in doubt considering that states would have to agree
on some of the most contentious issues such as definitions of terrorism and status
of individual members of groups.[83] Added to this is the concern over diminish-
ing existing protections and reducing restrictions on state behaviour.[84] The most
likely outcome of new treaty negotiations is either years of never-ending disagreement or adoption of a compromise set of rules that is relatively minimalist and far
removed from original hopes, as was the case in the adoption of Protocol II.[85] In
light of the difficulties of finding an answer in the realm of treaties, the possibility
of solution through customary international law must also be examined.

---

[79] 'I believe we need now to consider whether we—the international community in its widest
sense—need to re-examine these conventions. If we do not, we risk continuing to fight a 21st
Century conflict with 20th Century rules.' Reid addresses RUSI on '20th-Century Rules, 21st-
Century Conflict' 3 April 2006 available at <http://www.mod.uk/DefenceInternet/DefenceNews/
DefencePolicyAndBusiness/ReidAddressesRusiOn20thcenturyRules21stcenturyConflict.htm>.

[80] 'As you have said, the war against terrorism is a new kind of war. [...] In my judgement, this
new paradigm renders obsolete Geneva's strict limitations on questioning of enemy prisoners and
renders quaint some of its provisions [...]'—Memorandum, dated 25 January 2002, from Alberto
R Gonzales, Counsel to the President, to President Bush, reprinted in K Greenberg and J Dratel
(eds) n 72, *supra*, 118–121, 119.

[81] Interview, n 9, *supra*.

[82] Ratner, n 62, *supra*, 9–10; Roberts, n 3, *supra*, 240; Pejic, n 43, *supra*, 100; Sassoli,
'Transnational', n 16, *supra*, 20–21.

[83] Dworkin, n 61, *supra*; Wippman, n 72, *supra*, 11. For the start of some suggestions see Brooks,
n 1, *supra*, 755–60. See further discussion on an approach to discovering applicable rules, *infra*.

[84] Sassoli, 'Transnational, n 16, *supra*, 39; Dworkin, n 61, *supra*; Brooks, n 1, *supra*, 747.

[85] General Introduction to the *Commentary on the Additional Protocols of 8 June 1977 to the
Geneva Conventions of 12 August 1949* (Dordecht: Martinuus Nijhoff, 1987) 1319, paras 4412–17;
Ratner, n 62, *supra*, 17.

By virtue of the fact that states are speaking of a new type of situation there exists an inherent problem in searching for evidence of past consistent state practice, which would point to customary international law, relating directly to regulation of extraterritorial armed conflict against non-state actors, outside the traditional international and non-international paradigms. Furthermore, attempting to create a third category of conflict risks exacerbating the existing difficulties in classification and creating endless permutations of mixed situations.[86] It may instead be a more viable and productive route to attempt to identify a regulatory framework of customary rules which could be said to apply to any and all armed conflicts, whether they are referred to as international, non-international, or this new model of conflict. Unfortunately, the extensive ICRC study on customary international humanitarian law is not in itself sufficient to show the existence of such customary rules (although it will prove helpful) as it is largely built around the models of rules that apply in international and/or non-international armed conflicts,[87] and there may be a need for further exploration in order to reach the answers now sought. Further extensive study into the rules which might apply as minimum to all conflicts would hopefully also be able to address and clarify areas in which there is a need for more guidance. These include the question of whether customary international law contains rules pertaining to thresholds of applicability of IHL,[88] and also the matter of whether and when rules of customary international law would point to individual criminal responsibility in the context of conflicts which might not fit the traditional international and non-international paradigms. It is beyond the confines of the current work to try and establish a confirmed framework of customary rules spanning all conflicts, including those that fall outside the traditional models,[89] but the remainder of this chapter will nonetheless attempt to identify the basis for such an approach and propose the direction for its findings. A further clarification to be made is that this is not a suggestion of finding *lex ferenda* and whether we might be witnessing the formation of new rules, but rather a question of *lex lata* and whether customary rules already exist which might regulate these circumstances.

The idea of rules that apply to all types of conflict is not new, and its foundations can be found in the ICJ *Nicaragua* decision, which spoke of Common Article 3, despite it appearing in an article devoted to non-international armed conflicts, as constituting 'a minimum yardstick' which would also apply to international armed conflict.[90] As noted by Abi-Saab, 'This approach is not based

---

[86] See mention of internationalized internal armed conflicts, Ch 4, *supra*, nn 34, 35; see also Sassoli, 'Transnational', n 16, *supra*, 25.

[87] J Henckaerts and L Doswald-Beck, *Customary International Humanitarian Law vo. 1: Rules & vol II: Practice* (CUP: Cambridge, 2005).

[88] See n 93–95, *infra*, and accompanying text.

[89] Indeed, the ICRC study was the work of close to a decade with the involvement of hundreds of IHL experts from around the globe.

[90] *Case Concerning Military and Paramilitary Activities in and Against Nicaragua*, [1986] ICJ Rep 14, para 218.

on the legal classification of armed conflicts, in other words on the distinction between international and non-international armed conflicts'.[91] By virtue of the Court's reasoning one could argue that minimum yardsticks which 'reflect what the Court in 1949 called "elementary considerations of humanity"',[92] should equally apply to any type of armed conflict, including new ones which are said not to fit in the traditional international and non-international moulds. Whether this approach is limited to only Common Article 3, and precisely which rules might be considered as minimal yardsticks to always apply, will be examined further shortly.

First, however, before discussing the content of rules to regulate new conflicts, we must deal with the question of when these rules would apply. The rules of IHL are triggered by the existence of armed conflict and if a situation is not armed conflict then IHL does not apply. The only clearly recognized definitions of armed conflict speak of international and non-international conflicts.[93] In effect, to speak of IHL rules that would apply to armed conflicts which are neither international or non-international we must find a way to break out of the closed circle of rules of applicability. The treaty rules contain no other types of conflict and leave little room for other paradigms. The comprehensive attention to customary rules has largely been focused on the content of rules regulating the existing types of conflict, rather than on identifying customary rules on the threshold criteria for applying IHL,[94] although by the same token one might also argue that they do not contain an express obstacle to considering applicability of IHL to new circumstances. If it is accepted that situations such as certain of the US hostilities with Al-Qaeda and the Israel-Hezbollah conflict do not conform to the traditional models found in the Geneva Conventions, but are nonetheless armed conflicts,[95] then it is necessary to discuss precisely what criteria must be fulfilled for a situation to be considered armed conflict and to which any minimal rules of IHL would apply.

The threshold as defined for non-international conflicts (excluding the higher threshold of Protocol II) would appear to contain the appropriate minimum requirements for any situation involving a non-state actor to rise to the category of an armed conflict. That is to say there is a requirement for a certain level of violence and the opposing party must be sufficiently organized.[96] Even accepting that this exploration of the rules is in the context of the claims of new wars with new enemies, and that the latter might not be the traditional state or inter-

---

[91] R Abi–Saab, 'Humanitarian Law and Internal Conflicts: The Evolution of Legal Concern' in A Delissen and G Tanja (eds) *Humanitarian Law of Armed Conflict Challenges Ahead: Essays in Honour of Frits Kalshoven* (Martinus Nijhoff: Dordrecht 1991) 209–23, 222–3.

[92] The Court was referring to *Corfu Channel*, Merits, ICJ Rep 1949, 22.

[93] See Ch 4, *supra*.

[94] ICRC customary law study, n 87, *supra*. See also view of Rona, n 1, *supra*, 68–9.

[95] But see earlier discussion suggesting that all elements that are not international could be described as non-international. See also Rona, n 1, *supra*, 68–9.

[96] See section 5.1 of Ch 4, *supra*, on threshold for non-international armed conflicts.

nal rebel group, the bare minimum for an armed conflict must surely involve the existence of a defined and real opposing entity. States cannot be engaged in *de facto* armed conflicts with imaginary enemies. As stated by Sassoli, 'the existence of parties is one of the most fundamental elements that allow a situation to be classified as an armed conflict.'[97] Furthermore, in order to be considered a party to a conflict, it should be expected that a group demonstrate the necessary organizational and structural capacities and characteristics that would allow it to function as such.[98] An armed conflict against an enemy that is loosely defined and can endlessly encompass new groups in new places is in fact a conflict that knows no boundaries, has no beginning and can never have an end.[99] Accordingly, even without recourse to the legal definitions of a party to a conflict it should be obvious that the bare minimum for the existence of an armed conflict is to have a clearly defined and recognizable entity with which one is engaged in hostilities.

As for a requisite threshold of intensity of violence, clearly there must be one as states would otherwise be able to declare IHL applicable at will and engage in acts only permissible under IHL. Indeed, states do seem to recognize that it is not enough to merely claim that a given situation is an armed conflict and, particularly when dealing with a non-state actor, that there is a need to show that a certain threshold has been crossed. The US, for instance, has sought to support the case for a war on terror by pointing to the protracted high levels of violence over recent years, including various attacks against US targets around the globe,[100] and there was little question that the scale of fighting between Israel and the Hezbollah was clearly above the threshold for armed conflict.[101] It would seem, therefore, that the novelty of the situations does not completely relieve us of the need to fulfil the traditional minimal requirements of a threshold which must be crossed before a situation can be determined to be an armed conflict. There is, however, unlikely to be found at this stage any clear and objective agreement of precisely what the threshold is, and the debate here will be similar to the case of traditional non-international armed conflicts.[102]

On the matter of the threshold attention must be drawn to an additional concern that is unique to the circumstances under examination. In traditional (ie internal) armed conflicts threats presented by armed groups engaged in violence that are said to be sporadic or isolated, and below the threshold of armed conflict, can be countered through measures of law enforcement. When dealing with groups operating extraterritorially the possibilities for action are limited to either demanding action from the territorial state or moving towards the realm of armed conflict. This is a point at which the *ius ad bellum* and the *ius in*

---

[97] Sassoli, 'Transnational', *supra*, n 16, 11.
[98] See explanation of these concepts in Ch 4, nn 129–40, *supra*, and accompanying text.
[99] Brooks, n 1, *supra*, 745; Rona, n 1, *supra*.   [100] See nn 11, 22–28, *supra*.
[101] See discussion of this conflict in the Concluding Chapter, *infra*.
[102] Ch 4, n 107–19, *supra*, and accompanying text.

bello together face a similar question: how is a state to respond to a situation of violent activity from a non-state actor operating from the territory of another state which will not or cannot stop the group, when the actions of the group are said to be below the threshold of armed attack for the purpose of the *ius ad bellum*; and what are the rules that apply if forcible operations do commence, when the level of violence was perceived to be below the threshold of violence for the purpose of the armed conflict definition of the *ius in bello*? The *ius ad bellum* aspect of this problem was discussed in greater length in Part I of this work, and, as noted there, the current state of the law does not appear to make room for lowering the threshold that would allow states to engage in unilateral extra-territorial force against non-state actors.[103] Likewise, and for good reason,[104] whilst recognizing that this may be an imperfect situation, the threshold for applicability of IHL should not be lowered so as to render it meaningless.[105] However, should there be any future development or new interpretations as discussed in the *ius ad bellum* chapter, it will necessitate consideration of reper-cussions it might have on the *ius in bello*. As for the law as it stands, in light of all the above it is suggested here that if there should be discussion of new forms of conflict with non-state actors—however they are to be defined—so long as they are armed conflicts then they must conform to the minimal requirements of having an organized group as a party to the conflict and a threshold of vio-lence that must be crossed.

2.3 The rules for new types of conflict

In attempting to determine the specific rules applying to extraterritorial con-flicts against non-state actors the route chosen here, as indicated earlier, is to identify rules that would apply as a minimum to any armed conflict. Not only can the idea find support in the approach of the ICJ to Common Article 3,[106] but also from the US Department of Defense policy that '[m]embers of the DoD Components comply with the law of war during all armed conflicts, how-ever such conflicts are characterized, and in all other military operations.'[107] There would appear to be a growing acknowledgement that there are basic rules of IHL that apply to any type of conflict.[108] The ICRC study was of the opinion

---

[103] Although this is not without difficulty, as apparent from the discussion in Part I, *supra*.

[104] See n 60, *supra*, and accompanying text.

[105] For rules that would apply in these situations, see Chs 7 and 8, *infra*, on international human rights law.

[106] See n 90, *supra*.

[107] 'DoD Law of War Program', Department of Defense Directive no 2311.01E, 9 May 2006, para 4.1, available at <http://www.dtic.mil/whs/directives/corres/html/231101.htm>. See also J Rawcliffe and J Smith (eds) *The US Operational Law Handbook,* International and Operational Law Department, The Judge Advocate General's Legal Center and School, August 2006, 418.

[108] C Garraway, 'The "War on Terror": Do the Rules Need Changing?' Briefing Paper IL BP 06/02, The Royal Institute of International Affairs, September 2006, 10; Ratner, n 62, *supra*, 8–9.

that the majority of IHL rules can be said to be part of customary international law, applicable in both international and non-international armed conflict, with certain exceptions such as rules relating to individual status.[109] In the years prior to the publication of the ICRC Study, the ICTY gave a decision in which it elaborated on the laws of armed conflict which it found to be customary laws even in non-international armed conflict and, while not identical to the rules of international armed conflict, these represented significantly more than the barebones of Common Article 3.[110] This approach also finds support in the codification of the Rome Statute of the International Criminal Court, and its list of war crimes in non-international armed conflict.[111] According to the ICTY:

It follows that in the area of armed conflict the distinction between interstate wars and civil wars is losing its value as far as human beings are concerned. Why protect civilians from belligerent violence, or ban rape, torture or the wanton destruction of hospitals, churches, museums or private property, as well as proscribe weapons causing unnecessary suffering when two sovereign States are engaged in war, and yet refrain from enacting the same bans or providing the same protection when armed violence has erupted 'only' within the territory of a sovereign State? If international law, while of course duly safeguarding the legitimate interests of States, must gradually turn to the protection of human beings, it is only natural that the aforementioned dichotomy should gradually lose its weight.[112]

Much of the reasoning by the Tribunal as to transposing the essence of the rules of international conflicts and identifying them as applicable to non-international conflicts is equally pertinent when searching for rules that would apply as a minimal standard to all conflicts. As in the case of non-international armed conflict, the basic rules of IHL should be seen as applying to any other armed conflict involving non-state actors. In this respect, commentators have mentioned one or all of Common Article 3, Article 75 of Protocol I (fundamental guarantees during detention) and rules on conduct of operations.[113] Indeed, the framework of applicable rules is likely to go beyond Common Article 3 for much the same reasoning that lay behind the identification of rules for non-international armed conflict. While it would not be difficult to argue that rules on prisoner of war

---

[109] Although no study of such vast scope can be without some elements of disagreement. See examinations of the study in E Wilmshurst and S Breau (eds), *Perspectives on the ICRC Study on Customary International Humanitarian Law* (CUP: Cambridge, 2007); H Parks, 'The ICRC Customary Law Study: A Preliminary Assessment' 99 *American Society of International Law Proceedings*, Vol 99 (2005) 208.

[110] *Prosecutor v. Dusko Tadic*, Decision on the Defence Motion for Interlocutory Appeal on Jurisdiction, ICTY, 2 October 1995. But see Greenwood's comments on whether the Tribunal went further than it should have in C Greenwood, 'International Humanitarian Law and the *Tadic* Case' 7 *EJIL* 265 (1996) 277–78.

[111] Rome Statute of the International Criminal Court, 17 July 1998, Art 8.2(e).

[112] *Tadic*, n 110, *supra*, para 97.

[113] Garraway, n 108, *supra*, 10; Kretzmer, n 69, *supra*, 195; Murphy, n 45, *supra*, 34; Ratner, n 62, *supra*, 8–9.

status and the rights of combatants apply only to conflicts between states,[114] prohibitions on use of weapons causing superfluous injury and unnecessary suffering, for example, should still stand regardless of how the conflict is characterized. Obstacles will nevertheless remain on a number of fronts especially in relation to targeting of individuals but the difficulties raised by extraterritorial forcible measures, with regard to the questions of targeting, are not fundamentally different from those raised by similar operations against non-state actors, including civilians directly participating in hostilities in the context of international or non-international armed conflicts,[115] and the same rules should apply. This position should not be understood as claiming there are no difficulties in applying these rules. In fact it is quite the opposite—as will be seen in the following sections—the rules concerning which individuals can be targeted and under what circumstances are extremely complex, and there are ongoing debates and disputes on their interpretation. However, whatever solution or interpretation is found for these debatable rules, it will likely be the same whether it is a 'traditional' internal conflict or an extraterritorial one. Many of the questions that arise with regard to targeting individuals in the latter situations are equally raised in the classic debate over a state planning to target an individual who is a member of an armed opposition group in an internal conflict, dressed as a farmer by day and fighting by night against the government of his country.[116] Differences have nevertheless been mentioned with regard to matters such as responsibilities for local population in the fighting zone and transfer of detainees.[117] There are, moreover, naturally great differences as a result of the extraterritorial aspect, especially with regard to inter-state sovereignty matters and applicability of international human rights law, and these are addressed in the chapters dedicated to this. However, from the IHL point of view, insofar as there are many difficulties in interpreting rules such as the targeting of individuals, the essence of the problem, as will be seen in the following chapters, remains the same. Rather than calling for new laws on targeting these individuals, the answer lies in agreeing on the interpretation of the existing laws. Chapter 6 of this work will engage in further elaboration of the rules covering the primary areas of concern with regard to extraterritorial forcible measures.

Finally, to conclude the above chapters thus far, it should be emphasized again that the preferred approach suggested, is not to speak of new categories of conflict, but rather to interpret the existing rules of applicability and application so that any extraterritorial forcible measures rising to the level of armed conflict can be found to fit within the paradigms of international or non-international armed conflict. In most cases, conflicts between a state and a non-state actor would be classified as non-international armed conflicts. Should, however, there be an

---

[114] With the exception of Art 1.4 of Protocol I. See section 1 of Ch 6, *infra*, on individual status.

[115] See Ch 6, *infra*.   [116] See Ch 6, *infra*.

[117] Sassoli, 'Transnational', n 16, *supra*, 23–4.

insistence that there are situations of conflict which fall outside the traditional models, it is submitted in the current chapter that the rules of IHL will only apply once a certain threshold has been crossed and that, through customary international law, it is likely to be found that the rules regulating this new type of conflict will, at minimum, be similar to those applying in non-international armed conflicts.

6

Status of Individuals and the Regulation of Force

1. Individual status, categories and distinction

Under international humanitarian law ('IHL'), the use of force against individuals encompasses three crucial issues—the status of the individual; whether s/he is entitled to protection from attack; and the type of force and manner in which it is used. These will all be dealt with in this chapter.

Underpinning a large proportion of all IHL rules is the principle of distinction, regarded by the ICJ as one of the fundamental rules of armed conflict—'The cardinal principles contained in the texts constituting the fabric of humanitarian law are the following. The first is aimed at the protection of the civilian population and civilian objects and establishes the distinction between combatants and non-combatants'.[1]

The Commentary to Protocol I notes that the rule of protection and distinction is:

the foundation on which the codification of the laws and customs of war rests: the civilian population and civilian objects must be respected and protected in armed conflict, and for this purpose they must be distinguished from combatants and military objectives. The entire system established in The Hague in 1899 and 1907 (1) and in Geneva from 1864 to 1977 (2) is founded on this rule of customary law.[2]

Simply put, this means that all objects and people military are distinguished from all objects and people civilian. The division of objects and people into categories, will also mean that belonging to a certain category can be the most important determination with regard to the lawfulness of an individual being targeted.[3] In other words, an individual might be lawfully targeted and killed on account of his/her category of status rather than whether s/he poses an individual threat at that particular moment. Understanding this is crucial to understanding IHL as a whole—without accepting it, the IHL framework becomes incomprehensible.

---

[1] *Advisory Opinion on the Legality of the Threat or Use of Nuclear Weapons* [1996] ICJ Rep, 8 July 1996, para 78.

[2] Protocol I commentary, 598, 1863.   [3] See section 1.1, *infra*, on combatants.

The possible categories and protections which might apply in the case of individuals against whom a state is using extraterritorial force is, therefore, the primary focus of this section. The principle of distinction is of particular importance both in terms of targeting and the status of those captured. The issue of post-capture status is outside the scope of this work, but the problems of distinction with relation to targeting, and particularly relating to civilians taking part in hostilities and members of armed groups, will undergo extensive analysis in the coming sections.

The principle of distinction is more easily suited to international armed conflicts fought between states, in which it is expected that the military forces fight each other and civilians do not take part. In the context of non-international conflicts, whether traditional internal conflicts or extraterritorial conflicts against non-state actors, in which one of the parties is not a state military, some of the rules based on this principle—while still applicable and paramount[4]—become the object of controversial interpretations and debates.[5] As shown in the previous chapters, certain extraterritorial forcible measures against non-state actors can be defined as part of an armed conflict and regulated by IHL. These rules of IHL can, therefore, assist in the regulation and accountability for these operations. As will now be seen in this chapter, with regard to operations against non-state actors, there remains a huge obstacle in the actual interpretation of these rules.

The categories and rules mentioned in this opening section will receive detailed attention later, but a very brief introduction is necessary to set the backdrop for discussion. The principle of distinction in the laws of international armed conflict is based on the premise that an individual may either be a combatant or a civilian. The rules of non-international armed conflict are different in that they do not contain a definition of combatants, thus further compounding the disagreements over all matters relating to protections and entitlements based on an individual's status. Generally speaking, in international armed conflict combatants are legitimate targets during an armed conflict while civilians may never be intentionally attacked (subject to the qualification contained in the rule on civilians taking a direct part in hostilities[6]); combatants are immune from prosecution for acts that were in accordance with IHL while civilians can

---

[4] J Henckaerts and L Doswald-Beck, *Customary International Humanitarian Law, vol 1: Rules* (CUP: Cambridge, 2005) 3; Y Dinstein, C Garraway and M Schmitt, *The Manual on the Law of Non-International Armed Conflict: With Commentary* (International Institute of Humanitarian Law: San Remo, 2006) 11.

[5] See the examination of this in J Kleffner, 'From "Belligerents" to "Fighters" and Civilians Directly Participating in Hostilities—on the Principle of Distinction in Non-International Armed Conflicts One Hundred Years after the Second Hague Peace Conference' *Netherlands International Law Review* 315 (2007). Questions in the context of modern warfare more generally have also been raised. See R Brooks, 'War Everywhere: Rights, National Security Law, and the Law of Armed Conflict in the Age of Terror' 153 *University of Pennsylvania Law Review* 675 (2004) 730.

[6] See section 1.2, *infra*, on civilians.

be prosecuted for any act of participation. This distinction gives rise to di
ties when one of the parties to the conflict is not of uniformed soldiers or of any
kind of distinctly and overtly identifiable group and, more generally, in non-
international conflicts which lack the definition of combatants. In particular,
there are ongoing debates on how to deal with civilians who take a direct part in
hostilities and how to categorize members of armed groups.[7] The debates over
the use and meaning of terms such as 'unlawful combatants' is another hot-
bed of controversy and will also be dealt with in a dedicated section later. All
these topics encapsulate ongoing extensive debates, with implications for a far
wider sphere than covered in the present work and it is not possible to cover all
aspects of these debates in this chapter. The function of the following section is
to present the relevant concepts and understand the problems involved, especially insofar as they relate to the topic at hand.

1.1 Combatants

The definition of an individual as a combatant is crucial to two separate stages
of the conflict—it affects the decision of whether and how an individual can
be targeted during the fighting and it determines the treatment to which s/he is
entitled upon capture, especially with relation to the determination of prisoner
of war status. This current work is concerned with the use of force in operations
against non-state actors and, therefore, the discussion around combatants is limited here to those aspects of it affecting that first stage. The term combatant is
used to describe those who are recognized by the law as having the right to take
part in the fighting and who will be entitled to prisoner of war status if captured.[8]
The flip-side to being recognized as a combatant who has the right to take part
in the fighting is being a legitimate target who can be attacked at any time during the hostilities, provided s/he is not *hors de combat* (captured, shipwrecked,
sick or wounded).[9] The definitions of combatants and prisoners of war appear
only in the rules of international armed conflict. As for non-international armed
conflict, states are naturally reluctant to include in international law any recognition of individuals lawfully fighting against the state, and granted preferential

---

[7] See sections 1.3, *infra*, on direct participation of civilians and on members of armed groups.
[8] Geneva Convention relative to the Treatment of Prisoners of War (12 August 1949) 75 UNTS
135, entered into force 21 October 1950 (Geneva Convention III), Art 4; Protocol I, Arts 43, 44.
[9] Geneva Convention for the Amelioration of the Condition of the Wounded and Sick in
Armed Forces in the Field (12 August 1949) 75 UNTS 31, entered into force 21 October 1950
(Geneva Convention I), Arts 12, 13; Geneva Convention for the Amelioration of the Condition of
Wounded, Sick and Shipwrecked Members of Armed Forces at Sea (12 August 1949) 75 UNTS 85,
entered into force 21 October 1950 (Geneva Convention II) Arts 12,13; Geneva Convention III,
ibid, Arts 4, 13; Hague Convention (IV) Respecting the Laws and Customs of War on Land and
its annex; Regulations Concerning the Laws and Customs of War on Land (18 October 1907) 36
Stat 2277; 1 Bevans 631; 205 Consol TS 2773; Martens Nouveau Recueil (3d) 461, entered into
force 26 January 1910 (Hague Regulations) Art 4; however, see debate over notion of necessity and
whether it requires an attempt to detain, in the section 2.2, *infra*, on small-scale operations.

treatment if captured,[10] and it was feared that entitling rebels to prisoner of war status would prevent states from prosecuting them for taking up arms.[11] This does not necessarily mean, however, that all individuals in a non-international armed conflict are protected civilians and there are debates over the question of how to categorize members of armed groups—as something akin to combatants (minus immunity from prosecution) or as civilians who lose protection while taking part in hostilities.[12]

In the context of international armed conflicts, members of non-state groups fit into the definition of combatant if they are part of a militia or organization belonging to a party to the conflict[13] but unless this is a conflict under Article 1.4 of Protocol I,[14] belonging to a party to the conflict means belonging to a state, thereby not being non-state actors.[15] In any case, they would need to have a command structure, a fixed distinctive sign, be carrying arms openly and conducting their operations in accordance with the laws of war.[16] Another option would be if the individuals formed a *levée en masse,* a spontaneous mass uprising against the enemy invader.[17] The Protocol I definition extends the description to allow combatants to retain their status even if, in certain situations, they only reveal themselves to be carrying a weapon during each military engagement and whenever visible to the adversary while engaged in military deployment preceding the launch of attack.[18] Insofar as they are relevant, the various rules regarding fighting out of uniform, and 'unlawful combatancy' will be discussed in later sections.[19]

From all the cases raised, the only non-state actors who might be recognized as combatants under the laws of international armed conflict would be the Al-Qaeda members fighting with the Taliban in Afghanistan, and members of the Hezbollah fighting Israel in 2006. With both groups there appear, however, to be numerous matters that cast doubt on this possibility. With regard to the Hezbollah, there is first the question of whether this was an international armed conflict and, if so, whether their mode of operations could be described as in accordance with

---

[10]   J Pictet (ed), *Commentary on the Geneva Convention of 12 August 1949 for the Amelioration of the Condition of the Wounded and Sick in Armed Forces in the Field* (International Committee of the Red Cross: Geneva, 1958) 32; A Cassese, 'The Status of Rebels Under the 1977 Geneva Protocol on Non-International Armed Conflicts' 30 *ICLQ* 416 (1981) 421–2.

[11]   Notwithstanding, states engaged in non–international conflicts may decide of their own accord to agree on implementing prisoner of war rules (or an equivalent). On the Nigeria Biafran conflict see A Rosas, *The Legal Status of Prisoners of War: A Study in International Humanitarian Law Applicable in Armed Conflict* (The Finnish Academy of Science and Letters, Helsinki, 1976) 196–202, 277–8.

[12]   See section 1.3, *infra,* on direct participation of civilians, and on members of armed groups.

[13]   Geneva Convention III, n 9, *supra,* Art 4; Protocol I, Art 43.

[14]   But as noted earlier these types of conflict are unlikely to be relevant to this work.

[15]   See below for consideration of this in context of Al-Qaeda and Hezbollah.

[16]   Hague Regulations, n 9, *supra,* Art 1; Geneva Convention III, n 9, *supra,* Art 4.

[17]   Hague Regulations, n 9, *supra,* Art 2; Geneva Convention III, n 9, *supra,* Art 4.

[18]   Protocol I, Arts 43, 44.

[19]   See section 1.5, *infra,* on unlawful combatants, and on small scale operations by undercover units.

IHL.[20] An additional question, especially pertinent in the case of Al-Qaeda, is the requirement of having a distinctive sign.[21] Wearing Afghan clothes and a turban might distinguish them from US soldiers but the key is for the US soldiers to be able to distinguish the Al-Qaeda fighters from the civilian population.[22] The more lax approach taken in the Protocol definition would not apply since the US is not a party to the Protocol and this Article is not accepted as customary law. Moreover, if they are to be considered members of a group responsible for such acts as 11 September 2001, and stating as their agenda to commit further acts of this kind, then it becomes arguable whether they could be considered to belong to a group that conducts its operations in accordance with the laws of war.[23]

Generally speaking, it appears unlikely that individuals belonging to non-state actors as examined could be considered combatants as defined in international law, since this status would in most cases rely on them in fact fighting within a state structure and thereby in circumstances excluded from the current scope. In some cases, however, such as those mentioned above, the possibility of combatant status might arise in which case the requirements as defined earlier would have to be fulfilled. Other than these cases, as noted earlier, extraterritorial forcible measures against non-state actors are unlikely to be considered part of an international armed conflict, although they could be considered part of a non-international armed conflict. Legally qualifying as combatants under the laws applicable to non-international armed conflict is not an option since this set of rules does not contain a definition for combatants. The following sections will address the status of individuals not entitled to combatant status.

1.2 Civilians

Civilian persons, as with civilian objects, are not the subject of a descriptive definition within the law, but are defined by negation: anything which does not meet the definition of military is civilian. This is most clearly the case in the laws of

---

[20] See discussion in Concluding Chapter, *infra*.

[21] Y Dinstein, *The Conduct of Hostilities Under the Law of International Armed Conflict* (CUP: Cambridge, 2004) 49.

[22] R Goldman and B Tittemore, 'Unprivileged Combatants and the Hostilities in Afghanistan: Their Status and Rights Under International Humanitarian and Human Rights Law' American Society of International Law, Task Force on Terrorism, Task Force Papers, December 2002, 13; WH Parks, '"Special Forces" Wear of Non-Standard Uniforms' 4 *Chicago Journal of International Law* 493 (2003) 516–7; UK Ministry of Defence, *The Manual of the Law of Armed Conflict* (OUP: Oxford, 2004) 41–2.With regard to the Taliban, the point has been raised that it may have been enough to satisfy the legal criteria, if one could show that the Taliban and the Northern Alliance were able to recognize each other. See Goldman and Tittemore, 28.

[23] See the views over which of the criteria apply to the group as a whole, and which to individual members, and how this impacts upon their status: Goldman and Tittemore, *ibid*, 14–16, 29–30; Dinstein, nn 21, 35, *supra*, 43–4, 49; R Wedgwood, 'Military Commissions: Al Qaeda, Terrorism, and Military Commissions' 96 *AJIL* 328 (2002) 335; M Sassoli, 'Transnational Armed Groups and International Humanitarian Law' Program on Humanitarian Policy and Conflict Research, Harvard University, Occasional Paper Series no 6, Winter 2006, 17.

international armed conflict,[24] although it becomes a little more complex in non-international armed conflict due to the lack of definition for combatants.[25] Being in the legal category of civilian does not by any means leave a non-state actor who takes part in the fighting immune from attack. According to Article 51.3 of the First Protocol, which is regarded also as customary law,[26] civilians benefit from protection 'unless and for such time as they take a direct part in hostilities'. However, the interpretation of this rule is the subject of fierce debate.[27] This rule exists also for non-international armed conflict[28] and in all types of conflicts, including extraterritorial operations against non-state actors, as currently under examination, taking advantage of civilian appearance and of protections afforded to civilians raises numerous difficulties.[29] The primary challenge is finding a solution which does not blur the distinction between civilians and combatants and does not erode the protection needed by civilians. The following two sections deal with the interpretations of 'unless and for such time as they take a direct part in hostilities'. Issues related to 'unlawful combatants' and to members of armed groups will be dealt with in subsequent sections.

1.3 Direct participation

The first question is that of defining 'taking a direct part in hostilities'. Generally speaking, taking a direct part in the hostilities is understood to include carrying out an attack or actions such as laying mines, while not including supplying food or clothing to the forces, and with functions such as intelligence gathering and others being the subject of debate.[30] It has been noted at a meeting of experts on this subject, that, '[t]here seemed to be general agreement among the experts

---

[24] Protocol I, Arts 50, 52.

[25] ICRC customary law study, n 4, *supra,* 17. See further discussion in section 1.5, *infra,* on members of armed groups.

[26] ICRC customary law study, n 4, *supra,* 19–24; *The Public Committee against Torture in Israel and ors v. Israel and ors ('The Targeted Killings Case'),* HCJ 769/02, 13 December 2006, para 30.

[27] In fact, it has been at the centre of annual meetings of IHL experts, attempting to reach agreement over the interpretation of this rule. See *Third Expert Meeting on the Notion of Direct Participation in Hostilities,* Geneva, International Committee of the Red Cross and the TMC Asser Institute, 2005; *Fourth Expert Meeting on the Notion of Direct Participation in Hostilities,* Geneva, 27–8 November 2006, Summary Report, International Committee of the Red Cross and the TMC Asser Institute; *Fifth Expert Meeting on the Notion of Direct Participation in Hostilities,* Geneva, 5–6 February 2008, Summary Report, International Committee of the Red Cross; ICRC customary law study, n 4, *supra,* 23.

[28] Protocol II, Art 13.3; ICRC customary law study, n 4, *supra,* 19–24.

[29] See discussion in section 1.5, infra, on members of armed groups. Fischer mentions the civilian status as a precondition for success of terrorism, see H Fischer, 'The Status of Unlawful Combatants' in WP Heere (ed), *Terrorism and the Military: International Legal Implications* (Asser: The Hague, 2003) 101–06, 102.

[30] 'International Humanitarian Law and the Challenges of Contemporary Armed Conflicts' Report Prepared by the International Committee of the Red Cross, Geneva, 2003, 28–9. For a proposed list see APV Rogers, *Law on the Battlefield* (Manchester University Press: Manchester, 2004) 11–12. For detailed examination see *Third Expert Meeting on Direct Participation,* n 27, *supra.*

that direct participation in hostilities did not necessarily require the use of armed force and did not necessarily have to cause death, injury or destruction.'[31]

The outsourcing of certain functions by the military to civilian firms, and the technological advances that can allow someone sitting at a computer terminal to have immediate effect on the battlefield, are just two of the issues which compound the challenge of defining direct participation.[32] Within the context of operations against non-state actors the wider circle of the group is sometimes said to include collaborators who provide support, though don't carry out attacks.[33] The concept of collaboration is, however, a loose and subjective term and does not replace the need to show that the individual was taking a direct part in hostilities, as far as the interpretation of this rule has been agreed upon. Thus, for instance, strapping a bomb onto a suicide bomber's body might be considered direct participation whereas a civilian supplying food to members of a non-state armed group would not.[34] In the context of modern warfare, arguments have been raised along the lines of 'democratization of war', with civilians assuming growing involvement and responsibilities for the conduct of warfare. These arguments, perhaps disconcertingly, find their place on all sides of the debate, including governments, their critics and non-state groups,[35] some of whom might be said in fact to share the objective of widening the notion of who may be attacked. Further debates concern the potential loss of protection for civilians acting as voluntary human shields or those working in munitions factories.[36]

The International Committee of the Red Cross ('ICRC') has provided its interpretation of the constitutive elements of direct participation in hostilities as follows:

In order to qualify as direct participation in hostilities, a specific act must meet the following cumulative criteria:

1. The act must be likely to adversely affect the military operations or military capacity of a party to an armed conflict or, alternatively, to inflict death, injury, or destruction on persons or objects protected against direct attack (threshold of harm), and

---

[31] *Third Expert Meeting on Direct Participation*, n 27, *supra*, 14.

[32] *Third Expert Meeting on Direct Participation*, n 27, *supra*, 34–5; *Challenges of Contemporary Armed Conflicts*, n 30, *supra*, 30–1.

[33] Cayci asserts that terror organizations have 3 levels—leading staff; armed militants; collaborators. See S Cayci, 'Terrorist Warfare and the Law of Armed Conflict: A Guide for the Theatre Commander' in Heere, n 29, *supra*, 93–100, 95.

[34] '[M]ere contribution to the general war effort (eg by supplying food stuffs to combatants) is not tantamount to active participation in hostilities': see Dinstein, n 21, *supra*, 28.

[35] W H Parks, 'Air War and the Law of War' 32 *Air Force Law Review* 1 (1990) 121–35; for an analysis of the Al-Qaeda position see M Mohamedou, 'Non-Linearity of Engagement: Transnational Armed Groups, International Law, and the Conflict between Al Qaeda and the United States' Program on Humanitarian Policy and Conflict Research, Harvard University, July 2005, 4. See also Brooks n 5, *supra*, 730.

[36] Dinstein, n 21, *supra*, 124, 130–1. See problems with proportionality in section 2.1, *infra*, on large-scale operations. See discussion of voluntary human shields in *Interpretive Guidance on the Notion of Direct Participation in Hostilities under International Humanitarian Law*, International Committee of the Red Cross, 2009, 56–7.

2. There must be a direct causal link between the act and the harm likely to result either from that act, or from a coordinated military operation of which that act constitutes an integral part (direct causation), and

3. The act must be specifically designed to directly cause the required threshold of harm in support of a party to the conflict and to the detriment of another (belligerent nexus).[37]

There is nevertheless debate over how to categorize certain actions. Providing concrete training and instruction for the carrying out of a specific attack might also be considered as taking a direct part in certain circumstances, as might participation in the planning of an attack.[38] With regard to planning, however, aside from insider information or electronic surveillance it would be difficult for outside forces to recognize the time-frame of the act of planning taking place and to determine if an individual is, therefore, taking a part. Would there be a need for detailed knowledge of the discussion taking place? Perhaps it might be argued that a meeting between leaders and operatives is enough evidence to assert engagement in planning. That, however, would open the door for targeting members of this group any time two or more of them got together, which could just as easily be happening in the context of a social function. Some of these problems will be revisited, together with possible approaches to solutions, in the later section on members of armed groups.

Duration of loss of immunity

Resolving whether or not a civilian is taking direct part does not solve the predicament. Another formidable obstacle, and certainly a debatable one, is the need to define the time during which those who take direct part lose their immunity.[39] According to the rule, immunity is lost as long and for such time as the individual is taking a direct part. One of the greatest criticism of the rule on losing immunity is that it allows for a 'revolving door' of protection, giving individuals the ability to participate in attacks and then quickly regain immunity from counter attack until the next brief window in which they lose immunity through participation in another operation.[40] As a result, there is a view that those who participate in the hostilities should lose immunity from targeting for as long as the hostilities continue, similarly to combatant members of forces, and not only during participation in attack. The Israeli High Court of Justice, in the *Targeted Killings Case*, presented it as follows:

Again, it is helpful to examine the extreme cases. On the one hand, a civilian taking a direct part in hostilities one single time, or sporadically, who later detaches himself from

---

[37] ICRC *Interpretive Guidance, ibid,* 46, for detailed explanation see 46–65.

[38] *Third Expert Meeting on Direct Participation,* n 27, *supra,* 35; *Targeted Killings,* n 26, *supra,* para 37.

[39] For detailed examination see *Third Expert Meeting on Direct Participation,* n 27, *supra,* 59–68.

[40] *Challenges of Contemporary Armed Conflicts,* n 30, *supra,* 32; Fischer, n 29, *supra,* 103; Y Shany, 'Israeli Counter-Terrorism Measures: Are they "Kosher" under International Law?' in *Terrorism and International Law,* Ch 5, n 3, *supra,* 96–118, 104; Parks, 'Air War' n 35, *supra,* 118.

that activity, is a civilian who, starting from the time he detached himself from that activity, is entitled to protection from attack. He is not to be attacked for the hostilities which he committed in the past. On the other hand, a civilian who has joined a terrorist organization which has become his 'home', and in the framework of his role in that organization he commits a chain of hostilities, with short periods of rest between them, loses his immunity from attack 'for such time' as he is committing the chain of acts.[41]

The need to keep casualties down to a minimum is also part of an argument to allow targeting of these individuals outside the timeframe in which they take a direct part claiming that it would minimize collateral damage if they could be attacked, for instance, while travelling on a remote road rather than when sitting in a residential building putting together a bomb.[42] The link between direct participation and duration is of particular importance in the context of members of armed groups.[43] Considering the ongoing debates and subsequent uncertainty and lack of consensus on this rule it is no surprise that the Israeli High Court ultimately found that any determinations must be made on a case-by-case basis, and did not profess to offer a one-size-fits-all approach.[44]

The ICRC has taken the position that loss of protection for civilians is only for the limited duration of the specific act of direct participation in hostilities, with protection regained whenever the civilian is not engaged in direct participation. At the same time they have distinguished between civilians and members of organized armed groups, allowing for the latter to lose protection on the basis of a continuous combat function.[45]

1.4 Unlawful combatants / unprivileged belligerents

As explained above, there can be cases of individuals who do not qualify for combatant status despite being involved in the actual fighting. Lack of status will mean that they can be prosecuted for any act of violence, even if it is in accordance with IHL although, as is clear from the above and following sections, there are greater questions over when these individuals can be targeted. As for the legal definitions explicitly appearing in the treaties, if individuals are not combatants then they are civilians. Whilst there may be various interpretations and suggestions, the instruments of international law do not contain any defined legal category other than combatants and civilians.[46] Different terms have been used

---

[41] *Targeted Killings*, n 26, *supra*, para 39. See further in section 1.5, *infra*, on members of armed groups.

[42] Shany, n 40, *supra*, 104. On the risks to civilians created by the 'revolving door' problem, see also *Expert Meeting on the Right to Life in Armed Conflicts and Situations of Occupation*, The University Centre for International Humanitarian Law, Geneva, 2005, 40.

[43] See section 1.5, *infra*, on members of armed groups.

[44] *Targeted Killings*, n 26, *supra*, paras 40, 60.

[45] *Interpretive Guidance*, n 36, *supra*, 70–73. This approach will be further examined in section 1.5, *infra*, on members of armed groups.

[46] *Targeted Killings*, n 26, *supra*, para 28; *Anonymous v. Israel*, Supreme Court of Israel 6659/06, 11 June 2008, paras 12,14.

in the past and continue to be used to describe those who take part in the fighting without combatant status, including unlawful combatant, illegal combatant and unprivileged belligerent.[47] The terms are not new and the latter goes back at least as far as 1951.[48] These terms prove problematic for at least two reasons.

First, it is unclear what they are referring to and, in fact, they are sometimes used to describe two very different categories of persons. Dinstein states that a 'person who engages in military raids by night, while purporting to be an innocent civilian by day, is neither a civilian or a lawful combatant. He is an unlawful combatant.'[49] However, later in the same book, when speaking of 'the status of combatants who feign civilian status by removing their uniforms (or any other fixed distinctive emblem) and wear ordinary clothing',[50] Dinstein declares that '[u]nder customary international law, a combatant doing that becomes an unlawful combatant, i.e., he is denied the privileges of a prisoner of war status and exposed to the full rigour of the domestic penal system for any act of violence perpetrated by him in civilian clothes [...].'[51]

From the first example, it appears that the term 'unlawful combatant' could be used to refer to individuals who were never entitled to combatant status but are taking part in the fighting.[52] The last example describes persons who were lawful combatants but acted in such a way as to lose their status. In essence, the term unlawful combatant is being used in two ways—to describe combatants who lose their combatant status, or civilians who lose their civilian protection.

Secondly, these terms appear to confuse legal categories with factual descriptions. Legal categories are limited to those terms which are recognized and defined within the law as opposed to factual descriptions which are as limitless as are the endless permutations of reality. The point in common to be found in most uses of these terms, is that we are faced with individuals who are factually taking part in the fighting but who, for one reason or another, are not entitled to the privileges afforded to those who come within the rubric of 'combatants' as defined by law (namely immunity from prosecution for acts in accordance with IHL and POW status), or protection as civilians.[53] In other words, this is a factual description of persons, but it is not, in and of itself, a new legal categorization.

---

[47] A Roberts, 'The Laws of War in the War on Terror' *Israel Yearbook on Human Rights*, vol 32 (2003) 229–30.

[48] R Baxter, 'So-Called "Unprivileged Belligerency": Spies, Guerrillas and Saboteurs' 28 *British Yearbook of International Law* 323 (1951).

[49] Dinstein, n 21, *supra*, 29. See also the Israeli High Court, 'That is the law regarding unlawful combatants. As long as he preserves his status as a civilian—that is, as long as he does not become part of the army—but takes part in combat, he ceases to enjoy the protection granted to the civilian, and is subject to the risks of attack just like a combatant, without enjoying the rights of a combatant as a prisoner of war.' *Targeted Killings*, n 26, *supra*, para 31.

[50] *Ibid*, 203.   [51] *Ibid*. See also 233–4.

[52] K Dorman, 'The Legal Situation of "Unlawful / Unprivileged Combatants"' 849 *International Review of the Red Cross* 45 (2003) 46; *Targeted Killings*, n 26, *supra*, para 31.

[53] Goldman and Tittemore, n 22, *supra*, 4–5.

As far as recognized and defined legal categories are concerned, th
two—combatants and civilians.[54] As noted by the Supreme Court of Is...

With regard to the appellants' aforesaid arguments we should point out that the question of the conformity of the term 'unlawful combatant' to the categories recognized by international law has already been addressed in our case law in Public Committee against Torture in *Israel v. Government of Israel*, in which it was held that the term 'unlawful combatants' does not constitute a separate category but is a sub-category of 'civilians' recognized by international law.[55]

The 1951 article by Baxter lends support to the position that these so-called 'unlawful combatants' should be included in the same legal category as civilians:

Once it has been discovered that the accused is not entitled to treatment as a prisoner of war, there appears in most circumstances to be no reason in law to inquire whether the individual is a civilian or a disguised soldier, for it would appear in the latter case that the soldier, even in occupied territory, is to be regarded as having thrown in his lot with the civilian population and to be subject to the same rights and disabilities.[56]

In other words, the individual who was taking part in the fighting but is not a combatant should be viewed as a civilian who took part in the hostilities. The term used by Baxter is of 'unprivileged belligerents'. This is a factual description of persons who are taking part in the fighting, and who are not entitled to the privileges of combatants as defined by law.

Further points have been raised with regard to the possibility that IHL recognizes, even if implicitly, other categories of individuals in the context of detention rules[57] and in the rules of non-international armed conflict.[58] It is however submitted that this does not change the fact that pre-capture, certainly as far as the rules of targeting are concerned, no other category of person is described in the laws. In light of the above, the approach taken is that those individuals against whom the state is using forcible measures can fall into only one of two legal categories: combatants or civilians.

Nonetheless, states have referred to—on occasion even through legislation—the term 'unlawful combatant'.[59] The purpose of this term has been most apparent in two cases that came before the Israeli courts, which dealt with the legality

---

[54] See discussion of whether and how persons fall under one of these categories in M Sassoli, 'Use and Abuse of the Laws of War in the "War on Terrorism"' *Law and Inequality: A Journal of Theory and Practice* 22 (2004) 206–10.

[55] *Anonymous v. Israel*, n 46, *supra*, para 12.

[56] Baxter, n 48, *supra*, 340. Note that this article was written before the Additional Protocols.

[57] Roberts, n 47, *supra*, 229–30. S Murphy, 'Evolving Geneva Convention Paradigms in the "War on Terrorism": Applying the Core Rules to the Release of Persons Deemed "Unprivileged Combatants"' The George Washington University Law School Public Law and Legal Theory Working Paper no 239 (2007) 25.

[58] See discussion in section 1.5, *infra*.

[59] See Israel's *Internment of Unlawful Combatants Law, 5762–2002*, as presented and examined in detail in *Anonymous v. Israel*, n 46, *supra*.

of targeting alleged terrorists,[60] and of detention without trial until the end of hostilities.[61] However, as noted by the Israeli Supreme Court, despite the use of the term 'unlawful combatant' there is no clear evidence that international law contains this category of person.[62] Accordingly, it seems that in practice the term 'unlawful combatant' is primarily a rhetorical device used to justify certain policies on targeting and detention, rather than the implementation of a rule of international law. States might use a variety of rhetorical devices within domestic policies and laws, but the actions taken on the basis of these policies and laws must conform to the applicable international law. This is true whether it is in relation to targeting or detention. For example, while Israel has a law on detention of unlawful combatants, the key question regardless of the use of the term, is whether the resulting acts of detention adhere to appropriate international law, such as the laws on administrative detention of civilians during conflict. In other words, whilst the view taken here is that the use of 'unlawful combatant' should be avoided as it is not a category defined in international law, the focus of scrutiny should be on the actual practice of states which use it. If the use of the term is accompanied by a claim that these individuals are to be placed outside the framework of international law then it must be opposed. If, however, the state bases its actual practice on existing international law such as the framework of administrative detention of civilians, then contradictions with international law will largely have been avoided. Correspondingly, in the context of targeting, the issue can also be addressed through existing international law. Avoiding the term 'unlawful combatants' is in no way akin to claiming that the individuals are immune to any repercussions resulting from their participation in hostilities. Civilians may lose their civilian protection at times—as shown in the preceding and following sections—and thereby be subject to attack. The debate over the loss of civilian protection contains an impressively, and perhaps disconcertingly, wide margin of opinions. Those who use the term 'unlawful combatant' in order to ease the restrictions of targeting these individuals, could just as easily refrain from using the contentious term of 'unlawful combatant' and achieve the same end result within the debate on civilians taking a direct part in hostilities by adopting certain interpretations of the circumstances in which civilians lose protection.[63] This will be demonstrated in the following section on members of armed groups.

---

[60] *Targeted Killings*, n 26, *supra*.   [61] *Anonymous v. Israel*, n 46, *supra*.

[62] *Targeted Killings*, n 26, *supra*, para 28; *Anonymous v. Israel*, n 46, *supra*, paras 12, 14.

[63] 'As stated, other approaches are possible. I do not find a need to expand on them, since in light of the rules of interpretation proposed by President Barak, the theoretical distinction loses its sting. The interpretation proposed by my colleague President Barak in fact creates a new group, and rightly so. It can be derived from the combatant group ("unlawful combatants") and it can be derived from the civilian group. My colleague President Barak takes the second path. If we go his way, we should derive a group of international-law-breaking civilians, whom I would call "uncivilized civilians". In any case, there is no difference between the two paths in terms of the result, since the interpretation of the provisions of international law proposed by my colleague President Barak

1.5 The categorization of members of non-state groups

As concluded in the previous chapter, extraterritorial forcible measures against non-state actors which constitute an armed conflict are likely to be characterized as non-international armed conflict either directly or through customary rules based on the same pattern. In most cases the individuals against whom force is used will not be random civilians taking up arms but rather members of non-state groups. This section will attempt to set out the debate and possible interpretations as to how to categorize such individuals.[64]

In non-international armed conflicts, the question is whether members of armed and organized non-state groups should be viewed as either (i) civilians taking a direct part in hostilities, or (ii) as some form of category of fighters, akin to combatants in international armed conflict, albeit without the entitlement to prisoner of war status. The ICRC study on Customary Law affirms the uncertainty, noting that in non-international armed conflicts, 'practice is ambiguous as to whether members of armed opposition groups are considered members of armed forces or civilians.'[65] Arguments for seeing members of armed groups as something other than civilians often rest upon the assertion that the rules of non-international armed conflict, by virtue of containing protections for civilians, seem to implicitly recognize that there is another category of persons who are not civilian, even if not giving them a name. This argument finds support in the views of commentators, as well as in the commentary to Protocol II.[66] It also addresses an otherwise perceived imbalance that would have left members of state forces open to attack at any time, while regarding members of armed groups as civilians who might at times be protected.[67] Nonetheless, even if one is to accept this line of argument care must be taken with the terms used. The position has been described as follows, 'The logical conclusion of the definition of a non-international armed conflict as one between the armed forces of a state and an organized armed group is that members of both the armed forces and the organized armed group are combatants. While these combatants do not enjoy the privileges of combatants in an international armed conflict, they may be attacked

---

adapts the rules to the new reality. That interpretation is acceptable to me. It is a dynamic interpretation which overcomes the limitations of a black letter reading of the laws of war.' *Targeted Killings*, n 26, *supra*, opinion of Justice Rivlin, para 2. See also Sassoli, 'Use and Abuse', n 54, *supra*, 208–09.

[64] For detailed analysis of this topic see *Meeting on the Right to Life*, n 42, *supra*; Kleffner, n 5, *supra*.

[65] ICRC customary law study, n 4, *supra*, 17.

[66] Rogers, n 30, *supra*, 222–5; *Third Expert Meeting on Direct Participation*, n 27, *supra*, 43–4; Interpretive Guidance, n 36, *supra*, 27–36, 71–73; D Kretzmer, 'Targeted Killing of Suspected Terrorists: Extra-Judicial Executions or Legitimate Means of Defence?' 16 *EJIL* 171 (2005) 197–8; Kleffner, n 5, *supra*, 324–5; Protocol II, Commentary to article 13.3, para 4789, but see supporting and opposing opinion in *Meeting on the Right to Life*, n 42, *supra*, 35.

[67] ICRC customary law study, n 4, *supra*, 21.

by the other party to the conflict.'[68] It would, however, be preferable to frame this approach a little differently and it should be stressed that the term 'combatants' is better reserved for the definition it is given in the laws of international armed conflict, where it also entitles the individual to prisoner of war status upon capture. Since this privilege is not granted by the laws of non-international armed conflict, and even if one is to speak of non-civilians, it is perhaps better to use a term such as 'fighter' in order to avoid misusing the combatant definition of international armed conflicts.[69] This would avoid inappropriate use of the term combatant, although it would not yet solve the legal issue of how to categorize these individuals. Finally, it should also be noted that accepting that members of armed groups might be fighters or non-civilians, does not negate the possibility that there may also be individual civilians who are not members of the group and nevertheless take up arms and to whom the rule on loss of civilian protection would still apply.[70]

The approach describing members of organized armed groups as something other than civilians has gained considerable support by the recently published position of the ICRC. According to the ICRC, while in international armed conflicts individuals can only be combatants or civilians, the situation is different in non-international armed conflicts. In the latter, although the law does not contain a definition there is implicit recognition that there is a group of non-civilians. According to the ICRC, 'members of organized armed groups belonging to a non-State party to the conflict cease to be civilians for as long as they remain members by virtue of their continuous combat function.'[71]

An alternative position is that in the absence of a defined status for members of armed groups in non-international armed conflicts the individuals fighting against the state, including within organized armed groups, are defined as civilians taking a direct part in hostilities.[72] According to this approach, discussion over the question of when individuals can be targeted by the state, in the context of existing rules of non-international armed conflict, thus revolves around the question of civilians losing their immunity. As with the case of the debate over 'unlawful combatants', defining these persons as civilians does not necessarily mean adopting a position which overly restricts the state forces since, as will be seen below, the debate over loss of civilian protection encompasses a wide range of positions.

In effect, the duration of time during which immunity is lost, while separate from the definition of taking a direct part in hostilities, is nevertheless linked and

---

[68] Kretzmer, n 66, *supra*, 197–8.
[69] *Manual on the Law of Non-International Armed Conflict*, n 4, *supra*, 4. It should, however, be noted that in some languages it can be a challenge to find two separate words for combatant and fighter.
[70] Kleffner, n 5, *supra*, 336; Kretzmer, n 66, *supra*, 198–9.
[71] *Interpretive Guidance*, n 36, *supra*, 71.
[72] *Meeting on the Right to Life*, n 42, *supra*, 35–6.

affected by how the latter is interpreted. While it is impossible here to give full attention to every aspect of the ongoing debate over these questions, the various positions can be distilled into the following approaches:[73]

1. A narrow interpretation of the rule, in which taking a direct part involves only direct and active participation in attacks, eg firing a weapon. Loss of immunity occurs only while the individual is actually in the course of the action, and civilian immunity is regained once the attack is over.

2. An interpretation according to which direct participation includes all activities directly related to the attack and which form part of the hostile threat to the state forces, including for instance the planning, training and provision of direct support for the attacks. Loss of immunity occurs throughout the participation in any of these stages, although civilian immunity exists at all other times.

3. A wider interpretation, according to which the element of taking a direct part is defined as in either of the above, but loss of immunity occurs not only during the act, but also for as long as the individual continues and intends to continue to take a direct part in hostilities by engaging in these specific activities.

4. Perhaps the widest interpretation of all in which, regardless of individual proof of engagement in activities such as firing a weapon, it is the membership of an organized armed group in and of itself that leads to loss of civilian protection. The civilian immunity is therefore lost for such time as the individual continues to be an active member of the group, including possibly the duration of the armed conflict.

Nonetheless, whichever approach is chosen, whether one of the above or other possible approaches, the result is most likely to come up against one of the following obstacles:

(i) The narrower positions might give rise to the 'revolving door' criticism that they place the state forces at a disadvantage, allowing non-state actors to attack and then claim immunity from counter-attack, whilst leaving the state forces legitimate targets, and also restricting the state from ever engaging in preventative attacks.[74]

(ii) The wider interpretation of direct participation in (2), conversely, can be criticized for allowing the state an almost free hand in deciding who can be targeted. The term 'direct participation in hostilities' points to a limited

[73] For varying opinions and positions on when members of groups could be attacked, see *Expert Meetings on Direct Participation*, n 27, *supra*. For a different separation of approaches see Kleffner, n 5, *supra*, 330–5.

[74] ICRC customary law study, n 4, *supra*, 21; *Third Expert Meeting on Direct Participation*, n 27, *supra*, 44; Kleffner, n 5, *supra*, 332–3; K Watkin, 'Canada/United States Military Interoperability and Humanitarian Law Issues: Land Mines, Terrorism, Military Objectives and Targeted Killing' 15 *Duke Journal of Comparative and International Law* 281 (2005) 312.

range of activities.[75] Interpreting it to include more than these would make it possible for states to fit almost any desirable target into them, for example by claiming the individual was involved in planning.

(iii) There are obvious risks in (3) due to the lack of clarity caused by relying on the question of an individual's intent rather than his actions at a given time.

(iv) Approaches (1), (2) and (3) do not distinguish between categories of civilians and members of armed groups and, thereby, risk blurring the fundamental principle of distinction.[76]

(v) The membership approach has the advantage of recognizing that armed conflicts take place between parties to the conflict but raises questions over determining who is and is not a group member (and how one can prove disassociation from a group).[77] Furthermore it is, in effect, a form of having the cake and eating it—the state can attack group members whenever it sees fit just as if they were combatants under the laws of international armed conflict, but is under no obligation to give them prisoner of war status upon capture.[78]

(vi) Approaches that might address the latter point by resulting in similar rules on combatant status for international and non-international armed conflicts,[79] and consequently prisoner of war status, are not a viable option. States are unlikely to ever accept a rule which would, in effect, give advance impunity from prosecution even to armed groups and rebels that adhere to IHL and 'only' attack state military objects and personnel.

As noted earlier, the rules on these matters have been at the centre of many meetings of experts, and the ICRC has published its own interpretation of the rules.[80] According to this interpretation, in non-international armed conflicts members of organized armed groups are non-civilians. Members are 'individuals whose continuous function it is to take a direct part in hostilities ("continuous combat function")'.[81] These members 'cease to be civilians for as long as they remain

---

[75] See section 1.3, *supra*, on defining the activities.

[76] Kretzmer, n 66, *supra,* 198.

[77] For further elaboration of the advantages and disadvantages of the membership approach, see *Third Expert Meeting on Direct Participation*, n 27, *supra*, 48–51, 53–7, 63–5; Kleffner, n 5, *supra*, 332–3.

[78] Losing immunity for belonging to a military style organized non-state actor could perhaps be linked to the controversial concept of criminal organizations—for an example of some of the problems with this concept see the criticism by Judge Biddle in the discussion of criminal organizations in H Levie, *Terrorism in War—The Law of War Crimes* (Oceana Publications: New York, 1992) 411–21; Kretzmer, n 66, *supra*, 200.

[79] Brooks, n 5, *supra*, 755–8.

[80] *Expert Meetings on Direct Participation*, n 27, *supra*; *Challenges of Contemporary Armed Conflicts*, n 30, *supra*, 32–3; *Meeting on the Right to Life*, n 42, *supra*; *Interpretive Guidance*, n 36, *supra*. For further detailed analysis conducted in personal capacity by the same author as the ICRC report see N Melzer, *Targeted Killing in International Law* (OUP: Oxford, 2008) 300–53.

[81] *Interpretive Guidance*, n 36, *supra*, 16, 27–36.

members by virtue of their continuous combat function.'[82] The organized armed group is the military/armed wing of the non-state party and constitutes its *de facto* armed forces. Other non-fighting (eg political) wings of the non-state party are not considered part of the organized armed group. Individuals who are not members of the organized armed group are protected from attack unless, and for such time as, they take a direct part in hostilities. Whilst members of the armed groups have, as non-civilians, lost civilian protection, for others who are civilians the rule on loss of protection should be interpreted so that protection is lost only for the limited duration of a specific act of direct participation.[83]

This guidance by the ICRC attempts to address the concern over considering members of armed groups as civilians who, at times, would claim civilian protection whilst simultaneously addressing the desire to maintain the narrow interpretation of the rule on loss of protection by civilians. It, therefore, separates members of armed groups carrying out a continuous combat function from those civilians to whom the rule on direct participation would apply in its narrow form. The notion of continuous combat function is also designed to avoid the widest approach by which any membership of the group could lead to loss of protection. However, this guidance has not solved some of the most pressing questions whilst it may also have opened the door for further questionable interpretations.

The need to recognize the realities of combat while aiming to achieve the strongest protection possible for those who need it is at the heart of much of the work in the field of IHL, and is evident in the discussed ICRC document, as it is in the rest of the organization's work. In the context of direct participation in hostilities and categorization of members of armed groups this delicate and fateful balance must rule out the positions at either end of the spectrum of interpretations. On the one hand, applying the narrowest interpretation of the rule, even to members of armed groups, would ignore the realities of situations in which states might be faced with highly organized armed groups and in which the conduct of both parties mirrors high intensity conflicts between states. In these situations military encounters with members of armed groups are likely to be similar to any encounter between opposing forces, and not predicated on being allowed to open fire on the basis of individual direct participation at the given moment. On the other hand, applying a wide membership approach not based on any individual determination would lead, especially when faced with groups without overtly recognizable membership (eg through uniform) to the possibility of states using lethal force whenever they want against virtually whoever they want, so long as it is claimed the person was a member. A middle option is, therefore, necessary. One solution is the above-mentioned ICRC proposition which distinguishes between civilians and the specific members of armed groups who carry out continuous combat function. An alternative route would be to maintain a strict

[82] *Ibid*, 71.   [83] *Ibid*, 27–36, 70–3.

interpretation of the constitutive elements for acts to be considered as direct participation[84] while accepting a wider interpretation of the temporal aspect in the rule. In essence, this would mean interpreting the duration element so as to include the time in between repeated actions of direct participation, in that the individual is always likely to be preparing for the next engagement even when not in the midst of one. Members of armed groups would, therefore, be vulnerable to attack under similar conditions as in the ICRC document but they would continue to be considered legally as civilians.

A comparison between the position in the ICRC document on continuous combat function and this interpretation of direct participation is revealing. If one were to adopt the interpretation that loss of civilian protection occurs for as long as the individual is engaged in a string of direct participation acts, is the ICRC notion of continuous combat function still necessary? The perceived advantage of the ICRC approach is that by using the latter notion it enables application of the direct participation rule more narrowly for those individuals who are not regular members of a group. However, the implementation of the ICRC approach is likely to result in similar determinations as would have occurred applying the wider interpretation of the direct participation rule, as can be seen by examining the possible scenarios. If the individual X is an active member of an armed group taking regular part in direct acts of hostilities, then the ICRC continuous combat function approach would determine that he has lost protection for as long as he is so regularly engaged. Without using the continuous combat function approach, applying an interpretation of the direct participation rule that includes ongoing participation would also determine that X has lost protection for the whole period of ongoing participatory acts. If, however, X were a member of the group but not in a position that includes direct participation in hostilities, then both approaches would determine that he is protected as a civilian. Finally, if X is not a member of the group at all but nonetheless engages in an act of direct participation then the continuous combat function approach would determine him to be a civilian who loses protection only during the actual time of carrying out the act. This is the point at which the ICRC approach would supposedly offer better protection by applying the direct participation rule narrowly. However, even without this approach the above interpretation of the direct participation rule would not mean that X has lost protection for the whole conflict and in this scenario X would only lose protection during the act. The wider interpretation, as presented above, only widens the timeframe when dealing with individuals who are carrying out ongoing acts and continue to do so. Clearly there will be grave difficulties determining whether the individual intends to carry out further acts of direct participation or whether this was a single act, but then this same difficulty arises if one has to determine whether it is a single act or an example of continuous combat

---

[84] See discussion in section 1.3, *supra*, on direct participation.

function. The ICRC document resists the possibility of the wider notion of direct participation, since:

In operational reality, it would be impossible to determine with a sufficient degree of reliability whether civilians not currently preparing or executing a hostile act have previously done so on a persistently recurrent basis and whether they have the continued intent to do so again. Basing continuous loss of protection on such speculative criteria would inevitably result in erroneous or arbitrary attacks against civilians, thus undermining their protection which is at the heart of IHL.[85]

This is a primary consideration for keeping the interpretation narrow, while advancing the notion of continuous combat function to cover members of armed groups. Notably, the ICRC approach does not allow for targeting all members of a group but only those members of the armed wing who carry out continuous combat function. As such, and without published lists of active armed members, it is ultimately an individual determination based on the individual's actions.[86] Determining whether an individual is indeed carrying out a continuous combat function carries similar difficulties and risks as in the above quotation on determining intent of civilians. Even if not framed as such the ICRC's notion of continuous combat function thereby leads to the same pre-existing problem of how to determine an individual's ongoing intention, and the risk of this interpretation being open to abuse.

Moreover, despite the insistence at the start of the Guidance document that it only concerns the conduct of hostilities and does not relate to questions of post-capture status[87] once the ICRC proposes formulations according to which members of armed groups 'cease to be civilians',[88] it is hard to imagine that these will not be used to advance theories that the ICRC may not have wished to see. The pre-capture and post-capture stages are invariably linked, for example in the discussions over combatants and eligibility for prisoner of war status, and the stages cannot be entirely decoupled from each other. The use of a caveat at the start of the ICRC document stating that it should not be used for interpreting rules on persons deprived of their liberty is unlikely to deter those who may wish to do just that. International lawyers and governments will undoubtedly be using the ICRC notion of ceasing to be a civilian, in order to advocate for acceptance of the 'unlawful combatant' theories.[89] This is likely to be one unfortunate consequence of the new approach.

In light of the above, it should be stressed that the ICRC guidance document does not claim to be new law, but to 'reflect the ICRC's institutional position as to how existing IHL should be interpreted'.[90] Whilst it should be clear from the

---

[85] *Ibid*, 45.
[86] On the different views on what type of membership should be considered, and the practical difficulties raised, see *Fourth Expert Meeting*, n 27, *supra*, 22–32.
[87] *Interpretive Guidance*, n 36, *supra*, 10–11.   [88] *Ibid*, 71.
[89] See section 1.4, *supra*, on unlawful combatants.
[90] *Interpretive Guidance*, n 36, *supra*, 9.

current work that the ICRC's views are highly respected and in the vast majority of cases promoted, the position taken here with regard to the notion of direct
participation in hostilities does not fully adopt the positions in the ICRC document. There clearly is no straightforward answer as to the status and protections
afforded to individuals who may find themselves targeted in extraterritorial operations against non-state actors. All of the positions in the sections above can be
subjected to criticisms and questions, and indeed all these points and more have
been at the heart of years of debate beyond anything that can be captured in this
short section.[91] The current state of affairs means that many of the issues raised
here will remain subject to varying interpretations although, as raised in the section on 'unlawful combatants', some of these interpretations can seemingly take
different routes but on occasion arrive at similar conclusions. The position taken
here is that individuals can fall into only one of two legal categories—combatant
or civilian. While there may be implicit recognition of non-civilians in non-international armed conflicts a status akin to combatants is not presented in the law. In
situations in which individuals are taking part in the fighting without being eligi-
ble to combatant status, whether because it does not exist in the type of conflict at
hand or because the individuals do not meet the required criteria, they, therefore,
fall under the legal category of civilians. This does not preclude states (or indeed
commentators) from using other terms such as 'unprivileged belligerent', 'fighter',
'member of armed group' or anything else, but the actual practice of states both
during hostilities and post-capture, must be based on the existing legal categories
of status. There is clearly room for discomfort with this notion but the law as it
stands does not contain another category. The problem is particularly striking in
cases of high intensity conflict with uniformed armed groups controlling territory. Much of this stems from the understandable reluctance of states to consider
combatant status and immunity from prosecution for members of armed groups
in non-international conflicts. Combatants are part of the state apparatus and
benefit from the state's monopoly on resort to force while civilians have no right
to take part in hostilities. Members of armed non-state groups, therefore, fall into
the category of civilians who can be prosecuted for the very act of fighting. This
does not mean there are no consequences also with regard to protection from
attack during the conflict. Although they are clearly linked there must be differentiation between the debate over the name or category we assign to members
of armed groups, as opposed to the debate over reaching a workable approach to
implementing the rules on the ground. States are able to accept the existence of
the civilian-combatant dichotomy, and that certain fighters might fall into the
legal category of civilians, without it preventing them from advancing the laws
and policies they consider necessary.[92] It may be that discomfort will remain over

---

[91] *Expert Meetings*, n 27, *supra*.
[92] Including on controversial matters. See *Anonymous v. Israel*, n 46, *supra*, paras 12, 14;
Targeted Killings, n 26, *supra*, para 28.

labelling members of armed groups as legally belonging to the civilian category but that practical interpretations for implementing existing rules could nevertheless be found. A possible interpretation that would satisfy some concerns is one by which individuals who take an ongoing active part in the hostilities, whilst remaining within the IHL category of civilians, lose their protection for so long as they continue to be regularly engaged in these actions. The risk of this interpretation is that it blurs the distinction between combatants and civilians and exposes civilians to greater danger of being unjustifiably targeted. The ICRC's proposed solution attempts to alleviate this concern, but ultimately faces similar obstacles when it comes to determining whether an individual loses protection as a result of continuous combat function, and may have inadvertent repercussions on the debates over post-capture status as well as during hostilities.

The concerns of states facing armed groups are real as are the needs to ensure protection of civilians and leave them outside the field of combat. The existing approaches all have their faults and this clearly seems to be an area in which the law is in need of greater precision. There may be further developments in the future which might assist in this area. For example, stronger differentiation between low intensity and Protocol II type high intensity non-international conflicts, might allow for correspondingly differing interpretations of the rules on individual status—allowing for realistic approaches to high intensity conflicts without dragging down protection in the low intensity ones. The process of expert deliberations which culminated in the ICRC's own interpretive guidance cannot be the final endpoint and the law in this area remains in need of clarification.

Finally, as at the start of this chapter, it must again be stressed that all the above discussion on individual status, and the possibility of targeting individuals on the basis of a category to which they belong, will only become relevant in situations which amount to armed conflict. Outside of armed conflict these rules simply do not apply.[93]

2. IHL regulation of the conduct of fighting

The previous sections of this Part covered the circumstances and conditions for the applicability of IHL, the classifications of conflicts, and the categorization of those involved. The current section turns to the examination of the force used by the state against the non-state actor, and the rules that regulate the means and methods of conducting hostilities. As suggested previously, most situations of armed conflict covered here would fit within the framework of non-international armed conflict or be subjected to a similar set of rules under customary law. The same premise applies to the regulation of the conduct of the fighting as examined in this chapter. At a minimum any IHL rule considered to be customary

[93] See Part III, *infra*, on rules of international human rights law and law enforcement.

international law applying to all non-international armed conflict should also apply to armed conflicts that take the form of extraterritorial operations against non-state actors. This chapter will not engage in a lengthy repetition or analysis of the applicable law on conduct of hostilities but will instead identify key areas of concern which arise in the context of extraterritorial operations against non-state actors. The first of the following two sections focuses upon large-scale military operations and the subsequent section looks at issues arising from smaller scale operations aimed at specific individuals.

2.1 Large-scale military operations

Any large-scale military operations involving extensive use of force, be it in the form of armoured battalions, aerial bombardment or the like, must conform to the basic laws on conduct of hostilities. The rules appearing in this section—unless specifically indicated otherwise—are considered to be part of customary international law applicable to both international and non-international armed conflicts[94] even if their precise formulation is sometimes based upon the one found in specific instruments such as Protocol I. Accordingly, the following are among the rules applying to armed conflicts involving extraterritorial military attacks against non-state actors:[95]

(i) Attacks can only be directed at military objectives. Civilian objects and civilians cannot be the intended target of attack;[96]

(ii) indiscriminate attacks, which do not distinguish between military and civilian, are prohibited;[97]

(iii) feasible precautions must be taken in the planning and execution of attacks to minimize the effect upon civilians and civilian objects;[98]

(iv) any expected incidental harm to civilians or civilian objects must not be excessive in relation to the concrete and direct military advantage anticipated (the principle of proportionality);[99]

---

[94] Most of which appear in one form or another in some or all of the following: ICRC customary law study, n 4, *supra*; *Manual on the Law of Non-International Armed Conflict*, n 4, *supra*; *Prosecutor v. Dusko Tadic*, Decision on the Defence Motion for Interlocutory Appeal on Jurisdiction, ICTY, 2 October 1995; See also *UK Manual*, n 22, *supra*, 391. But see also Statute of the ICC for a more limited approach to the list of IHL rules for non-international armed conflicts.

[95] This is a partial list of a number of the most fundamental rules. For more exhaustive lists of rules, see ICRC customary law study, n 4, *supra* and *Manual on the Law of Non-International Armed Conflict*, n 4, *supra*.

[96] ICRC customary law study, n 4, *supra*, 25; *Manual on the Law of Non-International Armed Conflict*, n 4, *supra*, 18.

[97] ICRC customary law study, n 4, *supra*, 37, 40; S Oeter. 'Methods and Means of Combat' in D Fleck (ed), *The Handbook of Humanitarian Law in Armed Conflicts* (OUP: Oxford, 1995) 105–207, 120; *Manual on the Law of Non-International Armed Conflict*, n 4, *supra*, 20.

[98] ICRC customary law study, n 4, *supra*, 51, 56–7, 60; *Manual on the Law of Non-International Armed Conflict*, n 4, *supra*, 25.

[99] ICRC customary law study, n 4, *supra*, 46; *Manual on the Law of Non-International Armed Conflict*, n 4, *supra*, 22.

(v) it is prohibited to use unlawful weapons or to use means or methods which cause superfluous injury or unnecessary suffering.[100]

When conducting attacks against non-state actors the identification of the military objective can become problematic since the target might not appear in the form of a recognizable military base complete with signs, fences, armoured vehicles, and so on. The base camp of the armed group, and indeed its weapons storage and military facilities, might all be in locations that are no different from civilian dwellings and even shared with civilian housing. Moreover, if the group is operating from within the territory of a society in which civilians carry or use arms, even if not taking part in hostilities, identification of the target becomes even harder, as is evident from the cases in which it was alleged that the targets of US attacks were in fact wedding parties rather than militant camps.[101] This is true for any conflict involving non-state actors but is exacerbated in the case of extraterritorial operations, in which knowledge and information on the area of attack is more limited than in internal conflicts. While some militaries may have access to extensive satellite imagery this may not always be sufficient and is not the case for all armies. Nevertheless, these difficulties do not alter the applicable law and verification of the target as a military objective must precede any attack.

An even greater difficulty, and one for which the law does not provide a perfect solution, is in the context of the principle of proportionality and its application to cases in which the defender takes advantage of being surrounded by civilians. Proportionality in attack, whilst considered a fundamental principle of IHL,[102] is also one which is notoriously difficult to apply as it requires a balancing between the disparate elements of military advantage and civilian casualties.[103] It is undoubtedly a necessary principle since incidental harm to civilians can occur when targeting the military and, even though precision targeting has improved, it does not yet provide a legal or practical solution to ending collateral civilian casualties.[104] There must be a rule to limit such damage but in effect its application will likely only be clear in the extreme cases of obvious disproportion, or vice-versa, and arguable in the wide range in between.[105]

---

[100] ICRC customary law study, n 4, *supra*, 237, 244; *Manual on the Law of Non-International Armed Conflict*, n 4, *supra*,12.

[101] 'US justifies Afghan wedding bombing' *BBC News*, 7 September, 2002; 'Falluja raid "hits wedding party"' *BBC News*, 8 October, 2004.

[102] n 99, *supra*.

[103] Many have remarked on the difficulty of applying this principle, eg Final Report to the Prosecutor by the Committee Established to Review the NATO Bombing Campaign Against the Federal Republic of Yugoslavia, 2000, available at <http://www.un.org/icty/pressreal/nato061300. htm> para 48; *UK Manual*, n 22, *supra*, 25–6; Dinstein, n 21, *supra*, 122; Fischer, n 29, *supra*, 105–6; Kretzmer, n 66, *supra*, 201; Oeter, n 97, *supra*, 173; Rogers, n 30, *supra*, 20–1. For an extensive enquiry into the development of the rule see W Fenrick, 'The Rule of Proportionality and Protocol I in Conventional Warfare' 98 *Military Law Review* 91 (1982) and J Gardam *Necessity, Proportionality and the use of Force by States* (CUP: Cambridge, 2004).

[104] Roberts, n 47, *supra*, 213; Dinstein, n 21, *supra*, 126; Gardam, *ibid*, 103.

[105] Final Report to the Prosecutor, n 103, *supra*, para 48; *Targeted Killings*, n 26, *supra*, para 46.

A particular problem arises when the defender attempts to shield himself from attack through being surrounded by civilians (either by deliberately locating himself in civilian midst or by having civilians brought to surround him). When the civilians are willingly and actively taking part in this in order to shield the defender ('voluntary human shields') some would argue that they lose their civilian protection[106] but the greater problem arises when the civilians are not intentionally doing so. This situation has arisen more than once in the context of Israeli military operations against armed groups in Lebanon.[107] According to one description, during the conflict in 1982, the Palestinian Liberation Organization ('PLO') intentionally moved its weapons and forces into and near areas of civilians, churches and embassies, all in an effort to shield them from Israeli attack.[108] Using human shields in order to avoid being attacked is a clear violation of IHL, and the ICRC describes the act as 'the use of human shields requires an intentional co-location of military objectives and civilians or persons *hors de combat* with the specific intent of trying to prevent the targeting of those military objectives.'[109]

The legal effects of this violation for the attacker, as will be seen shortly, are disputable. First, however, it should be clarified that a military objective remains a legitimate target and that the abuse of the rules by the defender does not alter the categorization as such. As noted by Hampson:

If the adversary unlawfully places missile batteries in densely populated areas, the commander is not prohibited from attacking what is a lawful military objective. The unlawful act on the part of his adversary will determine *how* the attack is carried out, but not *whether* it takes place.[110]

Insofar as *how* to attack is concerned, the rule, as it appears in Protocol I, clearly states that abuse of the rules by the defender does not negate the attacker's obligation to apply the rules of IHL, including the principle of proportionality.[111] There can be a number of reasons for this. First, one may question the assessment of the Lebanon situation—or any other—as to whether the shielding was intentional for this purpose, and an inability to prove intent can serve to support the argument that this situation should not result in diminished protection for the civilians. Moreover, this would in effect be a form of punishing the civilians to the point of risk of death for acts they are not responsible for.[112] It also engages in balancing the actions of attackers and defenders rather than the idea

---

[106] Dinstein, n 21, *supra*, 130–1; M Schmitt, 'Targeting and Humanitarian Law: Current Issues' 34 *Israel Yearbook on Human Rights* 59 (2004) 95–6.

[107] For discussion of the recent hostilities in 2006 see Concluding Chapter, *infra*.

[108] Parks, 'Air War', n 35, *supra*, 165–6.

[109] ICRC customary law study, n 4, *supra*, 337–40.

[110] F Hampson, 'Means and Methods of Warfare in the Conflict in the Gulf' in P Rowe (ed), *The Gulf War 1990–91 in International and English Law* (Routledge: New York, 1993) 89–110, 92–3.

[111] Protocol I, Art 51.8.

[112] E Cannizaro, 'Contextualizing Proportionality: Jus ad Bellum and Jus in Bello in the Lebanon War' 864 *International Review of the Red Cross* 779 (2006) 790–1.

of IHL as balancing military necessity with humanity.[113] On the other hand, the approach of carrying on with the proportionality rule unchanged could be criticized for placing all the responsibility on the attacker for a situation he does not control, while allowing the defender to gain from abuse of the rules.[114] Views have, therefore, been expressed according to which the proportionality principle still applies (indeed any other view would be in direct contradiction to IHL) but that the assessment of whether it has been violated would take into account the specific circumstances and the defender's abuse of the prohibition of human shields. This could involve adjusting upwards the acceptable number of casualties to reflect the circumstances or the taking into account of the defender's actions at a later stage if the matter comes before a tribunal or investigation.[115] As noted at the start of this topic, the law here does not provide the perfect answer. The law often needs to be framed in guiding principles that cannot address every conceivable incident and its implementation must also rely upon the common sense and good faith of commanders faced with complex situations. Other than subscribing to some of the interpretations mentioned, even if the non-state group surrounds itself with civilians the state carrying out the extraterritorial military operation must abide by the principle of proportionality as by any other applicable rule of IHL.

2.2 Small-scale operations against individuals

Extraterritorial measures against non-state actors can often take the form of small scale operations directed against particular individuals, with the intention of capturing or even killing the target. Once again, for IHL to be applicable to such operations, they must be occurring as part of an armed conflict and, as examined earlier, this may not always be the case.[116] However, when the IHL framework is applicable, the rules discussed in this section will apply. It is of paramount importance to keep in mind the relevance of the determination of the individual's status whether s/he is a combatant; a civilian who has lost protection; or a protected civilian.[117] The legality of an operation designed for intentional use of force directed at individuals can hinge on the determination of their status and if the person is a protected civilian then intentional force against them will fail this initial stage of lawful validation.

The means and methods by which the operation is carried out can also affect its legality. In addition to the rules mentioned in the previous section (eg the legality of weapons used) operations against individuals are more likely to be carried out by smaller units of the special forces types and in a fashion that gives

---

[113] See comment by Schmitt in Rogers, n 30, *supra*, 129, fn 49.
[114] Parks, 'Air War', n 35, *supra*, 153–4, 162; Rogers, n 30, *supra*,129.
[115] Dinstein, n 21, *supra*, 130–1; Rogers, n 30, *supra*, 126–9; *UK Manual*, n 22, *supra*, 26; L Doswald-Beck, 'The Civilian in the Crossfire' 24 *Journal of Peace Research* 251 (1987).
[116] Ch 5, *supra*.   [117] Section 1, *supra*, on individual status.

rise to further potential concerns. Chief among these concerns is the question of operations carried out by undercover units. Insofar as extraterritorial operations against non-state actors might often occur without consent of the territorial state[118] they may well involve undercover units, including sending forces in civilian attire. An example of this type of operation is 'Operation Spring of Youth' in which Israeli commandos carried out a raid in Beirut, Lebanon in April 1973, against alleged members of Palestinian groups held responsible for attacks such as the killing of Israeli athletes in the 1972 Munich Olympics.[119] The military force, led by Ehud Barak,[120] dressed as civilians with Barak and others disguised as women, made their way to the location of their targets and carried out an operation resulting in the killing of targeted individuals, as well as other casualties.[121] In addition to questions over identity of the targets and casualties among civilians, when occurring in the context of armed conflict the use of civilian disguise in operations such as this risks being in violation of IHL.

While the military is generally presumed to be wearing uniform[122] it might not always need to be a traditional full military uniform provided the principle of distinction can be maintained and that the forces are recognizable as military forces rather than civilians.[123] Moreover, even if soldiers operate out of uniform or any recognizable attire this in itself is not necessarily a violation of IHL although it may lead to loss of eligibility for prisoner of war status[124] in conflicts in which this status is a possibility.[125] However, if the forces are disguising themselves as civilians in order to achieve an advantage (such as walking up to their target undetected) and kill the opposing individual this is likely to be a violation of the perfidy prohibition. Perfidy involves '[a]cts inviting the confidence of an adversary to lead him to believe that he is entitled to, or is obliged to accord, protection under the rules of international law applicable in armed conflict, with intent to betray that confidence,'[126] and 'the feigning of civilian, non-combatant status'[127] is an example of such acts. In the 1907 Hague Regulations there is a similar prohibition of treacherous killings or wounding,[128] while Protocol I includes also the feigning of protected status in order to effect a capture.[129] At least in the context of killing or wounding, this prohibition is part of customary international law, and is considered to apply also to non-international armed

---

[118]   See discussion in Part I, *supra*.

[119]   IHL may not have been applicable to this operation, depending on the interpretation of whether it was part of an armed conflict. If it was not an armed conflict then the use of force is regulated by the rules examined in Part III of the work. However, it serves as a useful example of the style of operation and methods used, as being discussed in this section.

[120]   Later to become prime minister.

[121]   'The Hunt for Black September' *BBC News*, 24 January 2006.

[122]   Parks, 'Special Forces' n 22, *supra*, 543.

[123]   K Ipsen, 'Combatants and Non–Combatants' in Fleck, n 97, *supra*, 65–104, 96–7; Parks, 'Special Forces' n 22, *supra*, 516–17, 539.

[124]   Dinstein, n 21, *supra*, 50, 203; Parks, 'Special Forces' n 22, *supra*, 512.

[125]   See section 1.1, *supra*, on combatants.   [126]   Protocol I, Art 37.   [127]   *Ibid.*

[128]   Hague Regulations, Art 23(b).   [129]   Protocol I, Art 37.

conflicts.[130] It is a war crime[131] as it corrodes the very foundation of IHL by violating the principle of distinction and removing any trust in the notion that protected persons must be kept out the cycle of violence.

To be clear, it is not the targeting of an individual that is necessarily unlawful, provided he is not a protected civilian,[132] nor is it necessarily a violation of IHL for a soldier to be out of uniform. The illegality arises when the forces carrying out the attack pretend to be entitled to protection as civilians (or as wounded personnel or other protected categories) with the intention of abusing the ensuing trust in order to kill or wound their target.[133] Provided that the above and all other rules of IHL on means and methods of conduct are adhered to the IHL framework does not prohibit the deliberate targeting of individuals who do not have civilian protection. Even the notion of proportionality does not completely prevent lethal force in this context as the IHL concept of proportionality (unlike the human rights understanding of the notion[134]) refers to the effect on surrounding civilians and objects and not the military target.[135] Proportionality, as defined in IHL, will, however, be relevant if the process of targeting individuals leads to casualties among surrounding civilians (for example, when individuals are targeted by carrying out a missile strike on their location). Notwithstanding the latter point, from a strict IHL point of view, intentional killings of individuals who are not protected civilians may therefore be lawful. Certain opinions have raised the possibility of requiring an attempt to detain before using force if and when this is possible.[136] The ICRC document on direct participation in hostilities suggests that the principles of military necessity and humanity may require an attempt to detain in certain circumstances.[137] This position has been extremely controversial for a number of reasons raised by many of the experts involved in deliberating the matter. These include the arguments that it misapplies the principle of military necessity; that it is an unwarranted incorporation of human rights notions into IHL; that it portrays what is only a potentially desirable policy as existing law, which it is not; and that it does not reflect the

---

[130] ICRC customary law study, n 4, *supra*, 221; *Manual on the Law of Non-International Armed Conflict*, n 4, *supra*, 43; *UK Manual*, n 22, *supra*, 391–2.

[131] ICC Statute, Arts 8.2(b)(xi) and 8.2(e)(ix).

[132] Rogers, n 30, *supra*, 44–5; Dinstein, n 21, *supra*, 199.

[133] Parks, 'Special Forces', n 22, *supra*, 541–2.

[134] The international human rights law notion of proportionality includes a measurement of the force used against the target individual, and not only the effect on surroundings. See discussion in Chapter 7, *infra*, as well as an additional notion of proportionality in the context of self-defence in Part I, *supra*.

[135] n 99, *supra*, 102–105 and accompanying text.

[136] *Third Expert Meeting on Direct Participation*, n 27, *supra*, 31, 43, 45–6, 56–7; *Targeted Killings*, n 26, *supra*, para 40; Kretzmer, n 66, *supra*, 201–04; *Meeting on the Right to Life*, n 42, *supra*, 35, 36; N Lubell, 'Challenges in Applying Human Rights Law to Armed Conflict', 860 *International Review of the Red Cross* 737, December 2005, 746–50.

[137] *Interpretive Guidance*, n 36, *supra*, 77–82. See also N Melzer *Targeted Killing in International Law* (OUP: Oxford, 2008) 278–99, 397–8.

practice on the ground and would be difficult to implement.[138] Other experts and, ultimately the ICRC, took the view that this was the correct interpretation of the IHL principles.[139] In support of this position, the ICRC document points out that indeed these principles might not create added restrictions in 'classic large-scale confrontations between well-equipped and organized armed forces or groups', but an attempt to detain could be possible in the case of 'an unarmed civilian sitting in a restaurant using a radio or mobile phone to transmit tactical targeting intelligence to an attacking air force' in an area controlled by the opposing party, despite this individual being considered to be directly participating in hostilities.[140] Undoubtedly this is factually correct but the debatable question is whether it leads to a legal obligation as opposed to a desirable practice. This is especially the case when taking into account that applying the IHL principles in this manner would mean that the same interpretation would apply with regard to operations against opposing combatants during international armed conflicts. The ICRC document speaks of situations in which there 'manifestly is no necessity for the use of lethal force'[141] but the question of how this is to be understood is less than clear. The situations on the ground will more often be somewhere in between the types of examples cited earlier. For example, a heavily armed platoon of 40 soldiers might spot an enemy patrol of three opposing soldiers encamped across the valley. With their significant number advantage and the fact that the enemy is unaware of them, they might be in a position to plan a swift operation to approach the enemy patrol undetected, surround them, and capture them without sustaining casualties. Alternatively, they could open fire from across the valley. It is unclear whether according to the ICRC position an attempt to detain must be considered in this scenario and there would be strong views that such a call would deviate from the widely accepted principles of IHL which allow for targeting of enemy combatants that are not *hors de combat*.[142] Additionally, separate to the interpretation of the IHL rule, there is also the question of how international human rights law might influence the requirements for the action to be considered lawful. While the applicability of international human rights law and the relationship between its rules and those of IHL can potentially assist in solving this question of lethal force as a first resort these,

---

[138] *Fifth Expert Meeting*, n 27, *supra*. 10–20; *Fifth Informal Expert Meeting, The Notion of Direct Participation in Hostilities under IHL, Expert Comments & Elements of Response Concerning the Revised Draft of the Interpretive Guidance on the Notion of Direct Participation in Hostilities*, International Committee of the Red Cross, Geneva, 5–6 February 2008, 39–42.

[139] *Expert Comments, ibid*, 41–2; *Fifth Expert Meeting, ibid*; *Interpretive Guidance*, n 36, *supra*, 77–82.

[140] *Interpretive Guidance*, n 36, *supra*, 80–1.   [141] *Interpretive Guidance*, n 36, *supra*, 82.

[142] The above views reflect a variety of arguments raised by the unnamed experts in the published reports. At the time of writing this issue is being raised and subjected to critique repeatedly at numerous IHL forums and a number of commentators—including some of the experts previously involved in the meetings—are known to be writing pieces for publication containing these and more arguments.

as will be seen in the following chapters, are equally controversial and debatable matters which are not yet fully resolved.

As for use of force in the context of attempts to detain an individual, the law of international armed conflict contains numerous rules for detention including detention of prisoners of war or civilians in occupied territory.[143] The latter situations are outside the scope of this work and, as noted in earlier chapters, extraterritorial operations against non-state actors are unlikely to come within the sphere of international armed conflicts in which individuals are entitled to prisoner of war status. Whilst the ICRC study has concluded that arbitrary detention is unlawful in both international and non-international armed conflicts[144] the rules of non-international conflicts do not in fact contain laws regulating the grounds for detention, but focus on treatment and trial of persons after they have been detained.[145] Extraterritorial conflicts with non-state actors, assuming they are not international armed conflicts, will therefore suffer from the same deficiency.[146] In internal armed conflicts states can detain according to their domestic law and international human rights law can assist in the determination of whether these conform to the prohibition of arbitrary detention. These detentions may take the form of administrative detention of individuals as a preventative security measure rather than in relation to a criminal charge.[147] To apply the same approach to extraterritorial operations, however, there must first be an examination of if and how international human rights law can apply and regulate extraterritorial acts of detention. This will be examined in Part III of this work.

---

[143] Geneva Convention I, Arts 30, 32; Geneva Convention II, Arts 36, 37; Geneva Convention III, Arts 21, 118; Geneva Convention IV, Arts 42, 78.

[144] ICRC customary law study, n 4, *supra*, 344.

[145] Common Article 3; Protocol II, Arts 4, 5, 6; F Hampson, 'Detention, the "War on Terror" and International Law' in H Hense (ed), *The Law of Armed Conflict: Constraints on the Contemporary Use of Military Force* (Ashgate: Aldershot, 2005) 131–70, 150. For further analysis of the rules of detention see J Pejic, 'Procedural Principles and Safeguards for Internment/Administrative Detention in Armed Conflict and Other Situations of Violence' 858 *International Review of the Red Cross* 375 (2005).

[146] Sassoli, 'Transnational' n 23, *supra,* 20; J Pejic, 'Terrorist Acts and Groups: a Role for International Law?' 75 *British Year Book of International Law* 71 (2004) 83–4.

[147] See discussion of this in Ch 7, *infra*, in the sections on deprivation of liberty and derogation.

Part II—Conclusion

This Part has dealt with the question of whether IHL can be used to regulate extraterritorial forcible measures against non-state actors and some of the main difficulties involved in regulating the use of force against them in situations which may come under this legal regime. In certain circumstances, extraterritorial force against non-state actors could be occurring in the context of armed conflict. Whilst perhaps not fitting perfectly within the traditional models of international and non-international armed conflicts, the rules of applicability for the latter should be interpreted so as to cover extraterritorial conflicts with non-state actors. If, however, these interpretations are not favoured then extraterritorial operations would nonetheless have to pass a threshold of violence and have organized parties involved in order to qualify as armed conflicts. The rules that would apply to these conflicts would be largely modelled upon the same rules that apply to non-international armed conflicts through customary international law.

Regardless of choice of model, decisions on who can be targeted will depend on the highly debatable interpretation of the rules—primarily those on direct participation in hostilities and categorization of members of armed groups. The difficulty in agreeing on direct participation and whether there is an obligation to capture does, however, leave the door open for controversial and opposing interpretations. The conduct of military operations, whether large scale or smaller operations of special forces, must adhere to the rules on conduct of hostilities, including the principle of proportionality and the prohibition of perfidy both of which are at risk of violation in these operations. Despite the claims of new types of conflicts and the need for new rules it appears that the greatest progress would be achieved by reaching consensus in the debates and controversies surrounding the interpretation of the existing rules, as can be evidenced in the questions over status of individuals. Finally, it must be kept in mind, before applying these rules to extraterritorial operations, that all of the above rules can only apply if the circumstances can be defined as an armed conflict. Otherwise, the IHL framework and the various rules in this chapter do not apply.

PART III

INTERNATIONAL HUMAN RIGHTS LAW

Introduction

International human rights law and the rules of law enforcement contain rules and guidelines on the use of force by the state against the individual. These can be found in binding treaties, such as the International Covenant on Civil and Political Rights ('ICCPR') and the European Convention on Human Rights ('ECHR'),[1] which contain articles prohibiting arbitrary deprivation of liberty and of life. Further, and far more detailed, instruments such as the Basic Principles on the Use of Force and Firearms by Law Enforcement Officials[2] do not have the legal status of a binding treaty but, nevertheless, contain many widely accepted rules and guidelines and can often serve as an authoritative interpretation of the less detailed treaty rules. Some of the rules, both in the treaties and other instruments, may also have the status of customary international law. In addition, many of the UN human rights mechanisms operate outside of the treaty sphere and play an important role in both monitoring and standard-setting. The rules of international human rights law are, therefore, potentially of high relevance to any assessment of forcible measures.

In previous chapters, it was the fact that we are dealing with measures taken against non-state actors that attracted most of the attention and it was the status of these actors that led to some of the problems dealt with. This Part is different. International human rights law is, by definition, designed to regulate the relationship between the state and the individual and, therefore, the fact that we are dealing with measures against non-state actors does not pose a serious obstacle. There are, however, other issues which come to the fore and which must be scrutinized carefully in order to assess the relevance of international human rights law.

First and foremost is the issue of extraterritoriality. The question is whether, and in what circumstances, the obligations contained in international human rights law can extend to measures taken outside the recognized borders of the state. If they can it will be necessary to examine what are the precise criteria and tests to determine whether any, or all, types of forcible measures covered can

---

[1] International Covenant on Civil and Political Rights (16 December 1966) 999 UNTS 171, entry into force 23 March 1976; Convention for the Protection of Human Rights and Fundamental Freedoms (4 November 1950) 213 UNTS 222; 312 ETS 5, entered into force 3 September 1953, as amended by Protocols nos 3, 5, 8, and 11 which entered into force on 21 September 1970, 20 December 1971, 1 January 1990, and 1 November 1998 respectively.

[2] UN Basic Principles on the Use of Force and Firearms by Law Enforcement Officials UN Doc A/CONF.144/28/rev.1 at 112 (1990), adopted by the 8th United Nations Congress on the Prevention of Crime and the Treatment of Offenders, Havana, Cuba, 27 August–7 September 1990.

come under the protection of the umbrella of human rights law. The majority of attention will be devoted to this issue.

If it is found that human rights obligations can, in certain circumstances, extend extraterritorially then an additional topic must be addressed in this Part, namely, the bearing of the relationship between international human rights law and IHL upon the forcible measures we are covering. In particular, there is the question of what happens to the human rights obligations which might be found applicable if some of these forcible measures are taken in the context of an armed conflict. In these circumstances it may be that the applicability and interpretation of certain human rights obligations could be affected by the existence of an armed conflict and the ensuing applicability of IHL.

7

The Principal Practices and Primarily Affected Rights

Before delving into the particular questions surrounding the applicability of international human rights law to these operations it is necessary to point out which human rights might actually be affected and why, therefore, the findings on the applicability of human rights obligations could carry significant weight.

As noted at the start, the extraterritorial forcible measures used by states against individuals often include state agents (acting outside their own sovereign territory) being responsible for one or more of the following: lethal or potentially lethal force; ill-treatment of persons in their custody; abduction and deprivation of liberty. They will be examined here in turn as will the possibility of restricting or derogating from these rights. As in previous chapters, the intent is not to engage in an elaborate analysis of all possible facets, but rather to identify the primarily relevant rights and draw out the specific aspects applicable to the issues being considered. The real and hypothetical scenarios for extraterritorial actions in the process of which other rights may also be affected are potentially infinite. The analysis presented in this chapter can also be transposed to the examination of additional rights, as called for in the circumstances. The subsequent and lengthier Chapter 8 will be devoted not to specific rights, but rather to the analysis of extraterritorial obligations, which would be applicable to virtually any discussion of rights affected. The current chapter sets aside the question of extraterritorial obligations, which will be covered in detail later, in favour of first understanding the potential relevance of human rights law and how these norms can seek to regulate force against individuals.

 Killings

Should the state attempt to kill an individual this would clearly raise the question of whether there has been a violation of the right to life. This fundamental right is to be found in every major human rights instrument.[3] The starting point

[3] Universal Declaration of Human Rights, Resolution 217 A(III); UN Doc A/810 91, UN General Assembly, 1948, Art 3; ICCPR, Art 6; African Charter on Human and Peoples' Rights

beyond question is that the state may not wantonly attempt to take the life of the individual.[4]

The right to life creates obligations for all states, usually through more than one source of law. The vast majority of states are party to the ICCPR,[5] and to its formulation that '[e]very human being has the inherent right to life. This right shall be protected by law. No one shall be arbitrarily deprived of his life.'[6]

In addition, the regional human rights instruments of Africa, the Inter-American system, and Europe all add another source of an obligation binding upon the majority of states in these continents. Within the instruments allowing for derogation from certain obligations in times of emergency, no room is made for derogation from the right to life.[7] UN members are also subject to the scrutiny of the non-treaty procedures, such as the UN Special Rapporteur on extrajudicial, summary or arbitrary executions.

Moreover, the right to life has been declared to be one of the human rights holding the status of a rule of customary international law.[8] Accordingly, the right to life is a human rights obligation binding upon all states, regardless of whether they are party to any particular treaty.

As will be seen below, the right to life does not automatically adjudge all loss of life by state action as a violation of international law. The provisions on the right to life contain a prohibition, the essence of which is to forbid extra-judicial executions or arbitrary killings.[9] A recurring principle in international human rights law is that any restrictions, exceptions or other actions which are likely to cause harm to individuals must be regulated through law.[10] In addition to the characteristic of occurring outside any judicial process or framework of law the term 'arbitrary' can be understood to 'include elements of inappropriateness, injustice

('ACHPR') (26 June 1981) OAU Doc CAB/LEG/67/3 rev.5; 1520 UNTS 217; 21 ILM 58 (1982), entered into force 21 October 1986, Art 4; American Convention on Human Rights (ACHR), (22 November 1969) 1144 UNTS 123, entered into force 18 July 1978, Art 4; ECHR, Art 2.

[4] See sections, *infra*, for discussion of possible exceptions, including the death penalty, war, and law enforcement.

[5] 165 states as of September 2009. See <http://treaties.un.org/Pages/ViewDetails.aspx?src= TREATY&mtdsg_no=IV-4&chapter=4&lang=en>.

[6] ICCPR, Art 6.

[7] ICCPR, Art 4; other than the ECHR provision for lawful acts of war ECHR, Art 15; ACHR, Art 27.

[8] BG Ramcharan, 'The Concepts and Dimensions of the Right to Life' 1–32, 3, 14–15; WP Gormley, 'The Right to Life and the Rule of Non-Derogatability: Peremptory Norms of *Jus Cogens*' 120–159 both in Ramcharan (ed) *The Right to Life in International Law* (Martinus Nijhoff: Dordrecht, 1985); D Kretzmer, 'Targeted Killing of Suspected Terrorists: Extra-Judicial Executions or Legitimate Means of Defence?' 16 *EJIL* 171 (2005) 185. See analysis in N Melzer *Targeted Killing in International Law* (OUP: Oxford, 2008) 184–221. Indeed commentators have even found it to be a norm of *jus cogens*, a peremptory norm of international law from which states cannot deviate, although this may not have received the same level of confirmation by judicial or quasi–judicial bodies as has the torture prohibition n 60, *infra*.

[9] *Ibid.* See also N Rodley, *The Treatment of Prisoners under International Law* (OUP Oxford, 1999), 182–3.

[10] ICCPR, Arts 6.2, 9.1, 12.3, 13, 14.7, 18.3, 19.3, 21, 22.2.

and lack of predictability', as individuals cannot know whether their behaviour is likely to lead to a situation in which they would lose their life at the hands of the state.[11] Insofar as this describes situations in which state authorities engage in random killings or killings not regulated by existing laws, this notion of arbitrariness is not dissimilar to that of being extra-judicial. Domestic laws must provide a framework regulating the use of force, lethal or otherwise, and the legitimacy of the measures permitted will be determined by reference to internationally recognized principles on how the force is to be used.[12] Unnecessary or disproportionate force, even if based on an existing domestic legal provision, can be declared to violate international human rights law.[13]

Situations which in certain circumstances might not violate the prohibitions, can be summarized as including:

(i) The carrying out of a lawfully imposed death penalty (unless the state is party to an instrument forbidding this, such as the Second Optional Protocol to the ICCPR, or the ECHR).[14]

(ii) Killings taking place during an armed conflict and which are lawful under IHL.[15]

(iii) If the force used was necessary and proportionate, and lethal force was not a first option.[16]

As for the first of these exceptions, sending state agents into the territory of another state in order to seek out and kill an individual would not comply

---

[11] In the context of a case concerning detention, the UN Human Rights Committee stated 'that "arbitrariness" is not to be equated with "against the law", but must be interpreted more broadly to include elements of inappropriateness, injustice and lack of predictability.' See *Van Alphen v. Netherlands*, Comm no 305/1988, UN Doc CCPR/C/39/D/305/1988, 15 August 1990, para 5.8.

[12] UN Basic Principles on the Use of Force and Firearms by Law Enforcement Officials, n 2, *supra*; *UN Code of Conduct for Law Enforcement Officials*, GA res 34/169 annex, 34 UN GAOR Supp (no 46) at 186; UN Doc A/34/46 (1979); *McCann and ors v. United Kingdom*, 21 EHRR 97, paras 147–9; Rodley, n 9, *supra*, 182–8.

[13] *Guerrero v. Colombia*, Comm no R.11/45, (A/37/40); UN Doc Supp no 40, 137 (1982) paras 13.1–13.3. See *infra* for further explanation of necessity and proportionality.

[14] Art 6.2 of the ICCPR accepts certain countries ratifying the covenant may have laws allowing for the Death Penalty and that these laws can continue to be in place so long as they conform to the requirements in this, and following, paragraphs. States Party to the Second Optional Protocol to the ICCPR are prohibited from carrying out the death penalty. See Second Optional Protocol to the International Covenant on Civil and Political Rights, aiming at the abolition of the death penalty, (15 December 1989) UN Doc A/RES/44/128, entered into force 11 July 1991; Protocol no 6 of the ECHR is also aimed at abolishing the death penalty. See Protocol no 6 to the Convention for the Protection of Human Rights and Fundamental Freedoms concerning the abolition of the death penalty, Strasbourg, 28 April 1983; see also, n 17, *infra*.

[15] *Legality of the Threat or Use of Nuclear Weapons*, Advisory opinion, ICJ Rep, 8 July 1996, para 25; ECHR, Art 15.2. For further discussion see Ch 9, *infra*.

[16] See all sources, nn 12, 13, *supra*. See also discussion later in this section on proportionality under international human rights law, which is a different notion to proportionality as described in the previous chapters on IHL.

with the requirements of a lawfully imposed death penalty.[17] The second exception—armed conflict—rests on the precise circumstances and the interpretation given to the parallel application of international human rights law and IHL, and will be explored in a later chapter devoted to this. In addition to the IHL reasoning, the third exception might prima facie offer another justification for taking forcible measures against individuals. We are, however, looking here at cases in which the state sends its agents on a mission to take a life, ie setting out with the intention to use *lethal* force. Operations of this type are likely to be clandestine but there have been sufficient known cases as to conclude that this does happen. For example, Israel's decision to track down and kill those responsible for the murder of its athletes at the Munich Olympics was made at the highest levels of government, apparently with a special committee convened to approve the killings.[18] Other examples are the allegations that Russia has sent its agents abroad on missions to kill individuals on numerous occasions, with well-known examples ranging from the murder of Trotsky in Mexico City in 1940;[19] allegations of government involvement in the killing of the Chechen leader Yanderbiyev by a bomb in Qatar in 2004;[20] radioactive poisoning of a dissident in London;[21] and the announcement by President Putin that Russian special services had been ordered to track down and 'eliminate' the individuals who had killed Russian diplomats in Iraq.[22]

[17] While the ICCPR article on the right to life contains an exception for death penalties, these must conform to all the procedural requirements of a fair trial. Extraterritorial targeted killings are likely to violate any number of the guarantees, such as imposition of the death penalty without any trial; *in absentia* proceedings without allowing the individual to raise a defence; lack of opportunity for appeal or pardon. Furthermore, carrying out the execution outside of a monitored and controlled environment may well also result in the action violating the prohibition of torture and cruel, inhuman or degrading treatment or punishment. For the connection between all these guarantees and capital punishment, see for example: *Mbenge v. Zaire*, Comm no 16/1977, (A/38/40) UN Doc supp no 40, 134 (1983); *Ng v. Canada*, Comm no 469/1991, UN Doc CCPR/C/49/D/469/1991 (1994); 'Safeguards Guaranteeing Protection of the Rights of Those Facing the Death Penalty', ESC Res 1984/50, annex, 1984 UN ESCOR Supp no 1 at 33; UN Doc E/1984/84 (1984).

[18] This has been widely reported in media and literature, see, eg, L Beyer, 'The Myths and Reality of Munich', *Time Magazine*, 4 December 04 2005. In an interview with Zvi Zamir the former head of the Mossad, he would not confirm this: 'Q) And what about Committee X, the famous ministerial body that was informed about each proposed liquidation and acted as a kind of special court for executions? A) Who said there was a Committee X? Q) Was there no such body? A) I will not comment on that. I will say only that the whole issue of whom to strike at was given meticulous consideration and the probable consequences were evaluated.' in Y Melman, 'Preventive measures' *Haaretz*, 17 February 2006.

[19] 'Lev Davidovich Trotsky' in *Dictionary of Political Biography* (OUP: Oxford, 2003).

[20] Qatar arrested two Russian men (and one more who was released due to his diplomatic status) who were said to have confessed and named the senior officers who sent them. See D Ignatius, 'In Qatar, Standing Up to Putin' *Washington Post*, 16 March 2004.

[21] Official involvement was not proven, though allegations were made against a former KGB officer, and there was no trial in the UK, following Russia's refusal of a UK extradition request. See details in 'Timeline: Litvinenko death case' on *BBC News online* available at <http://news.bbc .co.uk/1/hi/uk/6179074.stm>.

[22] 'Russia "to kill Iraq kidnappers"' *BBC News*, 28 June 2006, available at <http://news.bbc .co.uk/1/hi/world/middle_east/5125416.stm>.

By and large, it is hard to envisage how this could be the only available option and therefore fulfil the requirement of necessity. Even had all other non-forcible measures, such as extradition requests, already been attempted the leap from non-forcible measures directly to sending agents on a mission to kill is likely to fail the tests of necessity and proportionality.[23] Although necessity and proportionality are often heard in tandem, the two principles are not one and the same. As noted by Rodley, in the context of the right to life, the 'concept of necessity applies only to the hierarchy of coercive measures in which lethal or potentially lethal force is reserved as a last resort. It is complemented by the rule of *proportionality*, which applies to the nature of the law enforcement objective.'[24]

The requirement of necessity refers to the range of options available to achieve a certain aim. In the context of human rights protections, it would mean that if the measures taken will result in a possible violation of a right, it must be shown that these measures were necessary in order to achieve the legitimate objective. Once a measure has been deemed necessary, it must still conform to the principle of proportionality which measures whether the harm caused is proportionate to the sought objective. For example, preventing an individual from driving away when the police officer is trying to issue a parking ticket is a legitimate objective. If the individual is about to speed away and is not at arm's length from the police officer, then using a firearm may be the only way in which the police officer can prevent the person from escaping. In that sense, use of the firearm may be necessary in order to achieve the objective. However, firing a lethal weapon at someone attempting to avoid a parking ticket can hardly be said to be proportionate.[25] For the use of lethal force to be considered a proportionate measure, its objective should be the prevention of a real threat to life, and outside the preservation of life, lethal force is likely to be disproportionate.[26]

One of the cases mentioned provides an interesting (in other words complex) test for applying these principles. The incident in which the US intentionally targeted and killed individuals driving a jeep through a remote area of Yemen raises the question of whether a drastic measure of this type could ever conform to the human rights principle protecting the right to life. At the outset, it should be acknowledged that one must also address the question of whether international human rights law is applicable to measures of this type which take place outside

[23] The case of the targeted killings by the US in Yemen, might raise certain challenges to this presupposition, and these will be explored below.

[24] Rodley, n 9, *supra*, 185.

[25] This is a based on a similar example presented by Rodley, *ibid*.

[26] According to principle 9 of the 'UN Basic Principles on the Use of Force and Firearms by Law Enforcement Officials', 'Law enforcement officials shall not use firearms against persons except in self-defence or defence of others against the imminent threat of death or serious injury, to prevent the perpetration of a particularly serious crime involving grave threat to life, to arrest a person presenting such a danger and resisting their authority, or to prevent his or her escape, and only when less extreme means are insufficient to achieve these objectives. In any event, intentional lethal use of firearms may only be made when strictly unavoidable in order to protect life'. See also Rodley, n 9, *supra*, 188.

the state's sovereign territory. This crucial aspect will occupy the next, extensive, chapter. At this juncture, however, we shall assume for the sake of this analysis, that international human rights law can apply to such situations. What we are currently concerned with, assuming that human rights law does apply, is whether this action was necessarily a violation or could there have been circumstances which rendered it lawful?

Briefly, the facts of the case as publicized are as follows.[27] On 3 November 2002, a US Predator drone launched a Hellfire missile at a target in Yemen. The target of the missile was a vehicle travelling on a desert road. In the vehicle, were Qaed Salim Sinan al-Harethi,[28] an alleged Al-Qaeda leader, and five of his associates. It was alleged that al-Harethi was responsible for previous attacks, such as the one on the USS Cole.

Much of the justification presented for this case was predicated on it being part of the 'war on terror'.[29] It is, therefore, necessary to deal with a preliminary question as to whether this action was taken as part of an ongoing armed conflict. Whether actions taken under the umbrella of the 'war on terror', but outside the battlefields of Afghanistan or Iraq, can be considered to be part of an armed conflict is a matter that was subjected to examination in Part II of this work. As concluded in that section, there are serious difficulties in accepting measures of this type as armed conflict and strong arguments not to do so.[30] It is, nevertheless, a subject of controversy which cannot therefore be dismissed out of hand. For the purposes of the current chapter, suffice it to say that if a measure of this type would be considered part of an armed conflict, one would have to examine whether the taking of life was in accordance with IHL.[31] This would involve examination of issues such as whether the individuals were civilians or combatants and, if civilians, whether they had lost their protection at the time this attack was carried out.[32] If, however, the circumstances of this case are considered to fall outside the realm of the laws of armed conflict, then the examination of their legality must be under international human rights law.[33]

For the act not to have violated the right to life as defined in the ICCPR, it needs to have been carried out in accordance with the law, not be arbitrary, and

[27] W Pincus, 'US Strike Kills Six in Al Qaeda' *Washington Post,* 5 November 2002; S Hersh 'Manhunt' *The New Yorker,* 23 December 2002; 'CIA "killed al-Qaeda suspects" in Yemen' *BBC News,* 5 November 2002, available at <http://news.bbc.co.uk/2/hi/middle_east/2402479.stm>.

[28] His name has also been reported as Abu Ali al-Harithi.

[29] Condoleezza Rice on *Fox News Sunday,* 10 November 2002, available at <http://www .foxnews.com/story/0,2933,69783,00.html>; D Johnston and D Sanger, 'Threats and Responses: Hunt for Suspects; Fatal Strike in Yemen Was Based on Rules Set Out by Bush' *New York Times,* 6 November 2002.

[30] See Ch 5, *supra.* See also the final chapter, *infra,* for discussion of the possibility that this operation could be part of the Afghanistan conflict.

[31] See Ch 9, *infra,* on the relationship between IHL and human rights.

[32] See Ch 6, *supra.*

[33] See further discussion of the applying both frameworks in the context of the Yemen case, in the Concluding Chapter, *infra.*

have been necessary and proportionate.[34] It does not seem to have been arbitrary in the sense that this was not wanton random killing, but rather a planned intentional attack against a specific individual, although it is questionable whether it was according to law. The question of whether the targeted killing of alleged terrorists in the 'war on terror' contravenes domestic US law, and in particular the Executive Order 12333 banning assassinations, has arguments pointing to opposing answers and is beyond the scope of the current work.[35] However, it should be noted that if this measure were found to fall foul of domestic US law then the effect of it not being regulated by law would likely lead to a finding that it violated the right to life under international human rights law.[36] There could also be implications of legality if the measure was unlawful in the context of the inter-state sphere and the use of force on the territory of another state.[37] If, however, we were to conclude that this killing was regulated by law then the next step would be to examine the specifics of the case, namely whether the force used was necessary and proportionate.

At first glance it can be difficult to accept that immediate resort to lethal force could be either necessary or proportionate. Indeed, when viewing this case through human rights and law enforcement rules, the prima facie assessment, and one which has been voiced by critics of the operation, is that the intentional killing without attempting to arrest or even use lesser force would amount to an extra-judicial execution.[38] However, in order to examine whether such an

---

[34] See nn 9–26, *supra*, and accompanying text. See also analysis by Melzer, which further details the requirements so as to specifically mention the need for the operation to be preventative rather than punitive, and more. Melzer, n 8, *supra*, 222–39.

[35] The official view seems to be that there was legal authority for the strike. See D Johnston and D Sanger, n 29, *supra*; W Pincus, 'Missile Strike Carried Out with Yemeni Cooperation—Official Says Operation Authorized Under Bush Finding' *Washington Post,* 6 November 2002; Condoleezza Rice, n 29, *supra*. For examples of a variety of views on the relevance of the Executive Order on Assassinations, see: A McDonald, 'Terrorism, Counter-terrorism and the Jus in Bello' in M Schmitt and G Beruto (eds) *Terrorism and International Law: Challenges and Responses* (International Institute of Humanitarian Law, 2002) 57–74, 66–7; S Murphy 'International Law, the United States, and the Non-military "War" against Terrorism' 14 *EJIL* 347 (2003) 363. See also H Parks, 'Memorandum of Law: Executive Order 12333 and Assassination' *Army Law* (December 1989) 4.

[36] See earlier nn 9–13, *supra*, and accompanying text.

[37] See discussion of the potential link as outlined in the context of abductions in section 3, *infra*, and with regard to the *Yemen Case* in the Concluding Chapter, *infra*.

[38] See comments by Swedish Foreign Minister at the time, Anna Lindh, describing it as a 'summary execution' in B Whitaker 'Killing probes the frontiers of robotics and legality' *The Guardian,* 6 November, 2002; M Sassoli, 'Use and Abuse of the Laws of War in the 'War on Terrorism',' *Law and Inequality: A Journal of Theory and Practice,* 22 (2004) 212–13; H Duffy, *The 'War on Terror' and the Framework of International Law* (CUP: Cambridge, 2005) 342–3; Report of the Special Rapporteur on the promotion and protection of human rights and fundamental freedoms while countering terroris, Martin Scheinin, Mission to the United States of America/Advance edited version/A/HRC/6/17/Add.3, 25 October 2007, para 42; A McDonald, n 35, *supra,* 57–74, 66–7; Amnesty International, 'Yemen/USA: Government Must Not Sanction Extra–Judicial Executions', 8 November 2002 available at <http://web.amnesty.org/library/Index/ENGAMR5 11682002?open&of=ENGUSA>. It is worth noting that the Amnesty statement left open the possibility that there may have been circumstances which would have made it lawful: 'If this was the

operation is necessarily and automatically unlawful, let us posit the most extreme scenario that might give some support to a claim that it was necessary and proportionate. Let us assume it were to emerge that the individuals in the jeep were on their way to carry out an imminent devastating attack on the lives of hundreds of civilians; that they were driving through a remote part of Yemen to which there was no quick access, not even for the security forces of Yemen; that it was, therefore, impossible to carry out a detention operation; that the only way to stop them was by a missile launched from a distance; that there was no other less lethal option of targeting the jeep; and that if they were not targeted at that moment then it would be impossible to find them again before they carry out the impending attack. In other words, let us assume that the only way to prevent them from carrying out an imminent devastating attack was by targeting them in that fashion and at that point in time. Presented in this fashion, it might theoretically be possible to claim that an action of this type could be legitimate under the rules of human rights law as outlined earlier.[39] In the oft-cited European case of *McCann*, the actual act of deliberate lethal fire by British soldiers which killed Irish Republican Army ('IRA') members in Gibraltar was itself not unlawful,[40] although violations were found as a result of the planning and earlier stages of the operation which could have prevented the killings. It is, therefore, possible that in similar circumstances, in which there would not have been violations at earlier stages and soldiers would have found themselves in the same situation, a decision to use lethal force to prevent individuals from detonating a bomb might not be unlawful under international human rights law.[41] The specific circumstances must be reviewed on a case by case basis before conclusions are reached and justification for such measures is unlikely to be found in any but the most rare and exceptional situations.

Parts of the above claims regarding the Yemen incident do not appear too far removed from the facts publicized—they may well have been travelling in a remote area and could not have been stopped by any other means. Indeed, this appears to be the position of the government of Yemen.[42] However, there were

---

deliberate killing of suspects in lieu of arrest, in circumstances in which they did not pose an immediate threat, the killings would be extra-judicial executions in violation of international human rights law'.

[39] See also the analysis of the potential possibility of making a similar claim, in J Pejic 'Terrorist Acts and Groups: a Role for International Law?' 75 *British Year Book of International Law* 71 (2004), 90–1.

[40] See n 12, *supra*, paras 199–200.

[41] See also discussion of 'shoot to kill' policies in the context of suicide bombers, in which it is stated that 'the immediate use of lethal force may be justified' but that this can only follow stringent legal and procedural safeguards and carries many risks, in Report of the Special Rapporteur on extrajudicial, summary or arbitrary executions, Philip Alston, UN Doc E/CN 4/2006/53, 8 March 2006, para 51.

[42] The government of Yemen later stated that 'it had made every effort to bring these accused persons to justice'. See Report of the Special Rapporteur, on extrajudicial, summary or arbitrary executions, Asma Jahangir Addendum, Summary of cases transmitted to Governments and replies

reports that the Yemeni authorities had been tracking the men for months and relaying the information to the US,[43] which raises the question of whether there might in fact have been many chances to attempt to detain, rather than using a lethal strike. The other primary problem lies in the first points raised above, namely the fact that it is unclear whether there was any evidence that they presented an imminent threat of such magnitude that killing them was a proportionate measure. One can imagine a reluctance on the part of the US to reveal intelligence sources so as to provide detailed evidence as to what the individuals might have been planning, but there would be little reason to prevent the US administration from stating that there was some kind of imminent threat averted by this action. In fact, from the little that can be adduced from the supporters of this strike it appears that the main reasoning was that Abu Ali al-Harithi was a senior Al-Qaeda figure who had been involved in past attacks such as the one against the USS Cole in which 17 US sailors were killed and, it was claimed, would continue to play an active role in future Al-Qaeda acts of violence.[44] Past actions cannot justify a killing outside the process of trial and punishment and as for prevention, unless it is claimed that there is evidence of a particular imminent threat, then the primary claim appears to be one based on membership in a terrorist organization. Under IHL membership of an armed group could, in certain circumstances and depending on interpretations of combatant status and loss of civilian protection,[45] form part of an argument for justifying a killing, but international human rights law does not make room for such a possibility.

It is, therefore, submitted that, subject to the known facts, this killing was not lawful under the terms of the right to life as it appears in the ICCPR. Two caveats must however be mentioned—first, the above analysis does not completely rule out the possibility that measures taken in different circumstances and with additional evidence might in extreme circumstances not fall foul of human rights law; secondly, that this specific case probably stands a better chance when examined through the framework of IHL, although if that is based on the vague notion of a general 'war on terror' then there are strong reasons not to accept that it was part of an armed conflict and, therefore, not subject to being legitimized by IHL.[46]

---

received, UN Doc. E/CN 4/2004/7/Add.1, 24 March 2004, para 612; see also government comments that this was the fruit of collaboration between the security forces of Yemen and the US, and a measure of last resort. Human Rights Committee, 'Summary record of the 2283rd meeting', UN Doc. CCPR/C/SR.2283, 18 July 2005, para 19 (translated from the original French).

[43] B Whitaker, n 38, *supra*. In fact, the US may have been jointly tracking Al-Harethi, as part of a joint intelligence team with the Yemenis. See S Hersh n 27, *supra*.

[44] Pincus, n 27, *supra*; BBC, n 27, *supra*. The Yemeni government did, however, contend that 'The group had allegedly planned new acts of terrorism against oil, economic and strategic installations that would have adversely affected the international standing of Yemen, as well as its political and economic interests and external relations with other States.' Report of the Special Rapporteur, *ibid*.

[45] See Ch 6, *supra*.   [46] See Ch 5, *supra*.

It may also be the case that, unlike the Yemen incident, there is not a prior decision to use lethal force, for example if the state agents open fire in response to coming under attack by armed individuals. In these circumstances, under international human rights law, the lawfulness of the force used by the state agents will depend on the tests described above, including necessity and proportionality. However, sending state agents on a mission to take the life of an individual, whether in close quarters or by remote weapons, is most likely going to be a violation of the individual's right to life. This is clear from the texts of the human rights instruments and from the case law of human rights bodies.[47] With regard to this right, the remaining questions are whether the extraterritorial aspect or the existence of an armed conflict modify or change the applicability or content of this obligation. These questions will be the topic of the following chapters.

2. Torture and other ill-treatment

The prohibition of torture is perhaps the strongest of all restrictions placed on states through international human rights law. Unlike the right to life, it entertains no possibility of exception, whether through principles of proportionality and necessity, or even in times of war. Whilst there is no denying that the phenomenon of torture has not been eradicated, the legal prohibition is unequivocal. Article 7 of the ICCPR states that '[n]o one shall be subjected to torture or to cruel, inhuman or degrading treatment or punishment.'[48]

The European,[49] Inter-American[50] and African[51] human rights instruments all contain equally strong prohibitions. The importance of this prohibition is evident from the fact that it is one of the few human rights issues to be the subject of a dedicated UN treaty—the Convention against Torture and Other Cruel, Inhuman or Degrading Treatment or Punishment ('CAT'),[52] as well as specific regional treaties.[53] Torture is also prohibited under the laws of armed conflict whether with regard to prisoners of war,[54] protected civilians[55] or persons

---

[47] See nn 3, 12, 16, 23–26, and accompanying text, *supra*.   [48] ICCPR, Art 7.

[49] ECHR, Art 3.   [50] IACHR, Art 5(2).   [51] African Charter, Art 5.

[52] Convention against Torture and Other Cruel, Inhuman or Degrading Treatment or Punishment, (10 December 1984) 1465 UNTS 85, entered into force 26 June 1987 ('CAT').

[53] European Convention for the Prevention of Torture and Inhuman or Degrading Treatment or Punishment, CPT/Inf/C (2002) 1 (Part 1)—Strasbourg, 26.XI.1987 (Text amended according to the provisions of Protocols no 1 (ETS No 151) and no 2 (ETS No 152) which entered into force on 1 March 2002); The Inter-American Convention to Prevent and Punish Torture, entered into force on February 28, 1987.

[54] Geneva Convention relative to the Treatment of Prisoners of War (12 August 1949) 75 UNTS 135, entered into force 21 October 1950, Arts 17, 87; Protocol Additional to the Geneva Conventions of 12 August 1949, and Relating to the Protection of Victims of International Armed Conflicts (Protocol I), (8 June 1977) 1125 UNTS 3, entered into force 7 December 1978, Art 75.

[55] Geneva Convention relative to the Protection of Civilian Persons in Time of War (12 August 1949) 75 UNTS 287, entered into force 21 October 1950, Art 32.

detained in non-international armed conflicts,[56] and violation of this may result in a Grave Breach[57]—a particularly serious violation of the Geneva Conventions carrying strong enforcement obligations. The International Criminal Court has recognized torture as a war crime both in international and non-international armed conflict,[58] and as a crime against humanity.[59] The prohibition of torture can be regarded as a *jus cogens* rule—a peremptory norm of international law.[60]

Torture is defined in CAT as:

any act by which severe pain or suffering, whether physical or mental, is intentionally inflicted on a person for such purposes as obtaining from him or a third person information or a confession, punishing him for an act he or a third person has committed or is suspected of having committed, or intimidating or coercing him or a third person, or for any reason based on discrimination of any kind, when such pain or suffering is inflicted by or at the instigation of or with the consent or acquiescence of a public official or other person acting in an official capacity. It does not include pain or suffering arising only from, inherent in or incidental to lawful sanctions.[61]

Accordingly, for an act to constitute torture it must involve the following:

(i) The intentional infliction of severe physical or mental pain or suffering;
(ii) perpetrated by, or with the consent or acquiescence, of state agents;
(iii) inflicted for a specific purpose, such as gaining information, punishment or intimidation.

Torture is one form of ill-treatment, while other forms prohibited in the instruments of international human rights law are cruel, inhuman or degrading treatment or punishment. Some of the case law appears to view cruel, inhuman or degrading treatment or punishment as distinguished from torture on the basis of the latter involving a higher level of pain and suffering.[62] There is, however, strong support, as evidenced in the analysis of the premier leading experts on

---

[56] Common Article 3 to Geneva Conventions I–IV, supra and ibid; Protocol Additional to the Geneva Conventions of 12 August 1949, and Relating to the Protection of Victims of Non–International Armed Conflicts (Protocol II) (8 June 1977), 1125 UNTS 609, entered into force 7 December 1978, Art 4.

[57] Geneva Convention III, n 54, supra, Art 130; Geneva Convention for the Amelioration of the Condition of the Wounded and Sick in Armed Forces in the Field (12 August 1949) 75 UNTS 31, entered into force 21 October 1950, Art 50; Geneva Convention for the Amelioration of the Condition of Wounded, Sick and Shipwrecked Members of Armed Forces at Sea, (12 August 1949) 75 UNTS 85, entered into force 21 October 1950, Art 52; Geneva Convention IV, n 55, *supra*, Art 147.

[58] Rome Statute of the International Criminal Court, UN Doc 2187 UNTS 90, entered into force July 1, 2002, Arts 8.2(a)(ii), 8.2(c)(i).

[59] '[W]hen committed as part of a widespread or systematic attack directed against any civilian population, with knowledge of the attack' ICC Statute, Art 7.1(f).

[60] *Prosecutor v. Furundzija*, Trial chamber, ICTY IT–95–17/1, 10 December, 1998, paras 153–7; *Al-Adsani v. UK*, ECtHR, App no 35763/97, 21 November 2001, paras 60–1; Rodley, n 9, *supra*, 74.

[61] CAT, Art 1.

[62] *Ireland v. United Kingdom*, ECtHR, App no 5310/71, 18 January 1978, paras 167–68.

this matter—the previous UN Special Rapporteur on Torture, Sir Nigel Rodley, and the current Rapporteur, Manfred Nowak—for the distinction between cruel, inhuman or degrading treatment or punishment and torture to be made primarily on the basis of whether the ill-treatment was for a specific purpose prohibited by Article 1 of CAT.[63] In other words, once the pain or suffering intentionally inflicted has crossed the threshold so as to become severe, if inflicted for such purposes as described in CAT, it then violates the prohibition of torture. If the individual is exposed to intentional severe pain or suffering but not for these purposes, then it is in the realm of cruel, inhuman or degrading treatment or punishment.

In addition to the 'classic' examples of torture such as electric shocks, examples of acts which have been determined as torture or other prohibited ill-treatment, include methods such as severe beatings;[64] mock executions and mock amputations;[65] sensory manipulation and deprivation, and forced positions causing severe pain;[66] rape and other sexual violence.[67]

Recent times have seen the absolute character of the prohibition of torture being challenged in a number of ways. Whilst a detailed examination of such challenges is beyond the scope of this work, elements of these debates are occurring within the context of situations discussed therein. In a series of, now well publicized, documents,[68] the US administration contemplated, and at times attempted to redraw, the definitions of torture so as to allow for acts which would appear to be clearly prohibited under prevailing international law. Thus, for instance, in a memorandum later rescinded it was suggested that for an act to constitute torture, '[t]he victim must experience intense pain or suffering of the kind that is equivalent to the pain that would be associated with serious physical injury so severe that death, organ failure, or permanent damage

---

[63] N Rodley, 'The Definition(s) of Torture in International Law' in M Freeman (ed.), *Current Legal Problems 2002*, vol 55, 467–93 (OUP: Oxford, 2003); M Nowak, 'What Practices Constitute Torture?: US and UN Standards' 28 *Human Rights Quarterly* 809 (2006) 830–32.

[64] *Selmouni v. France*, ECtHR, App no 25803/94, 28 July 1999, paras 98–106.

[65] *Estrella v. Uruguay*, HRC Comm no 74/1980 (A/38/40) 17 July 1980 (1983), paras 1(6), 8(3), 10; *Mutabe v Zaire*, HRC Comm no 1244/19820 (A/39/40) 24 July 1984 (1984), para 10.2.

[66] 'Report of the Committee against Torture', General Assembly, Official Records, 52nd Session, Supp no 44 (A/52/44), paras 257–260; *Ireland v. UK*, Report of the Commission, 25 January 1976, Yearbook 792; *Ireland v. UK*, n 62, *supra*, paras 165–8; The Commission and the Court decisions were at odds whether the techniques under discussion constituted inhuman and degrading treatment or also torture, with the Court being of the opinion that it did not amount to torture on account of the threshold of severity between the concepts—however see nn 61, 62, 63 and accompanying text; 'Report of the Committee against Torture', A/56/44, 12 October 2001, para 186.

[67] *Aydin v. Turkey*, ECtHR, App no 23178/94, 25 September 1997, paras 80–8; *Furundzija*, n 60, *supra*, paras 264–9.

[68] K Greenberg and J Dratel, *The Torture Papers: The Road to Abu Ghraib* (CUP: New York, 2005); M Danner, *Torture and Truth* (Granta: London, 2005); J Jaffer and A Singh, *Administration of Torture: A Documentary Record from Washington to Abu Ghraib and Beyond* (Columbia University Press, 2007).

resulting in a loss of significant body function will likely result'.[69] A variety of specific techniques were proposed and examined by legal counsel. One particular memorandum from the Department of Justice to the CIA, approves the following: '(l) attention grasp, (2) walling, (3) facial hold, (4) facial slap (insult slap), (5) cramped confinement, (6) wall standing, (7) stress positions, (8) sleep deprivation, (9) insects placed in a confinement box, and (10) the waterboard'.[70] The latter technique involves the application of water to a cloth placed over an individual's face while s/he is tied to an inclined bench, in order to produce the perception of suffocation and drowning. 'Waterboarding' has come to epitomize the risk of sliding away from the torture prohibition back to the medieval torture racks. Whilst its legality was argued and its use sanctioned,[71] the subsequent US Administration revoked the authorization and the new President declared the practice to be torture.[72] Other techniques mentioned in the above memorandum, notably stress positions, wall standing and sleep deprivation, had previously arisen in legal cases concerning the practices of Israel and the UK.[73] The legitimacy of debating the use of questionable practices, some of which violate international law, has at times been facilitated by avoiding the term 'torture' in favour of euphemisms such as 'moderate physical pressure',[74] 'increased pressure phase'[75] and 'enhanced interrogation techniques'.[76]

Additional controversies over torture include the often mentioned 'ticking bomb' scenario[77] which has been at the centre of further debates in which suggestions have been made for authorization of torture, for example in the form

---

[69] 'Assistant Attorney General Jay Bybee Memo to Alberto Gonzales, Counsel to the President, August 1, 2002, Re: Standards of Conduct for Interrogation under 18 U.S.C.' reprinted in Greenberg and Dratel, *ibid*, 172–217, 183.

[70] Assistant Attorney General Jay Bybee Memo to John Rizzo, Acting General Counsel of the Central Intelligence Agency, August 1, 2002.

[71] 'CIA admit "waterboarding" al-Qaida suspects' *The Guardian*, 5 February 2008.

[72] Executive Order 13491 of 22 January 2009, *Federal Register*, vol 74, no 16, 27 January 2009; News Conference by the President, 29 April 2009, The White House, Office of the Press Secretary, 30 April 2009.

[73] *Ireland v. United Kingdom*, n 62, *ibid*; *The Public Committee Against Torture in Israel and ors v. the Government of Israel*, HCJ 5100/94, 53(4) P.D. 817 (1999).

[74] *PCATI v. Israel, ibid*.   [75] Bybee Memo, n 70, *supra*.

[76] CIA Office of Inspector General's Counterterrorism Detention and Interrogation Activities Report, 7 May 2004, 29–30, available at <http://www.aclu.org/human-rights_national-security/cia-office-inspector-generals-may-2004-counterterrorism-detention-and>.

[77] The essence of the debate surrounds the question of whether it would be legitimate to employ torture in order to extract information that would prevent an imminent devastating attack. For detailed examination see Y Ginbar, *Why Not Torture Terrorists? Moral, Practical and Legal Aspects of the 'Ticking Bomb' Justification for Torture* (OUP: Oxford, 2008); *Defusing the Ticking Bomb Scenario*, Association for the Prevention of Torture, 2007; H Shue, 'Torture in Dreamland: Disposing of the Ticking Bomb' 37 *Case Western Reserve Journal of International Law* 231 (2005); A Dershowitz 'Tortured Reasoning' in S Levinson (ed) *Torture* (OUP: Oxford, 2004) 257–80; O Gross 'Are Torture Warrants Warranted? Pragmatic Absolutism and Official Disobedience' 88 *Minnesota Law Review* 1481 (2004).

of 'torture warrants' for specific circumstances.[78] While strong arguments have been provided in defence against these challenges,[79] the practice of states raises concern that the torture prohibition is not perceived to be as absolute as some might hope.

One of the areas of concern which seems to have evolved in recent years, and is presented as a major problem, is the phenomenon of 'outsourcing' torture and colluding or turning a blind eye to its practice. In some instances this refers to the handing over of individuals to other countries, in the knowledge that they may be tortured there, and information handed back without the state agents having soiled their own hands.[80] Linked to this is the issue of using evidence which may have been gained through torture elsewhere. Of particular concern in the context of extraterritorial force is the matter of relocating the torture, whereby the individual is held outside state borders in a facility that is either controlled by an outside state or the territorial state, and in which agents of the outside state take part in the ill-treatment of the prisoner often in the context of abusive interrogation techniques.[81] In both these cases, the detention is often unacknowledged, which makes the individual even more vulnerable to such ill-treatment.[82]

The prohibition of torture is among the strongest that exist in human rights law, and the use of torture is legally and morally repeatedly condemned. Nonetheless, the debates over its precise definition and the concerns over indirect collusion with the practice, have contributed to an ongoing fraying at the edges of the prohibition and present a grave risk to protecting its inviolability.

3. Abductions and liberty and security of person

The essence of abduction operations is to apprehend an individual and usually whisk him/her away for interrogation and/or trial, back to the territory of the state which sent the agents or any other territory in which they are able to continue the next stage of the plan. As such, the human right most directly affected is the right to liberty. Despite this right being contained in all major human rights

[78] Dershowitz, *ibid*; A Dershowitz, 'The Torture Warrant: a Response to Professor Strauss' 48 *New York Law School Law Review* 275 (2004); Gross, *ibid*; R Posner, 'Torture, Terrorism, and Interrogation' in Levinson, *ibid*, 291–8.

[79] N Rodley, 'The Prohibition of Torture: Absolute Means Absolute' 34 *Denver Journal of International Law and Policy* 145 (2006); Rodley, n 9, *supra*; Shue, n 77, *supra*; Nowak, n 63, *supra*.

[80] D Priest and B Gellman, 'U.S. Decries Abuse but Defends Interrogations' *Washington Post* 26 December 2002; D Van Natta Jr, 'Questioning Terror Suspects in a Dark and Surreal World' *New York Times*, 9 March 2003.

[81] D Priest, 'CIA Holds Terror Suspects in Secret Prisons: Debate Is Growing Within Agency About Legality and Morality of Overseas System Set Up After 9/11' *Washington Post*, 2 November 2005; Van Natta, *ibid;* Human Rights First, *Ending Secret Detentions*, June 2004, available at <http://www.humanrightsfirst.org/us_law/PDF/EndingSecretDetentions_web.pdf>.

[82] See n 104, *infra*.

instruments, unlike the deprivation of life, intentional deprivation of liberty is an act commonly and frequently undertaken by states every time a person is detained or arrested. Close reading is, therefore, required in order to determine what it is exactly that is prohibited. Article 9 of the ICCPR sets out the underlying principle, '[e]veryone has the right to liberty and security of person. No one shall be subjected to arbitrary arrest or detention. No one shall be deprived of his liberty except on such grounds and in accordance with such procedure as are established by law.'

The African and Inter-American treaties contain similar provisions,[83] while the European Convention on Human Rights goes a step further and lays down the precise exceptions that may be permitted. Most of these involve arrest or detention, either following the decision of a competent court, or in order to bring an individual before a legal authority.[84] Depriving a person of their liberty not in accordance with these exceptions is likely to be considered an arbitrary deprivation of liberty and, therefore, unlawful. As with the right to life, a primary qualification is that any deprivation of liberty must be in accordance with law, and not be arbitrary.[85]

The right to freedom from arbitrary detention is not only to be found in all major treaties, but can also be considered one of the human rights that have acquired the status of customary international law.[86]

Three major issues arise from abduction operations, and they are, in chronological order:

(i) Whether there has been a breach of international law due to the violation of the sovereignty of another state;

(ii) whether there has been a violation of international human rights law with regard to the individual abducted;[87]

(iii) whether the act of abduction affects the legality of any ensuing trial taking place once the person is returned to the abducting state.

Although the first issue was dealt with in the earlier chapter on the inter-state relationship, as will be seen shortly, it retains a certain relevance to the analysis in this chapter. The third issue is a hotly debated one, and the subject of much case law and commentary, but concerns a question that falls outside the scope of

---

[83] ACHPR, Art 6; ACHR, Art 7.   [84] ECHR, Art 5.

[85] See discussion above on explanation of these concepts, nn 9–13, *supra*, and accompanying text.

[86] R Lillich 'The Growing Importance of Customary International Human Rights Law' 25 *Georgia Journal of International and Comparative Law* 1, 5–6; Restatement (Third) of the Foreign Relations Law of the United States, section 702, 1987 (referring to 'prolonged arbitrary detention'); 'No principle of international law is more fundamental than the concept that human beings should be free from arbitrary imprisonment' in *Rodriguiz-Fernandez v. Wilkinson*, 654 F.2d 1382 (10th Cir. 1981); Human Rights Committee, General Comment 24 (52), UN Doc CCPR/C/21/Rev.1/Add.6 (1994), para 8.

[87] Including a wide array of issues surrounding the abduction itself and other affected rights. See n 102–105, *infra*, and accompanying text.

a work dealing with legality of the extraterritorial measures themselves.[88] It is the second issue above that is of primary concern in this chapter.

One of the main questions is whether the extraterritorial abduction of an individual is 'arbitrary' or whether it can be considered to fall within the allowed exceptions. According to Higgins:

> From the perspective of an individual, his forcible detention and removal (whether or not from one jurisdiction to another, whether or not to stand trial) violate his human rights, in that everyone is entitled to security of the person and only to be restrained in accordance with due process.[89]

But could such an abduction nevertheless somehow fall within the permitted restrictions of liberty? A number of reasons suggest that such abductions are in most cases unlawful, although not necessarily in all.

It is worth recalling from an earlier chapter that enforcement measures of this kind,[90] taken without consent in the territory of another state, will in most cases be a violation of the sovereignty of the territorial state and, therefore, unlawful (unless the abduction took place on the high seas[91]). On the one hand, the inter-state relationship is a separate issue from the one relating to potential violations of the individual's rights, with which we are presently concerned.[92] On the other hand, this matter can in one respect actually affect the determination of a human rights violation: for the deprivation of liberty to be lawful under international human rights law, the act must take place in accordance with the law.[93] The governing principle is that a state's enforcement jurisdiction does not generally extend to carrying out extraterritorial enforcement measures in the territory of another state without consent,[94] even if there had originally been a domestic arrest warrant. Therefore, once the enforcement takes place extraterritorially in a manner that violates international law with regard to sovereignty, the illegality of the measure might permeate the human rights obligation and affect the determination of a violation of the right to liberty, in that it can be claimed that the deprivation of liberty was not in accordance with the law.[95] This point rests

---

[88] For discussion of these issues see amongst others J Paust, 'After Alvarez–Machain: Abduction, Standing, Denials of Justice, and Unaddressed Human Rights Claims' 67 *Saint John's Law Review* 551 (1993); M Shaw *International Law* (CUP: Cambridge, 2003) 604–07; M Feinrider, 'Kidnapping' in *Encyclopedia of Public International Law. vol III*, (Elsevier Science: Netherlands, 1997) 79–84.

[89] R Higgins, *Problems and Process: International Law and How We Use It* (Clarendon Press: Oxford, 1994) 70. See also Shaw, 'of course, any such apprehension would constitute a violation of the human rights of the person concerned': M Shaw, *ibid*, 605.

[90] See Part I, Chs 1 and 3, *supra*.

[91] Eg, in the case of *United States v. Yunis* 924 F. 2d 1086 (DC Cir. 1991).

[92] See more on this in Ch 8, *infra*, and text accompanying nn 78–80, 98–106.

[93] As seen in the treaty provisions above.

[94] I Brownlie, *Principles of Public International Law* (OUP: Oxford, 2003) 306 and see Ch 3, *supra*.

[95] *Ocalan v. Turkey*, App no 46221/99, 12 May 2005, para 85; though see *Stocke v. Germany*, App no 11755/85 (A/199), 12 October 1989, opinion of the Commission at para 162.

on the possibility of interpreting the requirement for lawfulness of an arrest to include international lawfulness as well as domestic lawfulness.

In a case which came before the UN Human Rights Committee, a Russian national (Mr Domukovsky) and a Georgian national (Mr Gelbakhiani) were abducted in Azerbaijan by Georgian agents, and taken back to Georgia for trial.[96] Georgia stated to the Committee that the arrests were based on warrants issued in Georgia, and that there was an agreement with Azerbaijan to allow for the arrests to take place.[97] The Committee was, however, not presented with evidence of any such agreement with Azerbaijan (and in fact counsel for the applicants submitted a letter from the Azerbaijani government indicating they had no knowledge of the arrests[98]), and therefore found that Georgia was responsible for an unlawful arrest, in violation of Article 9.1 of the ICCPR.[99] It should further be noted that whilst lack of consent by the territorial state might, as seen in *Domukovsky*, affect the legality of the arrest, this does not mean that existence of consent necessarily means that an arrest would be lawful. There are other factors which, as seen below, can affect the determination of legality.

Had consent from the territorial state been obtained, the unlawful encroachment upon the sovereignty of another state and the ensuing aspect of potential illegality on account of the inter-state relationship will have been avoided. If, in these circumstances, the abduction is carried out after a decision for the action is taken by a competent legal body from the outside state, would this still necessarily violate the human rights of the individual? In this case it is the due process aspect of the right that remains of primary concern.[100] Theoretically, it is possible to presuppose the existence of a process in which a matter is investigated, an arrest warrant issued, and an extraterritorial abduction ensues, and that the only difference between this and a 'regular' arrest made within the territory of the state is the fact that the person was detained outside the state borders. Should this be taking place with consent of the territorial state or on the high seas, and not in breach of the state's jurisdictional enforcement competence, there is a possibility that such an extraterritorial arrest might be lawful. For instance, whilst finding various other violations in the case, the European Court of Human Rights did not find any violation by virtue of the actual act of arrest of Ocalan by Turkish authorities in Kenya.[101] Nevertheless, it may well be the case that the specific means of abduction might involve disproportionate use of force; ill-treatment; inability to challenge lawfulness of detention; or that the relevant decisions were

---

[96] *Domukovsky and ors v. Georgia*, Comm no 626/1995, UN Doc CCPR/C/62/D/626/1995CCPR/C/62/D/626/1995, 29 May 1998.

[97] *Ibid*, paras 10.3 and 14.3.   [98] *Ibid*, para 11.1.

[99] *Ibid*, para 18.2. There is also the view that case indicates that arrests must be lawful under the laws of both state of the agents, and the territorial state. See S Joseph, J Schultz, and M Castan, *The International Covenant on Civil and Political Rights: Cases, Materials, and Commentary* (OUP: Oxford 2004) 309.

[100] Higgins, n 89, *supra*.   [101] *Ocalan*, n 95, *supra*, paras 92, 95–99.

not taken by the competent legal authorities—these are matters that will have to be determined on a case-by-case basis.

When scrutinizing a particular case of abduction there is a need to look out for the possibility of a number of additional violations. First, within the right to liberty and security, there are certain procedural requirements fundamental to the legality of any act of detention. The person detained must be informed of the reasons for the arrest—according to the ICCPR this should be at the time of arrest, and according to the ECHR it should be promptly.[102] Any person detained should be brought promptly before a judge (or other officer authorized by law).[103] The detention must be acknowledged and secret detentions run a risk of also violating the prohibition on disappearances.[104] The detained person must be treated humanely and be free from torture or cruel, inhuman or degrading treatment or punishment.[105] The abduction of Mordechai Vanunu, the nuclear programme secrets whistleblower, by Israeli agents in Italy, is an example of a case which appears to violate some of these rules. As reported by the media,[106] Vanunu was lured on false pretences by a female agent to fly from London to Rome.[107] After entering an apartment in Rome Vanunu was grabbed by Israeli agents, injected with a drug, and transported to Israel in a crate on board a ship. Clearly a number of the above rules on procedures of detention and ill-treatment appear to have been violated in the process of his abduction. Violations of this type would have rendered the abduction unlawful, whether or not Italy had consented to the Israeli operation.[108]

Finally, it should be noted that in certain cases, the deprivation of liberty might occur in the context of an armed conflict. If so, the rules of IHL will have to be consulted but, as noted in Chapter 6 of this work, there are situations in which IHL—despite being applicable—does not provide rules for the legitimate grounds of detention.[109] In these situations the detention might take the form of administrative detention of individuals on security grounds, which could be lawful under international human rights law. However, even if this occurs in the

---

[102] ICCPR, Art 9; ECHR, Art 5; ACHR, Art 7.   [103] *Ibid.*

[104] Of particular concern is the link between secret detention and torture. Human Rights Committee, General Comment no 20, Article 7, UN Doc HRI/GEN/1/Rev.1 at 30 (1994) para 11; International Convention for the Protection of All Persons from Enforced Disappearance, GA Res 61/177; UN Doc A/RES/61/177 (2006), adopted 20 December 2006. See detailed analysis of the relevant case law in Association for the Prevention of Torture, 'Incommunicado, Unacknowledged and Secret Detention Under International Law', 2006.

[105] ICCPR, Arts 7, 10; ECHR, Art 3; ACHR, Art 5; ACHPR, Art 5.

[106] For instance, see Y Melman, 'Capturing nuclear whistle-blower was "a lucky stroke" agents recall', *Haartez*, 21 April 2004.

[107] There was a decision not to kidnap him in London, so as not to strain the relationship between Britain and Israel, *ibid.*

[108] It appears that the Italian government had not approved this operation. 'Vanunu left Heathrow under his own name' *Sunday Times*, 28 December 1986.

[109] Ch 6, n 145, *supra.*

context of armed conflict it must not be arbitrary and,[110] as will be seen in the following section, there may be a need for derogation.

4. Derogation

Other than the prohibitions of torture and slavery, most human rights obligations contain elements of potential restrictions or exceptions. In addition to the derogation regime, which will be explained below, the non-absoluteness of rights can take a number of different forms:

- Some rights have the possibility of restriction built into the formulation of the right, such as the freedom of movement under the ICCPR, which allows for restriction on a number of grounds, including national security and public health.[111]

- Other rights, while not including an inbuilt formalization of legitimate grounds for restriction do, nevertheless, contain a description of specific types of actions that may be viewed as legitimate exceptions to the right. Thus, for instance, the right to life does not contain the possibility to restrict it on a list of general grounds, as seen in freedom of movement, but the ICCPR accepts that under certain conditions the death penalty would not violate the right to life,[112] and the ECHR lists further specific circumstances in which the taking of life might not contravene the legal obligation.[113]

- Moreover, when the language in which a right is formulated includes the term 'arbitrary', this further points to the fact that the freedom under discussion might not be absolute. This, for example, is the case with the right to liberty under the ICCPR which, as seen earlier,[114] is protected through the prohibition of *arbitrary* deprivation of liberty thus allowing for the possibility that the state may need to hold people in custody and can enact laws and procedures to allow for this.

All these formulations, while leading to possible restrictions and exceptions, are subject to strict requirements of necessity as defined within the rights,[115] and/or limited to the strict exceptions detailed in the provisions. An additional

---

[110] See discussion of arbitrariness throughout this section, and section 1, *supra*, on killings, n 7–11, and accompanying text; see also Ch 6, n 144, *supra*; see section 4, *infra*, for prohibition of arbitrary detention following a derogation.

[111] ICCPR, Art 12.3, 'The above-mentioned rights shall not be subject to any restrictions except those which are provided by law, are necessary to protect national security, public order (order public), public health or morals or the rights and freedoms of others, and are consistent with the other rights recognized in the present Covenant'.

[112] ICCPR, Art 6, nn 14, 17, *supra*, and accompanying text.   [113] ECHR, Art 2.

[114] See section 3, *supra*, on abductions and deprivation of liberty.

[115] Eg in ICCPR, Art 12, n 111, *supra*.

possibility comes in the form of reservations to treaties through which states signal in advance that they will be interpreting a right in a restrictive manner, or even not accepting a certain element of an obligation.[116]

A separate matter from the above is the mechanism of derogation. As described by Gross and Ni Aolain, derogation is 'the legally mandated authority of States to allow suspension of certain individual rights in exceptional circumstances of emergency or war'.[117] Article 4 of the ICCPR, Article 15 of the ECHR, and Article 27 of the ACHR, all set out the conditions for derogation. All Articles share some common features:

- There must be a serious public emergency. The European and American Conventions clearly mention war as an example of such emergency, whilst the ICCPR speaks of an emergency threatening the life of the nation. The precise definition of situations which allow for derogation is not entirely clarified, but it would appear to require an element of gravity of the situation, as is clear from the treaty references to war and threats to the life of the nation, in addition to the fact that by nature it is a regime of exception, and thus is not meant to be invoked to justify long-term restrictions outside of the limited state of emergency.[118] Moreover, the reference to war indicates that the context of the emergency may have an extraterritorial element.[119]

- The measures taken must be 'strictly required by the exigencies of the situation'.[120] According to the Human Rights Committee:

  This requirement relates to the duration, geographical coverage and material scope of the state of emergency and any measures of derogation resorted to because of the emergency. Derogation from some Covenant obligations in emergency situations is clearly distinct from restrictions or limitations allowed even in normal times under several provisions of the Covenant. Nevertheless, the obligation to limit any derogations to those strictly required by the exigencies of the situation reflects the principle of proportionality which is common to derogation and limitation

---

[116] The notion of reservations to human rights treaties raises complex problems of determining compatibility of reservations with the object and purpose of a treaty, as well as the validity of certain reservations and the repercussions of invalid reservations. See F Hampson, 'Reservations to Human Rights Treaties,' working paper submitted to the Commission on Human Rights pursuant to Sub–Commission decision 1998–113, E/CN 4/Sub.2/199/28; R Goodman, 'Invalid Reservations and State Consent' 96 *AJIL* 531 (2002); K Korekelia, 'New Challenges to the Regime of Reservations under the International Covenant on Civil and Political Rights' 13 *EJIL* 437 (2002).

[117] O Gross and F Ni Aolain, *Law in Times of Crisis* (CUP: Cambridge 2006) 257.

[118] Art 27 of the American Convention limits derogations to 'the period of time strictly required by the exigencies of the situation', and the Human Rights Committee also mention duration in General Comment no 29, n 121, *infra*.

[119] In the case of the ECHR in 1950, this is likely to have referred to international conflict. A problem, outside the scope of this work, arises over the question of derogation with regard to peace support operations, or when assisting another state with its own emergency, in which the nature of the emergency does not actually threaten the state taking the action.

[120] ICCPR, Art 4; ECHR, Art 15; IACHR, Art 27.

powers.[121]... [and]... This condition requires that States parties provide careful justification not only for their decision to proclaim a state of emergency but also for any specific measures based on such a proclamation. If States purport to invoke the right to derogate from the Covenant during, for instance, a natural catastrophe, a mass demonstration including instances of violence, or a major industrial accident, they must be able to justify not only that such a situation constitutes a threat to the life of the nation, but also that all their measures derogating from the Covenant are strictly required by the exigencies of the situation.[122]

- Procedural requirements also exist, under which the state must make a formal notification of the exact provisions from which it is derogating, and the reasons necessitating this measure.[123]

- Even in such times as derogation is allowed, there are certain rights from which it cannot be derogated. These rights are clearly defined in the derogation Articles of the Conventions.[124]

In relation to the issues of concern in this chapter, the prohibition of torture and other-ill-treatment, as well as the right to life, are amongst the list of nonderogable rights. With regards to torture and other ill-treatment, as this right does not have any inbuilt restrictions or exceptions, the non-derogabilty renders it as absolute as can be and under international law this right cannot be violated even in emergency or war. The right to life is also listed as a non-derogable right but, as noted earlier, the formulation of this right is different to that of torture as it allows for certain exceptions, such as deprivation of life occurring in the context of necessary and proportionate force in a law enforcement operation, or killings occurring during armed conflict and in accordance with the laws of armed conflict.[125] The right to liberty—the other primary right mentioned in this chapter—is, however, not included in the list of non-derogable rights as they appear in the Conventions, and indeed states have on occasion formally derogated from their obligations to this right.[126]

As noted earlier,[127] in the context of conflict and emergencies, recourse might be had to administrative detention for security reasons, in which an individual

---

[121] Human Rights Committee, General Comment no 29, States of Emergency (Article 4) UN Doc CCPR/C/21/Rev.1/Add.11 (2001) para 4.

[122] *Ibid* para 5.　　　[123] ICCPR, Art 4, para 3; ECHR, Art 15, para 3; ACHR, Art 27, para 3.

[124] Although certain rights appear as non-derogable in some treaties but not in others.

[125] The ECHR provision is formulated differently, in that the non-derogability of the right to life is 'except in respect of deaths resulting from lawful acts of war'. On the right to life during armed conflict, see Ch 9, *infra*, on human rights and IHL.

[126] Israel has entered a derogation from Art 9 in relation to the claim of emergency stretching back from the day of establishment of the State; the UK has derogated from Art 9 on a number of occasions in relation to Northern Ireland, and following the attacks of 11 September 2001. Other states that have entered Art 9 derogations at times include Algeria, Argentina, Azerbaijan, Bolivia, Chile, Colombia, Ecuador, Namibia, Nicaragua, Peru, Poland, Russia, Sri Lanka, Trinidad and Tobago, and Venezuela. Details are available in the United Nations Treaty Collection, at <http://treaties.un.org/Pages/ViewDetails.aspx?src=TREATY&mtdsg_no=IV-4&chapter=4&lang=en>.

[127] See nn 109, 110, *supra*, and accompanying text.

is held by executive decision and without criminal charge.[128] Since the ICCPR does not seem to explicitly rule out the possibility, and since it could be lawful under IHL,[129] it is unclear whether states need to derogate from the ICCPR when taking this measure.[130] Unlike the ICCPR the list of permitted grounds for detention under the ECHR[131]—which does not include administrative detention of this type—appears to lead to the need to derogate when taking this measure.[132]

The possibility of derogation does not allow unfettered discretion in denying all elements of this right even in times of emergency. As noted earlier, derogations are subject to necessity and proportionality and measures taken must, therefore, conform to these principles and meet the treaty demand of being 'strictly required by the exigencies of the situation'.[133] The Human Rights Committee, noted in its General Comment on States of Emergency that 'the mere fact that a permissible derogation from a specific provision may, of itself, be justified by the exigencies of the situation does not obviate the requirement that specific measures taken pursuant to the derogation must also be shown to be required by the exigencies of the situation.'[134]

Furthermore, there is the possibility that some rights, or specific elements of rights, which do not appear in the list of non-derogable ones may, nevertheless, not be derogated from. This is a proposition which cannot be hastily advanced without careful consideration since the list of derogable rights was debated during the drafting of the ICCPR and suggestions for inclusion of certain rights

---

[128] See discussion in J Pejic, 'Procedural Principles and Safeguards for Internment/Administrative Detention in Armed Conflict and Other Situations of Violence' 858 *International Review of the Red Cross* 375 (2005) 375–6.

[129] Ch 6, n 143, *supra*; See also Ch 9, *infra*, on the relationship between IHL and human rights law.

[130] Hampson notes that the 'The reservation made by India at the time of ratification and the derogation of the UK may imply that administrative detention is thought to be not normally lawful.' See F Hampson, 'Detention, the "War on Terror" and International Law' in H Hensel (ed) *The Law of Armed Conflict: Constraints on the Contemporary Use of Military Force* (Ashgate: Aldershot, 2005) 131–70, 143.

[131] The following are the permitted grounds under the ECHR: 'a person after conviction by a competent court'; 'for non-compliance with the lawful order of a court or in order to secure the fulfilment of any obligation prescribed by law'; 'for the purpose of bringing him before the competent legal authority on reasonable suspicion of having committed an offence or when it is reasonably considered necessary to prevent his committing an offence or fleeing after having done so'; 'detention of a minor by lawful order for the purpose of educational supervision or his lawful detention for the purpose of bringing him before the competent legal authority; detention of persons for the prevention of the spreading of infectious diseases, of persons of unsound mind, alcoholics or drug addicts or vagrants'; 'to prevent his effecting an unauthorised entry into the country or of a person against whom action is being taken with a view to deportation or extradition'.

[132] *Lawless v. Ireland*, ECtHR, 1 July 1961. In a case between Cyprus and Turkey, the European Commission raised the need for derogation in the context of detaining prisoners of war. See *Cyprus v. Turkey*, case nos 6780/74 and 6950/75, 10 July 1976; but see minority opinion in the same case.

[133] ICCPR, Art 4.   [134] General Comment no 29, n 121, *supra*.

were considered and rejected.[135] According to Dennis, this fact leads to the conclusion that 'the proposition that there are other nonderogable rights in the ICCPR in addition to the catalog of nonderogable rights provided in article 4(2) is doubtful'.[136] Nonetheless, there is strong reason to take the position that non-derogability is wider than the specific Articles listed in the Covenant. First, Article 4 requires that measures taken must not be inconsistent with other obligations under international law[137] and, as noted by the Human Rights Committee, this means that 'States parties may in no circumstances invoke article 4 of the Covenant as justification for acting in violation of humanitarian law or peremptory norms of international law'.[138] Accordingly, if international humanitarian law is applicable to a particular situation, then a restriction cannot be placed on a derogable right if it would result in violating an applicable principle of IHL. Furthermore, if certain rights or elements of a particular provision are now recognized as peremptory norms of international law then violating these rules would not be allowed, even if the said right does not appear in the list of non-derogable provisions.

Returning with this in mind to the question of freedom from arbitrary detention, it should be stressed that a notice of derogation alone will not provide a *carte blanche* for the state to ignore all its human rights obligations regarding detention. Juxtaposing two specific European cases will illustrate this point well. Following a UK derogation, in *Brannigan and McBride v. UK*, the Court accepted the lawfulness of detention without being brought before a judge for up to seven days;[139] in *Aksoy v. Turkey*, despite a derogation, the Court found that the prolonged detention (at least 14 days[140]) without seeing a judge was not lawful. In addition to the greater length of time, an aggravating factor in the Turkish case, as noted by the Court, was the lack of appropriate safeguards.[141] Accordingly, even if the provisions on detention are derogated from there are still minimal standards that must be met. The Human Rights Committee, in its discussion of measures that would not be permissible, stated that it would never be permitted for a state to take derogation measures amounting to arbitrary deprivation of liberty.[142] Although the Committee does not engage in an explanation of this the logic is fairly clear: even if states of emergency necessitate greater powers for the authorities to use temporary exceptional measures in the context of powers

---

[135] See for instance the discussion over Art 20 and aspects of Art 9 in Provisional Summary Record of the 196th Meeting, UN ESCOR Human Rights Committee, 6th sess, UN Doc E/CN 4/SR.196 (1950) paras 1–28.

[136] M Dennis, 'Application of Human Rights Treaties Extraterritorially to Detention of Combatants and Security Internees: Fuzzy Thinking All Around?' *ILSA Journal of International and Comparative Law* 459 (Spring 2006) 478–79.

[137] ICCPR, Art 4.   [138] General Comment no 29, n 121, *supra,* para 11.

[139] *Brannigan & McBride v. United Kingdom*, ECtHR, App nos 14553/89 and 14554/89, 26 May 1993.

[140] The exact start date of detention was disputed. *Aksoy v. Turkey*, ECtHR, App no 21987/93, 18 December 1996, paras 71–5.

[141] *Ibid*, paras 82–3.   [142] General Comment no 29, n 121, para 11.

of arrest and detention there is unlikely to be any reasoning which would lead to the necessity for randomly detaining persons, or for arresting and detaining individuals outside any framework regulated by law. *Arbitrary* detention would, therefore, not be 'strictly required by the exigencies of the situation'. The primary concern with extraterritorial detentions, as described earlier, is that they might transgress the prohibition of arbitrary detention. In as much as they would violate this rule, and accepting the Human Rights Committee's assertion of non-deviance from the rule, the mechanism of derogation would, therefore, not transform such actions from unlawful to lawful.

To summarize this chapter, it seems that the three rights of major concern with regard to extraterritorial forcible measures are the right to life; freedom from torture and other ill-treatment; and freedom from arbitrary detention. As for the first of these, if human rights law is the primary applicable framework then sending state agents on a mission to kill is almost always likely to involve a violation. The prohibition of torture and other ill-treatment is not subject to any legally justified exception and holding individuals in extraterritorial places of detention, over which there is little oversight, opens the door to potential abuse. Abductions might very well be deemed a form of arbitrary detention, especially if they take place on the territory of another state and without its consent, in addition to the fact that they may well involve a lack of adherence to the required safeguards. In the case of killings and detentions, the existence of allowed exceptions to the prohibitions leads to the need to conduct any assessment on a case-by-case basis. In addition, if these are occurring in the context of an armed conflict the rules of IHL may affect the legality.[143] To find a violation of international human rights law there must, however, also be an examination of the questions over human rights obligations applying to extraterritorial situations, as will be conducted in Chapter 8 of this work.

---

[143] See Part II, *supra*, on IHL; Ch 9, *infra*, on the relationship between IHL and human rights law; and the specific cases in the Concluding Chapter, *infra*.

8

Extraterritorial Applicability of
Human Rights Law

The largest potential obstacle to be dealt with when analysing the applicability of international human rights law in the current context is the issue of extraterritoriality and whether states are bound by human rights law when acting outside their borders. As will be seen, this question has long been the subject of debate and has arisen in a large number of cases. In order to better understand the problems raised by this question it needs to be broken down into separate issues, with some key distinctions made at the start.

Before proceeding with a detailed analysis, the fundamental question must be asked and answered—does the very concept of human rights obligations allow for the possibility that these obligations might include actions taken outside a state's sovereign territory? To answer this question one need not, at this early stage, delve into the intricacies of the specific circumstances, conditions and treaty requirements that could potentially bring about extraterritorial obligations—this will take place throughout the majority of the following sections of the chapter. Prior to a detailed analysis, we need only observe whether it is *ever* possible for extraterritorial obligations to exist at all.

The International Court of Justice ('ICJ'), the principal judicial organ of the United Nations, has clearly proclaimed more than once that states can be bound by human rights obligations in relation to activities they take on territory that is not their own. This was the finding in the *Advisory Opinion on the Wall*,[1] in the case of the *DRC v. Uganda*,[2] and more recently in *Georgia v. Russian Federation*.[3]

---

[1] *Legal Consequences of the Construction of a Wall in the Occupied Palestinian Territory*, Advisory Opinion, [2004] ICJ Rep, 9 July 2004, paras 107–13.

[2] *Armed Activities on the Territory of the Congo (Congo v. Uganda)*, 19 December 2005, paras 219–20.

[3] *Georgia v. Russian Federation*, Application of the International Convention on the Elimination of All Forms of Racial Discrimination, Request for the Indication of Provisional Measures, International Court of Justice, 15 October 2008. Of particular note is that while it mentions the lack of territorial reference in the treaty provisions at hand, the court makes a general statement about extraterritorial applicability of human rights obligations 'and whereas the Court consequently finds that these provisions of CERD generally appear to apply, like other provisions of instruments of that nature, to the actions of a state party when it acts beyond its territory', para 109.

The UN Human Rights Committee on numerous occasions (including individual cases,[4] its General Comment on the Nature of the General Legal Obligation on States Parties to the Covenant[5] and in scrutiny of country situations[6]) has clearly stated that extraterritorial activity can be subject to the obligations of international human rights law. Other, non-treaty-based, mechanisms of the UN have also determined that states can be bound by human rights obligations in the context of extraterritorial activities.[7] The European Court of Human Rights is no stranger to this conclusion either, as is evident in a number of cases.[8] Neither is the Inter-American system of human rights averse to speaking of extraterritorial obligations.[9] At the very least, this should be evidence enough that circumstances can exist in which one might argue that human rights obligations extend beyond a state's national borders. A large part of this chapter will, therefore, be devoted to examining these arguments and inquiring what, if any, are the conditions under which extraterritorial obligations might be considered applicable.

Within the question of applicability, there may be a difference between obligations created by treaties and those outside of the treaty sphere. The applicability of treaty provisions has an added value in that it brings into play the competence of judicial and quasi-judicial oversight mechanisms. In that respect, even if it would be possible to show the existence of obligations under customary international law, there is still a strong incentive to resolve the question of treaty applicability. In fact, as will be seen in the next two sections, much of the debate on the question of extraterritorial applicability of human rights obligations is contained within the case-law of treaty bodies, inquiring into whether they can in fact discuss extraterritorial operations within the parameters set out by their respective treaties.

The determination of applicability will also rest on the interpretation and understanding of a number of terms and tests. These include matters of

---

[4] *Delia Saldias de Lopez v. Uruguay*, Comm no 52/1979, UN Doc CCPR/C/OP/1 at 88 (1984); *Lilian Celiberti de Casariego v. Uruguay*, Comm no 56/1979, UN Doc CCPR/C/OP/1 at 92 (1984).

[5] Human Rights Committee, General Comment 31, UN Doc CCPR/C/21/Rev.1/Add.13 (2004), para 10.

[6] Human Rights Committee, 'Comments of The Human Rights Committee, Croatia', CCPR/C/79/Add.15, 28 December 1992, paras 7,9; Human Rights Committee 'Concluding Observations of the Human Rights Committee: Israel' UN Doc CCPR/C/79/Add.93, 18 August 1998.

[7] 'Report on the situation of human rights in Kuwait under Iraqi occupation', prepared by the Special Rapporteur of the Commission on Human Rights, W Kalin, in accordance with Commission resolution 1991/67i (E/CN 4/1992/26), 15 January 1992, paras 55–59; Report of the Special Rapporteur on the promotion and protection of human rights and fundamental freedoms while countering terrorism, M Scheinin, Mission to the United States of America/Advance edited version/A/HRC/6/17/Add.3, 25 October 2007.

[8] *Loizidou v. Turkey*, Preliminary Objections, 310 ECtHR, Series A, paras 62–4 (1995); *Cyprus v. Turkey*, ECtHR, App no 25781/94, 10 May 2001, para 77.

[9] *Alejandre Jr and ors v. Republica de Cuba* ('Brothers to the Rescue'), Case 11.589, Report no 86/99, OEA/Ser.L/V/II.106 Doc. 3 rev. at 586 (1999), para 23; *Coard and ors v. United States*, Case 10.951, Report no 109/99, IACHR, 29 September 1999, para 37.

jurisdiction, the questions of control over areas and over persons, and the possibility of a contextual approach to the nature of obligations. They will all be dealt with individually in the following sections. In light of the significance of treaty applicability to the question of oversight, and the fact that much of the debate over extraterritorial obligations has occurred in the context of treaty obligations, this will be the first subject to be examined.

Most international human rights treaties contain provisions setting out the scope of application for the obligations contained therein. For example:

Each State Party to the present Covenant undertakes to respect and to ensure to all individuals *within its territory and subject to its jurisdiction* the rights recognized in the present Covenant [emphasis added] (Article 2 of the ICCPR[10]).

The States Parties to this Convention undertake to respect the rights and freedoms recognized herein and to ensure to all persons *subject to their jurisdiction* the free and full exercise of those rights and freedoms [emphasis added] (Article 1 of the ACHR[11]).

The High Contracting Parties shall secure to everyone *within their jurisdiction* the rights and freedoms defined in Section I of this Convention [emphasis added] (Article 1 of the ECHR[12]).

The African Charter[13] does not contain similar wording, and speaks of recognizing and giving effects to the rights, without mentioning jurisdictional or territorial limitations.

Two key matters must be addressed:

(i) The ICCPR language is different from the others, in that it also mentions 'territory';
(ii) how is 'within their jurisdiction' to be understood?

1. The scope of application of the ICCPR

The phrasing of Article 2(1) of the ICCPR, which defines the scope of application using the words 'within its territory and subject to its jurisdiction', has been described as awkward,[14] and its precise meaning remains debatable. On the one hand, the Human Rights Committee, in its General Comment 31, clearly appears to have interpreted the phrase as positing two separate free-standing grounds for

---

[10] International Covenant on Civil and Political Rights (16 December 1966) 999 UNTS 171, entered into force 23 March 1976 ('ICCPR').

[11] American Convention on Human Rights (22 November 1969) 1144 UNTS 123, entered into force 18 July 1978 ('ACHR').

[12] Convention for the Protection of Human Rights and Fundamental Freedoms (4 November 1950) 213 UNTS 222; 312 ETS 5, entered into force 3 September 1953 (European Convention on Human Rights, 'ECHR').

[13] African Charter on Human and Peoples' Rights (26 June 1981) OAU Doc CAB/LEG/67/3 rev.5; 1520 UNTS 217; 21 ILM 58 (1982), entered into force 21 October 1986 ('African Charter')

[14] M Nowak, *UN Covenant on Civil and Political Rights* (2nd edn) (NP Engel: Germany, 2005) 43.

applicability of obligations, 'within its territory' *or* 'subject to its jurisdiction'.[15] The position of the Human Rights Committee, that the ICCPR obligations can apply extraterritorially, appears to be consistent and has been repeated on a number of occasions. In this General Comment, the Committee declares, in a manner that cannot be misconstrued, that:

States Parties are required by article 2, paragraph 1, to respect and to ensure the Covenant rights to all persons who may be within their territory and to all persons subject to their jurisdiction. This means that a State party must respect and ensure the rights laid down in the Covenant to anyone within the power or effective control of that State Party, even if not situated within the territory of the State Party. [...] This principle also applies to those within the power or effective control of the forces of a State Party acting outside its territory, [...]

Commenting on this provision, Theodor Meron noted that:

The legislative history of Article 2(1) does not support a narrow territorial construction. The leading study by Professor Buergenthal, now a member of the United Nations Human Rights Committee, argues that Article 2(1) should be read so that each party would have assumed the obligation to respect and ensure the rights recognized in the Covenant both 'to all individuals within its territory' and 'to all individuals subject to its jurisdiction.' This interpretation has almost never been questioned and has long ceased to be the preserve of scholars; it has obtained the imprimatur of the Human Rights Committee and UN rapporteurs.[16]

Indeed, whenever given the opportunity do so, the Committee has had little hesitation in applying this analysis to specific circumstances. Accordingly, it has found that Uruguay bore responsibility for the actions of its agents who had abducted an individual in Argentina;[17] that Israel bears responsibility for its actions in the West Bank that violate the Covenant;[18] and that Croatia was responsible for conditions of detention in Bosnia-Herzegovina.[19] In the context of the situation in the Former Yugoslavia, Rosalyn Higgins, at that time a member of the Committee and later President of the ICJ, noted that:

As regards the question of jurisdiction, the Committee had always maintained that States were responsible for ensuring respect for the human rights proclaimed in the Covenant when their representatives were implicated and when their acts affected human beings, even outside their national territory. Its practice in the matter was quite clear.[20]

---

[15] The Committee describes both of these as separate valid grounds for entering the scope of application, and in fact goes as far as restating the Covenant sentence, this time using the word *or:* 'who may find themselves in the territory or subject to the jurisdiction of the State Party.' General Comment 31, n 5, *supra*, para 10.

[16] T Meron, 'The 1994 U.S. Action in Haiti: Extraterritoriality of Human Rights Treaties', 89 *AJIL* 78 (1995) 79; see also T Buergenthal, 'To Respect and to Ensure: State Obligations and Permissible Derogations' in L Henkin (ed), *The International Bill of Human Rights* (Colombia University Press: New York, 1981) 72–7, 74.

[17] *Delia Saldias de Lopez v. Uruguay,* n 4, supra.   [18] See n 6, *supra*.

[19] See n 6, *supra*.

[20] Human Rights Committee, 'Summary record of the 1202nd meeting (second part), Consideration of reports submitted by States parties under article 40 of the Covenant: Croatia, Yugoslavia', UN Doc CCPR/C/SR.1202/Add.1, 15 April 1993, para 23.

On the other hand, the disjunctive interpretation has been criticized both by states and commentators,[21] leading some to the view that limits extraterritorial applicability.[22] Despite the Committee's clear position, not everyone accepts its interpretation. The most notable recent opposition comes from the United States,[23] with most of the arguments articulated by Michael Dennis,[24] an attorney for the Office of the Legal Adviser at the US Department of State. Two main strands of argument are presented against extraterritorial applicability of human rights obligations and both will now be examined.

The first point relates to the absence of state derogations in the context of extraterritorial operations. Dennis points out that:

What is even more important, although various overseas military missions involving States parties have been undertaken since the adoption of the Covenant, most recently in Iraq, Bosnia and Herzegovina, and the former Federal Republic of Yugoslavia (FRY), not one State has indicated, by making a derogation from those rights as provided under Article 4 of the Covenant, a belief that its actions abroad constituted an exercise of jurisdiction under the Covenant. All derogations under Article 4 have been lodged with respect to internal laws only.[25]

This appears to be a strong argument that states do not expect the ICCPR to be applicable in these circumstances. However, this argument is not as straightforward as it may at first seem. The examples cited by Dennis all involve military actions in the context of armed conflict. As Dennis later notes, an additional reason for the lack of derogations may be that the states concerned did not consider the human rights instruments as relevant to these operations, since in their

---

[21] 'Third periodic reports of States parties due in 2003', United States, UN Doc CCPR/C/USA/3, 28 November 2005, 109; M Dennis, 'Application of Human Rights Treaties Extraterritorially to Detention of Combatants and Security Internees: Fuzzy Thinking All Around?' *ILSA Journal of International and Comparative Law* 459 (Spring, 2006) 463, 466–7; Nowak, n 14, *supra*, 43 fn 78.

[22] US, *ibid*; Dennis, *ibid*. See the remarks by Waxman and Harris in Human Rights Committee, 'Consideration Of Reports Under Article 40 Of The Covenant (Continued), Second And Third Periodic Reports Of The United States Of America (Continued)', Summary Record of the 2380th Meeting, 18 July 2006, UN CCPR/C/SR.2380, 27 July 2006, paras 3,8. See also D Schindler, 'Human Rights and Humanitarian Law: Interrelationship of the Laws' 31 *American University Law Review* (1982) 935, 939.

[23] 'In short, the United States interprets human rights treaties to apply to persons living in the territory of the United States, and not to any person with whom agents of our government deal in the international community', J Rawcliffe and J Smith (eds), *The US Operational Law Handbook (August 2006)*, International and Operational Law Department, The Judge Advocate General's Legal Center and School, August 2006, 50; 'The Committee does not share the view expressed by the Government that the Covenant lacks extraterritorial reach under all circumstances': Human Rights Committee, 'Comments on United States of America', UN Doc CCPR/C/79/Add 50 (1995) para 19.

[24] Dennis, n 21, *supra*; M Dennis, 'Non-Application of Civil and Political Rights Extraterritorially During Times of International Armed Conflict' 40 *Israel Law Review* 453 (2007); M Dennis, 'ICJ Advisory Opinion on Construction of a Wall in the Occupied Palestinian Territory: Application of human rights treaties extraterritorially in times of armed conflict and military occupation', 99 *AJIL* 119 (2005).

[25] Dennis, n 21, *supra*, 468.

view they had been supplanted by international humanitarian law ('IHL').[26] This possibility goes to the heart of the debates over the parallel applicability of human rights law and IHL during armed conflict. The matter of the relationship between these bodies of law, and how to view human rights obligations during armed conflict will be the subject of analysis in Chapter 9 of this work. For now, it should be noted that if the extraterritorial measures occur during armed conflict then indeed one must clarify how and whether this fact might affect any potential human rights obligations.[27] It should also be noted, however, that not all extraterritorial operations take place in the context of armed conflict as is evident in some of the earlier examples.[28] If there is no armed conflict, then the possibility of deference to IHL cannot be the reason in these cases for a lack of derogations to the ICCPR. A more obvious reason would be the fact that certain types of operations, such as abductions and killings carried out by secret service agents, are activities which states are extremely unlikely to announce their prior intention to carry out, or even admit to *post-facto*.

A lack of derogations for extraterritorial measures taking place during armed conflict must, therefore, be considered in light of the debate regarding the relationship between international human rights law and IHL (which will be examined later), and the lack of derogations for extraterritorial operations against individuals not in the context of armed conflict is unlikely to point to anything other than a reluctance to draw attention to these operations. It is, therefore, submitted that the absence of derogations is in itself not conclusive evidence of a non-acceptance of extraterritorial applicability of human rights obligations, at least not outside the context of armed conflict. Moreover, if what states *do not* say is entered as evidence to support a particular position, one might also note the absence of a relevant reservation to the ICCPR by the US, despite the fact that the Human Rights Committee's practice in viewing the ICCPR as having extraterritorial applicability had already been established prior to the US ratification.[29] In fact, a number of states have indicated to the Human Rights Committee that they accept the applicability of Covenant obligations to extraterritorial circumstances involving their armed forces.[30] Indeed, as will be seen later in this chapter,

[26] Dennis, n 21, *supra*, 472. Dennis mentions that the US has raised both the above as reasons for not accepting extraterritorial applicability.

[27] See earlier discussion of derogations in Ch 7, *supra*, nn 116–30 and accompanying text. See also Ch 9, *infra*, on relationship between IHL and human rights.

[28] Eg, the abduction of Vanunu.

[29] Eg, the decision on *Delia Saldias de Lopez v. Uruguay*, n 4, *supra*, appeared in 1984. The US ratified the ICCPR in 1992.

[30] 'Wherever its police or armed forces are deployed abroad, in particular when participating in peace missions, Germany ensures to all persons that they will be granted the rights recognized in the Covenant, insofar as they are subject to its jurisdiction Germany's international duties and obligations, in particular those assumed in fulfilment of obligations stemming from the Charter of the United Nations, remain unaffected. The training it gives its security forces for international missions includes tailor-made instruction in the provisions of the Covenant.': 'Consideration of Reports Submitted by States Parties under Article 40 of the Covenant: International Covenant

there is plentiful evidence to support extraterritorial applicability in certain circumstances, although exactly which circumstances and through what legal interpretations is a matter of debate.

The second major criticism levelled at the notion of extraterritorial obligations, is that allowing for such obligations was never the intention of the drafters of the Covenant, and that in fact there should be no debate on this matter since the language they used was straightforward and can only be understood as excluding any extraterritorial applicability. Should there, nevertheless, be any question about this resort to the *travaux préparatoires* would, according to the holders of this opinion, confirm this interpretation.[31]

As to the language being straightforward, the existence of a debate and the fact that the Human Rights Committee, the primary body entrusted with overseeing the implementation of the Covenant, has a clear interpretation that differs from that of its critics should be evidence enough that one cannot brush aside the notion of extraterritorial obligations by claiming unequivocal language to the contrary. As for the *travaux préparatoires*, the words of Eleanor Roosevelt, the US representative at the drafting process (and then Chairperson of the Commission) during the discussion about adding the reference to within its territory, are offered by critics as support for denying extraterritorial obligations:

The purpose of the proposed addition was to make it clear that the draft Covenant would apply only to persons within the territory and subject to the jurisdiction of contracting States. The United States was afraid that without such an addition the draft Covenant might be construed as obliging the contracting States to enact legislation concerning persons who, although outside its territory were technically within its jurisdiction for certain purposes. An illustration would be the occupied territories of Germany, Austria and Japan: persons within those countries were subject to the jurisdiction of the occupying

on Civil and Political Rights: Comments by the Government of Germany to the Concluding Observations of the Human Rights Committee', UN Doc CCPR/CO/80/DEU/Add.1, 11 April 2005; 'Mr. Piermarini (Italy) said that the Penal Military Code of War had been amended to ensure that members of the armed forces and police officers who participated in international operations were aware of the local populations' rights under the Covenant': Human Rights Committee, Summary Record of the 2317th Meeting', UN Doc CCPR/C/SR.2317, 26 October 2005, para 39; Human Rights Committee, 'Concluding Observations of the Human Rights Committee, Italy' UN Doc CCPR/C/ITA/CO/5 (2006), para 3; Human Rights Committee, 'Concluding Observations of the Human Rights Committee, Poland', UN Doc CCPR/CO/82/POL (2004), para 3. However, multinational operations give rise to debate on other aspects—outside the scope of this work—of attribution and applicability: see, eg, *Behrami and Behrami v. France*, App no 71412/01 and *Saramati v. France, Germany and Norway,* Decision on admissibility, App no 78166/01, 2 May 2007. The Netherlands appear to have a taken a different position, noting that Art 2 of the ICCPR precludes the citizens of Srebrenica from coming within the scope of obligations of the Netherlands. 'Replies of the Government of the Netherlands to the concerns expressed by the Human Rights Committee in its concluding observations', UN Doc CCPR/CO/72/NET/Add.1, 29 April 2003, para 19.

[31] 'Third Periodic Report of States parties due in 2003, United States of America', Annex I – Territorial Scope of Application of the Covenant, remarks by Mr Harris in HRC Consideration of USA Reports, UN Doc CCPR/C/USA/3 28 November 2005, n 22, *supra*, para 8.

States in certain respects, but were outside the scope of the legislation of those States. Another illustration would be the case of leased territories: some countries leased certain territories from others for limited purposes, and there might be questions of conflicting authority between the lessor nation and the lessee nation.[32]

And:

That would limit the application of the covenant only to persons within its territory and subject to its jurisdiction. By this amendment the United Sates Government would not, by ratifying the covenant, be assuming an obligation to ensure the rights recognized in it to the citizens of countries under United States occupation.[33]

This may seem straightforward at first hand but, taken in context, it is rather less obvious that it excludes all extraterritorial obligations. The discussion that occurred during the drafting process did not cover the question of accountability for direct actions taken by state agents against individuals outside a state's sovereign territory. Rather, the discussion focused upon whether the Covenant could obligate states parties to *ensure all its provisions* to individuals who were not in their territory. Of primary concern was the question whether state A could be obligated to ensure the Covenant provisions to its own nationals living in state B, as can be seen in the text of the drafting process. The response to the above second quotation from Eleanor Roosevelt, and the ensuing discussion, proceeded as follows:

Mr Mendez (Philippines) remarked that a United States citizen abroad would surely be entitled to claim United States jurisdiction if denied the rights recognized in the covenant.[34]

Eleanor Roosevelt then responded:

if such a case occurred within the territory of a State party to the covenant, the United States Government would insist that the State should honour its obligations under the covenant; if, however, the State in question had not acceded to the covenant, the United States Government would be unable to do more than make representations on behalf of its citizens through the normal diplomatic channels. It would certainly not exercise jurisdiction over a person outside its territory.[35]

This was repeated once more in an exchange between Mrs Roosevelt, and the Yugoslavian representative Mr Jevremovic.[36] The representative of Uruguay, Mr Oribe, agreed with the US position, voicing the opinion that:

Since no State could provide for judges, police, court machinery, etc. in territory outside its jurisdiction, it was evident that States could effectively guarantee human rights only to

---

[32] UN ESCOR Human Rights Committee, Summary Record of the 138th Meeting, UN Doc E/CN 4/SR.138 (1950) paras 33–4.

[33] UN ESCOR Human Rights Committee, Summary Record of the 194th Meeting, UN Doc E/CN 4/SR.194 (1950) para 14.

[34] *Ibid*, para 15.   [35] *Ibid*, para 16.   [36] *Ibid*, paras 28, 29.

those persons residing within their territorial jurisdiction. For that reason the Uruguayan delegation would support the United States amendment.[37]

The support for inclusion of reference to territory can, therefore, be understood in the context of states being concerned that they would be unable to provide the guarantees necessary for implementing all of the Covenant's provisions in territories in which they did not have the powers to do so. This is also the case for post-World War II occupied territories in which, additionally, there was the difficulty of individuals who were not fully within the legislative powers of the US.[38] The ICJ has confirmed this reading:

> The travaux préparatoires of the Covenant confirm the Committee's interpretation of Article 2 of that instrument. These show that, in adopting the wording chosen, the drafters of the Covenant did not intend to allow States to escape from their obligations when they exercise jurisdiction outside their national territory. They only intended to prevent persons residing abroad from asserting, vis-à-vis their State of origin, rights that do not fall within the competence of that State, but of that of the State of residence.[39]

It appears, therefore, that the drafters, when deciding to add the reference to territory, wished to avoid the risk that the Covenant would create positive duties outside the scope of a state's authority and ability to execute such obligations. This is a very different question from circumstances in which state agents are actively taking measures which appear to contradict the rights protected by the Covenant. In essence, this is about recognizing that the concept of human rights obligations contains requirements of a different nature, namely those of positive and negative obligations. Positive obligations are those that require the state to take a specific action in order to give effect to an individual's human rights, such as building schools and courts, and training teachers and judges. Negative obligations do not require active measures, but rather demand that the state does not take actions that would impede an individual's right, for example, not to randomly pull a person off the street and torture them to death.[40] The drafters appeared to be concerned that states should not be encumbered with positive duties in territories where they do not have the authority or power to do so, but it is primarily the latter scenario of negative obligations with which we are currently

---

[37] *Ibid,* para 30.

[38] See the remarks by N Rodley, member of the Human Rights Committee, in HRC Consideration of USA Reports, n 22, *supra,* para 65. See also Nowak, n 14, *supra,* 43; and analysis of this in Human Rights First, 'Submission to HRC, 18 January 2006, Re: Follow-Up to Human Rights First's October 18, 2005 Memorandum to the Human Rights Committee', 18 October 2005. See also D McGoldrick, 'Extraterritorial Application of the International Covenant on Civil and Political Rights' in F Coomans and M Kamminga (eds), *Extraterritorial Application of Human Rights Treaties* (Intersentia: Antwerp, 2004) 41–72, 66.

[39] *Wall,* n 1, *supra,* para 109.

[40] In fact, within most rights it is possible to identify both positive and negative elements. For more detailed discussion of negative and positive obligations, see section 3, *infra,* on contextual approach.

concerned,[41] and attempts to refit the original drafting discussions onto these different circumstances cannot provide a ready answer.

Another argument against extraterritorial applicability is that, had the intention been to include extraterritorial applicability, the drafters of the human rights instruments could have used the language found in the IHL Geneva Conventions, in which the state parties 'undertake to respect and to ensure respect for the present Convention in all circumstances'.[42] Since they did not follow this example, then they cannot have intended extraterritorial applicability.[43] This argument has two weaknesses. First, as will be seen shortly, the case-law and indeed the views of virtually all commentators testify to an agreement that there are at least some circumstances in which human rights treaties will apply extraterritorially. Secondly, IHL treaties designed to regulate international armed conflict must of course apply extraterritorially, since the extraterritoriality is an almost inherent component of such armed conflict. They are built upon obligations imposed on belligerent parties in relation to categories of persons and objects (civilians, combatants, military objectives and so on) in the context of the international armed conflict and, therefore, do not require the same type of provision on the scope of obligations as the human rights instruments. Human rights treaties are not premised upon protections for categories of persons as in IHL, but on all persons subject to the authority of the state. There is probably little reason to object to the view that human rights treaties are primarily designed to regulate behaviour within the state since, unlike in international armed conflicts, this is the main sphere in which the states will be acting. It is only natural that the language in the respective treaties reflects the primary design. That does not, however, lead to the automatic deduction that a human rights treaty is necessarily always limited to the territory of the state, but only to the fact that this was the primary anticipated sphere for most of its application. As noted, and as will be further expanded upon in this chapter, there is substantial support for arguing that the applicability of human rights treaties can sometimes cross borders although there is a need to clarify the circumstances in which that might happen.

In denying the extraterritorial applicability of the obligations, Dennis borrows support by quoting Nowak's position on this matter.[44] It is true that in one of his footnotes Nowak expresses criticism of the disjunctive interpretation of the phrase 'within its territory and subject to its jurisdiction'[45] but, once again, a proper examination of the context shows that Nowak's views are in contradiction to Dennis' assertion. Criticism of the disjunctive interpretation is understandable in light of the above discussion of the difference between creating the obligation

---

[41] In extraterritorial situations which amount to control of territory, such as military occupation, there may be call for positive obligations. This will be raised briefly in the following sections, although, as will be explained, most of these situations are outside the scope of this work.

[42] Common Article 1 of the Geneva Conventions.

[43] The argument was made with regard to the European Convention, but this question can equally be asked of the other human rights treaties. *Bankovic and ors v. Belgium and ors*, ECtHR, App no 52207/99, 2001, para 75.

[44] Dennis, n 21, *supra*, 466–7.   [45] Nowak, n 14, *supra*.

to positively ensure all Covenant rights to persons outside the state's territory, as opposed to the question of responsibility for specific extraterritorial actions that affect specific rights. Even if the phrase 'within its territory and subject to its jurisdiction' is interpreted to include an element of territorial limitation for the overall scope of the Covenant[46] (and there are additional reasons that the disjunctive interpretation presents problems),[47] accepting this position still does not lead to accepting that states cannot be held responsible for any extraterritorial actions. Nowak is in fact unequivocally clear on this point:

When States parties, however, take actions on foreign territory that violate the rights of persons subject to their sovereign authority, it would be contrary to the purpose of the Covenant if they could not be held responsible. It is irrelevant whether these actions are permissible under general international law (e.g. sovereign acts by diplomatic or consular representatives, or in border traffic or by border officials in customs-free zones; actions by occupation forces in accordance with the rules of the law of war) or constitute illegal interference, such as the kidnapping of persons by secret service agents.[48]

Dennis also seeks support in the views of Tomuschat, a member of the Human Rights Committee whose individual opinion in the case of the Uruguayan abduction in Argentina appeared to contain some criticism of the majority opinion. Once again, the bottom line of Tomuschat's opinion is in fact opposed to the point that Dennis and the US position are attempting to promote. Tomuschat's criticism concerns the grounds on which the Committee reached their conclusion, and in particular the reliance on Article 5 of the Covenant.[49] In that respect, Tomuschat interprets the origin of the territorial reference, saying that it was meant 'to restrict the territorial scope of the Covenant in view of such situations where enforcing the Covenant would be likely to encounter exceptional obstacles.'[50] Any reliance on Tomuschat should, however, also reflect the fact that Tomuschat concurred with the majority view finding Uruguay responsible for violating the Covenant obligations in the context of an extraterritorial operation, since:

To construe the words 'within its territory' pursuant to their strict literal meaning as excluding any responsibility for conduct occurring beyond the national boundaries would, however, lead to utterly absurd results. [...] Never was it envisaged, however,

---

[46] E Schwelb, 'Civil and Political Rights: The International Measures of Implementation' 62 *AJIL* 827 (1968) 863; E Mose and T Opsahl, 'The optional Protocol to the International Covenant on Civil and Political Rights' 21 *Santa Clara Law Review* 271 (1981) 297.
[47] Nowak, n 14, *supra*, 43, fn 78.   [48] Nowak, n 14, *supra*, 44.
[49] Article 5 states that '1. Nothing in the present Covenant may be interpreted as implying for any State, group or person any right to engage in any activity or perform any act aimed at the destruction of any of the rights and freedoms recognized herein or at their limitation to a greater extent than is provided for in the present Covenant; 2. There shall be no restriction upon or derogation from any of the fundamental human rights recognized or existing in any State Party to the present Covenant pursuant to law, conventions, regulations or custom on the pretext that the present Covenant does not recognize such rights or that it recognizes them to a lesser extent.'
[50] Individual opinion of C Tomuschat *Delia Saldias de Lopez v. Uruguay*, n 4, *supra*.

to grant States parties unfettered discretionary power to carry out wilful and deliberate attacks against the freedom and personal integrity of their citizens living abroad. Consequently, despite the wording of article 2 (l), the events which took place outside Uruguay come within the purview of the Covenant.[51]

In summary thus far, it appears that the grounds for denial of ICCPR applicability to extraterritorial operations, as expressed by Dennis and the US position, are not as firm as they are presented to be, and on closer inspection actually uncover support for the possibility of extraterritorial applicability.

There is an additional argument which lends strong support to accepting that such obligations may in certain circumstances exist under the Covenant. Much of the above debate centred upon the supposed intention of the drafters as it appears in the *travaux préparatoires*. Recourse to the *travaux préparatoires* is indeed an acceptable avenue for treaty interpretation but, according to Article 32 of the Vienna Convention on the Law of Treaties, it is in fact only a supplementary mode of interpretation:

Recourse may be had to supplementary means of interpretation, including the preparatory work of the treaty and the circumstances of its conclusion, in order to confirm the meaning resulting from the application of article 31, or to determine the meaning when the interpretation according to article 31:

(a) Leaves the meaning ambiguous or obscure; or
(b) Leads to a result which is manifestly absurd or unreasonable.[52]

Article 31 which contains, therefore, the primary method for interpretation, declares in paragraph 1 that '[A] treaty shall be interpreted in good faith in accordance with the ordinary meaning to be given to the terms of the treaty in their context and in the light of its object and purpose.'[53] The Article continues and elaborates upon the need to also take into account the preamble, later agreements, and relevant practice.

Applying Article 31 of the Vienna Convention to the question at hand, Rodley notes that:

The ordinary meaning of article 2 was the one given to it by the Committee, and the context included any subsequent practice in the application of the treaty which established the agreement of the States parties regarding its interpretation. It did not include the travaux préparatoires, which were a supplementary means of interpretation under article 32 of the Convention. *The object and purpose were laid down clearly in the preamble to the Covenant and consisted in protecting humans from the overreaching power of States.*[54]

The argument of adhering to the object and purpose of the Covenant, therefore, offers strong reinforcement for accepting that there may be circumstances

---

[51] *Ibid*; see also C Tomuschat, *Human Rights: Between Idealism and Realism* (OUP: Oxford, 2003) 108–10.
[52] Vienna Convention on the Law of Treaties, (23 May 1969) 1155 UNTS 331, entered into force 27 January 1980, Art 32.
[53] *Ibid*, Art 31.   [54] Remarks by Rodley, n 38, *supra* (emphasis added).

in which the Covenant obligations must be applied to the scrutiny of extraterritorial activities, and has the support of numerous commentators, including Meron, Frowein, and others.[55] Referring to the case law of human rights bodies and the ICJ applying human rights law to extraterritorial scenarios, Cassese confirms that:

[it] is consistent with the object and purpose of human rights obligations: they aim at protecting individuals against arbitrariness, abuse, and violence, regardless of the location where the State conduct occurs.[56]

The historical context of egregious atrocities against individuals both within *and outside sovereign territory* (including territories occupied by Germany) in which the modern human rights treaties were developed, together with the underlying principle of universality, are further evidence that the object and purpose of the treaty cannot be said to exclude the possibility of extraterritorial obligations.[57] Allowing states to escape responsibility for causing direct intentional harm to individuals on the sole grounds of geographical location of the abuse would, therefore, fly in the face of the principles that are the object and purpose of the ICCPR. As noted by Nowak:

[…] a State party would thus need only to shift its repressive acts (e.g., construction of a concentration or torture camps) to the territory of a friendly neighbouring State in order to avoid its responsibility under the Covenant.[58]

In light of all of the above, and in conclusion of this section, it is submitted that the reference to 'within its territory' in Article 2 of the ICCPR may limit the scope of the Covenant, in that states cannot be obligated to ensure all the rights in circumstances in which they do not have the power or authority to do so. This phrase does not, however, exclude the possibility that extraterritorial measures by state agents can be scrutinized in light of Covenant obligations, and give rise to responsibility for violations. Indeed, the very object and purpose of the Covenant would be severely undermined if states could evade responsibility by relocating their abuse of individuals.

The above points are of direct relevance also to the UN Convention against Torture ('CAT').[59] Article 2 of CAT declares that '[E]ach State Party shall take effective legislative, administrative, judicial or other measures to prevent acts of torture *in any territory under its jurisdiction*' [emphasis added].

There is, however, a significant difference in the case of CAT. This Convention also creates obligations with regard to establishing criminal jurisdiction and

---

[55] Meron, n 16, *supra*, 80–1; J Frowein, 'The Relationship between Human Rights Regimes and Regimes of Belligerent Occupation' 28 *Israel Yearbook on Human Rights* 1 (1998) 6; Rodley, *ibid*; Nowak, n 14, *supra*, 44, 859; O Ben-Naftali and Y Shany, 'Living in Denial: The Application of Human Rights in the Occupied Territories' 37 *Israel Law Review* 17 (2003–04).

[56] A Cassese, *International Law* (OUP: Oxford, 2005) 386.

[57] Ben-Naftali and Shany, n 55, *supra*, 62–4.   [58] Nowak, n 14, *supra*, 859.

[59] Convention against Torture and Other Cruel, Inhuman or Degrading Treatment or Punishment (10 December 1984) 1465 UNTS 85, entered into force 26 June 1987.

bringing proceedings against perpetrators of torture, including in cases in which the torture occurred outside the state's territory.[60] Accordingly, states cannot argue that the CAT prohibition of torture does not bind their agents acting extra-territorially if, at the same time, they accept the obligation to initiate criminal proceedings against these individuals. Indeed, the illegality of torture wherever it occurs is hard to dispute and, in its submission to the Committee against Torture, the US declares that '[T]he U.S. Government does not permit, tolerate, or condone torture, or other unlawful practices, by its personnel or employees under any circumstances. U.S. laws prohibiting such practices apply both when the employees are operating in the United States and in other parts of the world.'[61]

The CAT obligations are not, however, free from disagreement with regard to their extraterritorial applicability. States have argued that a number of obligations other than the torture prohibition itself, do not apply outside their own territory. This includes the Article 16 prohibition of 'other acts of cruel, inhuman or degrading treatment or punishment which do not amount to torture as defined in article I'. Referring to this article of CAT, the US noted that it only applied to territory under its jurisdiction, and that it did not accept that *de facto* control fell under this.[62] The Committee against Torture did not accept this position, and the Committee took the view that 'the provisions of the Convention expressed as applicable to "territory under the State party's jurisdiction" apply to, and are fully enjoyed, by all persons under the effective control of its authorities, of whichever type, wherever located in the world.'[63]

The extraterritorial applicability of these disputed provisions can be subjected to a similar line of reasoning as taken earlier with regard to the ICCPR, in that denying their applicability would seem to contradict the very notion of the protections that international human rights law seeks to achieve. Notwithstanding, as with the ICCPR and other treaties, there is still need for further analysis of the conditions under which extraterritorial applicability might exist and, in particular, of the notion of being within a state's jurisdiction in the context of human rights obligations. The majority of the remaining sections of the current chapter will be devoted to this examination.

[60] CAT, Arts 5, 6, 7, 8, 9.

[61] 'Consideration of Reports Submitted by States Parties Under Article 19 of the Convention, Second Periodic Reports of States Parties due in 1999', Addendum, United States of America, UN Doc Cat/C/48/Add.3, 29 June 2005, para 7. For details of steps taken, see paras 45–52.

[62] 'List of issues to be considered during the examination of the second periodic report of the United States of America, Response of the United States of America', Committee Against Torture, 36th Session, 1–19 May 2006, 87. See also statement of UK delegation to CAT in 'UNCAT Hearing: Provisions of lists of issues to state parties', Committee Against Torture, 33rd Session, 15–26 November 2004, 22.

[63] 'Consideration of Reports Submitted by States Parties Under Article 19 of the Convention, Conclusions and Recommendations of the Committee against Torture, United States of America' UN Doc CAT/C/USA/CO/2, 25 July 2006, para 15. See also Committee Against Torture, 'General Comment no 2: Implementation of article 2 by States parties', UN Doc.CAT/C/GC/2 24 January 2008, para 16.

A further argument against applicability of human rights obligations, rests upon the view that they do not apply during armed conflict, in which times IHL should be the sole source of rules.[64] There are a number of reasons why this argument is not enough to deny extraterritorial human rights obligations. First, it is the case, as described in Chapter 5 of this work, that there may be debates as to whether particular situations are to be determined as armed conflict or not, thus leaving the applicability of IHL unclear. Second, international human rights law does not cease to be of relevance at the outset of armed conflict, and human rights obligations can exist during these times, as will be seen in the later chapter devoted to this matter. It should however be noted that if the circumstances in which the state actions take place are those of armed conflict, then any analysis of whether human rights violations have occurred would also have to take into account the parallel applicability of IHL and the ways in which this may, or may not, affect the relevant human rights.[65] Finally, not all extraterritorial forcible measures against individuals occur in the context of armed conflict (as can be seen in the earlier example of Vanunu). If these measures are not part of an armed conflict, then IHL will not apply. International human rights law is the primary framework that provides rules for restraining states from using abusive force against individuals in these circumstances.

2. The conditions for extraterritorial applicability of human rights law

The discussion thus far has pointed to the fact that the concept of applying international human rights law to extraterritorial operations is indeed a reality that has support even in the seemingly more restrictive ICCPR, and in the views of international courts and human rights monitoring bodies. The next stage is, therefore, to examine under what circumstances and conditions can one claim that international human rights law applies to a situation in which a state is acting extraterritorially. As noted earlier, the human rights treaties speak of affording protection to individuals who are subject to the state's jurisdiction. Accordingly, the first step of the analysis should be to examine this concept.

2.1 The meaning of 'within their jurisdiction'

It is advantageous, at the start of any debate on issues of jurisdiction, to repeat the words of Brownlie, who says of jurisdiction (and of sovereignty) that there is a:

... terminology which is not employed very consistently in legal sources such as works of authority or the opinions of law officers, or by statesmen, who naturally place political

---

[64] *Consideration of Reports*, *ibid*, para 14.
[65] See Ch 9, *infra*, on relationship between IHL and human rights.

meanings in the foreground. The terminology as used by lawyers is also unsatisfactory in that the complexity and diversity of the rights, duties, powers, liberties, and immunities of states are obscured by the liberal use of omnibus terms like 'sovereignty' and 'jurisdiction'.[66]

As will be seen, jurisdiction is a term used in more than one way, and the meaning has, therefore, to be understood in the context within which it is being used. Brownlie does later provide a clear starting point to understand the term when he says that '[j]urisdiction is an aspect of sovereignty and refers to judicial, legislative, and administrative competence.'[67] Generally speaking, most of the references to jurisdiction refer to it as a form of competence or authority to take a certain action.[68] Within this, jurisdiction can refer to different types of action, most notably the authority to make rules or laws, which can be described as prescriptive or legislative jurisdiction, and the authority to ensure compliance with the laws, described as enforcement or prerogative jurisdiction.[69]

Most of the discussion on jurisdiction is concerned with the competence to create laws and enforce them, and much of this occurs in the context of criminal jurisdiction. In this context, the clearest basis for exercise of jurisdiction rests on territoriality—states can regulate daily life within their own territory by legislating and enforcing the rules.[70] There are certain matters that can fall outside the jurisdictional authority of the state, such as diplomatic immunities,[71] but generally speaking states have a virtually free reign to exercise jurisdiction within their territory. Extraterritorial legislative jurisdiction is also acceptable to a certain degree, based on additional principles of jurisdiction. These are based on nationality (a national abroad can be the subject of jurisdiction); passive personality (jurisdiction over acts in which the victim was a national); the protective principle (jurisdiction over acts abroad which affect state security); and jurisdiction over certain international crimes (such as war crimes).[72] The first and last of these principles have a strong basis in international law (even if the actual exercise of jurisdiction under these principles is sometimes at the centre

---

[66] Although Brownlie does add that 'a degree of uniformity of usage does exist and may be noticed'. See I Brownlie *Principles of Public International Law* (OUP: Oxford, 2003) 105–6. For an examination of the different uses of the term jurisdiction see M Milanovic, 'From Compromise to Principle: Clarifying the Concept of State Jurisdiction in Human Rights Treaties' 8 *Human Rights Law Review* 411 (2008).

[67] *Ibid*, 297.

[68] M Dixon and R McCorquodale, *Cases & Materials on International Law* (OUP: Oxford, 2003) 268; 'In its broadest sense, the jurisdiction of a State may refer to its lawful power to act and hence to its power to decide whether and, if so, how to act.'; B Oxman, 'Jurisdiction of States' in *Encyclopedia of Public International Law, vol III*, (Elsevier Science: Netherlands, 1997) 55–60, 55.

[69] Brownlie, n 66, *supra*, 297; Shaw, n 72, *infra*, 572; Dixon and McCorquodale, *ibid*. Some commentators add a further division to include adjudicative jurisdiction to describe the specific competence of courts.

[70] Brownlie, n 66, 297; Oxman, n 68, *supra*, 56.

[71] Cassese, n 56, *supra*, 98–123; Dixon and McCorquodale, n 68, *supra*, 301–47.

[72] Brownlie, n 66, *supra*, 301–05. M Shaw *International Law* (CUP: Cambridge, 2003) 584–97.

of controversy[73]) and are clear indications that extraterritorial jurisdiction does exist. It should be noted that the extraterritorial aspect is contained in the *legislative* jurisdiction. States can, in these circumstances, create laws relating to extra-territorial actions or people who are abroad. Extraterritorial *enforcement*, however, is a separate affair and is generally regarded as prohibited.[74] For example, a state might have the legislative jurisdictional competence to pass a law prohibiting its nationals from committing murder abroad, and can place an individual on trial for this crime committed abroad once the individual is back in the state, but it does not generally have the enforcement jurisdictional competence to send its police officers to arrest the person while abroad.[75]

When human rights treaties speak of securing the rights of persons 'within the jurisdiction', how is jurisdiction to be understood? Can these treaty obligations cover forcible measures taken outside state territory? At the outset, it should be recognized that there is a certain difficulty in transposing the above discussion of jurisdiction into the realm of human rights obligations. In the context of criminal jurisdiction, as referred to above, jurisdiction is used to denote the competence of the state to take an action. In human rights treaties, jurisdiction is referred to from a different angle, this time focusing on the responsibility of states towards an individual. Taking the earlier example of the abduction of Vanunu, according to the general principles of jurisdiction referred to earlier, Israel may have had the legislative jurisdictional competence for the laws that made it a crime for Vanunu to be divulging state secrets to journalists, even if his act took place in London. It did not, however, have the enforcement jurisdictional authority to abduct Vanunu from Italy in order to put him on trial for the crime. These are crucial jurisdictional matters but, insofar as human rights law is concerned, there is yet a third jurisdictional question and that is whether, at the time of the abduction, Vanunu can be considered to have been within Israel's jurisdiction as understood in the human rights treaties, thus leading to a conclusion that Israel had a responsibility not to violate his rights.

Under the nationality jurisdiction principle, it might be argued that the state agents were, from the start, within the jurisdiction of the state and that the state has responsibility for their actions even if these take place beyond its borders.[76] Attribution is, however, only one component of state responsibility for an

---

[73] See for instance *Democratic Republic of the Congo v. Belgium ('Arrest Warrant of April 11th 2000')*, Judgment, Merits, para 78.D.2; 41 ILM 536 (2002).

[74] See R Higgins *Problems and Process: International Law and How We Use It* (Clarendon Press: Oxford, 1994) 73; above discussion concerning abductions; Dixon and McCorquodale, n 68, *supra*, 268; see discussion in Ch 3 of Part I.

[75] Though there may be exceptions or allowances based for instance on consent of the territorial state. See Dixon and McCorquodale, n 68, *supra*, 268; Shaw, n 72, *supra*, 572–3; Oxman, n 68, *supra*, 59. See the discussion of this in Ch 3 of Part I, *supra*. See also the possibility of enforcement in context of piracy, n 154–162, *infra*, and accompanying text.

[76] See, eg, discussion of attribution in *Case Concerning Military and Paramilitary Activities in and Against Nicaragua*, [1986] ICJ Rep 14.

internationally wrongful act, the other being a breach of an international obligation.[77] As far as human rights treaties are concerned, the existence of obligations are not dependent on whether the *agent* is within the jurisdiction, but on the individual at the receiving end—the alleged *victim* of the violation needs to be within the jurisdiction.[78] This appears quite clear from the wording of the treaties, as quoted above.[79] In light of this it is generally necessary to establish the circumstances in which an individual victim might be considered within the jurisdiction of the state. An additional possibility is that a breach of obligation might be found through customary international law obligations not to violate human rights—this will be explored in a later section.

One of the criticisms of the extraterritorial extension of human rights treaty obligations is that the individuals who have allegedly suffered a violation were not in the first place within the jurisdiction of the state, and therefore the state owed them no obligation.[80] It is certainly true that before the state acts the individual who is about to be affected might not come within the jurisdiction of the state—at least not according to the classic principles of jurisdiction as appeared earlier.[81] However, the primary conclusion one should draw from this line of thinking is that, by taking this action, the state may well have overstepped its authority to exercise enforcement jurisdiction and encroached upon the sovereignty of the territorial state.[82] This is a separate issue from whether, in the process of taking the action, the state might have violated the rights of the individual. The action has already taken place and arguing *post-facto* that the state did not have initial jurisdiction over the individual, and should not have taken the action, is of real significance to the inter-state aspect of the problem, but of little help in answering the problem of the individual alleging the violation. Along that vein, when discussing *Bankovic*,[83] Scheinin points out that the court discussed the permissibility of the state exercising jurisdiction beyond its territory, rather than the consequences of exercise of authority, and views this as a problem since the question put to the court was not whether the states were entitled to take action but whether there were human rights obligations if they did so.[84]

---

[77] 'Draft articles on responsibility of states for internationally wrongful acts', International Law Commission at its 53rd session (2001) Art 2.

[78] C Greenwood, 'Remarks, Bombing for Peace: Collateral Damage and Human Rights', 96 *American Society of International Law Proceedings* 95 (2002) 100.

[79] The UN Convention against Torture contains a particular feature which sets it apart, in that it includes an obligation to bring perpetrators of torture to justice on the basis of a link to the offender, without necessitating a jurisdictional link to the victim. See CAT, n 59, *supra*, Art 5.

[80] McGoldrick, n 38, *supra*, 43.

[81] See discussion of jurisdiction in section 2.1, *supra*. See also McGoldrick, n 38, *supra*, 45.

[82] See n 75, *supra*, and accompanying text; See also Ch 3, *supra*.

[83] In this case, the relatives of persons killed in a NATO bombing of the RTS television and radio station in Belgrade filed an application with the ECtHR against the European members of NATO. The Court found the application inadmissible (see further mention throughout this chapter).

[84] Similarly, Scheinin also notes that the Human Rights Committee did not ask whether Iran was entitled to issue a fatwa against Salman Rushdie, and presumed Iran would be responsible for results even if harm was befallen to him outside Iran. See M Scheinin, 'Extraterritorial Effect of

Human rights bodies, as will be seen shortly, have approached the notion of being 'within the jurisdiction' in two ways. The first is by determining that certain situations appear to qualify as circumstances in which the state is in fact exercising a form of jurisdictional authority over a territory, even if this is not sovereign territory, as in the case of military occupation. The second approach revolves around the concept that, by exercising control and authority over an individual, the person is brought within the jurisdiction of the state for the purpose of human rights obligations. This will be explored in further detail below.

The first situation, in which there is clear support for extraterritorial applicability of human rights obligations, is when a state exercises effective control over territory outside its borders, most clearly when a state has been recognized as an occupying power. Strong support for this is found in the case-law of human rights bodies as well as the ICJ. These include the situation of Israel and the Occupied Palestinian Territories, about which the ICJ and UN Human Rights bodies have clearly stated the applicability of UN human rights treaties;[85] the ICJ decision finding that human rights law obligations were applicable to Uganda in areas of Eastern DRC;[86] the UN Special Rapporteur's report on the Iraqi occupation in Kuwait;[87] and the finding of the European Court of Human Rights that Turkey's human rights obligations under the ECHR extended to its control of Northern Cyprus.[88] This approach can be based on certain situations of effective control being analogous to territorial jurisdiction, at least with regard to the power and authority to enforce rules,[89] primarily since, in this type of situation, the state takes on responsibilities on a governmental scale and the circumstances are in many ways analogous to the state's own territory.[90]

Situations in which the state exercises effective control over a territory have been defined as outside the scope and will, therefore, not be analysed in detail but, in the context of this chapter, they do serve to demonstrate that human rights obligations can extend extraterritorially.[91] Other types of situation in

the International Covenant on Civil and Political Rights' in F Coomans and M Kamminga, n 38, *supra*, 73–81, 79–80.

[85] *Wall*, n 1, *supra*, paras 107–12; Human Rights Committee: Israel, n 6, *supra*; Committee on Economic, Social and Cultural Rights, 'Concluding Observations of the Committee on Economic, Social and Cultural Rights: Israel' E/C.12/1/Add.69, 31 August 2001.

[86] *DRC v. Uganda*, n 2, *supra*, paras 216–20. The Court seems to go further, and the decision can be read as finding extraterritorial applicability of international human rights law also in areas outside Ituri, ie outside of occupied territory.

[87] Special Rapporteur, n 7, *supra*, paras 55–9.

[88] *Loizidou v. Turkey*, n 8 *supra*; *Cyprus v. Turkey*, n 8, *supra*.

[89] 'Jurisdiction analogous to territorial jurisdiction may be exercised over areas leased by a State in accordance with the terms of the lease or, for some purposes, over areas subject to military occupation' Oxman, n 68, *supra*, 57.

[90] *Bankovic*, n 43, *supra*, para 71. See also the discussion in section 3, *infra*, on contextual approach to obligations.

[91] Situations of effective control over territory also raise the question of whether the state might be obligated to ensure all human rights obligations—positive and negative. See *ibid* and discussion in section 3, *infra*, on contextual approach to obligations.

which there is considerable support for applying human rights obligations, concern cases involving diplomatic or consular agents, or craft or vessels registered in the state or flying its flag.[92] The relevance of these situations will be returned to later in this chapter. Indeed, in addition to control of territory, there is ample case law supporting further instances in which individuals not in the territory of a state might, nevertheless, be considered within its jurisdiction for the purpose of determining the existence of an obligation under human rights law. The recurring proposition in these cases is that, in certain circumstances, the action taken by the state agent brings the individual at the receiving end of the action into the jurisdiction of the state.[93] This approach can be understood as implying that the action which the state (through its agents) takes against the individual is a form of exercise of enforcement jurisdiction, whether lawful or unlawful and, as such, the individual at that point in time is within the jurisdiction of the state as far as human rights treaties are concerned.[94] The action may have exceeded the accepted authority of the state (and that may have implications insofar as the inter-state relationship is concerned[95]) but that does not alter the fact that the state has carried out an enforcement type action.

The Inter-American Commission of Human Rights chose to formulate their reasoning in a case concerning individuals who had been detained by US forces operating in Grenada, and formulated the grounds for this approach as follows:

While the extraterritorial application of the American Declaration has not been placed at issue by the parties, the Commission finds it pertinent to note that, under certain circumstances, the exercise of its jurisdiction over acts with an extraterritorial locus will not only be consistent with but required by the norms which pertain. The fundamental rights of the individual are proclaimed in the Americas on the basis of the principles of equality and non-discrimination—'without distinction as to race, nationality, creed or sex'. Given that individual rights inhere simply by virtue of a person's humanity, each American State is obliged to uphold the protected rights of any person subject to its jurisdiction. While this most commonly refers to persons within a State's territory, it may, under given circumstances, refer to conduct with an extraterritorial locus where the person concerned is present in the territory of one State, but subject to the control of another State—usually through the acts of the latter's agents abroad. In principle, the inquiry turns not on the presumed victim's nationality or presence within a particular geographic

---

[92] See discussion in section 2.2, *infra*, on acts of diplomatic or consular agents.

[93] *Cyprus v. Turkey* (unreported) App no 6780/74 and No 6950/75, 26 May 1975, para 8; *X v. United Kingdom* (unreported) App no 7547/76, 15 December 1977; *Alejandre v. Cuba*, n 9, *supra*, para 23; *Coard v. US*, n 9, *supra*, para 37; *Issa and ors v. Turkey*, App no 31821/96, 16 November 2004, para 72.

[94] In a recent article Milanovic offers an alternative understanding of this, based on interpreting the term of jurisdiction in human rights treaties as being different to other notions of jurisdiction in international law, and essentially referring to the factual exercise of power: see Milanovic, n 66, *supra*.

[95] See above and Part I, *supra*.

area, but on whether, under the specific circumstances, the State observed the rights of a person subject to its authority and control.[96]

The European Commission of Human Rights described the concept thus:

[...] authorised agents of a State not only remain under its jurisdiction when abroad, but bring any other person 'within the jurisdiction' of that State to the extent they exercise authority over such persons. Insofar as the State's acts or omissions affect such persons, the responsibility of that State is engaged.[97]

2.2 Authority and control over individuals

Acts of diplomatic and consular agents

According to the European Court of Human Rights, in addition to control of territory, 'other recognised instances of the extraterritorial exercise of jurisdiction by a state include cases involving the activities of its diplomatic or consular agents abroad and on board craft and vessels registered in, or flying the flag of, that State.'[98] In the case of *X v. UK*, the European Commission of Human Rights acknowledged that an affected individual can be said to have been brought into the jurisdiction of the state when stating that, 'even though the alleged failure of the consular authorities to do all in their power to help the applicant occurred outside the territory of the United Kingdom, it was still 'within the jurisdiction' within the meaning of Article 1 of the Convention'.[99]

Extraterritorial applicability of human rights obligations in these circumstances appears to have support even within the context of a more limited approach to extraterritorial obligations.[100] What is it about the cases involving

---

[96] *Coard and ors v. United States*, n 9, *supra*, para 37. It should be noted that the American Declaration does not contain an article setting down the conditions for applicability as found in the American Convention and other treaties quoted above. Nonetheless, the above view sets out an understanding of the term jurisdiction which is pertinent to the discussion at hand. *American Declaration of the Rights and Duties of Man*, OAS Res XXX, adopted by the Ninth International Conference of American States (1948), reprinted in Basic Documents Pertaining to Human Rights in the Inter-American System, OEA/Ser.L.V/II.82 doc 6 rev.1 at 17 (1992).

[97] The decision referred to a German national who alleged unlawful detention on account of being tricked into returning to Germany where he was subsequently arrested. The application was rejected on the fact and the Court (to which the application was referred by the Commission) did not find in favour of the applicant either. See *Stocke v. Germany*, Case no 28/1989/188/248, 19 March 1991.

[98] *Bankovic*, n 43, para 73.

[99] *X v. UK*, n 93, *supra*. The case concerned a British national's complaint that the British Consulate in Jordan had failed to adequately assist her in recovering her daughter from the Jordanian father. The application failed on the facts, since the Commission assessed that the consular authorities had indeed attempted to help.

[100] For instance in the determination of the European Court in *Bankovic*, n 43, *supra*, para 73, and the UK High Court in *Al-Skeini and ors v. Secretary of State for Defence* [2004] EWHC 2911, 14 December 2004, para 270. The case then went before the Court of Appeals, see *Al-Skeini and ors v. Secretary of State for Defence* [2005] EWCA Civ 1609, Court of Appeal, 21 December 2005; and the House of Lords, see *Al-Skeini and ors* (Respondents) *v. Secretary of State for*

diplomatic or consular agents, that might distinguish them from other cases, for instance from an undercover agent abducting an individual on foreign soil? The primary reasoning would appear to be that the former situation:

> ...occurs by reason of the exercise of State authority in or from a location which has a form of discrete quasi-territorial quality, or where the State agent's presence in a foreign State is consented to by that State and protected by international law: such as diplomatic or consular premises, or vessels or aircraft registered in the respondent State.[101]

Had embassies and other diplomatic premises been considered to be territory of the foreign state, there would be a clear and strong argument that these situations qualify for applicability of human rights obligations. However, behind the convoluted term 'discrete quasi-territorial quality', is the fact that while the premises of diplomatic missions enjoy various protections and immunities from local law,[102] they nevertheless are part of the territory of the local state and under its sovereignty,[103] with the diplomatic staff therefore acting as extraterritorial agents. Accordingly, the key distinction between cases involving diplomatic or consular agents and some other cases is, as noted in the above quotation, that diplomatic or consular agents are operating with the consent of the local state. This brings us back to the need to distinguish between the two categories of relationships—the inter-state relationship and that of the state to the individual. The issue of consent for the actions of diplomatic or consular agents belongs to the domain of inter-state relationships as governed by the appropriate rules of international law.[104] Determining an alleged violation of a human rights obligation is an issue residing primarily in the sphere of the relationship between the state and the individual in accordance with international human rights law. Whether or not the extraterritorial agents acted with consent affects the inter-state relationship and may involve a breach of an international obligation towards the local state, but it should not be the determining factor as to whether the state agents violated the rights of an individual.[105] As Nowak stated, in an earlier quotation, '[I]t is irrelevant whether these actions are permissible under general international law [...].'[106] Furthermore, the issue of consent relates primarily to the question of whether

---

Defence (Appellant); *Al-Skeini and ors* (Appellants) *v. Secretary of State for Defence* (Respondent) (Consolidated Appeals) [2007] UKHL 26, 13 June 2007, para 109.

[101] *Al-Skeini*, High Court, *ibid*, para 270.

[102] Vienna Convention on Diplomatic Relations (18 April 1961) 500 UNTS entered into force on 24 April 1964, Art 22.

[103] Cassese, n 56, *supra*, 114; *Al-Skeini*, High Court, n 100, *supra*, para 169.

[104] Such as the Vienna Convention, n 102, *supra*.

[105] There may be certain connections, as noted in Ch 7, section 3, *supra*, on abductions, in that the inter-state illegality serves to show that the measure against the individual was not in accordance with the law. If there is a connection between the two spheres, it would therefore seem to work in the opposite direction—the lack of consent might strengthen the possibility of the act being a human rights violation, rather than serve as a reason for claiming human rights law does not apply.

[106] Nowak, n 14, *supra*, 44.

the state was allowed to take the measure in the first place, rather than answering what obligations exist when it does take action.[107]

Arguing that the applicability of human rights law obligations is dependent on whether the agents were acting with consent of the territorial state leads, in effect, to the unsavoury conclusion that a state whose agents act with consent of the territorial state must conform to human rights law obligations in its dealings with individuals, while the state that acts unlawfully in respect of the inter-state relationship is rewarded with being outside the purview of human rights law in respect of the measures it takes. In other words, by breaching the sovereignty of the territorial state, the outside state would shed itself of responsibilities under human rights law. This interpretation is at best problematic, if not highly dubious, in that it creates an incentive for states to act unlawfully. Lack of authority for the initial action cannot be grounds for evading responsibility for the results.

Instead, it is suggested here that, while acts taken by diplomatic or consular staff are distinguishable in that they are less likely to involve a breach of sovereignty towards the territorial state, they are of less relevance in determining the applicability of human rights law obligations. If such circumstances can give rise to extraterritorial obligations towards individuals, then obligations towards individuals in circumstances involving non-diplomatic personnel might also exist. In fact, the citation used as support for the claim that extraterritorial human rights obligations can be attached to actions of diplomatic or consular personnel actually supports a wider and less limited contention:

It is clear, in this respect, from the constant jurisprudence of the Commission that authorised agents of a State, *including* diplomatic or consular agents, bring other persons or property within the jurisdiction of that State to the extent that they exercise authority over such persons or property. Insofar as they affect such persons or property by their acts or omissions, the responsibility of the State is engaged.[108]

Diplomatic or consular agents are but one possibility among others, as is apparent from the word 'including'. They are, perhaps, the clearest example but not the only one. Indeed, case-law of the human rights bodies goes beyond actions of diplomatic personnel and includes a variety of circumstances in which it is claimed that extraterritorial actions of state agents can lead to the individuals affected by their actions being considered within the jurisdiction of the outside state with respect to human rights obligations. Examples range from extraterritorial abduction and ill-treatment of an individual by Uruguay in Argentina,[109] to the shooting down by Cuba of civilian aircraft outside Cuban airspace.[110] The deciding factor shared by all these cases is not the official title (eg diplomatic personnel) of the extraterritorial agents, or whether they had consent from the territorial state,

---

[107] See discussion in text, *infra*, and mention in nn 82, 84, *supra*, and accompanying text.

[108] *X v. UK*, n 93, *supra*, emphasis added.   [109] *Lopez v. Uruguay*, n 4, *supra*.

[110] *Alejandre v. Cuba*, n 9, *supra*.

but the determination that the circumstances involved an element of authority and power over the individual, and this is what led the individual to be brought into the jurisdiction of the state with respect to the existence of human rights law obligations. A further observation is that in cases concerning diplomatic or consular personnel, the affected individual may have been the initiator of contact with the state (eg applying for a visa) whereas, in the forcible measures situations, it is often the other way around—the state seeks the individual and exercises power over him/her without the individual's consent. Taking that distinction into account, one might argue that if the former cases qualify for bringing persons into the jurisdiction of the state then the latter cases, in which the individual was not even given the choice of interaction with the state agents, should all the more so be equally considered.

Detention

The view that human rights obligations can extend extraterritorially when an individual is under the authority or control of the state, has support in many cases of the human rights bodies, including the European Commission of Human Rights, the European Court of Human Rights, the UN Human Rights Committee and the Inter-American Commission on Human Rights, as well as domestic courts.[111] It is this element of control or authority that consequently leads to the individual being considered within the jurisdiction of the state for the purpose of human rights obligations. The Human Rights Committee uses the expression 'power or effective control' when stating that 'a State party must respect and ensure the rights laid down in the Covenant to anyone within the power or effective control of that State Party, even if not situated within the territory of the State Party.'[112] Although it has been argued that the European *Bankovic Case* adopted a more restricted approach which may negate the authority or control test,[113] the continuing reiteration in various forms of this approach in numerous earlier and later cases (as will be seen) in addition to cases and opinions of other human rights bodies,[114] provides ample support for the contention that exercise by state agents of authority or control over an individual can bring him/her into the jurisdiction of the state for the purposes of human rights obligations. It is, therefore, necessary to try to understand the precise meaning of this test.

Holding an individual in an extraterritorial prison or detention facility is a clear example of having authority or control. During the *Bankovic* pleadings, Christopher Greenwood, acting as counsel for the UK and speaking on behalf of the respondent states, and therefore arguing to limit extraterritorial applicability

---

[111] See cases mentioned, nn 93, 109, *supra*; *Al-Skeini* Court of Appeal, n 100, *supra*, paras 81, 96. The UK Court gave support for this test under a different title—the doctrine of state agent authority.

[112] General Comment 31, n 5, *supra*, para 10.

[113] Most notably in *Al-Skeini*, High Court and House of Lords judgments, both n 100, *supra*.

[114] See nn 111, 93, 109, *supra*, and Ch 7, n 95, *supra*; n 140, *supra*.

of the ECHR, accepted that 'a prisoner is the archetypal example of someone who comes within the jurisdiction of the detaining State which exercises the most extreme type of control over him'.[115]

In the six consolidated cases of *Al-Skeini and ors* the UK government, before the House of Lords, accepted that in relation to one of the cases the individual may have come within the jurisdiction of the UK.[116] This was the case of Baha Mousa, a hotel receptionist in Basra, Iraq, who was detained by British forces, taken to a military base, and beaten to death by British soldiers. The other five cases were incidents involving British troops patrolling the streets and troops raiding a house. Whilst rejecting the other five applications, the UK courts found that, in the case of Baha Mousa, the state's responsibilities under the European Convention on Human Rights were engaged. Thus, the High Court, the Court of Appeals and the House of Lords, all appear to confirm the extraterritorial applicability of international human rights law obligations in relation to death in detention.[117]

A number of cases confirm that human rights obligations extend to extraterritorial places of detention. In addition to *Al-Skeini*, these include the case of *Hess v. UK* concerning the treatment of the Nazi leader, Rudolf Hess, who was being held in a Berlin prison controlled by the US, UK, France and the USSR. The application failed primarily in the context of resolving responsibility in a situation of joint administration, but the Commission noted that:

[...] in the present case the exercise of authority by the respondent Government takes place not in the territory of the United Kingdom but outside its territory. [...] The Commission is of the opinion that there is in principle, from a legal point of view, no reason why the acts of British authorities in Berlin should not entail the liability of the United Kingdom under the Convention...[118]

---

[115] Verbatim record of the hearing 24 October 200 cited in M O'Boyle, 'The European Convention on Human Rights and Extraterritorial Jurisdiction: A Comment on "Life After Bankovic"' in Coomans and Kamminga, 125–39, n 38, *supra*, 138. See also the submissions of the respondent governments in *Bankovic*, n 43, *supra, para* 37. See also *Al-Skeini*, High Court, n 100, *supra*, paras 286–8; *Hess v. United Kingdom* (1975) 2 D&R 72; *Coard*, n 9, *supra*; *Request for Precautionary Measures Concerning the Detainees at Guantanamo Bay, Cuba* IACHR, 12 March 12, 2002; 41 ILM (2002) 532.

[116] Statement of Case on behalf of the Respondent / Cross Appellant, *Al-Skeini* House of Lords, n 100, *supra*, para 106. However, the state contested the applicability of the UK Human Rights Act to all six cases, Baha Mousa included.

[117] See n 100, *supra*. In the house of Lords judgment, Lord Brown agreed with the Divisional Court that the reasoning for the detention exception was that a detention facility was a similar exception as embassies and consulates, whilst the court of Appeal found that Mr Mousa could have come within control and authority of the UK from the moment of his arrest. See *Al-Skeini*, House of Lords, n 100, *supra*, paras 107, 132. The question of persons being held outside formalized detention facilities will be examined in the next section.

[118] *Hess v. UK*, n 115, *supra*, 73. More recently one should note the difficulties (outside the scope of this work—posed by attribution and human rights obligations in the context of detentions overseas by multi-national forces, peace-support operations, and UN Security Council mandated operations. See *Behrami and Behrami v. France*, App no 71412/01 and *Saramati v. France, Germany and Norway*, Decision on admissibility, App no 78166/01, 2 May 2007.

The case of *Coard*, concerning persons held by US forces operating in Grenada, is an additional example in which human rights obligations were found applicable to extraterritorial detention.[119] Another situation involving the US revolves around the many detainees held in Guantanamo Bay in Cuba. Whilst the US Government has rejected the applicability of international human rights law to these detainees, the UN and Inter-American human rights bodies have resolutely taken the position that human rights obligations do apply.[120]

Detention in formal facilities, with *de jure* or *de facto* control over the facility and individuals within it would clearly, therefore, bring the individuals within the jurisdiction of the state for the purpose of human rights obligations.[121] The above cases have in common that the detained individuals were all held for periods ranging from days to years in extraterritorial detention. However, the extraterritorial aspect of an act of detention can also be much briefer. In the case of *Ocalan v. Turkey*, Ocalan, then leader of the Kurdistan Worker's Party ('PKK') was arrested by Turkish forces in Kenya before being flown back to Turkey for trial and imprisonment. In the words of the European Court of Human Rights:

> The Court notes that the applicant was arrested by members of the Turkish security forces inside an aircraft registered in Turkey in the international zone of Nairobi Airport. It is common ground that, directly after being handed over to the Turkish officials by the Kenyan officials, *the applicant was under effective Turkish authority and therefore within the 'jurisdiction' of that State for the purposes of Article 1 of the Convention, even though in this instance Turkey exercised its authority outside its territory.*[122]

Whilst the Court notes that the actual act of arrest occurred in a Turkish aircraft, it also clearly takes the position that exercising effective authority over the

---

[119] See n 9, *supra*. As noted above, the American Declaration does not contain a provision on jurisdiction. The Commission's opinion has, nevertheless, included an examination of this issue, and is relevant to the determination of detainees being considered within the jurisdiction of a state.

[120] Special Rapporteur on protection of human rights while countering terrorism n 7, *supra*, paras 6–10; Report of the Chairperson-Rapporteur of the Working Group on Arbitrary Detention, Leila Zerrougui; the Special Rapporteur on the independence of judges and lawyers, Leandro Despouy; the Special Rapporteur on torture and other cruel, inhuman or degrading treatment or punishment, Manfred Nowak; the Special Rapporteur on freedom of religion or belief, Asma Jahangir; and the Special Rapporteur on the right of everyone to the enjoyment of the highest attainable standard of physical and mental health, Paul Hunt, E/CN 4/2006/120, 27 February 2006, para 11; *Detainees in Guantanamo Bay, Cuba; Request for Precautionary Measures*, IACHR, 13 March 2002). The fact that the Guantanamo detention facility is on territory leased by the US places it in the category of territories over which the level of control is similar to that of national territory, and therefore outside the scope of this work as defined in the first chapter. It is, nevertheless, mentioned here briefly since it is referred to as an example in which authority and control over detained persons can meet the requirement of extraterritorial human rights obligations.

[121] The ECtHR *Al-Saadoon* admissibility decision raises the question of *de facto* control over detention facilities. See *Al-Saadoon and Mufdhi v UK*, Decision on Admissibility, App no 61498/08, paras 87–88.

[122] *Ocalan v. Turkey*, App no 46221/99, 12 May 2005, para 91, emphasis added.

individual, in extraterritorial circumstances, brings that individual within the state's jurisdiction insofar as its human rights treaty obligations are concerned.

Ocalan, like the other cases on detention discussed above, concerned a formalized measure, taking place in accordance with some form of official policy openly acknowledged by the state. Not all extraterritorial deprivations of liberty occur in conditions of this type, especially when involving clandestine or questionable operations. Could human rights obligations also extend to individuals who find themselves in the hands of state agents operating in the latter circumstances? As seen in the next section, the case law suggests that they can.

Authority or control outside formally acknowledged detention facilities

The case of *Issa v. Turkey* concerned Iraqi shepherds found dead in the hills of Northern Iraq. Their families alleged that Turkish forces operating in the area had detained and killed them. The Court found that there was not enough evidence to prove these allegations but clearly indicated that, had the facts been present, it could have found Turkey to be in violation of the Convention, for extraterritorial unlawful detention and/or killings. The court noted that 'a State may also be held accountable for violation of the Convention rights and freedoms of persons who are in the territory of another State but who are found to be under the former State's authority and control through its agents operating—*whether lawfully or unlawfully*—in the latter state.[123]

As can be seen from *Ocalan* and *Issa*, the exercise of control or authority over individuals, resulting in human rights obligations under the European Convention, does not require that this control be exercised within the four walls of a formally recognized detention facility. Extraterritorial clandestine detentions were also the subject of cases before the UN Human Rights Committee. In *Lopez v. Uruguay*[124] and *Casariego v. Uruguay*[125] the Committee was faced with cases in which Uruguayan agents had abducted and secretly detained individuals in Argentina and Brazil, respectively, before taking them back to Uruguay. In both cases, the Committee declared that:

Article 2 (1) of the Covenant places an obligation upon a State party to respect and to ensure rights 'to all individuals within its territory and subject to its jurisdiction', but it does not imply that the State party concerned cannot be held accountable for violations of rights under the Covenant which its agents commit upon the territory of another State, whether with the acquiescence of the Government of that State or in opposition to it.[126]

---

[123] *Issa*, n 93, *supra*, para 71, emphasis added. [124] *Lopez v. Uruguay*, n 4, *supra*.
[125] *Casariego v. Uruguay*, n 4, *supra*.
[126] *Casariego, ibid*, para 10.3; *Lopez*, n 4, *supra*, para 12.3. One of the Committee members, Tomuschat, disagreed with the explanation the Committee gave for this statement, but agreed with the conclusion that in this case there had been a violation See discussion of this in nn 49–51, *supra*, and accompanying text.

With regard to cases such as *Ocalan*, it has been argued that co-operation with local authorities as part of an official procedure to detain and bring the person back for trial is a primary factor in explaining why there might be support for extraterritorial obligations.[127] As discussed earlier, the consent of the territorial state is pertinent to the inter-state rules on violation of sovereignty, but should not be a determining factor in the assessment of extraterritorial applicability of human rights obligations.[128] Indeed, in the cases mentioned above, it is clearly indicated that the human rights obligations were not dependent upon consent of the territorial state. Neither, as can be seen from the cases described immediately above, should the applicability be influenced by the question of whether the individual was detained in a formal detention facility, in a cave in the mountains or held secretly in a city apartment. The determining factor, which all the described cases share, is that an individual is being held powerless in direct control of agents of the state.

Regarding the types of forcible measures with which we are concerned here, it would thus appear that extraterritorial abductions and ill-treatment of detainees could clearly fulfil the criteria of the authority or control test, and that human rights obligations are attached to these situations.

Beyond being physically in the hands of state authorities, what else would constitute exercise of authority? Some of the European Commission's cases mention state agents affecting a person (or property) by their acts or omissions.[129] This formulation is perhaps a little too wide, and claiming that anyone affected by *any* act (or omission!) of any state agent is thereby within state jurisdiction is a claim which might be difficult to sustain. According to Lawson, although restricting the test only to legal authority is too narrow since this might exclude *de facto* control (as discussed above[130]) referring to 'anybody affected' goes too far.[131] Lawson suggests that 'if there is a direct and immediate link between the extraterritorial conduct of a state and the alleged violation of an individual's rights, then the individual must be assumed to be "within the jurisdiction", within the meaning of Article 1, of the State concerned'. An example he provides of such a link is the case of *Xhavara*, in which an Italian warship collided with a boat of Albanian asylum seekers heading for Italy, resulting in the death of 58 people who had been on the

---

[127] Lord Brown was of the view that 'both *Sánchez Ramirez v France* (1996) 86–A DR 155 and *Freda v Italy* (1980) 21 DR 250 (the authorities there referred to) also concerned irregular extradition, one a revolutionary known as Carlos (the Jackal), the other an Italian Each was taken into custody abroad, respectively by French police in Khartoum and by Italian police in Costa Rica, and flown respectively in a French military airplane to France and in an Italian Air force plane to Italy. In each case, as in *Ocalan*, the forcible removal was effected with the full cooperation of the foreign authorities and with a view to the applicant's criminal trial in the respondent state.' in *Al-Skeini*, House of Lords, n 100, *supra*, para 119.

[128] Although it might influence certain aspects of it. See Ch 7, n 88–97, *supra*, and accompanying text.

[129] Eg in *X v. UK*, n 93, *supra*.   [130] *Lopez v. Uruguay*, n 4, *supra*; *Issa*, n 93, *supra*.

[131] R Lawson, 'Life After Bankovic: On the Extraterritorial Application of the European Convention on Human Rights' in Coomans and Kamminga, 83–123, n 38, *supra*, 103–04.

Albanian ship.[132] It is worth noting that acts of omission can also come within this rubric—for instance, not feeding a detainee.[133] While Lawson's suggestion is not a water-tight definition of the test, and one can question how to understand 'direct and immediate link', the precise interpretation and result may have to be determined on a case-by-case basis.[134] Scheinin has a similar but differently formulated approach, according to which 'facticity determines normativity',[135] as do Ben-Naftali and Shany with their 'conduct oriented approach'.[136] The key to such approaches can be found in the state's control over whether to act in a way which has a direct foreseeable adverse impact on the individual. It is not only a question of overall control over an individual or the territory in which s/he is located, but can also be of power over a specific aspect of the individual's circumstances in such a way as to be controlling their right(s).[137] Clearly there is room to further develop the above approaches, with questions such as whether one could use these tests in order to assert that a state's domestic economic subsidy policy has a direct effect on labourers in a developing country. In this context, Ben-Naftali and Shany suggest that 'considerations of fairness and expediency require that states would not bear responsibility for indirect or unforeseen consequences of their actions in areas outside their control.'[138] The exact limits of these tests may still need to be worked out, nonetheless it is submitted that they provide a useful approach to consider. Furthermore, the types of forcible measures examined within the current scope fall within the less debatable end of the spectrum for these tests in that the direct effect of forcible measures, such as abductions and killings, is fairly clear. In the context of the questions raised this is, therefore, of clear relevance to assessing applicability of human rights obligations to extraterritorial use of force in measures such as targeted killings.

If the state agents gained physical control of the individual prior to carrying out the killing then it would clearly follow from the above analysis that the person is within their authority and subject to their control. This certainly seems

---

[132] The Italian captain was in fact tried in Italy for manslaughter. See *Xhavara and ors v. Italy and Albania,* Decision, (unreported) App no 39473/98, 11 January 2001 (summary available on Information Note no 26 on the case-law of the Court, January 2001). Greenwood points out that the decision on jurisdiction in this case was based on there being an agreement between the two countries on shipping inspections. Greenwood, n 78, *supra,* 103.

[133] See section 3, *infra,* on contextual approach.

[134] Rules of international law, even those designed to protect the innocent, are not immune from being formulated in a manner that leaves much room for interpretation and a need for common sense and good faith in application to specific cases. For instance, the IHL determination of proportionality in attack rests on balancing between foreseeable civilian casualties and a 'concrete and direct military advantage'. Protocol Additional to the Geneva Conventions of 12 August 1949, and Relating to the Protection of Victims of International Armed Conflicts (Protocol I) (8 June 1977) 1125 UNTS 3, entered into force 7 December 1978, Art 51.

[135] Scheinin, n 84, *supra,* 75–7.

[136] 'In our view, a sensible interpretation of the term "jurisdiction" would equate it with the actual or potential exercise of governmental power vis-à-vis all affected individuals', Ben-Naftali and Shany, n 55, *supra,* 62–3.

[137] Scheinin, n 84, *supra,* 75–7. [138] Ben-Naftali and Shany, n 55, *supra,* 64.

to be a legitimate conclusion from the case of *Issa*,[139] and it is confirmed in the more recent admissibility decision of the European Court in the case of *Isaak*.[140] Anastassios Isaak was allegedly beaten to death, at the hands of Turkish Republic of Northern Cyprus ('TRNC') and Turkish security personnel during a demonstration, and this occurred in the neutral buffer zone in Cyprus. The Turkish government argued that it could not be held responsible for acts that occurred in the buffer zone, which was outside Turkey's jurisdiction.[141] The Court explicitly recognized that this was not within Turkey's territory, but was of the opinion that the control exercised over Isaak by Turkish agents, brought him within the state's jurisdiction for the purpose of human rights obligations:

At the outset, the Court notes that the area in which the acts complained of took place belonged to the neutral UN buffer zone.[142]

And:

In the present case, the Court must therefore ascertain whether Anastassios Isaak came under the authority and/or effective control, and therefore within the jurisdiction, of the respondent State as a result of the acts of the Turkish and 'TRNC' soldiers and/or officials. The Court notes that the applicants provided written Statements from independent eyewitnesses describing the alleged course of events leading to the killing of Anastassios Isaak. In particular, UNFICYP members Police Officer Flood, Sergeant Carney and Superintendent Cosgrave were unequivocal in their Statements that Turkish-Cypriot policemen had actively taken part in the beating of Anastassios Isaak. This is also confirmed by the aforementioned reports of UNFICYP and the UN Secretary-General concerning the demonstration and, further, the video recording and photographs submitted by the applicants. In the latter, three 'TRNC' policemen and a Turkish or Turkish-Cypriot military/police officer in camouflage uniform can be seen beating Anastassios Isaak with the civilian demonstrators. Moreover, it transpires from the case-file that despite the presence of the Turkish armed forces and other 'TRNC' police officers in the area, nothing was done to prevent or stop the attack or to help the victim.

In view of the above, *even if the acts complained of took place in the neutral UN buffer zone, the Court considers that the deceased was under the authority and/or effective control of the respondent State through its agents* (see Issa and Others, cited above). It concludes, accordingly, that the matters complained of in the present application fall within the 'jurisdiction' of Turkey within the meaning of Article 1 of the Convention and therefore entail the respondent State's responsibility under the Convention.[143]

The greater question is with regard to targeted killings occurring at a distance, without the individual being physically in the hands of the agents. The *Bankovic* decision appears to suggest that aerial bombardment does not bring the affected individuals into the jurisdiction of the bombarding state(s). In fact, it is possible

---

[139] *Issa*, n 93, *supra*.
[140] *Maria Isaak and ors v. Turkey*, Decision on Admissibility, ECtHR, App no 44587/98, 28 September 2006.
[141] *Ibid*, 18.   [142] *Ibid*, 20.   [143] *Ibid*, 21, emphasis added.

to read this decision as negating the whole authority or control test, and limiting extraterritorial applicability only to effective control of territory and the diplomatic exceptions.[144] This approach is, however, in conflict with the above arguments and the extensive case-law supporting the use of authority or control test. While some may take the view that any conflicts within the case-law should be resolved in favour of *Bankovic*,[145] others would disagree with parts of the Court's conclusions.[146] It is suggested here that this one decision on admissibility cannot easily override all other European cases before it and—more importantly—after it, which made clear use of the authority or control test, as well the pronouncements of other bodies.[147] Briefly, it should be clarified here that even if one were to take the approach that *Bankovic* was wrongly decided insofar as admissibility is concerned, this does not mean that the applicants would necessarily have won the case. As will be seen in the later section on the relationship between human rights law and IHL, in circumstances such as in this case, any assessment of the legality of the operation would have to take into account an examination of its lawfulness under the laws of armed conflict.[148]

It is submitted here that the appropriate test for circumstances of this kind is the exercise of authority or control over the individual in such a way that the individual's rights are in the hands of the state. If state agents, even if acting from a distance, are able to carry out their plan to target individuals with intent to take life, this might amount to a form of authority or control over the life of the individual. In a case covering circumstances such as these, in which Cuban military aircraft shot down civilian planes outside Cuban airspace, the Inter-American Commission found 'conclusive evidence that agents of the Cuban State, although outside their territory, placed the civilian pilots of the "Brothers to the Rescue" organization under their authority' and subsequently

---

[144] *Bankovic*, n 43, *supra*, paras 59–60.

[145] *Al-Skeini*, High Court, n 100, *supra*, paras 265–72; *Al-Skeini*, House of Lords, n 100, *supra*, para 127.

[146] See, eg, Scheinin, n 84, *supra* and Lawson, n 131, *supra*; Ben-Naftali and Shany, n 55, *supra*, 80–86; E Roxstrom, M Gibney, and T Einarsen, 'The NATO Bombing Case (Bankovic et al v. Belgium et al.) and the Limits of Western Human Rights Protection' 23 *Boston University International Law Journal* 55; L Loucaides, 'Determining the Extra-territorial Effect of the European Convention: Facts, Jurisprudence and the Bankovic Case' 4 *European Human Rights Law Review* 391 (2006); H Hannum 'Remarks, Bombing for Peace: Collateral Damage and Human Rights', 96 *American Society of International Law Proceedings* 95, (2002) 96–9.

[147] Including *Issa*, n 93, *supra*; *Isaak*, n 140, *supra*; *Ocalan*, n 122, *supra*; *Coard*, n 9, *supra*; General Comment 31, n 5, *supra*.

[148] This would entail an examination of whether the targeted station was a legitimate military objective and if so, whether the attack was carried out in accordance with the rules of targeting, such as proportionality (if the first part of the question as to it being a military objective is answered in the negative, then it is unlawful regardless of questions of proportionality). One might hazard a guess that one of the motivations for the Court to rule the case inadmissible was precisely their reluctance to embark upon an extensive analysis of IHL rules—the mandate and competence of human rights bodies in matters of IHL raises a number of difficulties, see N Lubell, 'Challenges in Applying Human Rights Law to Armed Conflict', 860 *International Review of the Red Cross* 737, December 2005. See also O'Boyle, n 115, *supra*, 135.

found a violation of the right to life.[149] Limiting authority or control to cases in which the individual is physically in the hands of the state agents would cause the determination of a violation to rest on the method of killing chosen by the state.[150] As explained by Scheinin, the control of the individual is equally achieved by 'a cruise missile, an anthrax letter sent from the neighbouring country, a sniper's bullet in the head from the distance of 300 meters, or a poisoned umbrella tip on a crowded street'.[151] In other words '[the]"modality of delivery" is not decisive'.[152]

Denying the applicability of international human rights law to cases of killing from a distance, by claiming that it does not involve control, creates an incentive for states to evade applicability of obligations by choosing one method of killing over another. Moreover, it means that while a state that detains an individual must adhere to human rights law, if it kills him/her without first detaining, it might avoid any such scrutiny.[153] This approach means, for example, that should a suspected terrorist be on the high seas and a state sends out a naval vessel, by boarding the individual's vessel and detaining him/her, they would bring the person within their jurisdiction but should they torpedo the individual's boat and sink it (killing all on board) there would be no violation of human rights law. This result shows why such limitations cannot stand and that authority and control should be interpreted to include not only situations in which an individual is physically in the hands of the state agents. The key is not the physical distance between the agents and the individual, but rather the power over the individual that is exercised by the agents. Killings, such as some of those dealt with here, can answer the requirements of the authority or control test.

As can be seen in the above mentioned case involving the Cuban air force, extraterritorial situations can occur not only on the territory of other states but also in international airspace or on the high seas. In the latter, forcible measures can take place against criminal activities such as drug smuggling and piracy. As noted earlier, actions of this type are generally regarded as a form of law

---

[149] See n 93, *supra*, paras 25, 53. Similarly to the case of *Coard* in cases brought under the American Declaration there is no treaty provision on jurisdiction, however the Commission did choose to articulate why it was of the opinion that the human rights obligations applied extraterritorially. The case is being cited above in the context of determining the possible interpretations of control over an individual.

[150] Scheinin, n 84, *supra*, 77.

[151] *Ibid*, 77–8. The reference to a poisoned umbrella tip is grounded in reality, in the case of Bulgarian dissident Georgi Markov who was said to have been jabbed with a poisoned umbrella tip while walking along Waterloo Bridge in 1978. The KGB and the Bulgarian secret police were alleged to have been involved.

[152] Scheinin quoting McDougal in M McDougal and F Feliciano, *The International Law of War: Transnational Coercion and World Public Order* (New Haven Press and Martinus Nijhoff Publishers: New Haven & Dordrecht, 1994) cited in Scheinin, *ibid* 77.

[153] 'Attempts by the respondent governments in *Bankovic* to distinguish *Issa* rested on the at best tenuous argument that the victims were technically in the custody of Turkish forces and therefore within Turkish "jurisdiction"—simply shooting suspects is apparently immune from scrutiny, so long as you are careful not to arrest them first!' Hannum, n 146, *supra*, 98.

enforcement.[154] Indeed, the mission objective of counter-piracy operations in the Horn of Africa is to protect shipping and when pirates are encountered force is used 'to deter, prevent and intervene in order to bring to an end acts of piracy and armed robbery' and to detain with a view to prosecute.[155] As such, the regulation of force would be in accordance with the law enforcement model. The level of force and types of weapons employed may well rise beyond the usual domestic crime scenarios—the arsenal of pirates off the Somali coast has included rockets and grenade launchers.[156] Nonetheless, this force is to be used in accordance with the law enforcement approach of the scaled use of force, and with lethal force only as a last option.[157] The international law regulatory framework for this type of force is found within international human rights law. The unusual location for these operations does not remove them from the oversight of this framework. The above arguments on extraterritorial applicability of human rights obligations equally cover these circumstances. Indeed, practice points to an acceptance that human rights obligations remain relevant. The UK has acknowledged the possibility of human rights obligations with regard to detained pirates,[158] as has the European Union in the context of its counter-piracy operation.[159] In the *Medvedyev Case*, which concerned the seizure by French naval forces of a ship suspected of engaging in drug trafficking, the European Court of Human Rights noted that the persons detained on the ship were to be considered within the jurisdiction of France for the purposes of the Convention, despite being outside French territory.[160]

The obligations to respect international human rights law once the pirates have been captured is, therefore, clear as is the fact that these obligations do not begin only once the pirate is in the state's territory and must be respected already on

---

[154] See discussion in section on identifying the parties to the conflict in section 5.2 of Ch 4, *supra*.

[155] Acts Adopted under Title V of the EU Treaty Council Joint Action 2008/851/CFSP of 10 November 2008, on a European Union military operation to contribute to the deterrence, prevention and repression of acts of piracy and armed robbery off the Somali coast, Art 2. See also the description of NATO Counter Piracy Operation Ocean Shield at <http://www.shipping.nato.int/CounterPir/Operations>. See also UK Foreign and Commonwealth Office position in 'Frequently asked questions about Piracy', 'Q—Under what circumstances will the Royal Navy capture and detain pirates? A—If it is considered that there is sufficient evidence on which to charge suspected pirates they will be detained and subsequently transferred to a regional state for prosecution The UK has an arrangement with the Kenyan and Seychelles government which allows the transfer of suspected pirates to these countries. Conversely, if after thorough investigation there is insufficient evidence on which to charge suspected pirates, they will be released', available at <http://www.fco.gov.uk/en/global-issues/conflict-prevention/piracy/faq>.

[156] 'NATO frees 20 hostages; pirates seize Belgian ship', *Associated Press*, 18 April 2009; 'U.S. Navy warships exchange gunfire with suspected pirates off Somali coast' *Seattle Times*, 19 March 2006.

[157] See discussion of rules on use of force in section 1 of Ch 7, *supra*, on killings.

[158] 'Pirates can claim UK asylum' *The Sunday Times*, 13 April 2008.

[159] Acts Adopted under Title V, n 155, *supra*, Art 12. See also D Guilfoyle *Shipping Interdiction and the Law of the Sea* (CUP: Cambridge, 2009) 268–71.

[160] *Medvedyev and ors v. France*, Judgment, App no 3394/03, 10 July 2008, para 50.

the seized vessel. The remaining question is, then, whether these rules also apply to the earlier moments in which force is being used when first confronting and then boarding the pirate ship. The answer here should be affirmative. As seen earlier, the use of force must be governed from the first moment. If one were to argue that the human rights framework does not apply to firing at the ship from a distance and only applies once the ship has been boarded, this would mean that states could torpedo and drown all pirate ships with no attempt to capture and bring to justice. While this may have been acceptable in the past, modern society has preferred to do away with such summary executions. Applying human rights obligations of necessity and proportionality to these circumstances does not create unmanageable restrictions for counter-piracy operations, and conforms to accepted approaches to use of force in these situations.[161] The law enforcement framework allows for use of weapons and for the force necessary to seize ships or deal with hostage situations. Moreover, human rights bodies are capable of recognizing the challenges presented by operations at sea and interpreting obligations in a suitable manner, as is apparent from the recognition in two cases of 'wholly exceptional circumstances' which necessitated a longer than usually acceptable period before the detained persons were brought before a judge.[162] Accordingly, operations of this type would be treated as one example of extraterritorial forcible operations to which international human rights law must apply.

An additional matter to be noted is the question of whether determination of control over an individual is linked to the existence of other viable options. In other words, is the finding of control dependent on whether the state agent has the possibility to arrest the individual rather than shooting him/her. To answer this, let us imagine two scenarios in both of which an individual is about to launch a grenade into a busy cafe, and a state security officer sees the individual and fires at him before he can throw the grenade. In scenario (a), the officer was 10 yards away on the same surface, and would have been able to approach the individual from behind and overpower him without firing a shot. In scenario (b), the officer and individual were on adjacent but separate rooftops, and the officer had no way of getting physically closer, so there was no alternative way of stopping the individual without firing at him. It is submitted here that in both cases the security officer had equal control over whether to take the individual's life by firing a lethal weapon at him, and accordingly in both cases the right to life is engaged. The difference between the two cases is not whether the right to life comes into play, but instead relates to the question of determining whether the right has been violated. Even if the above scenarios took place in the territory of a different state (than that of the security officer) or somewhere such as the neutral buffer

---

[161] According to case law and custom, force in interdiction at sea is usually expected to conform to the basic principles of minimum force (including prior warning) and necessity. See discussion of this in Guilfoyle, n 159, *supra*, 265–94.

[162] *Rigopoulos v. Spain*, Decision, App no 37388/97, ECHR 1999–II. See also *Medvedyev*, n 160, *supra*, para 68.

zone as in the case of *Isaak*,[163] by virtue of deliberately targeting and firing at the individual the state agent could be said to have brought the individual within the jurisdiction of the state insofar as the right to life is concerned. The availability of alternatives to firing is nonetheless highly relevant to a different issue, that of determining whether the shooting was conducted in a manner which violated the right, which goes back to the earlier discussion of use of force and the right to life, and to the principles of necessity and proportionality.[164] The right to life is thus engaged in both cases, but the outcome of a determination of violation might rest on the existence of alternatives to opening fire.

Two problems with this approach still need to be mentioned:

(i) Does this approach create complications with regard to military operations by introducing human rights law on to the battlefield?
(ii) Precisely which obligations are created when the test is fulfilled—are the state agents required to provide the full range of human rights obligations?

As for the question of military operations two points must be made. First, it should be recalled that this test for extraterritorial applicability of human rights law demands that the state agents have the authority or control over the individual. Fighting between opposing forces on a chaotic battlefield, with both sides under fire and returning fire, is usually unlikely to satisfy this criterion. However, the detention of an opposing combatant, or a situation in which a sniper is calmly aiming at an opposing combatant in a situation away from the battlefield, might both be examples in which control is found. This brings us to the second point. In situations of armed conflict, to which IHL is applicable, even though human rights obligations may well exist their interpretation must take into account the existence of detailed IHL rules especially designed for these particular circumstances. Therefore, although the authority or control test might lead to the existence of a right to life obligation towards the combatant seen through the rifle scope of the sniper, at the same time, if the targeting was in accordance with an applicable IHL rule allowing this operation, then the right to life may not have been violated.[165] This relationship between human rights law and IHL will be dealt with in greater detail in the next chapter of this work. The second question, on the range and extent of the obligations owed, is the subject of the following section.

3. A contextual approach

When, in an extraterritorial situation, an individual comes within state jurisdiction for the purpose of human rights law, one might wonder if this means that

---

[163] See n 140, *supra*.
[164] See section 1 of Ch 7, *supra*, on killings and the right to life.
[165] See Part II, *supra*, for more detailed analysis, including some of the problems in applying this rule in certain situations.

the state must now act positively to ensure the individual receives the full range of human rights obligations. Here a distinction must be made between territory under effective control, and the test of authority or control over individuals. In the former (which is outside the scope and therefore only mentioned briefly) when the state has the power to govern the territory, human rights law treats the state's obligations as analogous to those in national territory. This implies that the state must work towards securing the full range of human rights protections[166] although in cases such as military occupation there may be a question over the precise nature of the fulfilment of certain rights.[167] However, when state agents acting extraterritorially have temporary authority and control over an individual such an extensive requirement may be difficult to sustain. On the one hand, it might not be feasible to require state agents who have temporarily detained an individual to begin ensuring a right to form a trade union while, on the other hand, as shown, they could be responsible for a potential violation of the right to liberty. An 'all or nothing' approach in these situations is therefore not appropriate.[168]

A useful approach to clarifying this issue is through the concept mentioned earlier of positive and negative obligations although, as will be seen, this too has its problems. The identification of positive and negative obligations is not a means to differentiate between groups of rights. It is rather that within most rights there are both positive and negative elements. These distinctions are often understood through referring to the three-tiered approach of respect, protect and fulfil. The UN Committee on Economic, Social and Cultural Rights has detailed the obligations contained within a number of rights using this approach. For example, with regard to the right to health, the Committee notes that:

The right to health, like all human rights, imposes three types or levels of obligations on States parties: the obligations to respect, protect and fulfil. In turn, the obligation to fulfil contains obligations to facilitate, provide and promote. The obligation to respect requires States to refrain from interfering directly or indirectly with the enjoyment of the right to health. The obligation to protect requires States to take measures that prevent

---

[166] 'It follows that, in terms of Article 1 of the Convention, Turkey's "jurisdiction" must be considered to extend to securing the entire range of substantive rights set out in the Convention and those additional Protocols which she has ratified, and that violations of those rights are imputable to Turkey'. See *Cyprus v. Turkey*, n 8, *supra*.

[167] Eg, there are problems with regard to the question of whether human rights law obliges an occupying power to fulfil economic and social rights to a level similar to its national territory. Lubell, n 148, *supra*, 742–4. Problems can also arise with regard to defining control over an area, including defining the starting and ending point of the control, and control over limited and small parts of territory.

[168] Ben-Naftali and Shany, n 55, *supra*, 64–5; Meron recognizes that not all ICCPR obligations are equally suited to extraterritorial application. See Meron, n 16, *supra*, 80. See the opinion of Lord Justice Sedley 'it is not an answer to say that the UK, because it is unable to guarantee everything, is required to guarantee nothing' in *Al-Skeini*, Court of Appeal, n 100, *supra*, para 197. But see Lord Rodger, *Al-Skeini* House of Lords, n 100, *supra*, para 79; and *Bankovic*, n 43, *supra*, para 75.

third parties from interfering with article 12 guarantees. Finally, the obligation to fulfil requires States to adopt appropriate legislative, administrative, budgetary, judicial, promotional and other measures towards the full realization of the right to health.[169]

A similar approach has been mentioned with regard to other rights.[170] Accordingly, obligations to protect and fulfil would usually be positive duties to act and take certain measures, while the obligation to respect is a negative duty to refrain from direct action that would violate a right. Positive measures would usually necessitate a combination of resources and authority to act and it is, therefore, understandable that states cannot generally be called upon to fulfil the rights of all peoples, including those in other sovereign territories.[171] With regard to negative obligations, or the duty to respect, it has been argued that, by the very nature of universality of human rights, such obligations are owed by states to everyone, regardless of territory.[172] The theoretical and practical foundations of this approach are noted by Shue:

Negative duties—duties not to deprive people of what they have rights to—are, and must be, universal. A right could not be guaranteed unless the negative duties corresponding to it were universal, because anyone who lacked even the negative duty not to deprive someone of what she has rights to would, accordingly, be free to deprive the supposed right-bearer. Universal negative duties, however, are no problem (if 'opportunity costs' are ignored). I can easily leave alone at least five billion people, and as many more as you like.[173]

One way of then implementing this approach, as presented by Roxstrom, Gibney and Einarsen, would be that the concept of jurisdiction is deemed necessary to determining a state's positive obligations, but is irrelevant to negative obligations.[174] However, the approach of relying on negative obligations in the context of some of the extraterritorial situations described may not be enough to guarantee basic rights. The type and circumstances of control over an individual may demand positive action. For example, when an individual is held extraterritorially for any period longer than a few hours, s/he will need the state agents to

---

[169] Committee on Economic, Social and Cultural Rights, 'General Comment no 14, The right to the highest attainable standard of health' (22d session, 2000), UN Doc E/C.12/2000/4 (2000) para 33.
[170] 'Like civil and political rights, economic, social and cultural rights impose three different types of obligations on States: the obligations to respect, protect and fulfil. Failure to perform any one of these three obligations constitutes a violation of such rights.' in para 6 of T van Boven, C Flinterman, I Westendorp (eds), 'The Maastricht Guidelines on Violations of Economic, Social and Cultural Rights', SIM Special no 20, Netherlands Institute of Human Rights, 1996; Committee on Economic, Social and Cultural Rights, 'General Comment no 12, Right to adequate food', 20th session (1999) UN Doc E/C.12/1999/5 (1999) para 15; Committee on Economic, Social and Cultural Rights, General Comment no 13, The right to education, 21st session (1999), UN Doc E/C.12/1999/10 (1999) paras 46–7.
[171] See detailed discussion of this in Roxstrom and ors, n 146, *supra*, 72–5. See also view of Henkin, cited *ibid*, fn 66.
[172] *Ibid*.   [173] H Shue, 'Mediating Duties' 98 *Ethics* 687 (1988) 690.
[174] Roxstrom and ors, n 146, *supra*, 75.

take the positive action of providing food in order to survive.[175] Therefore, while accepting that the positive-negative distinction is highly pertinent, and that state agents acting extraterritorially should not actively violate an individual's rights, there is still a possibility that the state would have certain positive duties. What is needed is a contextual approach to obligations. As noted by Lawson, there is a need for a '"gradual" approach to the notion of "jurisdiction": the extent to which contracting parties must secure the rights and freedoms of individuals outside their borders is proportionate to the extent of their control over these individuals.'[176]

Indeed, a contextual approach to jurisdiction and obligations is not a concept foreign to human rights bodies. Cases before both the UN Human Rights Committee and the European Court of Human Rights have made use of a notion of contextual jurisdiction and obligations. The Committee, in the case of *Gueye v. France*, noted that 'the authors are not generally subject to French jurisdiction, except that they rely on French legislation in relation to the amount of their pension rights'.[177]

The European Court, in the case of *Ilaşcu v. Moldova and Russia*, accepted that the level of obligations is linked to the precise circumstances, and is therefore variable rather than all or nothing, noting that '[n]evertheless such a factual situation reduces the scope of that jurisdiction in that the undertaking given by the State under Article 1 must be considered by the Court only in the light of the Contracting State's positive obligations towards persons within its territory'.[178]

The ICJ, in its Advisory Opinion on the *Wall*, noted that in some areas of the West Bank, although Israel may have transferred some powers regarding economic, social and cultural rights to the Palestinian Authority, it nevertheless had responsibilities not to actively impede human rights and '[f]urthermore, it is under an obligation not to raise any obstacle to the exercise of such rights in those fields where competence has been transferred to Palestinian authorities.'[179]

In light of all the above, it is suggested that states must refrain from taking direct action that would violate rights of persons even if the actions take place extraterritorially. Furthermore, the authority or control test for state agents acting extraterritorially brings the affected individuals within the jurisdiction of the state and creates obligations under human rights law, but only with regard to those rights for which the individual is directly dependent on the power exercised

---

[175] One could argue that intentionally starving a person is an action, and therefore this still falls under the negative obligations (to refrain from starving a person), but it could also be unintentional, or under a claim of not having the resources to provide food, ie more clearly a matter of requiring positive steps to fulfil a right.

[176] Lawson, n 131, *supra*, 120; Scheinin also speaks of a contextual assessment of factual control, n 84, *supra*, 76–7.

[177] *Ibrahima Gueye and ors v. France*, Comm no 196/1985, UN Doc CCPR/C/35/D/196/1985 (1989) para 9.4.

[178] *Ilaşcu and ors v. Moldova and Russia*, ECtHR, Appl no 48787/99, 8 July 2004, para 333.

[179] *Wall*, n 1, *supra*, para 112.

by the agents. Extraterritorial abductions would, for instance, create obligations with regard to the rights to liberty and humane treatment.

4. Regional—*espace juridique*

A further issue, raised in particular by regional conventions, is whether they can create obligations for actions occurring outside their specific geographical region, or whether they are limited to influencing activities within their pre-defined *espace juridique*. In *Bankovic*, the Court Stated that:

> In short, the convention is a multi-lateral treaty operating…in the legal space (*espace juridique*) of the contracting States…The FRY clearly does not fall within this legal space. The convention was not designed to be applied throughout the world, even in respect of the conduct of contracting States. Accordingly, the desirability of avoiding a gap or vacuum in human rights' protection has so far been relied on by the court in favour of establishing jurisdiction only when the territory in question was one that, but for the specific circumstances, would normally be covered by the convention.[180]

However, this approach is not entirely consistent with both earlier and later cases. In the 1992 case of *Drozd*, the Court did not see a problem of principle in discussing alleged violations occurring in Andorra, which was not a party to the ECHR.[181] In the post-*Bankovic* cases of *Issa* and of *Ocalan*,[182] again the Court did not appear to believe that that it was impossible to find violations of the European Convention for acts occurring in Iraq or Kenya. Similarly, the Inter-American Commission made a finding of violation of human rights in a case which occurred in international airspace.[183] These cases provide sufficient support for the view that human rights obligations contained in regional instruments can potentially extend extraterritorially into areas outside the geographical space of the regional systems.[184] In other words, one could argue that the regional element of these instruments affects the determination of which states can become a party, rather than the location of potential violations. As for the ICCPR, which is a universal treaty, the obligations apply extraterritorially to all individuals within the power or effective control (ie the authority and control test) of the

---

[180] *Bankovic*, n 43, *supra*, para 80.

[181] The Court found that it lacked jurisdiction *ratione loci*, but then went on to inquire whether the acts complained of can be attributed to France or Spain acting extraterritorially. See *Drozd and Janousek v. France and Spain* (1992) 14 EHRR 745, paras 84, 89, 91.

[182] *Ocalan*, n 122, *supra*.   [183] *Alejandre v. Cuba*, n 9, *supra*, para 25.

[184] For further detailed arguments, see Lawson n 131, *supra*, 113–15; Roxstrom and ors, n 146, *supra*. While the UK High Court recognized the inconsistencies, but chose to side with Bankovic (see *Al-Skeini*, n 100, *supra*, paras 276–7) the Court of Appeal did recognize that the Convention could apply outside the *espace juridique* (see *Al-Skeini Appeal*, n 100, *supra*, paras 90–6). See also *Alejandre v. Cuba*, which occurred in international airspace, ie not in the territory of any state within the Inter-American system, n 9, *supra*.

state, and there appears to be no geographical limitation to areas belonging to state parties.[185]

5. Non-treaty-based extraterritorial human rights obligations

The debate in the earlier sections of this chapter was largely focused on the question of treaty obligations, including the competence of human rights treaty monitoring bodies to review cases with an extraterritorial dimension. The mandate of these bodies is determined and qualified by the treaties from which they derive their authority. Consequently, if one were to adopt a more restrictive conclusion than has been reached above, this would result in a view that limits the competence of the treaty bodies with respect to extraterritorial situations. It would not necessarily negate the possibility that states may have extraterritorial human rights obligations, outside the context of specific treaties and their monitoring bodies.

There are many non-treaty-based international human rights bodies, which instead derive their authority from the UN Charter. Whilst some of these bodies, such as the Human Rights Council (and its predecessor the Commission on Human Rights), might be seen to reflect the opinions of governments there are also a number of mechanisms comprised of individuals generally operating as independent human rights experts. These have included the former UN Sub-Commission on the Promotion and Protection of Human Rights and the Special Procedures operating with thematic or specific country mandates. The practice of these bodies clearly indicates that they do not view human rights obligations as being limited by territorial boundaries. For example, the Special Rapporteur on the Promotion and Protection of Human Rights and Fundamental Freedoms while Countering Terrorism has reviewed extraterritorial targeted killings by the US;[186] a report of the Sub-Commission took the view that human rights obligations can extend extraterritorially;[187] the Special Rapporteur on Extrajudicial, Summary or Arbitrary Executions has expressed concern over allegations of actions by Sudan in Chad, the US in Pakistan and Iraq, and Uzbekistan in Kyrgyzstan.[188]

Moreover, most of the questions in earlier sections of this chapter on the extraterritorial applicability of human rights obligations are raised as a result of the specific language and conditions set by treaties. While the vast majority of

---

[185] General Comment 31, n 5, *supra*, para 10. See also Scheinin's view on this, n 84, *supra*, 77.

[186] Special Rapporteur on protection of human rights countering terrorism, n 7, *supra*, para 42.

[187] F Hampson and I Salama, 'Working paper on the relationship between human rights law and international humanitarian law', UN Sub-Commission on the Promotion and Protection of Human Rights, E/CN.4/Sub.2/2005/14, 21 June 2005, paras 78–92.

[188] 'Report of the Special Rapporteur on extrajudicial, summary or arbitrary executions, Philip Alston Addendum, Summary of cases transmitted to Government and replies received', HRC/4/20/Add.1.

states are party to treaties that contain these obligations, there is a theoretical possibility that a state engaging in extraterritorial forcible measures will not be a party to human rights treaties. As noted in the previous chapter, most of the human rights concerns raised by the activities covered relate to human rights obligations that can be considered part of customary international law. The question then becomes whether human rights obligations that have the status of customary international law also extend extraterritorially. The customary status of rules of applicability, as opposed to the rules of content, can be complicated to determine.[189] While treaty sources contain rules on when and how the obligations apply, discussion of custom is usually confined to the content of the obligations. However, certain sources and state practice can assist in answering our question. The Universal Declaration of Human Rights[190] ('UDHR') has often been cited as a source of customary human rights obligations.[191] The UDHR does not have a clause restricting the obligations territorially, and in Article 2 states that:

Everyone is entitled to all the rights and freedoms set forth in this Declaration, without distinction of any kind, such as race, colour, sex, language, religion, political or other opinion, national or social origin, property, birth or other status.

Furthermore, no distinction shall be made on the basis of the political, jurisdictional or international status of the country or territory to which a person belongs, whether it be independent, trust, non-self-governing or under any other limitation of sovereignty.

The UDHR elaborates on the UN Charter purpose of striving towards universal respect for human rights.[192] It should also be recalled that regardless of whether or not they have ratified specific human rights treaties, all member states of the UN are bound by the terms of the Charter of the United Nations. At the outset, in Article 1 of the Charter, respect for human rights is declared to be one of the purposes of the UN. Furthermore, Article 55(c) of the Charter calls for: 'universal respect for, and observance of, human rights and fundamental freedoms for all without distinction as to race, sex, language, or religion', with Article 56 then making clear that 'all Members pledge themselves to take joint

---

[189] Eg, this may be one of the reasons the ICRC study on customary rules of IHL focused on content rules of IHL, but did not cover the customary status of applicability rules. See J Henckaerts and L Doswald-Beck *Customary International Humanitarian Law, vol. 1* (CUP: Cambridge, 2005).

[190] Universal Declaration of Human Rights, Resolution 217 A(III); UN Doc A/810 91, UN General Assembly, 1948.

[191] BG Ramcharan. *The Concept and Present Status of the International Protection of Human Rights: Forty Years After the Universal Declaration* (Nijhoff: Dordrecht, 1989); R Lillich, 'The Growing Importance of Customary International Human Rights Law' 25 *Georgia Journal of International and Comparative Law* 1, 1–9. A distinction should, however, be made between regarding the UDHR as a whole as reflecting customary international law, as opposed to speaking of particular rules therein having attained this status.

[192] Charter of the United Nations, June 26, 1945, 59 Stat. 1031, T.S. 993, 3 Bevans 1153, entered into force Oct. 24, 1945, paras 1,55.

and separate action in co-operation with the Organization for the achievement of the purposes set forth in Article 55'.

The Charter does not limit itself to speaking of respect for human rights only of persons within the state, but adopts a universal approach of joint recognition of the importance of respecting human rights. States that actively take forcible measures such as deliberate killings of individuals (outside the recognized exceptions raised earlier[193]) would thereby be acting in stark violation of their commitments under the UN Charter to respect human rights. Indeed, the ICJ has in the past found that the UN Charter can impose human rights obligations upon a state acting outside its own sovereign territory:

> Under the Charter of the United Nations, the former Mandatory had pledged itself to observe and respect, in a territory having an international status, human rights and fundamental freedoms for all without distinction as to race. To establish instead, and to enforce, distinctions, exclusions, restrictions and limitations exclusively based on the grounds of race, colour, descent or national or ethnic origin which constitute a denial of fundamental human rights is a flagrant violation of the purposes and principles of the Charter.[194]

Fundamental human rights obligations have also been described as obligations *erga omnes*, meaning that all states have an interest in securing their protection, even in and by other states.[195] If protection of certain rights is a matter of *erga omnes* obligation then it is not unreasonable to assert that, if state A is to have a vested interest in state B's protection of human rights within state B, it cannot at the same time be allowed to send agents into state B and commit the same violations for which it could be admonishing state B were it to commit them itself. The duty of positive action to fulfil human rights obligations would naturally lie primarily with sovereign states (and is accordingly reflected in their treaty obligations). States, as noted earlier,[196] are limited legally and practically in their power and authority to take positive actions in the territory of other states. However, the fact that all states are obligated to strive towards universal protection clearly indicates that they should not be taking steps in the opposite direction by violating human rights in other countries. The fundamental notion of universality would be undermined by claiming that states have no human rights obligations to individuals outside their jurisdiction.[197] Forcible measures that appear to violate

---

[193] See section 1, of Ch 7, *supra*, on killings and the right to life.

[194] *Legal Consequences for States of the Continued Presence of South Africa in Namibia (South West Africa) notwithstanding Security Council Resolution 276 (1970)*, Advisory Opinion of 21 June 1971, ICJ Rep 1971 16, para 131.

[195] *Barcelona Traction, Light and Power Co, Ltd Case (Belgium v. Spain)*, 1970 ICJ Rep 4, 32, 5 February 1970; General Comment no 31, n 5, *supra*, para 2; *DRC v. Uganda*, n 2, *supra*, separate opinion of Judge Simma at para 35. See also *Reservations to the Convention on the Prevention and Punishment of the Crime of Genocide*, Advisory Opinion, 28 May 1951, 23.

[196] See text accompanying nn 32–51, *supra*. See also above section 3, *supra*, on contextual approach.

[197] D Kretzmer, 'Targeted Killing of Suspected Terrorists: Extra-Judicial Executions or Legitimate Means of Defence?' 16 *EJIL* 171 (2005) 185.

customary human rights obligations, such as the right to life would, therefore, be likely to be in breach of customary international law, whether committed domestically or extraterritorially.

The extraterritorial applicability of customary human rights obligations also has state support, with the US Operational Law Handbook (2006) declaring that:

If a 'human right' is considered to have risen to the status of customary international law, then it is likely considered binding on U.S. State actors wherever such actors deal with human beings. According to the ReStatement (Third) of Foreign Relations Law of the United States, international law is violated by any State that 'practices, encourages, or condones' a violation of human rights considered customary international law. The ReStatement makes no qualification as to where the violation might occur, or against whom it may be directed.[198]

In addition, as noted by Kretzmer:

While a State party's treaty obligations are a function of the scope of application defined in the particular treaty, some of the substantive norms in human rights treaties that have been ratified by the vast majority of States in the world, have now become peremptory norms of customary international law. The duty to respect the right to life is surely one of these norms. A State's duty to respect the right to life (as opposed to its duty to ensure that right) follows its agents, wherever they operate.[199]

In summary, human rights obligations can extend extraterritorially not only through the interpretations of the relevant human rights treaty provisions, but also through customary international law and obligations outside specific human rights treaties. Since forcible measures, such as killings and torture, are in fact a subject of customary international law, extraterritorial measures of this type can amount to a violation of international human rights law obligations, regardless of treaty applicability and how it is interpreted. The debate over extraterritorial effect of human rights treaties is paramount to the determination of the competence of treaty monitoring bodies to scrutinize the cases but, regardless of the outcome of this debate, if the affected right is part of customary international law then, by taking the extraterritorial forcible measure, a state may have violated its international legal obligations.

---

[198] *The US Operational Law Handbook*, n 23, *supra*, 47.
[199] Kretzmer, n 197, *supra*, 184–5.

9

Concurrent Applicability of International Humanitarian Law and International Human Rights Law

Although international human rights law can be applicable to extraterritorial operations, its actual use as regulatory framework is not yet assured. This could also depend on whether the particular situation was classified as part of an armed conflict and on the interpretation of the relationship between human rights law and international humanitarian law ('IHL'). In other words, by reaching the conclusion that human rights obligations can extend extraterritorially—even to certain actions taken by military forces—determination of whether any human rights have been violated will still need to take into account the possibility of other applicable rules that may supersede or change the interpretation of a human rights obligation.

At the outset of this section, it should be recalled that the use of force in an extraterritorial operation does not automatically lead to the conclusion that we are faced with an armed conflict. The analysis below of the relationship between human rights law and IHL is only relevant to circumstances of armed conflict, which then bring about the applicability of IHL. Many of the examples of extra-territorial forcible measures cited occurred in non-conflict or debatable situations[1] in which IHL might not apply, and the sole candidate for a legal framework to regulate the use of force would, therefore, be human rights law. The debate over the 'war on terror' is a case in point,[2] and actions taken in that context may or may not come within the sphere of IHL applicability, depending on the facts and their interpretation. If the extraterritorial measures are occurring outside the context of an armed conflict, then the regulation of forcible measures must be in accordance with their interpretation in human rights law and the rules of law enforcement.

Whilst IHL is only applicable during armed conflict, international human rights law, conversely, applies at all times from peace to armed conflict and any

---

[1] Eg the abduction by Israel of Vanunu was not part of an armed conflict, and the US killing of alleged terrorists in Yemen was at least debatable as to whether this was part of an armed conflict. See discussion in Chs 5 and 7, *supra* and in the Concluding Chapter, *infra*.

[2] See examination in Ch 5, *supra*.

point on the blurred scale between them. In the past, there was a vibrant debate surrounding the contention that international human rights law is the law of peacetime and IHL is the law of war.[3] Although this debate has not completely subsided, and there are still expressions of the view that human rights law has limited use in times of armed conflict,[4] the majority of commentators are of the opinion that human rights law continues to apply during armed conflict. Support for continued applicability of international human rights law during armed conflict can be found in virtually every direction we turn, from the positions of states at the Teheran Conference in 1968[5] and the Security Council,[6] through to current commentators,[7] and to the various international and regional judicial and quasi-judicial bodies, including the UN Human Rights Committee,[8] the UN Committee on Economic, Social and Cultural Rights,[9] the Inter-American Commission on Human Rights, the Inter-American Court of Human Rights[10] and the International Court of Justice (on three occasions).[11] This continued applicability of human rights law is firmly rooted in the human rights treaties themselves, as can be seen in the rules regarding derogations. The International Covenant on Civil and Political Rights ('ICCPR'), the European Convention

---

[3] GIAD Draper, 'The relationship between the human rights regime and the law of armed conflicts', 1 *Israel Yearbook of Human Rights* 191 (1971); K Suter, 'An Inquiry into the Meaning of the Phrase "Human Rights in Armed Conflicts"' 15 *Revue de Droit Pénal Militaire et de Droit de la Guerre* 393 (1976).

[4] M Dennis, 'ICJ Advisory Opinion on Construction of a Wall in the Occupied Palestinian Territory: Application of human rights treaties extraterritorially in times of armed conflict and military occupation', 99 *AJIL* 119 (2005).

[5] *Human Rights in Armed Conflicts*, International Conference on Human Rights, Teheran, Res XXII, 12 May 1968.

[6] '[...] essential and inalienable human rights should be respected even during the vicissitudes of war' Security Council Resolution no 237 (1967) of 14 June 1967.

[7] L Doswald-Beck and S Vité, 'International Humanitarian Law and Human Rights Law' 293 *International Review of the Red Cross* 94 (1993); RE Vinuesa, 'Interface, Correspondence and Convergence of Human Rights and International Humanitarian Law' *Yearbook of International Humanitarian Law, vol 1* (TMC Asser Press: The Hague, 1998) 69–110; C Droege, 'The Interplay Between International Humanitarian Law and International Human Rights Law in Situations of Armed Conflict', 40 *Israel Law Review* 310 (2007); R Provost *International Human Rights and Humanitarian Law* (CUP: Cambridge 2002). For recent detailed analysis see F Hampson and I Salama, 'Working paper on the relationship between human rights law and international humanitarian law', UN Sub-Commission on the Promotion and Protection of Human Rights, E/CN.4/Sub.2/2005/14, 21 June 2005.

[8] Human Rights Committee, General Comment no 29, States of Emergency (Article 4), UN Doc CCPR/C/21/Rev.1/Add.11 (2001) para 3.

[9] The Committee on Economic, Social and Cultural Rights, 'Concluding Observations of the Committee on Economic, Social and Cultural Rights: Israel', UN Doc E/C.12/1/Add.69., 31 August 2001.

[10] *Bámaca-Velásquez v. Guatemala*, 2001 IACHR Series C no 70 at 28, 25 November 2000; *Abella v. Argentina*, Case 11.137, IACHR, Report no 55/97, OEA/Ser.L/V/II.95 Doc 7 rev. at 271.

[11] *Legality of the Threat or Use of Nuclear Weapons*, Advisory opinion, ICJ Rep 1996, 8 July 1996, para 25; *Legal Consequences of the Construction of a Wall in the Occupied Palestinian Territory*, Advisory opinion [2004] ICJ Rep, 9 July 2004, para.106; *Case Concerning Armed Activities on the Territory of the Congo (Democratic Republic of the Congo v. Uganda)*, Judgment, ICJ General List No 116, 2005 (19 December 2005) para 216.

on Human Rights ('ECHR') and the American Convention on Human Rights ('ACHR') allow for certain derogations from obligations in times of 'public emergency which threatens the life of the nation'[12] 'war or other public emergency threatening the life of the nation'[13] and 'war, public danger, or other emergency that threatens the independence or security of a State Party.'[14] The derogations can only occur in a specified framework of rules and safeguards, and certain rights cannot be derogated from at all, leaving it clear that the human rights treaties remain in operation during these times.[15]

Accordingly, in times of armed conflict there are two frameworks of international law with concurrent application. As seen in this and the previous part, these two frameworks have significant differences, and joint application is, therefore, not a straightforward affair. The clearest example, and one which is directly relevant, is the way these legal frameworks approach the question of lethal force against an individual. As seen in Chapter 6 of this work, in an armed conflict IHL can allow for lethal use of force, provided the individual is a 'legitimate target' such as a combatant. With regard to civilians taking a direct part in the hostilities, it would appear that they too can be subjected to lethal force, although the time frame and circumstances when this would be lawful are subject to debate.[16] IHL therefore allows a belligerent party in certain cases to use, as a first option, lethal force against an individual who fulfils a certain general group criteria (eg is a combatant of the opposing party), even if he/she does not individually pose an immediate threat.[17] By contrast, under human rights law and the rules of law enforcement, non-violent means must be the first option and, if violence is used, then force should always be at the minimum level possible with use of lethal force only when strictly unavoidable—for instance in order to protect life.[18] Lethal force cannot, therefore, be a first choice and, in fact, should be the last option. There must also be a reason for the use of force against the particular individual.[19] Other differences include the notion of proportionality,[20] which under IHL is used primarily with reference to the 'side-effects' and collateral damage, ie the effect upon people and objects other than the target,[21] whereas in

---

[12] International Covenant on Civil and Political Rights (16 December 1966) 999 UNTS 171, entered into force 23 March 1976, Art 4.

[13] Convention for the Protection of Human Rights and Fundamental Freedoms (4 November 1950) 213 UNTS 222; 312 ETS 5, entered into force 3 September 1953, Art 15.

[14] American Convention on Human Rights (22 November 1969) 1144 UNTS 123, entered into force 18 July 1978, Art 27.

[15] See section 4 of Ch 7, *supra*, on derogation.

[16] See discussion in Ch 6, *supra*.

[17] *Ibid*. But see also Ch 6, section 2.2, on small scale operations for debate over necessity in use of force in these contexts.

[18] See section 1, of Ch 7, *supra*, on killings and the right to life.   [19] *Ibid*.

[20] N Lubell, 'Challenges in Applying Human Rights Law to Armed Conflict', 860 *International Review of the Red Cross* 737 (December 2005) 745–6.

[21] See explanation of this in the chapter on IHL.

law enforcement, in addition to the effect on others, proportionality also refers to the effect of the force on the targeted individual.[22]

How then can the simultaneous application of two different rules be resolved? The International Court of Justice, in its Advisory Opinion on the Legality of the Threat or Use of Nuclear Weapons, stated that while the ICCPR continues to apply even in time of war, IHL would then be used as *lex specialis* when coming to determine whether a violation has actually occurred.[23] The principle of *lex specialis* means that a specific rule prevails over a more general rule. There are, however, a number of different ways to implement this principle. For instance as a conflict resolving tool for choosing one rule over another (*lex specialis derogat legi generali*), as a complementary approach (*lex specialis complementa*), or as a method advocating use of the specific rule as an interpretative tool for the general one.[24] On two later occasions, the ICJ clarified that its intention was not to introduce this principle in order to say that IHL, as a whole, replaces all use of international human rights law, but that the applicable rules for each situation must be determined on a case by case basis. It stated that 'some rights may be exclusively matters of international humanitarian law; others may be exclusively matters of human rights law; yet others may be matters of both these branches of international law.'[25]

Accordingly, when looking for an answer as to whether a bombarded building was a military objective, IHL is the only framework containing the appropriate definition. When seeking a detailed understanding of the components of a fair trial, international human rights law is the framework that can provide the answer.

The position of the UN Human Rights Committee with regard to the ICCPR further supports the notion that IHL does not completely replace international human rights law, but that the two operate together with the ability to complement each other:

the Covenant applies also in situations of armed conflict to which the rules of international humanitarian law are applicable. While, in respect of certain Covenant rights, more specific rules of international humanitarian law may be specially relevant for the purposes of the interpretation of Covenant rights, both spheres of law are complementary, not mutually exclusive.[26]

---

[22] Ch 7, n 22–24 and accompanying text, *supra*; CK Boyle, 'The Concept of Arbitrary Deprivation of Life' in Ramcharan (ed), *The Right to Life in International Law* (Martinus Nijhoff: Dordrecht, 1985) 221–44, 239–40.

[23] *Nuclear Weapons*, n 11, *supra*, para 25.

[24] For a detailed analysis of the *lex specialis* rule and its application in the context of human rights and IHL, see N Prud'homme, 'Lex Specialis: Oversimplifying a More Complex and Multifaceted Relationship?', 40 *Israel Law Review* 356 (2007).

[25] *Wall*, n 11, *supra*, para 106; *DRC v. Uganda*, n 11, *supra*, para 216.

[26] Human Rights Committee, General Comment no 31, UN Doc CCPR/C/21/Rev.1/Add.13 (2004), para 11.

Notwithstanding its contribution towards a coherent approach to concurrent application, the ICJ's formulation leaves some problems unanswered. It has been noted that talk of *lex specialis* is in our case an oversimplification and is perhaps an inept approach to the question of the IHL–human rights relationship. This doctrine can work well within a single legal framework such as a domestic legal system, but the principle does not apply itself with equal success to attempts to solve the relationship between different branches of international law.[27] There is a vagueness and ambiguity that too easily lends itself to legal manipulation. Indeed, it is hard to find agreement on the meaning and implementation of this rule, and interpretations tend to vary considerably and on occasion even to contradict.[28]

Although a detailed analysis of this is outside the scope of the subject under examination, it is clear that unresolved questions remain on a wide range of issues. For example, Schabas raises an issue which presents a marked difference between the bodies of law with regard to the nexus between the aims and the means.[29] IHL is indifferent to the *ius ad bellum*—the laws on the resort to force[30]—but human rights law cannot be indifferent to it, since there is an assumption of a right to peace, and also because under human rights law the legitimacy of the aims is part of the test for lawfulness of the means. Accordingly, there may be killings that take place in armed conflict and are lawful under IHL, but the application of human rights law might be expected to look also at the background for the use of force, and whether legitimate aims are being pursued, which would then include the *ius ad bellum* question of whether this may have been an unlawful war of aggression. Whilst this could theoretically require attention when addressing it from the perspective of human rights law, such an approach challenges the reasoning behind the separation between the *ius ad bellum* and the *ius in bello*, and could effectively undermine the adherence to the rules of conduct during hostilities.[31]

Another example of an area in need of further resolve is the protection of economic, social and cultural rights during armed conflict. Once it is clear that human rights obligations continue to apply during conflict, there is no convincing legal justification for excluding economic, social and cultural rights from this understanding. The International Court of Justice has affirmed the applicability

[27] Prud'homme, n 24, *supra*.

[28] See the variety of views expressed in *Expert Meeting on the Right to Life in Armed Conflicts and Situations of Occupation*, International Conference Centre, Geneva: The University Centre for International Humanitarian Law, Geneva, September 2005, 18–20.

[29] W Schabas, 'Lex specialis? Belt and suspenders? The Parallel Operation of Human Rights Law and the Law of Armed Conflict, and the Conundrum of Jus ad Bellum', 40 *Israel Law Review* 592 (2007) 606–13.

[30] See the discussion on the connection between the legal frameworks in the Introduction, *supra*.

[31] For further discussion of this issue, see Schabas, n 29, *supra*. If the conduct of party to a conflict were to be assessed less favourably on account of an *ius ad bellum* determination, there is a risk it would see no benefit in adhering to the *ius in bello* at all. See the discussion on the connection between the legal frameworks in the Introduction, *supra*.

of economic, social and cultural rights obligations in a situation to which IHL is applicable,[32] so outright dismissal of those rights whenever IHL becomes applicable is not a tenable position. The ICJ Advisory Opinion thus provided further support to the already existing views of the UN Committee on Economic, Social and Cultural Rights on their applicability.[33] The actual application of these obligations is less clear. Whilst the notion of progressive realization and practical considerations may stand in the way of total fulfilment of these rights, certain core obligations do exist. Moreover, it is possible that in certain areas, such as a detailed understanding of health related obligations, it is human rights law that must be used as the primary tool on account of its greater developed case law and interpretations.[34]

Some of the difficulties arise most clearly in the context of judicial or quasi-judicial bodies needing to address the specifics of particular cases. In particular, the role and ability of human rights bodies to address situations of armed conflict has come under scrutiny. Bodies created through specific treaties will usually have their mandate restricted to monitoring violations of those treaties, whilst other bodies such as those created through the UN Charter mechanisms, will have less of a direct restriction on the scope and type of violations they can address.[35] Indeed, the challenges created by the concurrent applicability of international human rights law and IHL are often at their most acute in the context of specific bodies attempting to clarify which rules they should be using to analyse cases before them. Accordingly, one avenue for resolving many of these situations, could be to approach concurrent applicability not in search of a pure single legal theory with a single solution for all circumstances, but rather as a combination of legal principles whose application rests upon the context and the body required to address them. In other words, concurrent applicability of the two bodies of law would be addressed with different legal tools based on the body carrying out the assessment.[36] Depending on how the various rules are interpreted, this would not necessarily entail reaching different results despite approaching the situation through different primary rules.[37] Notwithstanding this approach,

---

[32] *Wall*, n 11, *supra*, paras 107–12.

[33] 'Concluding Observations of the Committee on Economic, Social and Cultural Rights: Israel', E/C.12/1/Add.69, 31 August 2001.

[34] For more on these and other related issues see Lubell, n 20, *supra* and S Vite, 'The Interrelation of the Law of Occupation and Economic, Social and Cultural Rights: The Examples of Food, Health and Property' 871 *International Review of the Red Cross* 629 (2008).

[35] For further discussion of the ways in which human rights bodies have addressed situations of armed conflict, and some of the associated challenges, see A Reidy, 'The Approach of the European Commission and Court of Human Rights to International Humanitarian Law' 324 *International Review of the Red Cross* 513 (1998); Lubell, n 20, *supra*; D O'Donnell, 'Trends in the application of international humanitarian law by United Nations human rights mechanisms', 324 *International Review of the Red Cross* 481 (1998).

[36] For the development and detailed elaboration of this theory, see N Prud'homme, *International Humanitarian Law and International Human Rights Law: From Separation to Complementarity* (PhD thesis in progress, draft on file with author).

[37] See for example discussion of the Yemen incident in the Concluding Chapter.

there are bodies such as the ICJ and national courts, which are not restricted to one of the two particular frameworks. Governments and their militaries also need to know how to determine the precise nature of the rules that will apply to their planned actions.

In the context of the situations focused on here, the concurrent applicability of the two frameworks of law is clearer than in some of the above mentioned problem areas, but not in all circumstances. When the extraterritorial forcible measures are on the scale of a full-blown armed conflict (as in the US military operations against Al-Qaeda fighters in the early stages of the recent war in Afghanistan or the fighting between the Israeli military and Hezbollah fighters in Lebanon during the summer of 2006) then the rules governing forcible measures such as aerial bombardment would be those found in IHL, even if they appear foreign to the rules of human rights law.[38] International human rights law is not equipped to provide regulation for determining what is, and is not, a military objective. The appropriate definitions are to be found only in IHL. Likewise, the legality of certain weapons; the necessary precautions to be taken before and during attacks; and a host of other guiding rules all come from the framework of IHL. Conversely, when the situation is not one of armed conflict, as in the abduction of Vanunu,[39] then IHL does not apply, and only the rules of international human rights law are applicable. The difficulties of concurrent applicability emerge more clearly in situations such as the US targeting of the individuals in the jeep driving through Yemen.[40] The first question that needs answering in this case is whether IHL applies at all—it is a matter of debate whether this operation can be attributed to an armed conflict.[41] Assuming, for the sake of argument, that this operation is to be regarded as part of an armed conflict and therefore that IHL is applicable, there would then be the question of whether the targeted individuals were legitimate targets under IHL, either as combatants or civilians who had lost their protection.[42] Finally, were it to be concluded that under IHL they could indeed be targeted, then it should be recalled that the traditional approach as formulated by the ICJ, would be that the deprivation of life during armed conflict is regulated by IHL as it is the *lex specialis*.[43] It would, therefore, appear that, subject to accepting certain interpretations of applicability of IHL and the status of the individuals concerned, one might argue that killings such as these could have a lawful basis in IHL (although one would also have to take into account all the IHL rules discussed in earlier chapters, including proportionality, distinction, perfidy and others). This conclusion sits, for some, very uneasily with

---

[38] See discussion in Ch 6, *supra*.

[39] See discussion in Ch 7, section 3, on abductions and deprivation of liberty.

[40] See discussion on killings and right to life in section 1 of Ch 7, *supra*, and the Concluding Chapter, *infra*.

[41] See discussion of the possible existence of a 'war on terror' and other related issues in Ch 5, *supra*.

[42] See Ch 6, *supra*.   [43] *Nuclear Weapons*, n 11, *supra*.

the idea that human rights law was also applicable, in the expectation that this type of direct recourse to lethal force would not be lawful under the rules of law enforcement.[44]

It is cases such as this that exemplify the need for further analysis of the relationship between IHL and human rights law and the search for additional tools and models of interpretation for the concurrent application. There are numerous attempts by scholars in the field examining a wide variety of issues relating to concurrent application, that go far beyond the scope of issues presently covered and, although there are many views and approaches, there is no agreed solution.[45] Accepting the complete dominance of IHL in these situations, combined with the possibility of existing interpretations of the threshold of armed conflict and determinations of individual status, risks creating situations in which it would be too easy for states to claim that individuals are not protected civilians and that they are part of an armed conflict, and can therefore be targeted with a shoot-to-kill approach.[46] The predominant view based on observations of past years has been that states tended not to accept the classification of armed conflict and deny that the threshold had been reached.[47] Recent years, however, indicate that this tendency may be turning in the opposite direction. States have realized that invoking IHL appears to give them a freer hand and a wider range of options in the choice and methods of using force. Nowhere is this clearer than in the pursuit of the 'war on terror', in which the categorization as armed conflict and ensuing invocation of IHL rules were used to support lethal measures against individuals.[48] Israel's policy of targeted killings and the legitimacy (albeit with restrictions) granted to it by the Supreme Court, also rests on similar foundations.[49] Assertions of the applicability and ensuing predominance of IHL carry a risk of abuse and cannot always be accepted at face value. The opposite solution, of advocating the use of the human rights law approach, might seem more suitable for

[44] See discussion of reasons for illegality under human rights law, in section 1 of Ch 7, *supra*. But also see there for the theoretical possibility that such operations might not always be in violation. See also further discussion in the Concluding Chapter.

[45] In addition to other sources mentioned in this chapter, two recent journal volumes dedicated to this topic, and which contain a number of engaging articles, are *Israel Law Review*, vol 40(2) (2007) and *International Review of the Red Cross*, vol 871 (2008). See also Prud'homme, n 36, *supra*; D Kretzmer, 'Targeted Killing of Suspected Terrorists: Extra-Judicial Executions or Legitimate Means of Defence?' 16 *EJIL* 171 (2005). For a comprehensive analysis comparing the two bodies of law see R Provost, *International Human Rights and Humanitarian Law* (CUP: Cambridge, 2002).

[46] This problem has been raised not only in the context of counter-terror operations, but also with regard to non-international armed conflicts. Kretzmer, *ibid*, 200. See also discussion in *Expert Meeting*, n 28, *supra*, 34–41; Lubell, n 20, *supra*, 749.

[47] See T Meron, *Human Rights in Internal Strife: Their International Protection* (Grotius: Cambridge, 1987) 47. See also analysis of acceptance of Common Article 3, in L Moir, *The Law of Internal Armed Conflict* (CUP: Cambridge, 2008) 67–88.

[48] See Ch 5, *supra*.

[49] *The Public Committee against Torture in Israel and ors v. Israel* ('*The Targeted Killings Case*'), Judgment, HCJ, 769/02, 13 December 2006.

operations such as the one in Yemen, but the law enforcement framework would not lend itself as easily to operations on the scale of the battles in Afghanistan, in which surely it could not be maintained that a soldier on the battlefield can only fire in immediate self-defence of himself or others?[50] This would entail a complete upheaval of some of the rules that lie at the heart of IHL and of the very concept of how wars are fought, to such a degree as to change the nature of war itself. Leaving aside the attractiveness this might hold for some, it is clearly the case that the long-established IHL rules for regulating armed conflict cannot presently be easily reconstructed or even discarded.

Another approach would be along the lines of the 'Mixed Model' suggested by Kretzmer, in which the availability of alternative options must be taken into account before lethal force against alleged terrorists operating from another state can be legitimate.[51] This argument seems to allow for retention of crucial elements of the law enforcement and human rights law approach without promoting impractical solutions. However, the basis under IHL for this approach is unclear, since there is considerable support for the understanding that the rules of IHL do not operate under the presumption that non-lethal measures must be adopted before shooting an individual categorized as a legitimate target. This debate arose recently in the ICRC position on direct participation in hostilities, and was explored in Chapter 6 of this work. Significantly, the ICRC position would appear to endorse an interpretation of the IHL principles themselves as potentially requiring attempts to detain, in certain circumstances, even when faced with individuals without civilian protection.[52] The ICRC position does not, therefore, explicitly rely on the human rights approach—although some of the criticism directed at it suggests that it is in fact using human rights notions rather than IHL.[53] Clarification of the IHL rules and adoption of certain interpretations in relation to individual status and loss of protection might, therefore, present one avenue for solution but, as discussed previously, this interpretation of IHL seems unlikely to gain widespread support in the near future. If the rules of IHL are seen as allowing for direct lethal

---

[50] Although some views would appear to lead in that direction—see FF Martin, 'Using international human rights law for establishing a unified use of force rule in the law of armed conflict', *Saskatchewan Law Review*, vol 64, 2001, 347. But see responses in J Paust, 'Colloquy on the law of armed conflict: The unified use of force and exclusionary rules—The right to life in human rights law and the law of war', and in LC Green, 'Colloquy on the law of armed conflict: The unified use of force and exclusionary rules—The "unified use of force rule" and the law of armed conflict: A reply to Professor Martin', both in *Saskatchewan Law Review*, vol 65, 2002, 411 and 427.

[51] For a full explanation of this approach, and the other requirements it entails, see Kretzmer, n 45, *supra*, 201. In relation to the possibility of requiring to apprehend when feasible before lethally targeting, see also the approach of Ben-Naftali and Shany in O Ben-Naftali and Y Shany, 'Living in Denial: The Application of Human Rights in the Occupied Territories' 37 *Israel Law Review* 17 (2003–04) 107–08. See also discussion of the possibility of requiring arrest attempt prior to force, in *Expert Meeting*, n 28, *supra*, 17–8, 39–41. See also L Doswald-Beck, 'The Right to Life in Armed Conflict: Does International Humanitarian Law Provide all the Answers?' 864 *International Review of the Red Cross* 881 (2006); see also further sources and discussion of this in Ch 6, *supra*.

[52] See section 2.2 of Ch 6 on small scale operations.   [53] *Ibid*.

force against categories of persons, then in situations to which IHL is applicable, any approach combining the frameworks would need to overcome the argument that it would be placing a restriction on acts that applicable laws do not prohibit. Nonetheless, it is submitted here that an approach based on the assertion that, in situations such as the Yemen incident, an attempt to detain should be made before lethal force can be used, should indeed be advocated as a matter of policy, even if a legal requirement cannot be identified. Until a legal formulation can be agreed upon (if at all) at a minimum it is possible to advance arguments requiring attempts to detain when circumstances permit as desirable practice, even if not always a legally binding obligation. Progress towards a legal solution lies in a combination of areas. First, in certain circumstances there may in fact be an argument that the situation at hand is not one to which IHL is applicable (eg in some cases of the 'war on terror') and that human rights law, therefore, provides the only relevant framework.[54] Secondly, if IHL does apply, there is clearly room for further development of a methodological approach allowing for a coherent and consistent interpretation of the concurrent application of international human rights law and IHL.[55] Thirdly, there may be room within IHL itself to develop further interpretations. One of the difficulties raised in the debates over necessity, as outlined earlier, is that the same principles could be argued with regard to international armed conflicts. States are unlikely to accept that they must attempt to detain opposing combatants before using lethal force.[56] Perhaps further development in differentiation between interpretations of rules based on typology of conflicts might assist in this area. All these points impact upon each other and additional potential solutions can involve a combination of them. For example, rethinking the classification and applicability of IHL would inevitably involve clarifying the default legal regime and the possible interactions.[57]

Many of the problems discussed are not solely a matter of the ambiguous relationship between IHL and international human rights law, but are in fact largely due to lack of clarity within IHL itself. Where IHL is clearer, one is less likely to encounter problems of concurrent applicability. The determination of whether the object of a particular attack fell under the definition of military objectives does not present us with this type of problem, as the rules of IHL are not in major doubt. Likewise, where there is a rule of IHL for which there is also a similar

---

[54] See discussion in Chs 5 and 7, *supra*.

[55] For further views of this see, eg, the articles in a dedicated issue of the *Israel Law Review* (based on a conference held in Jerusalem in May 2006) including Droege, n 7, *supra*; Prud'homme, n 24, *supra;* Schabas, n 29, *supra;* N Lubell, 'Parallel Application of International Humanitarian Law and International Human Rights Law: An Examination of the Debate' 40(2) *Israel Law Review* 648 (2007). See also Doswald-Beck, n 51, *supra*; Kretzmer, n 45, *supra*.

[56] See discussions in sections 1.5 and 2.2 of Ch 6, *supra*.

[57] For development of this type of approach, see D Kretzmer, 'Rethinking Application of International Humanitarian Law in Non-International Armed Conflicts' 42(1) *Israel Law Review* 1 (2009).

parallel rule of human rights law—as in the prohibition of torture—it is not controversial to use the more highly developed field of human rights law to determine the definition of which acts actually constitute torture. When dealing with the use of lethal force by one combatant against another on the battlefield of an international armed conflict, there is little controversy over accepting that the right to life under human rights law must be interpreted so as to accept the IHL rules which could allow for such killings.[58] These are all because the above IHL rules themselves are not a subject of major dispute. The situation changes markedly once we turn to those areas in which IHL itself is unclear. One of the greatest areas of concern that arises in the debates over concurrent applicability relates to the use of force against individuals who are not combatants engaged in an international armed conflict. The primary question posed is whether there must be a law enforcement paradigm of attempting to detain and using minimal force necessary, or whether certain individuals can be targeted with direct lethal force. There are also implications for the status and treatment of such individuals if they are detained. The question of use of force, as examined in previous chapters in this work, encompasses numerous areas of contention within IHL itself, including: whether or not the situation at hand could be classified as an armed conflict to which IHL would then apply; whether membership of an armed group, other than an army or militia in international armed conflict, could entail a status similar to combatants insofar as the individual would be a legitimate target at all times during the conflict; how such membership is to be defined and determined; and the activities and duration of time for which civilians lose their protection on account of direct participation in hostilities. As a result of these longstanding areas of debate,[59] even if human rights law did not concurrently apply, we would remain with controversy and contradicting opinions over the applicable law. The introduction of concurrent applicability of human rights law into these debates and the ensuing opinions generated by it, tend to reflect positions and approaches already existing within the internal IHL debates. Moreover, any proposed solution to concurrent applicability in these situations which incorporates use of IHL rules, will have little effect if those rules themselves are still a subject of controversy.

In summary, in the context of the measures examined here, many of the difficulties of concurrent applicability of human rights law and IHL can, in fact,

---

[58] Whether this is achieved through the principle of *lex specialis*, or as an interpretation of one rule through the other, is not as crucial here, as the practical result is the same.

[59] See Part II on IHL. Whilst there should be hope and real attempt at progress, it is worth noting that there is no shortage of issues that were recognized as problems long ago but have not yet found a solution, eg while there has been much progress in development of IHL in relation to non-international armed conflict, comments concerning the status of individuals made over 30 years ago remain pertinent: 'international law can responsively order internal conflict only if it, first, provides uniform rules for the conduct of military operations therein and, second, provides rules for the classification and treatment of non-combatants'. J Bond, *The Rules of Riot: Internal Conflict and the Law of War,* (Princeton University Press: Princeton, 1974) 137.

be said to reflect problem areas in IHL itself regardless of the concurrent applicability of human rights law. These issues, as seen in earlier chapters, are continuously being debated, and any progress in clarifying them would be of significant assistance in determining the appropriate applicable rules for operations described in this section. Accordingly, the solution to some of these problems lies less in legal theories of concurrent applicability and more in the realm of solving long-standing debates within IHL.

Part III—Conclusion

Extraterritorial forcible measures taken against non-state actors are, prima facie, capable of leading to human rights violations, in particular of the right to life and freedoms from arbitrary detention, torture and other ill-treatment. International human rights law is precisely designed to safeguard individuals against measures which may amount to unlawful killings, arbitrary deprivation of liberty and torture. However, the treaties in which these obligations are contained appear, at first sight, to place certain restrictions on the scope of these obligations, restrictions which may also place territorial limitations. As seen in this Part, while the primary focus of the obligations is indeed towards individuals within the territory of the state, in certain circumstances obligations can, and do, exist towards individuals located outside the state's recognized borders. Extraterritorial obligations can be found not only when a state exercises effective control over territory of another state, but also when state agents exercise authority or control over an individual, thereby bringing the individual within state jurisdiction as determined by human rights treaties. In the latter circumstances, should the individual's rights be directly in the control of the state agent, then the state is obligated to observe those rights which are in its power to uphold. The obligation not to take action—including extraterritorially—which directly contravenes fundamental human rights, can be found in the basic concepts of human rights as stated in the UN Charter and through customary international law. State agents on a mission in the territory of another state cannot, therefore, act in a way which would be directly in breach of the rights to life, liberty or freedom from torture. If they do so their state may be liable for a breach of international human rights law. Lastly, should these forcible measures be taking place in the context of an armed conflict, then the determination of whether human rights law has been violated may depend also on whether the particular measure is permitted under IHL, and how the applicability of IHL affects the interpretation of the human rights obligation.

Concluding Chapter

The legality of extraterritorial use of force against non-state actors must take into account a number of different frameworks and rules. Whether or not the sending state violated the sovereignty of the territorial state will be determined according to the framework outlined in Part I of this work. Unless a case can be made for self-defence following an armed attack (or arguably to prevent a specific imminent attack) and that any response occurs only after the territorial state has proved unable or unwilling to take action, then it is likely that forcible operations on the territory of another state will violate the fundamental UN Charter prohibition on use of force.

The rules and principles of international humanitarian law, examined in Part II, will assist in determining whether the situation is to be considered an armed conflict. If it is, then the model of non-international armed conflict appears the most appropriate, whether *de jure* applicable or through analogous application of its rules as a minimal set of international humanitarian law ('IHL') rules applicable to non-traditional models of conflict. The rules of IHL will not, however, be applicable unless a certain intensity of violence and level of organization exists. If it is an armed conflict the rules on conduct of hostilities will regulate the force, although there are differing interpretations on a number of the rules, in particular in relation to the categorization of individual members of armed groups.

The framework of international human rights law, analysed in Part III of this work, applies at all times. It is submitted that human rights obligations apply also to extraterritorial situations and that when a state has authority or control over an individual it is obligated to observe those rights which are directly in its power to uphold. Should the circumstances amount to armed conflict then the applicability of international humanitarian law can affect the interpretation and obligations of human rights law, although the precise relationship between the bodies of law is not completely resolved.

The different legal frameworks are necessary for understanding the applicable laws, but the reality of the situations examined does not exist in identifiable boxes of distinct legal categories. The frameworks may be many, but an incident under examination is just one. Any single set of circumstances must be examined from numerous angles simultaneously if we are to have a more complete understanding of how to address the problems. This necessitates an examination of how all the different frameworks might apply and there were, therefore, three parts devoted to them. In addition, the junctures at which the frameworks overlap and might affect each other have been pointed out throughout the chapters. The overall picture that emerges from the different frameworks and the connections between them can be seen in the following two brief examinations of specific cases, that of the large-scale conflict between Israel and the Hezbollah in the summer of 2006, and of more limited scale of operations in the form of the targeted strikes against individuals as exemplified by the US strike in Yemen in 2002 and the drone strikes in recent years in Pakistan.

1. Israel—Hezbollah 2006

In the summer of 2006, Israel and the Lebanese armed group of Hezbollah were engaged in a conflict which saw extensive casualties and aerial bombing causing large scale destruction in Lebanon; ground operations which effectively emptied southern Lebanese villages; and thousands of Hezbollah rockets raining down on Israel, leading to mass internal displacement of civilians in the north of the country.[1] Israel's actions were predicated on a claim of self-defence.[2] Before proceeding with the examination, the first problem to be addressed here is whether Hezbollah was indeed a non-state actor, since its political wing had government seats and it has been a key player wielding significant power in Lebanon. There can be differing opinions on this,[3] but certain government statements and positions on both sides of the border suggest it is not unfounded to approach the situation as one involving a non-state actor and in which the Lebanese government was not itself a party to the conflict, and that Hezbollah was perhaps even acting against its government.[4] Accepting, as suggested in Part I, that there can be self-defence against non-state actors, it appears that Hezbollah's actions at the start of this affair (12 July 2006) can be seen as an armed attack. As reported by a UN

---

[1] See Report of the Special Rapporteur on extrajudicial, summary or arbitrary executions, Philip Alston; the Special Rapporteur on the right of everyone to the enjoyment of the highest attainable standard of physical and mental health, Paul Hunt; the Representative of the Secretary-General on human rights of internally displaced persons, Walter Kälin; and the Special Rapporteur on adequate housing as a component of the right to an adequate standard of living, Miloon Kothari, Mission to Lebanon and Israel, UN Doc A/HRC/2/7, 7–14 September 2006; Report of the Commission of Inquiry on Lebanon pursuant to Human Rights Council resolution S-2/1, UN Doc A/HRC/3/2, 23 November 2006 (this report focussed on Israeli actions and the effects in Lebanon); Human Right Watch, n 10, *infra*.

[2] Statement by Ambassador Dan Gillerman, Permanent Representative during the open debate on 'The Situation in the Middle East', United Nations, New York, 8 August 2006.

[3] See analysis in Report of the Commission, n 1, *supra*, paras 56–7, containing reasoning that could support an argument for seeing the Hezbollah as a state organ.

[4] The Lebanese government stated that is was not aware of the incident, was not responsible for it, and did not endorse it. Identical letters, dated 13 July 2006, from the Chargé d'affaires a.i. of the Permanent Mission of Lebanon to the United Nations addressed to the Secretary-General and the President of the Security Council, UN Doc A/60/938–S/2006/518; Israel, while placing responsibility on Lebanon, viewed itself as being in engaged in conflict with Hezbollah and not the Lebanese Government. Israeli Government, Cabinet Communique, 16 July 2006, available on website of Israeli Ministry for Foreign Affairs at <http://www.mfa.gov.il/MFA/Government/Communiques/2006/Cabinet+Communique+16-Jul-2006.htm>. See also Statement by Ambassador Dan Gillerman, Permanent Representative during the open debate on 'The Situation in the Middle East', Security Council, New York, 31 July 2006, stating that 'Israel has no quarrel with Lebanon. Israel has no battle with Lebanon. Israel has no war with Lebanon'.

mandated Commission of Inquiry, 'The situation began when Hezbollah fighters fired rockets at Israeli military positions and border villages while another Hezbollah unit crossed the Blue Line, killed eight Israeli soldiers and captured two.'[5] The combination of the rocket attacks on top of the attack of a military unit would appear to go beyond a small border incident. Furthermore, it would appear that Lebanon, as the territorial state, was either unwilling or unable to prevent these and further attacks.[6] If, however, it were to be claimed that this was a border incident which did not amount to an armed attack, then Israel would not have been allowed to respond in self-defence and was in violation of the fundamental prohibition regarding resort to force.[7]

That the hostilities between Israel and Hezbollah rose above the level required for armed conflict is uncontroversial, as is the fact that Hezbollah displays the requisite organizational capabilities and characteristics in order to qualify as a party to a conflict.[8] This being the case, the primary rules for regulating the use of force are those found in IHL. As concluded above, international human rights law may still be applicable if, for example, Israeli forces gain authority and control over individuals in Lebanon during the operations. However, any applicable rule of human rights law would have to be interpreted in light of the relevant provisions of IHL.[9]

Perhaps the most debatable aspect of this conflict is its characterization, thus reflecting the questions raised in Part II over how to define extraterritorial conflicts with non-state actors. Views exist in relation to this particular conflict supporting each of the possibilities, as either international or non-international armed conflict.[10] The approach taken here would deem this conflict to have been a non-international one. This is a point at which the differentiation between the legal frameworks must be stressed. The resort to force by Israel on Lebanese soil is a matter for the *ius ad bellum*, and is separate from the question of classification of the conflict for the purpose of the *ius in bello*. Under the rules of the *ius ad bellum* the first question, as indicated above, is whether Israel had a right to self-defence

---

[5] Report of the Commission, n 1, *supra*, para 40.

[6] The Security Council had repeatedly urged Lebanon to assert control and authority in the South. See Security Council Resolution no 1583, adopted by the Security Council at its 5117th meeting, on 28 January 2005, UN Doc S/RES/1583 (2005); Security Council Resolution no 1614, adopted by the Security Council at its 5241st meeting, on 29 July 2005, UN Doc S/RES/1614 (2005); Security Council Resolution no 1655, adopted by the Security Council at its 5362nd meeting, on 31 January 2006, UN Doc. S/RES/1655 (2006).

[7] See discussion in Ch 3, *supra*, of dilemmas in responding to an incident which is deemed less than an armed attack.

[8] This is evident in the facts and approach taken by virtually all the reports on the conflict.

[9] See discussion in the previous chapter on the relationship between the two frameworks.

[10] For an approach that appears to see it as an international armed conflict, see Report of the Commission, n 1, *supra*, para 60; the Israeli government based its actions on the laws of international armed conflict, see testimony of Brigadier General A Mendelblit, Israeli Military Advocate General, before the *Winograd Commission of Inquiry into the Events of Military Engagement in Lebanon 2006* available at <http://www.vaadatwino.org.il/statements.html#null>; For an examination that also raises the possibility of non-international armed conflict, see Human Rights Watch, 'Why They Died: Civilian Casualties in Lebanon during the 2006 War' Vol 19, no 5(E), September 2006, 31–2.

following what appeared to be an armed attack by the Hezbollah. Assuming it did the exercise of this right must pass the test of necessity, which in this case rested on the inability or unwillingness of the Lebanese government to prevent the attacks by the Hezbollah. A further question is whether the exercise of self-defence was carried out within the limits of proportionality. To be clear, this is with regard to proportionality under the *ius ad bellum*, which is separate to the question of proportionality of specific attacks under the *ius in bello*. The proportionality under the *ius ad bellum*, measures the overall scale of the response in light of the prevailing need to end the attacks.[11] The scale and nature of Israel's attacks in Lebanon, particularly the decision to carry out heavy attacks in areas other than the Hezbollah-controlled South, are those which would raise questions of proportionality in the resort to force. If it is the case that this was disproportionate, Lebanon would have a claim against Israel, who despite having the initial right to self-defence, may have exercised it in a manner that violated the rules of the *ius ad bellum*. This is a separate matter from the classification of the conflict under the *ius in bello*. If the hostilities themselves were between Israel and the Hezbollah as a non-state actor, with Lebanon taking no active part—and both states accepting that the conflict is between Israel and the Hezbollah, rather than Lebanon—then according to the analysis in Chapter 4 of this work these hostilities between a state and a non-state actor should be regarded as a non-international armed conflict.

The fact that force is used on the territory of another state cannot alone lead to an automatic conclusion of the existence of an international armed conflict, if there is no fighting between the states. There may or may not be a violation of the *ius ad bellum*, but that is a separate matter from the classification of conflict under the *ius in bello*. The latter depends upon the existence of hostilities and the identity of the parties. The possibility of the *ius ad bellum* being violated is not an automatic trigger for an international armed conflict—for example, Israel's abduction of Eichmann was an illegal use of force on Argentinean territory, but Israel and Argentina were not considered to be engaged in international armed conflict as a result. Determinations and classifications under *ius ad bellum* and *ius in bello* are separate issues and any link between them must not lead to automated inferences.

Nonetheless, in cases such as the current one, it might be argued that some of the Israeli attacks were against targets that are more readily associated with the Lebanese state than with Hezbollah, thus indicating the existence of an international armed conflict. Moreover, if Israel is regarded as having been in occupation of South Lebanon at the later period of the conflict, then at that point the rules of international armed conflict may come into play, as the existence of occupation does not rest upon resistance by the state.[12] However, notwithstanding the possibility of an international armed conflict evolving between Israel and Lebanon,

---

[11] See discussion in section 4 of Ch 2, *supra*, on proportionality.

[12] See Geneva Convention relative to the Protection of Civilian Persons in Time of War (12 August 1949) 75 UNTS 287, entered into force 21 October 1950 (Geneva Convention IV) Art 2; The scope of the current examination focuses, however, on actions that do not amount to occupation of foreign territory.

this would be separate from the non-international armed conflict between Israel and Hezbollah.

As seen in Chapter 6 of this work, insofar as the regulation of hostilities is concerned, most of the rules of conduct would be similar regardless of the classification.[13] However, an important effect of the characterisation of the conflict concerns the individual status of the members of Hezbollah. If it is not an international armed conflict they cannot have the legal status of combatants, which does not exist in these types of conflicts,[14] and which leads to the question of if, and when, they could legitimately be targeted.[15] Situations such as these, in which there is a full-scale armed conflict with an organized entity consisting of trained fighters in a military-style organization from command structure to uniform,[16] are one of the reasons for the search to clarify the categorization of members of armed groups.[17] Examinations of this conflict did not regard Hezbollah fighters as civilians, though the lack of clarity over the correct legal label to be applied is apparent in the fact that they are referred to both as 'fighters' and, at times, as 'combatants'.[18] Nonetheless, whilst it is certainly of benefit to make the factual distinction between the Hezbollah fighters and civilians not taking part in the conflict, there is considerable difficulty in declaring that the former belong to a categorization that has no definition in existing law. Without repeating the earlier debate on the correct categorization of these individuals, both of the primary solutions discussed in the earlier chapter—the continuous combat function, or the interpretation of civilians directly participating in hostilities—could mean that members of the armed wing of Hezbollah who were engaged in the fighting were not entitled to civilian protection and could be targeted during the hostilities.

The adherence to the laws on the conduct of hostilities was of major concern in this conflict. The respect for the *ius in bello* principle of proportionality and the targeting decisions by Israel in response to the alleged launching of rockets

---

[13] In this regard, it is noteworthy that one of the UN Reports is of the opinion that 'While the qualification of the conflict as international or non-international is complex, this report is mainly based on international customary law applicable in both forms of conflict.' Report of the Special Rapporteurs, n 1, *supra*, para 23.

[14] If it was an international armed conflict, there might still be debate over whether they fulfilled the requirements for this status. See section 1.1 in Ch 6, *supra*, on combatants.

[15] This also has bearing on the question of POW status for those captured. POW status is outside the scope of this work. For further information on the status, treatment and trial of captured Hezbollah fighters, see cases of the Israeli Supreme Court, *Srur and ors v. the State of Israel,* Case nos 8780/06 and 8984/06 (in Hebrew).

[16] Although the uniforms were not always worn, they did exist and were in use during some of the fighting between Israel and the Hezbollah. See mention in Human Rights Watch, n 10, *supra*, 60–1.

[17] See discussion concerning members of armed groups, in Ch 6, *supra*.

[18] The Report of the Special Rapporteurs, n 1, *supra*, para 37, spoke of Israel not distinguishing Hezbollah fighters from civilians. See, eg, also Human Rights Watch, n 10, *supra*, mentioning Hezbollah 'combatants' and 'fighters', 60–1. It should also be noted that this refers to the fighters, as opposed to other members of the wider Hezbollah organization who may be involved in social welfare or other non-fighting activities.

from inside Lebanese villages were central to the question of possible violations of international law.[19] As seen in Chapter 6 of this work, this is an area of contention as to the interpretation of the law but, nevertheless, many of the enquiries into conduct during this conflict have indicated that Israel's attacks violated international humanitarian law.[20] Without going further into a lengthy analysis of this conflict[21] it appears, on the one hand, to present a type of situation in which extraterritorial force against non-state actors illustrates certain controversial issues that arose in earlier chapters—namely the right of self-defence against armed groups and the characterization of the ensuing conflict. On the other hand, it also demonstrates that interpretations exist which prove these to be not insurmountable legal hurdles, and that the major debates flowing from this conflict in fact concern a more straightforward analysis of whether or not the parties committed violations of clearly applicable rules of IHL. Many of the determinations of the alleged violations, as evidenced in the examinations of the conflict, revolve around disputes over the facts of what was targeted, and for what reason, more than debates over the applicable law. The next type of case to be examined does, however, throw into the air a more complex set of legal questions.

2. Targeted killings in Yemen and strikes in Pakistan

The US has, on a number of occasions, engaged in strikes aimed at specific individuals in the context of the 'war on terror'.[22] The targeting of an alleged Al-Qaeda leader and five others in November 2002 was by a missile fired at their vehicle travelling on a desert road in Yemen.[23] The inter-state aspect of this case is unclear since it is not certain whether the Yemeni government gave prior authorization for the missile strike.[24] If they did not give their consent, then absent any evidence of the

---

[19] Report of the Commission, n 1, *supra*, para 2; Report of the Special Rapporteurs, n 1, *supra*, para 46, 58; Statement by Ambassador Dan Gillerman, Permanent Representative During the open debate on 'The Situation in the Middle East' Security Council, New York, 30 July 2006; Human Rights Watch, n 10, *supra*.

[20] Report of the Commission, n 1, *supra*; Report of the Special Rapporteurs, n 1, *supra*; Human Rights Watch, n 10, *supra*. These reports (other than the first) also addressed violations of IHL by Hezbollah.

[21] See Report of the Special Rapporteurs, n 1, *supra*; Report of the Commission, n 1, *supra*; Human Rights Watch, n 10, *supra*.

[22] 'US bombs Islamist town in Somalia' *BBC News,* 3 March 2008; W Pincus, 'U.S. Strike Kills Six in Al Qaeda' *Washington Post,* 5 November, 2002; F Bokhari, 'Pakistan tries to ease tension after US attack' *Financial Times,* 16 January 2006.

[23] For a description of the incident see Pincus, *ibid*; S Hersh, 'Manhunt' *The New Yorker,* 23 December 2002; 'CIA "killed al-Qaeda suspects" in Yemen' *BBC News,* 5 November 2002.

[24] The government of Yemen later stated that it had been engaged in joint operations with the US tracking the group, and that the measure was taken in the context of cooperation with the US. See Report of the Special Rapporteur, on extrajudicial, summary or arbitrary executions, Asma Jahangir Addendum, Summary of cases transmitted to Governments and replies received, UN Doc E/CN.4/2004/7/Add.1, 24 March 2004, para.612. It also stated that the operation was the fruit of collaboration between the security forces of Yemen and the US, see Human Rights Committee, Summary record of the 2283rd meeting, UN Doc CCPR/C/SR.2283, 18 July 2005, para 19

US first seeking action from the Yemeni government, use of force in Yemen would not conform to the requirement of necessity.[25] Whether or not there was a violation of the rules covering the inter-state relationship, there will in either case remain the question over the appropriate model for regulating the use of force—law enforcement or armed conflict—and whether different results would be given by the two frameworks. In addition to the suggestion that international human rights law can be applied to extraterritorial operations of this type, the analysis of this case in Part III concluded that under the law enforcement model, as encapsulated in international human rights law, the intentional killing of the individuals is likely to have been unlawful. The primary reasoning was based on the action being neither necessary nor proportionate according to the applicable rules.[26] The possibility was, however, left open that international human rights law might allow for a lethal strike of this type in cases in which there was a clear imminent serious threat which could not be averted by other means.[27] As for IHL, viewing this through the IHL framework can only occur if the situation is part of an armed conflict. If not, the assessment ends with the conclusion from the rules of international human rights law. The possibility that this operation was part of a 'war on terror' classified as an armed conflict was examined in Chapter 5 of this work. There are serious misgivings over reaching a positive answer to this, and a loosely defined 'war on terror' cannot provide grounds to classify this operation as part of an armed conflict.[28] If, however, this operation is tied into a specific existing armed conflict, such as the conflict in Afghanistan, then it could be argued that IHL does apply. Armed conflicts can, and do, spill over borders. The possibility of the Afghan conflict crossing borders is evidenced most clearly on the borders with Pakistan, with actions by the US against Taliban targets in Pakistan.[29] Just as the Taliban forces can relocate and operate from Pakistan, members of the opposing party to the conflict could theoretically also operate from Yemen. It must be stressed that this does not, however, lead to a *carte blanche* to strike at any individual in any country and a number of criteria must first be answered. Individuals do not carry the battlefield away with them whenever they relocate to a different territory, otherwise there would be no possibility to disengage from an armed conflict. Rather, it is a question of whether the conflict activities themselves have also relocated. In other words, only if the individual or group are continuing to engage in the armed conflict from their new location, then operations taken against them could be considered to be part of the armed conflict. This could be the case for Taliban fighters engaged in the Afghan conflict but operating from Pakistan. IHL could, therefore, apply in operations

---

(translated from the original French). However, one may question whether the general co-operation and joint tracking of the group also means that the actual decision to use lethal force and carry out the missile strike was itself a joint decision or even one in which there was advance consultation.

[25] For further elaboration of this requirement see Ch 2, *supra*.

[26] This is due to the fact that, according to reports, there may have been opportunities to detain the persons earlier and also because it is unclear that they actually posed an imminent threat. See discussion in Ch 7, *supra*.

[27] *Ibid.*   [28] See discussion of the 'war on terror' in Ch 5, *supra*.

[29] ' "US strike" kills Taleban leader' *BBC News*, 27 October 2008.

against them should the targeted individuals or groups meet this requirement. If the US attacks are being launched against persons not involved in the Afghan conflict to which the US is party then they cannot be considered legitimate targets under IHL since this framework would not apply between them and the US. For example, it appears that one of the targets of a strike in Pakistan was the head of the Islamic Movement of Uzbekistan.[30] This individual was alleged to have been taking part in the Afghan conflict by targeting foreign forces in Afghanistan but,[31] if that was not the case, then the IHL rules on targeting could not be invoked to justify the strike. Targeting individuals allegedly linked to Al-Qaeda under the vague notion of a 'war on terror' would not provide legitimate grounds for attacks.[32] Furthermore, if the targeted individuals are being targeted on account of their actions within Pakistan,[33] there would need to be both a determination of an armed conflict in Pakistan, and a request from the Pakistani government for the US to be taking part in the conflict alongside the government.[34]

If these actions are found to take place within the context of an armed conflict the actual use of lethal force in these strikes rests primarily on the interpretation of the IHL rules relating to status of members of armed groups, direct participation, and the contentious debates over requiring lesser means first.[35] Additional concerns are raised about the proportionality of these strikes. There are differing reports on the number and composition of casualties from the strikes.[36] Some of these reports suggest that other than the individuals who are the intended targets there regularly appear to be a far larger number of additional individuals killed or injured in these strikes—a large proportion of whom may have been civilians who were taking no part in hostilities.[37] If the latter numbers are correct, then there would be a strong case that many of the strikes violated the principle of proportionality. In addition to the above, the drone strikes raise a wide variety of further issues, such as the legal implications of a drone being operated by the CIA, since only combatants are given the right to participate in hostilities.[38] An additional concern is that the legal and

---

[30] 'Uzbek rebel "killed" in Pakistan"' *BBC News*, 2 October 2009.   [31] *Ibid.*

[32] See Ch 5, *supra.*

[33] As appears to be the case on occasion, for example see '"Drone attack" kills Taliban wife' *BBC News*, 5 August 2009.

[34] See later discussion on questionable consent from the Pakistani government.

[35] See discussion on all these throughout Ch 6, *supra.*

[36] D Kilcullen and A Exum, 'Death From Above, Outrage Down Below' *New York Times*, 16 May 2009; B Roggio and A Mayer, 'Analysis: A look at US airstrikes in Pakistan through September 2009' *The Long War Journal*, 1 October, 2009.

[37] Kilcullen and Exum, *ibid.*

[38] Protocol Additional to the Geneva Conventions of 12 August 1949, and Relating to the Protection of Victims of International Armed Conflicts (Protocol I) (8 June 1977), 1125 UNTS 3, entered into force 7 December 1978, Art 43(2); APV Rogers, *Law on the Battlefield* (Manchester University Press: Manchester, 2004), 45-6; G Rona, 'Interesting Times for International Humanitarian Law: Challenges From the "War on Terror"' *Fletcher Forum of World Affairs*, 27:2 (2003) 64–5. Essential problems include whether the CIA operatives can be targeted for directly participating in the hostilities and what would be their status if captured.

ethical field may need to catch up with technological developments in the area of unmanned and robotic warfare.[39]

A separate question is the legality of the operations under the rules of the *ius ad bellum* which would regulate the decision to resort to forcible measures in the first place. If the territorial state consents to the operations, as arguably was the case in Yemen,[40] then these rules will not have been violated. The situation in Pakistan exemplifies the challenges in determining whether consent was given in light of contradictory statements and reports. Some of these point to a difference between public condemnation of the attacks, which may be necessary for internal political reasons, and the simultaneous approval given behind closed doors.[41] Identifying the consent presents a primarily factual difficulty rather than a legal one. If the territorial state does not consent to the measures, then use of force must pass all the tests outlined in Part I of this work, including a need to use force in order to respond to attacks which have crossed the threshold of armed attack, and the test of necessity which would include the territorial state being unwilling, or unable, to end the attacks taking place from its soil. Without these the use of force in the territory of another state will have been unlawful under the *ius ad bellum*. It is the strict adherence to these rules that must provide a safeguard against overzealous resort to extraterritorial force.

Returning to the Yemen case, should one take the position that IHL applied to this operation the legality of this attack would primarily depend on the categorization of the targeted individuals. Targeting them could be lawful under IHL if they are seen to be non-civilians (if one accepts the corresponding interpretation concerning members of armed groups)[42] or if they had lost civilian protection on account of direct participation in hostilities. For the latter, there would have to be wide interpretation of the duration of time during which protection is lost.[43] Determination of legality under an applicable rule of IHL could then affect the determination of whether human rights law had been violated.[44]

The answer may lie in determining the inapplicability of IHL to small scale operations, that cannot readily be claimed to be part of a larger and definable ongoing armed conflict,[45] whilst simultaneously accepting that in extreme circumstances international human rights law might allow for resort to lethal force.[46] This approach does away with the debate over which framework to choose but accepts the harsh reality that, in certain cases, lethal force might be the only option and be necessary and proportionate. It would then depend on an assessment under international human rights law as to whether a particular

---

[39] For description of these developments, see PW Singer, *Wired for War: the Robotics Revolution and Conflict in the 21st Century* (Penguin Press: London, 2009).

[40] See n 24 *supra*.

[41] D Ignatius, 'A Quiet Deal With Pakistan' *Washington Post*, 4 November 2008; B Ghosh and M Thompson, 'The CIA's Silent War in Pakistan' *Time*, 1 June 2009.

[42] See discussion concerning members of armed groups, in Ch 6, *supra*.

[43] See section 1.3 of Ch 6, *supra*, on direct participation.

[44] See Ch 9, *supra*, on relationship between IHL and international human rights law.

[45] See discussion of the 'war on terror' in section 1 of Ch 5, *supra*.

[46] See this possibility in the examination of the Yemen case in Ch 7, *supra*.

operation was lawful. Alternatively, if the situation is interpreted as falling within the scope of applicability of IHL, and seen as being subject to both IHL and human rights law, there could be an attempt to adopt interpretations that could provide similar results within both frameworks.[47] Accordingly, if international human rights law is understood to allow for lethal force in extreme situations of preventing an imminent serious attack in circumstances which offer no alternative, and IHL is interpreted so as to allow the targeting of members of armed groups only on the basis of the rule on loss of protection during such time as they are taking a direct part in hostilities (which could include the wider timeframe following one attack and leading up to the next one), then this would bring us closer to similar conclusions under the two frameworks. They would, nevertheless, not be identical due to the human rights approach to lethal force only as a last option. Moreover, the chances for similar conclusions would drift even further away if other interpretations were favoured, allowing for targeting all members of groups regardless of their precise activities, at any time.[48] Approaches proposed by some, and discussed in Chapter 6 of this work, suggest a particular understanding of the notion of necessity in IHL[49] which might in some circumstances result in similar interpretations to human rights law.[50] Nonetheless, there are strong views that the law as it stands points to a deep ravine between international human rights law and IHL, in that the latter accepts that targeting decisions can be based not just on individual activity but also on the category to which a person belongs.[51]

Following the above, it appears that whether or not each of the frameworks applies can be of major significance since IHL and human rights law can lead to differing conclusions. The debates over operations such as this, and over the 'war on terror' in general,[52] demonstrate the lack of consensus and difficulty in achieving certainty on this matter. Discerning the appropriate rules and potential confusion over how to regulate use of force have been identified as real problems that must be addressed.[53] While concurrent applicability of human rights and IHL is

---

[47] See also discussion of the need for 'a holistic approach to the law' in the context of the two frameworks in C Garraway, 'The "War on Terror": Do the Rules Need Changing?' Briefing Paper IL BP 06/02, The Royal Institute of International Affairs, September 2006, 10.

[48] See discussion in Ch 6 *supra*.

[49] See discussion in section on small-scale attacks, Ch 6, section 2.2, *supra*.

[50] Indeed, it was this similarity that also caused some of the opposition to these proposals. *Ibid.*

[51] *Ibid.*

[52] See the exchange of opinions between the US and the UN Special Rapporteur on Extrajudicial Killings, concerning a similar case of an alleged killing of an individual on the Pakistan-Afghanistan border by the US in 2005, as reflected in 'UN Expert on Extrajudicial Killings tells United States War on Terror could Undermine Human Rights Accountability' UNHCHR Press Release, 28 March 2007; on the Yemen incident see M Sassoli, 'Use and Abuse of the Laws of War in the "War on Terrorism"' *Law and Inequality: A Journal of Theory and Practice* 22 (2004) 214; Rogers, *ibid*; A McDonald, 'Terrorism, Counter-terrorism and the Jus in Bello' in M Schmitt and G Beruto (eds) *Terrorism and International Law: Challenges and Responses* (International Institute of Humanitarian Law, 2002); Rona, *ibid*, 62–5; on the 'war on terror' see Ch 5, *supra*.

[53] Garraway, n 47, *supra*; K Watkin, 'Controlling the Use of Force: A Role for Human Rights Norms in Contemporary Armed Conflict' 98 *AJIL* 1 (2004) 1–2.

a legal reality, the lack of an agreed approach to interpretation leads to difficulties of implementation in practice. Regulation and scrutiny are hard to achieve since the various international bodies, whose work is predicated on a mandate based in one of the two frameworks, can find themselves operating outside their mandate or having to scrutinize laws they are less accustomed to.[54] More importantly, throughout the chapters it has been clear that there are inherent problems within the frameworks and internal difficulties such as the status of members of armed groups in IHL, and extraterritorial scope of applicability of human rights law, on which there is much disagreement. Before constructing new models, we must first try and resolve the difficulties posed by the lack of clarity within the building blocks that are being used.

All three legal frameworks are of relevance to operations such as these. The resort to a forcible operation on the territory of another state will be governed by the *ius ad bellum*. If the situation is one of armed conflict, then the rules of IHL will apply to the way in which the force is used. If it is not part of an armed conflict then international human rights law will provide the sole regulatory framework for assessing the legality of the use of force. If IHL were applicable then the concurrent applicability of the two frameworks could affect the interpretation of the specific rules.

A final word of caution must be given with regard to operations such as the ones discussed. The above debate concerned itself with the applicable rules of international law and whether there could be circumstances in which these types of operation might be legal. Notwithstanding the outcome of that debate, it should be borne in mind that being legal does not always equal being wise. Political and military decision makers would do well not to base their decision solely on whether it would be lawful. Depending on the circumstances, concerns of political strategy; effects on public perception and the international community; questions of ethics and morality; and many more considerations should be taken into account,[55] and may well provide reason not to carry out such operations even when they might be lawful.

3. Concluding comments

From the issues examined throughout, it is clear that in each of the analysed frameworks, there are a number of contentious matters. These include the legality of states responding extraterritorially to attacks by non-state actors; the question

---

[54] Eg the European Court of Human Rights would have to develop an expertise and ability to apply IHL and the ICRC faces questions of international human rights law. For an elaborate analysis of the relationship between IHL and human rights law, and how this is affected by the monitoring bodies in question, see N Prud'homme, *International Humanitarian Law and International Human Rights Law: From Separation to Complementarity* (PhD thesis in progress, draft on file with author).

[55] Eg, see concerns over the policy of drone strikes in Pakistan in Kilcullen and Exum, n 36, *supra*.

of whether extraterritorial forcible measures can be categorized as an armed conflict, and of what type; the interpretation of certain rules of IHL, in particular on the status and laws allowing the targeting of members of armed groups; and the extraterritorial applicability of international human rights law obligations, and how these are affected when IHL also applies.

Two key areas were identified in which the law could be argued to lack the clarity necessary to match perceived threats. The first is with regard to the possibility for states to respond to violence from non-state actors operating from other territories, but whose actions might be interpreted as not reaching a threshold of armed attack, and against whom the territorial state is unwilling or unable to act itself. As noted at the end of Part I, the law as it stands rules out unilateral force other than through the prism of self-defence, which does not exist without an armed attack. While there will be those who rue this standpoint and see it as tying the hands of states that are in need of action, there is doubtless stronger reason for maintaining this threshold and preventing descent into unbridled endless forcible incursions into other states. Another area of contention relates to the status of individuals under IHL, in particular with regard to members of armed groups. Various interpretations were presented, and some were preferred over others as a matter of identifying existing law, but all solutions on offer have their own flaws and entail certain risks.

These issues notwithstanding, most of the other areas in which there initially seemed to be problems particular to the situation being examined were found, upon inspection, to have solutions that, at least in the current analysis, were considered to be relatively satisfactory. This was the case with the existence of a right of self-defence against non-state actors; with extraterritorial applicability of human rights obligations; and with the possibility of applying—either directly or as an analogous minimal standard—the rules of non-international armed conflict to extraterritorial conflicts against non-state actors.

The challenge of this analysis has been to identify the wide variety of primary issues that must be addressed across all three legal frameworks and, where possible, to suggest potential approaches that may be adopted in order to achieve coherent regulation of extraterritorial force against non-state actors. In so doing, it has been apparent that not only must all three frameworks be addressed, but so must the links between them. In some cases it is necessary to differentiate between the frameworks, and identify the legality or illegality under one set of rules in a manner separate from issues raised within other frameworks. On other occasions, the determinations under one framework can have a direct impact on another. Each of the frameworks plays a different role in the regulation of this type of extraterritorial force and each can only answer the expectations that belong to its own sphere. The rules of the *ius ad bellum* provide the primary regulatory framework for assessing the legality of the very resort to force on the territory of another state, rather than IHL and international human rights law. It is, therefore, to the *ius ad bellum* framework that we must turn for the crucial role of limiting unnecessary extraterritorial force. Strict adherence to the principle of necessity in the exercise of self-defence and rejection of theories allowing for a vague notion of pre-emptive force will serve well in this regard.

If, and when, force is used IHL and international human rights law may provide the rules for oversight. The rules of IHL offer a regulatory framework for force in the context of armed conflict but are focused upon the manner in which the force is used, rather than the decision to resort to extraterritorial force in the first place. Outside of armed conflict situations the main regulatory framework will be international human rights law. It is primarily through international human rights law that the relationship and obligations of the state towards individuals must be assessed. The obligations of international human rights law must be considered to cover extraterritorial circumstances as a consistent interpretation of the underlying principles of this body of law. When an individual's rights are directly in the control of state agents then the state is obligated to observe those rights which are in its power to uphold. Absent the applicability of IHL, which may modify the human rights obligations in situations of armed conflict, international human rights law and its rules on use of force will provide the necessary framework for regulation.

The primary conclusions of the examination are, therefore, twofold. First, a number of the unique legal challenges posed by the use of extraterritorial force against non-state actors can be adequately addressed by adopting particular interpretations within the current frameworks of applicable international law. Secondly, this examination has highlighted existing problems in international law which must be addressed in order to reach a coherent and consistent approach not only to these operations but also in a wider context. Thus, for example, the problem of how to categorize members of armed groups under IHL is vital to the situation under examination but is also a fundamental and pre-existing problem in the context of armed conflicts.

In light of this, the extraterritorial use of force against non-state actors, including as part of a 'war on terror', must not be seen as a stimulant for embarking on searches for new rules which would apply to these specific situations. There are abundant existing laws which apply to these situations and can serve to regulate them. Nonetheless, within these are areas of the law which present real challenges, and have been recognized as such regardless of these specific operations and situations.

The solution to clarity in the regulation and scrutiny of extraterritorial use of force against non-state actors lies, therefore, first and foremost in the finding of acceptable interpretations to wider existing problems. Once further progress is reached in these departments it may well become apparent that any calls for new laws in the specific context of extraterritorial force against non-state actors will become redundant. In the meantime, certain challenges were found to have adequate solutions in the existing law, whilst others will remain subject to ongoing debates over their interpretation.

Bibliography

1. International treaties and instruments

African Charter on Human and Peoples' Rights (26 June 1981) OAU Doc CAB/ LEG/67/3 rev.5; 1520 UNTS 217; 21 ILM 58 (1982), entered into force 21 October 1986.

American Convention on Human Rights (22 November 1969) 1144 UNTS 123, entered into force 18 July 1978.

American Declaration of the Rights and Duties of Man, OAS Res XXX, adopted by the Ninth International Conference of American States (1948), reprinted in Basic Documents Pertaining to Human Rights in the Inter-American System, OEA/ Ser.L.V/II.82 doc.6 rev.1 at 17 (1992).

Charter of the United Nations (26 June 1945) 59 Stat 1031; TS 993; 3 Bevans 1153, entered into force 24 October 1945.

Convention against Torture and Other Cruel, Inhuman or Degrading Treatment or Punishment (10 December 1984) 1465 UNTS 85, entered into force 26 June 1987.

Convention for the Protection of Human Rights and Fundamental Freedoms (4 November 1950) 213 UNTS 222; 312 ETS 5, entered into force 3 September 1953.

Declaration on Principles of International Law Concerning Friendly Relations and Co-operation among States in accordance with the Charter of the United Nations, GA res 2625, Annex 25 UN GAOR, Supp (no 28); UN Doc A/5217 at 121 (1970).

European Convention for the Prevention of Torture and Inhuman or Degrading Treatment or Punishment, CPT/Inf/C (2002) 1 (Part 1)—Strasbourg, 26.XI.1987 (Text amended according to the provisions of Protocols no 1 (ETS No 151) and no 2 (ETS No 152) which entered into force on 1 March 2002).

Geneva Convention for the Amelioration of the Condition of the Wounded and Sick in Armed Forces in the Field (12 August 1949) 75 UNTS 31, entered into force 21 October 1950.

Geneva Convention for the Amelioration of the Condition of Wounded, Sick and Shipwrecked Members of Armed Forces at Sea (12 August 1949) 75 UNTS 85, entered into force 21 October 1950.

Geneva Convention relative to the Protection of Civilian Persons in Time of War (12 August 1949) 75 UNTS 287, entered into force 21 October 1950.

Geneva Convention relative to the Treatment of Prisoners of War (12 August 1949) 75 UNTS 135, entered into force 21 October 1950.

International Convention for the Protection of All Persons from Enforced Disappearance, GA Res 61/177; UN Doc A/RES/61/177 (2006), adopted 20 December 2006.

International Convention for the Suppression of the Financing of Terrorism (9 December 1999) GA Res 109, UN GAOR, 54th session, Supp no 49; UN Doc A/54/49 (vol I) (1999); S Treaty Doc no 106–49 (2000); 39 ILM 270 (2000), entered into force 10 April 2002.

International Convention for the Suppression of Terrorist Bombing, GA Res 164, UN GAOR, 52nd session, Supp no 49 at 389; UN Doc A/52/49 (1998), entered into force 23 May 2001.

International Covenant on Civil and Political Rights (16 December 1966) 999 UNTS 171, entered into force 23 March 1976.

Protocol Additional to the Geneva Conventions of 12 August 1949, and relating to the Protection of Victims of International Armed Conflicts (Protocol I) (8 June 1977) 1125 UNTS 3, entered into force 7 December 1978.

Protocol Additional to the Geneva Conventions of 12 August 1949, and relating to the Protection of Victims of Non-International Armed Conflicts (Protocol II) (8 June 1977), 1125 UNTS 609, entered into force 7 December 1978.

Regulations Annexed to the Hague Convention (IV) Respecting the Laws and Customs of War on Land, 1907.

Rome Statute of the International Criminal Court, UN Doc 2187 UNTS 90, entered into force 1 July 2002.

Second Optional Protocol to the International Covenant on Civil and Political Rights, aiming at the abolition of the death penalty (15 December 1989) UN Doc A/RES/44/128, entered into force 11 July 1991.

The Inter-American Convention to Prevent and Punish Torture, entered into force on 28 February 1987.

United Nations Convention on the Law of the Sea (10 December 1982) 1833 UNTS 3, entered into force 16 November 1994.

UN Basic Principles on the Use of Force and Firearms by Law Enforcement Officials, UN Doc A/CONF.144/28/rev.1 at 112 (1990).

UN Code of Conduct for Law Enforcement Officials, GA Res 34/169 annex, 34 UN GAOR Supp (no 46) at 186; UN Doc A/34/46 (1979).

Universal Declaration of Human Rights, Resolution 217 A(III); UN Doc A/810 91, UN General Assembly, 1948.

Vienna Convention on Diplomatic Relations (18 April 1961) 500 UNTS entered into force on 24 April 1964.

Vienna Convention on the Law of Treaties (23 May 1969) 1155 UNTS 331; 8 ILM 679 (1969); 63 *American Journal of International Law* 875 (1969), entered into force 27 January 1980.

2. Other international and governmental documents

'A More Secure World: Our Shared Responsibility', Report of the Secretary-General's High-Level Panel on Threats, Challenges and Change, UN Doc A/59/565, 2004.

Acts Adopted under Title V of the EU Treaty Council Joint Action 2008/851/CFSP of 10 November 2008, on 'a European Union military operation to contribute to the deterrence, prevention and repression of acts of piracy and armed robbery off the Somali coast'.

Ago, R., 'The internationally wrongful act of the State, source of international responsibility (part 1)' Addendum to the 8th report on state responsibility by the Special

Rapporteur, 32nd session of the ILC (1980); UN Doc A/CN.4/318/Add.5–7 (extract from the *Yearbook of the International Law Commission 1980, Vol II(1)*).

Baroness Symons written answer to Lord Kennet, Hansard, Column WA140, 16 November 1998.

CIA Office of Inspector General's Counterterrorism Detention and Interrogation Activities Report, 7 May 2004, available at <http://www.aclu.org/human-rights_national-security/cia-office-inspector-generals-may-2004-counterterrorism-detention-and>.

'Commentaries to the draft articles on Responsibility of States for internationally wrongful acts', International Law Commission, 53rd session (2001), (extract from the 'Report of the International Law Commission on the work of its Fifty-third session', Official Records of the General Assembly, 56th session, Supp no 10 (A/56/10), chp.IV.E.2), November 2001, 80–122).

Committee on Economic, Social and Cultural Rights, 'The right to adequate food', General Comment no 12, 20th session, UN Doc E/C.12/1999/5 (1999).

—— 'The right to education', General Comment no 13, 21st session, UN Doc E/C.12/1999/10 (1999).

—— 'The right to the highest attainable standard of health', General Comment 14, 22nd session, UN Doc E/C.12/2000/4 (2000).

—— 'Concluding Observations of the Committee on Economic, Social and Cultural Rights: Israel' E/C.12/1/Add.69, 31 August 2001.

'Consideration of Reports Submitted by States Parties Under Article 19 of the Convention, Conclusions and Recommendations of the Committee against Torture, United States of America' UN Doc CAT/C/USA/CO/2, 25 July 2006, para 15. See also Committee Against Torture, 'General Comment no 2: Implementation of article 2 by States parties', UN Doc.CAT/C/GC/2 24 January 2008.

'Consideration of Reports Submitted by States Parties Under Article 19 of the Convention, Second Periodic Reports of States Parties due in 1999', Addendum, United States of America, UN Doc Cat/C/48/Add.3, 29 June 2005.

'Consideration of Reports Submitted by States Parties under Article 40 of the Covenant: International Covenant on Civil and Political Rights: Comments by the Government of Germany to the Concluding Observations of the Human Rights Committee' UN Doc CCPR/CO/80/DEU/Add.1, 11 April 2005.

'DoD Law of War Program' Department of Defense Directive Number 2311.01E, 9 May 2006.

'Draft Articles on Responsibility of States for internationally wrongful acts', International Law Commission, 53rd session (2001) (extract from the 'Report of the International Law Commission on the work of its Fifty-third session', Official Records of the General Assembly, 56th session, Supp no 10 (A/56/10), chap IV.E.1, November 2001).

Extrajudicial, summary or arbitrary executions, Report of the Special Rapporteur, Philip Alston UN Doc. E/CN.4/2006/53, 8 March 2006.

'Final Report to the Prosecutor by the Committee Established to Review the NATO Bombing Campaign against the Federal Republic of Yugoslavia' ICTY, 2000.

Foreign and Commonwealth Office Paper, 'Is intervention ever justified?' Foreign Policy Document no 148, 1986 (reprinted in part in 57 *British Yearbook of International Law* 614).

'Fragmentation of International Law: Difficulties Arising from the Diversification and Expansion of International Law' Report of the Study Group of the International Law Commission, finalized by Martti Koskenniemi, UN Doc A/CN.4/L.682, 13 April 2006.

Human Rights Committee, 'Comments of the Human Rights Committee: Croatia' UN Doc CCPR/C/79/Add.15, 28 December 1992.

—— 'Comments on United States of America' UN Doc CCPR/C/79/Add 50 (1995).

—— 'Concluding Observations of the Human Rights Committee: Israel' UN Doc CCPR/C/79/Add.93, 18 August 1998.

—— 'Concluding Observations of the Human Rights Committee: Italy' UN Doc CCPR/C/ITA/CO/5 (2006).

—— 'Concluding Observations of the Human Rights Committee: Poland' UN Doc CCPR/CO/82/POL (2004).

—— 'Consideration of reports submitted by States parties under article 40 of the Covenant: Croatia, Yugoslavia' Summary record of the 1202nd meeting (second part) UN Doc CCPR/C/SR.1202/Add.1, 15 April 1993.

—— 'Consideration of Reports Under Article 40 Of The Covenant (Continued), Second And Third Periodic Reports Of The United States Of America (Continued)' Summary record of the 2380th Meeting, 18 July 2006, UN Doc CCPR/C/SR.2380, 27 July 2006.

—— General Comment no 20, UN Doc HRI/GEN/1/Rev.1 at 30 (1994).

—— General Comment no 24 (52), UN Doc CCPR/C/21/Rev.1/Add.6 (1994).

—— General Comment no 29, States of Emergency (Article 4), UN Doc CCPR/C/21/Rev.1/Add.11 (2001).

—— General Comment no 31, UN Doc CCPR/C/21/Rev.1/Add.13 (2004).

—— 'Summary record of the 2283rd meeting', UN Doc CCPR/C/SR.2283, 18 July 2005.

—— 'Summary record of the 2317th Meeting', UN Doc CCPR/C/SR.2317, 26 October 2005.

Human Rights in Armed Conflicts, International Conference on Human Rights, Teheran, Res no XXII, 12 May 1968.

Identical letters, dated 13 July 2006, from the Chargé d'affaires a.i. of the Permanent Mission of Lebanon to the United Nations addressed to the Secretary-General and the President of the Security Council, UN Doc. A/60/938-S/2006/518.

International Maritime Organization, 'Code of Practice for the Investigation of the Crimes of Piracy and Armed Robbery Against Ships 2001' Resolution A.922(22).

—— 'Reports on Piracy and armed robbery against ships'.

Israeli Government, Cabinet Communique, 16 July 2006.

—— 'Hizbullah attack' Special Cabinet Communique, 12 July 2006.

Letter, dated 27 July 1842, from Mr. Webster to Lord Ashburton, Department of State, Washington.

Letter, dated 6 August 1842, from Mr. Webster to Lord Ashburton, Department of State, Washington.

Letter, dated 25 May 1993, from the Permanent Representative of the Islamic Republic of Iran to the United Nations Addresses to the Secretary General UN Doc. S/25843.

Letter, dated 20 August 1998, from the Permanent Representative of the United States of America, to the United Nations, Addressed to the President of the Security Council, UN SCOR, 53d session at 1, UN Doc S/1998/780.

Letter, dated 7 October 2001, from the Permanent Representative of the United States of America, to the United Nations, Addressed to the President of the Security Council, UN SCOR, 56th session at 1; UN Doc S/2001/946 (2001).

'List of issues to be considered during the examination of the second periodic report of the United States of America, Response of the United States of America', Committee Against Torture, 36th Session, 1–19 May 2006, 87. See also statement of UK delegation to CAT in 'UNCAT Hearing: Provisions of lists of issues to state parties', Committee Against Torture, 33rd Session, 15–26 November 2004.

Lord Goldsmith, Attorney General of the UK, House of Lords, Hansard, column 370, 21 April 2004.

Memorandum, dated 22 January 2002, from Jay S Bybee, Assistant Attorney General, to Alberto R Gonzales, Counsel to the President, and William J Haynes Ii, General Counsel of the Department of Defense in *The Torture Papers: The Road to Abu Ghraib*, Dratel, K. and Greenberg, J. (eds) 118–21 (Cambridge University Press: New York, 2005).

Memorandum, dated 25 January 2002, from Alberto R Gonzales, Counsel to the President, to President Bush in *The Torture Papers: The Road to Abu Ghraib*, Dratel, K. and Greenberg, J. (eds) 118–21 (Cambridge University Press: New York, 2005).

Mueller, R., 'From 9/11 to 7/7: Global Terrorism Today and the Challenges of Tomorrow', Transcript of Chatham House Event, 7 April 2008.

'The National Defense Strategy of the United States of America' US Department of Defense, March 2005.

'The National Security Strategy of the United States of America' The White House, September 2002.

NATO Press Release 124, 12 September 2001, available at <http://www.nato.int/docu/pr/2001/p01-124e.htm>.

NATO Counter Piracy Operation Ocean Shield, available at <http://www.shipping.nato.int/CounterPir/Operations>.

Press Conference on Special Working Group on Crime of Aggression, UN Department of Public Information, News and Media Division, New York, 13 February 2009.

'Protect, Respect and Remedy: a Framework for Business and Human Rights, Report of the Special Representative of the Secretary-General on the issue of Human Rights and Transnational Corporations and other Business Enterprises, John Ruggie', UN Doc A/HRC/8/5, 7 April 2008.

Provisional Summary Record of the 196th Meeting, UN ESCOR Human Rights Committee, 6th session, UN doc, E/CN.4/SR.196 (1950).

Rawcliffe, J. and Smith, J. (eds), *The US Operational Law Handbook*, International and Operational Law Department, The Judge Advocate General's Legal Center and School, August 2006.

'Remarks by Alberto R Gonzales Counsel to the President Before the American Bar Association Standing Committee on Law and National Security' Washington DC, 24 February 2004.

'Replies of the Government of the Netherlands to the concerns expressed by the Human Rights Committee in its concluding observations', UN Doc CCPR/CO/72/NET/Add.1, 29 April 2003.

Report of the Chairperson-Rapporteur of the Working Group on Arbitrary Detention, Leila Zerrougui; the Special Rapporteur on the independence of judges and lawyers,

Leandro Despouy; the Special Rapporteur on torture and other cruel, inhuman or degrading treatment or punishment, Manfred Nowak; the Special Rapporteur on freedom of religion or belief, Asma Jahangir; and the Special Rapporteur on the right of everyone to the enjoyment of the highest attainable standard of physical and mental health, Paul Hunt, E/CN.4/2006/120, 27 February 2006.

Report of the Commission of Inquiry on Lebanon pursuant to Human Rights Council resolution S-2/1, UN Doc.A/HRC/3/2, 23 November 2006.

Report of the Committee against Torture, General Assembly, Official Records, 52nd session, Supp No 44 (A/52/44).

Report of the Committee against Torture (A/56/44) 12 October 2001.

Report of the Human Rights Committee, vol 1 (A/50/40) (Supp).

Report of the Special Rapporteur on extrajudicial, summary or arbitrary executions, Asma Jahangir Addendum, Summary of cases transmitted to Governments and replies received, UN Doc. E/CN.4/2004/7/Add.1, 24 March 2004.

Report of the Special Rapporteur on extrajudicial, summary or arbitrary executions, Philip Alston, Addendum, Summary of cases transmitted to Government and replies received, UN Doc E/CN 4/2006/53, 8 March 2006.

Report of the Special Rapporteur on extrajudicial, summary or arbitrary executions, Philip Alston; the Special Rapporteur on the right of everyone to the enjoyment of the highest attainable standard of physical and mental health, Paul Hunt; the Representative of the Secretary-General on human rights of internally displaced persons, Walter Kälin; and the Special Rapporteur on adequate housing as a component of the right to an adequate standard of living, Miloon Kothari, Mission to Lebanon and Israel, UN Doc A/HRC/2/7, 7–14 September 2006.

Report of the Special Rapporteur on the promotion and protection of human rights and fundamental freedoms while countering terrorism, Martin Scheinin, Mission to the United States of America/Advance edited version/A/HRC/6/17/Add.3, 25 October 2007.

Report of the Special Representative of the Secretary-General on the issue of Human Rights and Transnational Corporations and other Business Enterprises, Addendum, Corporations and Human Rights: a Survey of the Scope and Patterns of Alleged Corporate-Related Human Rights Abuse, UN Doc. A/HRC/8/5/Add.2, 23 May 2008.

Report of the Special Working Group on the Crime of Aggression, UN Doc. ICC-ASP/7/20/Add.1.

Report on the situation of human rights in Kuwait under Iraqi occupation, prepared by the Special Rapporteur of the Commission on Human Rights, Kalin, W., in accordance with Comm Res no 1991/67i (E/CN.4/1992/26), 15 January 1992.

Resolution adopted by the Security Council at its 868th Meeting on 23 June 1960 (on questions relating to the case of Adolf Eichmann), UN Doc S/4349.

Resolution 1583 (2005) adopted by the Security Council at its 5117th meeting, on 28 January 2005, UN Doc. S/RES/1583 (2005).

Resolution 1614 (2005) adopted by the Security Council at its 5241st meeting, on 29 July 2005, UN Doc. S/RES/1614 (2005).

Resolution 1655 (2006) adopted by the Security Council at its 5362nd meeting, on 31 January 2006, UN Doc. S/RES/1655 (2006).

'Responsibility for the Terrorist Atrocities in the United States, 11 September 2001—an Updated Account', UK Government press release.

Restatement (Third) of the Foreign Relations Law of the United States, section 702, 1987.

'Safeguards Guaranteeing Protection of the Rights of Those Facing the Death Penalty', ESC Res 1984/50, annex, 1984 UN ESCOR Supp no 1 at 33, UN Doc E/1984/84 (1984).

Secretary of Defense, Donald Rumsfeld, 'US National Military Strategic Plan for the War on Terrorism', Chairman of the Joint Chiefs of Staff, Washington DC 20318, 1 February 2006.

Secretary Rumsfeld Speaks on '21st Century Transformation' of US Armed Forces (transcript of remarks and question and answer period), Remarks as Delivered by Secretary of Defense Donald Rumsfeld, National Defense University, Fort McNair, Washington, DC, Thursday, 31 January 2002.

Security Council Resolution no 237 (1967), 14 June 1967.

Security Council Resolution no 487 (1981), 19 June 1981.

Security Council Resolution no 1368 (2001), adopted by the Security Council at its 4370th meeting, 12 September 2001.

Security Council Resolution no 1373 (2001), adopted by the Security Council at its 4385th meeting, 28 September 2001.

Security Council Resolution no 1846 (2008) adopted by the Security Council at its 6026th meeting, UN Doc S/RES/1846, 2 December 2008.

Security Council Resolution no 1851 (2008), adopted by the Security Council at its 6046th meeting, UN Doc S/RES/1851, 16 December 2008.

Security Council Official Records, 31st Year, 1939th Meeting, 9 July 1976, New York, UN Doc S/PV.1939 (1976).

Security Council Official Records, 31st Year, 1940th Meeting, 12 July 1976, New York UN Doc S/PV.1940(OR).

Statement by Ambassador Dan Gillerman, Permanent Representative, Emergency Session, Security Council, New York, 5 October 2003.

Statement by Ambassador Dan Gillerman, Permanent Representative, During the open debate on 'The Situation in the Middle East', Security Council, New York, 30 July 2006.

Statement by Ambassador Dan Gillerman, Permanent Representative, During the open debate on 'The Situation in the Middle East', Security Council, New York, 31 July 2006.

Statement by Ambassador Dan Gillerman, Permanent Representative, During the open debate on 'The Situation in the Middle East', United Nations, New York, 8 August 2006.

Statement of the Organization of American States, 'Support for the Measures of Individual and Collective Self-Defense Established in Resolution Rc.24/Res. 1/01', Oea/Ser.F/Ii.24, Cs/Tiar/Res. 1/01, 16 October 2001.

UN ESCOR Human Rights Committee, Summary Record of the 138th Meeting, 6th session, UN Doc, E/CN.4/SR.138 (1950).

UN ESCOR Human Rights Committee, Summary Record of the 194th Meeting, 6th session, UN Doc, E/CN.4/SR.194 (1950).

Testimony of Brigadier General Mendelblit, A., Israeli Military Advocate General, before the Winograd Commission of Inquiry into the Events of Military Engagement in Lebanon, 2006.

'Third periodic reports of states parties due in 2003', United States of America, UN Doc CCPR/C/USA/3, 28 November 2005.

'Transnational Terrorism: The Threat to Australia' Government of Australia, 2004.

UK Foreign and Commonwealth Office position in frequently asked questions about Piracy: available at <http://www.fco.gov.uk/en/global-issues/conflict-prevention/piracy/faq>.

UK Secretary of State for Defence Reid addresses RUSI on '20th-Century Rules, 21st-Century Conflict', 3 April 2006.

UN Expert on Extrajudicial Killings tells United States War on Terror could Undermine Human Rights Accountability, UNHCHR Press Release, 28 March 2007.

US Department of Defense Military Commission Instruction no 2: Crimes and Elements for Trials by Military Commission, Section 5C, 30 April 2003.

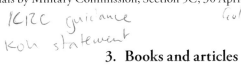

ICRC guidance   *Goldstone*
Koh statement

3. Books and articles

Abi-Saab, R., 'Humanitarian Law and Internal Conflicts: The Evolution of Legal Concern' in Delissen, A. and Tanja, G. (eds) *Humanitarian Law of Armed Conflict Challenges Ahead: Essays in Honour of Frits Kalshoven* (Martinus Nijhoff: Dordrecht, 1991).

Abramovsky, A., 'Extraterritorial Abductions: America's 'Catch And Snatch' Policy Run Amok' 31 *Virginia Journal of International Law* 151 (1991).

Alexandrov, S., *Self-Defense Against the Use of Force in International Law* (Kluwer Law International: The Hague, 1996).

Bassiouni, C., 'Legal Control of International Terrorism: A Policy-Oriented Assessment' 43 *Harvard International Law Journal* 83 (2002).

Baxter, R., 'So-Called "Unprivileged Belligerency": Spies, Guerrillas and Saboteurs' 28 *British Yearbook of International Law* 323 (1951).

Bellinger, J., 'Legal Issues in the War on Terrorism' International Humanitarian Law Project Lecture Series, London School of Economics, 31 October 2006.

X Ben-Naftali, O. and Shany, Y., 'Living in Denial: The Application of Human Rights in the Occupied Territories' 37 *Israel Law Review* 17 (2003–4).

Bethlehem, D., 'International law and the use of force: the law as it is and as it should be', written evidence submitted by Daniel Bethlehem QC, Director of Lauterpacht Research Centre for International Law, University of Cambridge Select Committee on Foreign Affairs, Minutes of Evidence, 8 June 2004.

Bond, J., *The Rules of Riot: Internal Conflict and the Law of War* (Princeton University Press: Princeton, 1974).

Bothe, M., 'Terrorism and the Legality of Pre-emptive Force' 14 *European Journal of International Law* 227 (2003).

Bowett, D., *Self-Defence in International Law* (Manchester University Press: Manchester, 1958).

—— 'Reprisals Involving Recourse To Armed Force', 66 *American Journal of International Law* 1 (1972).

Boyle, CK., 'The concept of arbitrary deprivation of life' in BG Ramcharan (ed.), *The Right to Life in International Law* (Nijhoff: Dordrecht, 1985).

Bradford, W., '"The Duty to Defend Them": A Natural Law Justification for the Bush Doctrine of Preventive War' 79 *Notre Dame Law Review* 1365 (2004).

Brooks, R., 'War Everywhere: Rights, National Security Law, and the Law of Armed Conflict in the Age of Terror' 153 *University of Pennsylvania Law Review* 675 (2004).

Brownlie, I., *International Law and the Use of Force by States* (Oxford University Press: Oxford, 1963).

—— *Principles of Public International Law* (Oxford University Press: Oxford, 2003).

Buergenthal, T., 'To Respect and to Ensure: State Obligations and Permissible Derogations' in Henkin, L. (ed.) *The International Bill of Human Rights* (Colombia Univerity Press: New York, 1981).

Burke, J., *Al-Qaeda: Casting a Shadow of Terror* (IB Tauris: London, 2003).

Cannizaro, E., 'Contextualizing Proportionality: Jus ad Bellum and Jus in Bello in the Lebanon War' 864 *International Review of the Red Cross* 779 (2006).

Cassese, A., 'The Status of Rebels Under the 1977 Geneva Protocol on Non-International Armed Conflicts' 30 *International & Comparative Law Quartely* 416 (1981).

—— *International Law* (Oxford University Press: Oxford, 2005).

Cayci, S., 'Countering Terrorism and International Law: the Turkish Experience' in Schmitt, M. and Beruto, G. (eds) *Terrorism and International Law: Challenges and Responses* (International Institute of Humanitarian Law, 2002), 137–46.

—— 'Terrorist Warfare and the Law of Armed Conflict: A Guide for the Theatre Commander' in WP Heere (ed.), *Terrorism and the Military: International Legal Implications* (Asser: The Hague, 2003) 93–100.

Chesney, R., 'National Insecurity: Nuclear Material Availability And The Threat Of Nuclear Terrorism' 20 *Loyola of Los Angeles International and Comparative Law Review* 29 (1997).

Clapham, A., *Human Rights Obligations of Non-State Actors* (Oxford University Press: Oxford, 2006).

D'Amato, A., 'Editorial Comment: Israel's Air Strike upon the Iraqi Nuclear Reactor' 77 *American Journal of International Law* 584 (1983).

Dalton, J., 'What is War?: Terrorism as War after 9/11' 12 *ILSA Journal of International and Comparative Law* 523 (2006).

Danner, M., *Torture and Truth* (Granta: London, 2005).

Delahunty, R., 'Paper Charter: Self-Defense and the Failure of the United Nations Collective Security System' 56 *Catholic University Law Review* 871 (2007).

Delbruck, J., 'Proportionality', Encyclopaedia of Public International Law, Vol. 7 (Elsevier Science Publishers: 1984).

Dennis, M., 'ICJ Advisory Opinion on Construction of a Wall in the Occupied Palestinian Territory: Application of human rights treaties extraterritorially in times of armed conflict and military occupation', 99 *American Journal of International Law* 119 (2005).

—— 'Application of Human Rights Treaties Extraterritorially to Detention of Combatants and Security Internees: Fuzzy Thinking All Around?' *ILSA Journal of International and Comparative Law* 459 (Spring 2006).

—— 'Non-Application of Civil and Political Rights Extraterritorially During Times of International Armed Conflict' 40 *Israel Law Review* 453 (2007).

Dershowitz, A., 'Tortured Reasoning' in Levinson, S. (ed.), *Torture* (Oxford University Press: Oxford, 2004) 257–80.

—— 'The Torture Warrant: a Response to Professor Strauss' 48 *New York Law School Law Review* 275 (2004).

Dinstein, Y., 'Dinstein, Comment' at the conference *Terrorism as a Challenge for National and International Law*, Max-Planck Institute for Comparative Public Law and International Law in Heidelberg, 24–5 January 2003.

—— 'Ius Ad Bellum Aspects of the "War on Terrorism"' in WP Heere (ed.), *Terrorism and the Military: International Legal Implications* (Asser: The Hague, 2003).

—— *The Conduct of Hostilities Under the Law of International Armed Conflict* (Cambridge University Press: Cambridge, 2004).

—— *War, Aggression, and Self-Defence* (Cambridge University Press: Cambridge, 2005).

—— Garraway, C. and Schmitt, M., *The Manual on the Law of Non-International Armed Conflict: With Commentary* (International Institute of Humanitarian Law: San Remo, 2006).

Dixon, M. and McCorquodale, R., *Cases and Materials on International Law* (Oxford University Press: Oxford, 2003).

Dorman, K., 'The Legal Situation of "Unlawful/Unprivileged Combatants"' 849 *International Review of the Red Cross* 45 (2003).

Doswald-Beck, L., 'The Legal Validity of Military Intervention by Invitation of the Government' 56 *British Yearbook of International Law* 189 (1985).

—— 'The Civilian in the Crossfire' 24 *Journal of Peace Research* 251 (1987).

—— 'The Right to Life in Armed Conflict: Does International Humanitarian Law Provide all the Answers?' 864 *International Review of the Red Cross* 881 (2006).

—— and Vité, S., 'International Humanitarian Law and Human Rights Law' 293 *International Review of the Red Cross* 94 (1993).

Draper, GIAD., 'The relationship between the human rights regime and the law of armed conflicts' 1 *Israel Yearbook on Human Rights* 191 (1971).

Droege, C., 'The Interplay Between International Humanitarian Law and International Human Rights Law in Situations of Armed Conflict' 40 *Israel Law Review* 310 (2007).

Duffy, H., *The 'War on Terror' and the Framework of International Law* (Cambridge University Press: Cambridge, 2005).

Dworkin, A., 'Revising the Laws of War to Account for Terrorism: The Case Against Updating the Geneva Conventions, On the Ground That Changes Are Likely Only to Damage Human Rights' *FindLaw's Legal Commentary*, 4 February 2003, available at <http://writ.findlaw.com/commentary/20030204_dworkin.html>.

—— 'Military Necessity and Due Process: The Place of Human Rights in the War on Terror' in Wippman, D. and Evangelista, M. (eds), *New Wars, New Laws?* (Transnational Publishers: New York, 2005).

Expert Meeting on the Right to Life in Armed Conflicts and Situations of Occupation, The University Centre for International Humanitarian Law, Geneva, 2005.

Feder, N., 'Reading the U.N. Charter Connotatively: Toward a New Definition of Armed Attack' 19 *New York University Journal of International Law and Politics* 395 (1987).

Feinrider, M., 'Kidnapping' in *Encyclopedia of Public International Law Vol III*, (Elsevier Science: Netherlands, 1997).

Fenrick, W., 'The Rule of Proportionality and Protocol I in Conventional Warfare' 98 *Military Law Review* 91 (1982).

Finch, G., 'Mexico and the United States' 11 *American Journal of International Law* 399 (1917).

Finkelstein, M., 'Legal Perspectives in the Fight Against Terror—The Israeli Experience' 1 *IDF Law Review* 341 (2003).

Fischer, H., 'The Status of Unlawful Combatants' in WP Heere (ed.), *Terrorism and the Military: International Legal Implications* (Asser: The Hague, 2003) 101–6.

Franck, T., 'Editorial Comments: Terrorism and the Right of Self-Defense', 95 *American Journal of International Law* 839, 840 (2001).

—— *Recourse to Force: State Action Against Threats and Armed Attacks* (Cambridge University Press: Cambridge, 2002).

—— and Lockwood, B., 'Preliminary Thoughts towards an International Convention on Terrorism' 68 *American Journal of International Law* 69 (1974).

Frowein, J., 'The Relationship between Human Rights Regimes and Regimes of Belligerent Occupation' 28 *Israel Yearbook of Human Rights* 1 (1998).

Gardam, J., *Necessity, Proportionality and the use of Force by States* (Cambridge University Press: Cambridge, 2004).

Garraway, C., 'Discussion' in WP Heere (ed.), *Terrorism and the Military: International Legal Implications* (Asser: The Hague, 2003).

—— 'The "War on Terror": Do the Rules Need Changing?' Briefing Paper IL BP 06/02, The Royal Institute of International Affairs, September 2006.

HP Gasser, 'Internationalized Non-international Armed Conflicts: Case Studies of Afghanistan, Kampuchea, and Lebanon', 33 *American University Law Review* 145 (1983).

Geiss, R., 'Asymmetric Conflict Structures' 864 *International Review of the Red Cross* 757 (2006).

Gill, T., 'The Eleventh of September and the Right of Self-Defense' in WP Heere (ed.), *Terrorism and the Military: International Legal Implications* (Asser: The Hague, 2003).

Gillard, E., 'The Complementary Nature of Human Rights Law, International Humanitarian Law and Refugee Law' in Schmitt, M. and Beruto, G. (eds) *Terrorism and International Law: Challenges and Responses* (International Institute of Humanitarian Law, 2002).

Ginbar, Y., *Why Not Torture Terrorists? Moral, Practical, and Legal Aspects of the 'Ticking Bomb' Justification for Torture* (Oxford University Press: Oxford, 2008).

Goldman, R. and Tittemore, B., 'Unprivileged Combatants and the Hostilities in Afghanistan: Their Status and Rights Under International Humanitarian and Human Rights Law' American Society of International Law Task Force on Terrorism, Task Force Papers, December 2002.

Goodman, R., 'Invalid Reservations and State Consent' 96 *American Journal of International Law* 531 (2002).

Gormley, WP., 'The Right to Life and the Rule of Non-Derogatability: Peremptory Norms of Jus Cogens' in Ramcharan (ed.), *The Right to Life in International Law* (Martinus Nijhoff: Dordrecht 1985) 120–59.

Gray, C., *International Law and the Use of Force* (Oxford University Press: Oxford, 2004).

Green, LC., 'Colloquy on the law of armed conflict: The unified use of force and exclusionary rules—The "unified use of force rule" and the law of armed conflict: A reply to Professor Martin', 65 *Saskatchewan Law Review* 427 (2002).

Greenberg, K. and Dratel, J. (eds), *The Torture Papers: The Road to Abu Ghraib* (Cambridge University Press: New York 2005).

Greenwood, C., 'The Relationship between Ius ad Bellum and Ius in Bello' 9 *Review of International Studies* 221 (1983).

—— 'The Concept of War in Modern International Law' 36 *International Comaprative Law Quarterly* 283 (1987).

—— 'Scope of Application of Humanitarian Law' in Fleck, D. (ed.), *The Handbook of Humanitarian Law in Armed Conflicts* (Oxford University Press: Oxford, 1995) 39–63.

—— 'International Humanitarian Law and the Tadic Case' 7 *European Journal of International Law* 265 (1996).

—— 'Remarks, Bombing for Peace: Collateral Damage and Human Rights', 96 *American Society of International Law Proceedings* 95, (2002).

—— 'International Law and the Pre-emptive Use of Force: Afghanistan, Al-Qaida, and Iraq', 4 *San Diego International Law Journal* 7, 17 (2003).

Gross, O., 'Are Torture Warrants Warranted? Pragmatic Absolutism and Official Disobedience' 88 *Minnesota Law Review* 1481 (2004).

—— and Ni Aolain, F., *Law in Times of Crisis* (Cambridge University Press: Cambridge, 2006).

Grotius, H., *Law of War and Peace (De Jure Belli ac Pacis)* originally published in 1625, English translation by John W Parker (Cambridge, 1853).

Guilfoyle, D., *Shipping Interdiction and the Law of the Sea* (Cambridge University Press: Cambridge, 2009).

Hampson, F., 'Means and Methods of Warfare in the Conflict in the Gulf', in Rowe, P. (ed.), *The Gulf War 1990–91 in International and English Law* (Routledge: New York, 1993).

—— 'Reservations to Human Rights Treaties,' working paper submitted to the Commission on Human Rights pursuant to Sub-Commission decision 1998–113, E/CN.4/Sub.2/199/28.

—— 'Detention, the "War on Terror" and International Law' in Hensel, H. (ed.), *The Law of Armed Conflict: Constraints on the Contemporary Use of Military Force* (Ashgate: Aldershot, 2005) 131–70.

—— and Salama, I., 'Working paper on the relationship between human rights law and international humanitarian law', UN Sub-Commission on the Promotion and Protection of Human Rights, E/CN.4/Sub.2/2005/14, 21 June 2005.

Hannum, H., 'Remarks, Bombing for Peace: Collateral Damage and Human Rights', 96 *American Society of International Law Proceedings* 95 (2002).

Hargrove, J., 'Appraisals of the ICJ's Decision: Nicaragua v. United States (Merits)' 81 *American Journal of International Law* 135 (1987).

Henckaerts, J. and Doswald-Beck, L., *Customary International Humanitarian Law Vol. 1: Rules* (Cambridge University Press: Cambridge, 2005).

Henkin, L., 'The Reports of the Death of Article 2(4) are Greatly Exaggerated' 65 *American Journal of International Law* 544 (1971).

Higgins, R., 'The Attitude of Western states Towards Legal Aspects of the Use of Force' in Cassese, A. (ed.), *The Current Legal Regulation of the Use of Force* (Martinus Nijhoff: Dordrecht 1986).

—— *Problems and Process: International Law and How We Use It* (Clarendon Press: Oxford, 1994).

Hoffman, B., 'Terrorism Trends and Prospects' in Lesser, I., Hoffman, B., Arquilla, J., Ronfeldt, D. and Zanini, M., *Countering the New Terrorism* (RAND: Santa Monica, 1999).

Ipsen, K., 'Combatants and Non-Combatants' in Fleck, D. (ed.), *The Handbook of Humanitarian Law in Armed Conflicts* (Oxford University Press: Oxford, 1995) 65–104.

Jaffer, J. and Singh, A., *Administration of Torture: A Documentary Record from Washington to Abu Ghraib and Beyond* (Columbia University Press, 2007).

Jennings, R., 'The Caroline and McLeod Cases' 32 *American Journal of International Law* 82 (1938).

—— and Watts, A. (eds), *Oppenheim's International Law Ninth Edition Vol. 1 Peace*, (Longman: London, 1992).

Jinks, D., 'September 11 and the Laws of War' 28 *Yale Journal of International Law* 1(2003).

—— 'The Applicability of the Geneva Conventions to the "Global War on Terrorism"' 46 *Virginia Journal of International Law* 165 (2005).

Joseph, S., Schultz, J. and Castan, M., *The International Covenant on Civil and Political Rights: Cases, Materials, and Commentary* (Oxford University Press: Oxford 2004).

Keijzer, N., 'Terrorism as a Crime' in WP Heere (ed.) *Terrorism and the Military: International Legal Implications* (Asser: The Hague, 2003).

Klabbers, J., 'Rebel with a Cause? Terrorists and Humanitarian Law' 14 *European Journal of International Law* 299 (2003).

Kleffner, J., 'From "Belligerents" to "Fighters" and Civilians Directly Participating in Hostilities—on the Principle of Distinction in Non-International Armed Conflicts One Hundred Years after the Second Hague Peace Conference' *Netherlands International Law Review* 315 (2007).

Koplow, D., 'That Wonderful Year: Smallpox, Genetic Engineering, and Bio-Terrorism' 62 *Maryland Law Review* 417 (2003).

Korekelia, K., 'New Challenges to the Regime of Reservations under the International Covenant on Civil and Political Rights' 13 *European Journal of International Law* 437 (2002).

Kretzmer, D., 'Targeted Killing of Suspected Terrorists: Extra-Judicial Executions or Legitimate Means of Defence?' 16 *European Journal of International Law* 171 (2005).

Kunz, J., 'Individual and collective Self-Defense in Article 51 of the charter of the United Nations' *AJIL Editorial Comment* 872 (1947).

Lawson, R., 'Life After Bankovic: On the Extraterritorial Application of the European Convention on Human Rights' in Coomans, F. and Kamminga, M. (eds), *Extraterritorial Application of Human Rights Treaties* (Intersentia: Antwerp, 2004) 83–123.

WK Lietzau, 'Combating Terrorism: Law Enforcement or War?' in Schmitt, M. and G Beruto (eds) *Terrorism and International Law: Challenges and Responses* (International Institute of Humanitarian Law, 2002).

Lillich, R., 'The Growing Importance of Customary International Human Rights Law' 25 *Georgia Journal of International and Comparative Law* 1.

Lippman, M., 'The Trial of Adolf Eichmann and the Protection of Universal Human Rights under International Law' 5 *Houston Journal of International Law* 1 (1982).

—— 'The New Terrorism and International Law' 10 *Tulsa Journal of Comparative and International Law* 297 (2003).

Loucaides, L., 'Determining the Extra-territorial Effect of the European Convention: Facts, Jurisprudence and the Bankovic Case' 4 *European Human Rights Law Review* 391 (2006).

Lubell, N., 'Challenges in Applying Human Rights Law to Armed Conflict' 859 *International Review of the Red Cross* 737 (December 2005).

—— 'Parallel Application of International Humanitarian Law and International Human Rights Law: An Examination of the Debate' 40(2) *Israel Law Review* 648 (2007).

Martin, F.F., 'Using international human rights law for establishing a unified use of force rule in the law of armed conflict', 64 *Saskatchewan Law Review* 347 (2001).

McDonald, A., 'Terrorism, Counter-terrorism and the Jus in Bello' in Schmitt, M. and G Beruto (eds) *Terrorism and International Law: Challenges and Responses* (International Institute of Humanitarian Law, 2002).

McGoldrick, D., *From '9-11' to the 'Iraq War 2003'* (Hart: Oxford, 2004).

—— 'Extraterritorial Application of the International Covenant on Civil and Political Rights' in Coomans, F. and Kamminga, M. (eds), *Extraterritorial Application of Human Rights Treaties* (Intersentia: Antwerp, 2004) 41–72.

Meron, T., 'The 1994 U.S. Action in Haiti: Extraterritoriality of Human Rights Treaties', 89 *American Journal of International Law* 78 (1995).

Milanovic, M., 'From Compromise to Principle: Clarifying the Concept of State Jurisdiction in Human Rights Treaties' 8 *Human Rights Law Review* 411 (2008).

Mohamedou, M., 'Non-Linearity of Engagement: Transnational Armed Groups, International Law, and the Conflict between Al Qaeda and the United States' Program on Humanitarian Policy and Conflict Research, Harvard University, July 2005.

Moir, L., *The Law of Internal Armed Conflict* (Cambridge University Press: Cambridge, 2008).

Moore, JB., 'The Caroline (exchange of diplomatic notes between Great Britain, Ashburton, and the United States, Webster 1942)' 2 *Digest of International Law* 409, 412 (1906).

Mose, E. and Opsahl, T., 'The optional Protocol to the International Covenant on Civil and Political Rights' 21 *Santa Clara Law Review* 271 (1981).

Mullerson, R., '*Jus Ad Bellum: Plus Ça Change (Le Monde) Plus C'est La Même Chose (Le Droit)*?' 7 *Journal of Conflict and Security Law* 149 (2002).

Murphy, S., 'Contemporary Practice of the United States Relating to International Law, Legal Regulation of Use of Force: Terrorist Attacks on World Trade Center and Pentagon' 96 *American Journal of International Law* 237 (2002).

—— 'International Law, the United States, and the Non-military 'War' against Terrorism' 14 *European Journal of International Law* 347 (2003).

—— 'Self-Defense and the Israeli Wall Advisory Opinion: An Ipse Dixit from the ICJ?' 99 *American Journal of International Law* 62 (2005).

—— 'Evolving Geneva Convention Paradigms in the "War on Terrorism": Applying the Core Rules to the Release of Persons Deemed "Unprivileged Combatants"' The George Washington University Law School Public Law and Legal Theory Working Paper no 239 (2007).

Myjer, E. and White, N., 'The Twin Towers Attack: An Unlimited Right to Self-Defence?' 7 *Journal of Conflict and Security Law* 5 (2002).

Neff, S., *The Rights and Duties of Neutrals* (Manchester University Press: Manchester, 2000).

Nowak, M., *UN Covenant on Civil and Political Rights* (2nd ed.) (NP Engel: Germany, 2005).

—— 'What Practices Constitute Torture?: US and UN Standards' 28 *Human Rights Quarterly* 809 (2006).

O'Boyle, M., 'The European Convention on Human Rights and Extraterritorial Jurisdiction: A Comment on "Life After Bankovic"' in Coomans, F. and Kamminga, M. (eds) *Extraterritorial Application of Human Rights Treaties* (Intersentia: Antwerp, 2004) 125–39.

O'Brien, W., 'Reprisals, Deterrence and Self-Defense in Counterterror Operations' 30 *Virginia Journal of International Law* 421 (1990).

O'Connell, ME., 'War and Armed Conflict: Evidence of Terror' 7 *Journal of Conflict and Security Law* 19 (2002).

—— 'When Is a War Not a War? the Myth of the Global War on Terror,' *ILSA Journal of International and Comparative Law* 12 (2006).

Oeter, S., 'Methods and Means of Combat' in Fleck, D. (ed.) *The Handbook of Humanitarian Law in Armed Conflicts* (Oxford University Press: Oxford 1995) 105–207.

Oxman, B., 'Jurisdiction of States' in *Encyclopedia of Public International Law Vol III* (Elsevier Science: Netherlands, 1997) 55–60.

Parks, H., 'Memorandum of Law: Executive Order 12333 and Assassination' *Army Law* 4 (December 1989).

—— 'Air War and the Law of War' 32 *Air Force Law Review* 1 (1990).

—— 'Special Forces' Wear of Non-Standard Uniforms' 4 *Chicago Journal of International Law* 493 (2003).

—— 'The ICRC Customary Law Study: A Preliminary Assessment' 99 American Society of International Law Proceedings 208 (2005).

Paulus, A. and Vashakmadze, M., 'Asymmetrical War and the Notion of Armed Conflict—A Tentative Conceptualization' 873 *International Review of the Red Cross* 95 (2009).

Paust, J., 'Responding Lawfully to International Terrorism: The Use of Force Abroad' 8 *Whittier Law Review* 711 (1986).

—— 'After Alvarez-Machain: Abduction, Standing, Denials of Justice, and Unaddressed Human Rights Claims' 67 *Saint John's Law Review* 551 (1993).

—— 'Colloquy on the law of armed conflict: The unified use of force and exclusionary rules—The right to life in human rights law and the law of war', 65 *Saskatchewan Law Review* 411 (2002).

—— 'Use of Armed Force against Terrorists in Afghanistan, Iraq, and Beyond' 35 *Cornell International Law Journal* 533 (2002).

Pejic, J., 'Terrorist Acts and Groups: a Role for International Law?' 75 *British Year Book of International Law* 71 (2004).

—— 'Procedural Principles and Safeguards for Internment/Administrative Detention in Armed Conflict and Other Situations of Violence' 858 *International Review of the Red Cross* 375 (2005).

Pellet, A., '"No, This is not War!" The Attack on the World Trade Center: Legal Responses' *European Journal of International Law Discussion Forum*, 3 October 2001.

Pictet, J., (ed.), *Commentary on the Geneva Convention of 12 August 1949 for the Amelioration of the Condition of the Wounded and Sick in Armed Forces in the Field* (International Committee of the Red Cross: Geneva, 1958).

Pokempner, D., 'The "New" Non-State Actors in International Humanitarian Law' 38 *George Washington International Law Review* 551 (2006).

Posner, R., 'Torture, Terrorism, and Interrogation' in Levinson, S. (ed.) *Torture* (Oxford University Press: Oxford 2004) 291–8.

Poulantzas, N., *The Right of Hot Pursuit in International Law* (Kluwer Law International: The Hague, 2002).

Pratt, AN., '9/11 and Future Terrorism: Same Nature, Different Face' in Schmitt, M. and G Beruto (eds) *Terrorism and International Law: Challenges and Responses* (International Institute of Humanitarian Law, 2002).

Provost, R., *International Human Rights and Humanitarian Law* (Cambridge University Press: Cambridge, 2002).

Prud'homme, N., 'Lex Specialis: Oversimplifying a More Complex and Multifaceted Relationship?' 40 *Israel Law Review* 356 (2007).

—— *International Humanitarian Law and International Human Rights Law: From Separation to Complementarity* (PhD thesis in progress, draft on file with author).

Pugh, M., 'Legal Aspects of the Rainbow Warrior Affair' 36 *International & Comparative Law Quarterly* 655 (1987).

Ramcharan, BG., 'The Concepts and Dimensions of the Right to Life', in Ramcharan (ed.) *The Right to Life in International Law* (Nijhoff: Dordrecht, 1985) 1–32.

—— *The Concept and Present Status of the International Protection of Human Rights: Forty Years After the Universal Declaration* (Nijhoff: Dordrecht, 1989).

Randelzhofer, A., 'Article 2(4)' in Simma, B. (ed.), *The Charter of the United Nations, A Commentary* (Oxford University Press: Oxford, 1994) 108–9.

—— 'Article 51' in Simma, B. (ed.), *The Charter of the United Nations, A Commentary* (Oxford University Press: Oxford, 1994) 661–78.

Ratner, S., 'Revising the Geneva Conventions to Regulate Force by and Against Terrorists: Four Fallacies' 1 *Israel Defense Forces Law Review* 7 (2003).

Record, J., 'Bounding the Global War On Terrorism' US Strategic Studies Institute, December 2003.

Reid, J., 'Twenty-First Century Warfare—Twentieth Century Rules' 151 *The RUSI Journal* 3 (2006).

Reidy, A., 'The Approach of the European Commission and Court of Human Rights to International Humanitarian Law' 324 *International Review of the Red Cross* 513 (1998).

Reisman, M., 'Criteria for the Lawful Use of Force in International Law' 10 *Yale Journal of International Law* 279 (1985).

Roberts, A., 'The So-Called "Right" of Humanitarian Intervention' *Yearbook of International Humanitarian Law* (2000) 3–52.

—— 'The Laws of War in the War on Terror' *Israel Yearbook on Human Rights* 32 (2003), 193–245.

Rodley, N., *The Treatment of Prisoners under International Law* (Oxford University Press: Oxford, 1999).

—— 'The Definition(s) of Torture in International Law' in Freeman, M. (ed.), *Current Legal Problems 2002* (Oxford University Press: Oxford, 2003) 467–93.

—— 'The Prohibition of torture: Absolute Means Absolute' 34 *Denver Journal of International Law and Policy* 145 (2006).

—— and Cali, B., 'Kosovo Revisited: Humanitarian Intervention on the Fault Lines of International Law 7 *Human Rights Law Review* 275 (2007).

Rogers, APV., *Law on the Battlefield* (Manchester University Press, Manchester 2004).

—— 'Humanitarian Intervention and International Law' 27 *Harvard Journal of Law and Public Policy* 725 (2004).

Rona, G., 'Interesting Times for International Humanitarian Law: Challenges from the "War on Terror"' 27 *Fletcher Forum of World Affairs* 2 (2003).

Rosas, A., *The Legal Status of Prisoners of War: A Study in International Humanitarian Law Applicable in Armed Conflict* (The Finnish Academy of Science and Letters: Helsinki, 1976).

Roxstrom, E., Gibney, M. and Einarsen, T., 'The NATO Bombing Case (*Bankovic and ors. v. Belgium and ors.*) and the Limits of Western Human Rights Protection' 23 *Boston University International Law Journal* 55.

Sands, P., 'International Law and the Use of Force', written evidence submitted by Professor Philippe Sands QC, to Select Committee on Foreign Affairs, 1 June 2004.

Sassoli, M., 'Transnational Armed Groups and International Humanitarian Law' Program on Humanitarian Policy and Conflict Research, Harvard University, Occasional Paper Series, no 6, Winter 2006.

Sassoli, M., 'Use and Abuse of the Laws of War in the "War on Terrorism"' *Law and Inequality: A Journal of Theory and Practice* 22 (2004).

Saul, B., 'Attempts to Define "Terrorism" in International Law' 52 *Netherlands International Law Review* 57 (2005).

Schabas, W., 'Lex specialis? Belt and suspenders? The Parallel Operation of Human Rights Law and the Law of Armed Conflict, and the Conundrum of Jus ad Bellum' 40 *Israel Law Review* 592 (2007).

Schachter, O., 'The Extraterritorial Use of Force Against Terrorist Bases' 11 *Houston Journal of International Law* 309 (1988–9).

Scheinin, M., 'Extraterritorial Effect of the International Covenant on Civil and Political Rights' in Coomans, F. and Kamminga, M. (eds) *Extraterritorial Application of Human Rights Treaties* (Intersentia: Antwerp, 2004) 73–81.

Schindler, D., 'The Different Types of Armed Conflicts According to the Geneva Conventions and Protocols', 163 *Recueil Des Cours* 117 (1979).

—— 'International Humanitarian Law and Internationalized Internal Armed Conflicts', 22 *International Review of the Red Cross* 255 (1982).

—— 'Human Rights and Humanitarian Law: Interrelationship of the Laws' 31 *American University Law Review* (1982).

Schmitt, M., 'Counter-Terrorism and the Use of Force in International Law' The Marshall Center Papers no 5, The George C Marshall European Center for Security Studies.

—— 'Computer Network Attack and the Use of Force in International Law: Thoughts on a Normative Framework' 37 *Columbia Journal of Transnational Law* 885 (1999).

—— 'Targeting and Humanitarian Law: Current Issues' 34 *Israel Yearbook on Human Rights* 59 (2004).

—— and Beruto, G. (eds) *Terrorism and International Law: Challenges and Responses* (International Institute of Humanitarian Law, 2002).

Schondorf, R., 'Extra-State Armed Conflicts: Is There a Need for a New Legal Regime?' 37 *New York University Journal of International Law and Politics* 1 (2004).

Schwelb, E., 'Civil and Political Rights: The International Measures of Implementation' 62 *American Journal of International Law* 827 (1968).

Scott, J., 'The American Punitive Expedition into Mexico' 10 *American Journal of International Law* 337 (1916).

Shany, Y., 'Israeli Counter-Terrorism Measures: Are they "Kosher" under International Law?' in Schmitt, M. and Beruto, G. (eds) *Terrorism and International Law: Challenges and Responses* (International Institute of Humanitarian Law, 2002).

Shaw, M., *International Law* (5th edn) (Cambridge University Press: Cambridge, 2003).

Shue, H., 'Mediating Duties' 98 Ethics 687 (1988).

—— 'Torture in Dreamland: Disposing of the Ticking Bomb' 37 *Case Western Reserve Journal of International Law* 231 (2005).

Singer, PW., *Wired for War: the Robotics Revolution and Conflict in the 21st Century* (Penguin Press: London, 2009).

Sievert, RJ., 'War on Terrorism or Global Law Enforcement Operation?' 78 *Notre Dame Law Review* 307 (2003).

Spieker, H., 'Twenty-five years after the adoption of Additional Protocol II: Breakthrough or failure of humanitarian legal protection?' in *Yearbook of International Humanitarian Law, Vol 4* (TMC Asser Press: The Hague, 2001).

Stewart, J., 'Towards a Single Definition of Armed Conflict in International Humanitarian Law: A Critique of Internationalized Armed Conflict', 850 *International Review of the Red Cross* 313 (2003).

Suter, K., 'An Inquiry into the Meaning of the Phrase "Human Rights in Armed Conflicts"' 15 *Revue de Droit Pénal Militaire et de Droit de la Guerre* 393 (1976).

Tams, C., 'The Use of Force against Terrorists' 20 *European Journal of International Law* 359 (2009).

Thompson, R., *Defeating Communist Insurgency: Experiences from Malaya and Vietnam: Studies in International Security no 10* (Chatto and Windus: 1966).

Tomuschat, C., *Human Rights: Between Idealism and Realism* (Oxford University Press: Oxford, 2003).

'Transnationality, War and the Law: A Report on a Roundtable on the Transformation of Warfare, International Law, and the Role of Transnational Armed Groups' Program on Humanitarian Policy and Conflict Research, Harvard University, April 2006.

Treves, T., 'Piracy, Law of the Sea, and Use of Force: Developments off the Coast of Somalia' 20 *European Journal of International Law* 399 (2009).

UK Ministry of Defence, *The Manual of the Law of Armed Conflict* (Oxford University Press: Oxford, 2004).

Van Boven, T., Flinterman, C., and Westendorp, I. (eds) 'The Maastricht Guidelines on Violations of Economic, Social and Cultural Rights 1996', SIM Special no 20, Netherlands Institute of Human Rights (1998).

de Vattel, E., *The Law of Nations, Applied to the Conduct and Affairs of Nations and Sovereigns,* Vol IV (7th edn) (J Chitty translation, 1849).

Vinuesa, RE., 'Interface, Correspondence and Convergence of Human Rights and International Humanitarian Law' *Yearbook of International Humanitarian Law Vol 1* (TMC Asser Press: The Hague, 1998).

Vite, S., 'The Interrelation of the Law of Occupation and Economic, Social and Cultural Rights: The Examples of Food, Health and Property' 871 *International Review of the Red Cross* 629 (September 2008).

Waldock, H., 'The Regulation of the Use of Force by Individual States in International Law' 81 *Recueil des Cours* 455 (1952).

Watkin, K., 'Controlling the Use of Force: A Role for Human Rights Norms in Contemporary Armed Conflict' 98 *American Journal of International Law* 1 (2004).

—— 'Canada/United States Military Interoperability and Humanitarian Law Issues: Land Mines, Terrorism, Military Objectives and Targeted Killing' 15 *Duke Journal of Comparative and International Law* 281 (2005).

Wedgwood, R., 'Military Commissions: Al Qaeda, Terrorism, and Military Commissions' 96 *American Journal of International Law* 328 (2002).

Wharton, *Criminal Law, vol I* (12th edn) (The Lawyers Co-operative Publishing Co: Rochester, NY, 1932).

Wilmshurst, E. (ed.), 'Principles of International Law on the Use of Force by States in Self-Defence' The Royal Institute of International Affairs, Chatham House, October 2005.

—— and Breau, S., (eds) *Perspectives on the ICRC Study on Customary International Humanitarian Law* (Cambridge University Press: Cambridge, 2007).

Wippman, D., 'Do New Wars Call for New Laws?' in Wippman, D. and Evangelista, M. (eds) *New Wars, New Laws?* (Transnational Publishers: New York, 2005).

[handwritten: Melzer / Cassese for PCATI / Showy on PCATI]

4. Miscellaneous, NGO documents, news and other organizations

'11 Pirates Seized by French Navy' *New York Times*, 15 April 2009.

'Abu Nidal' in Thackrah, J., *Dictionary of Terrorism* (Routledge: London, 2004) 1–3.

Amnesty International, 'Yemen/USA: Government Must Not Sanction Extra-Judicial Executions', 8 November 2002.

Beyer, L., 'The Myths and Reality of Munich' *Time Magazine*, 4 December 2005.

'CIA Holds Terror Suspects in Secret Prisons: Debate Is Growing Within Agency About Legality and Morality of Overseas System Set Up After 9/11' *Washington Post*, 2 November 2005.

'Capturing nuclear whistle-blower was "a lucky stroke", agents recall' *Haaretz*, 21 April 2004.

Condoleezza Rice on *Fox News Sunday*, 10 November 2002.

'DR Congo Troops to Uganda Border' *BBC News*, 5 October 2005.

'"Drone attack" kills Taliban wife' *BBC News*, 5 August 2009.

'Ethiopia urged to leave Somalia' *BBC News*, 27 December 2006.

Excerpts from interview with Charles Allen, Deputy General Counsel for International Affairs, US Department of Defense, by Anthony Dworkin, 16 December 2002, available at <http://www.crimesofwar.org/onnews/news-pentagon-trans.html>.

Exploring Criteria and Conditions for Engaging Armed Non-State Actors to Respect Humanitarian Law and Human Rights Law, Geneva, 5 June 2007, conference report available at <http://www.genevacall.org/resources/conference-reports/conference-reports.php>.

'Falklands war (1982)' in *The Oxford Companion to Military History* (Oxford University Press: Oxford, 2004).

'Falluja raid "hits wedding party"' *BBC News*, 8 October 2004.

'Farc aura of invincibility shattered' *BBC News*, 1 March 2008.

Fifth Expert Meeting on the Notion of Direct Participation in Hostilities, Geneva, 5–6 February 2008, Summary Report, International Committee of the Red Cross.

'For Many Israelis, Assassination Is Only as Bad as Its Execution' *Washington Post*, 12 October, 1997.

Fourth Expert Meeting on the Notion of Direct Participation in Hostilities, Geneva, 27–8 November 2006, Summary Report, International Committee of the Red Cross and the TMC Asser Institute.

'France detains Somali pirates, U.S. to boost fight' *Reuters*, 15 April 15, 2009.

Ghosh, B. and Thompson, M., 'The CIA's Silent War in Pakistan' *Time*, 1 June 2009.

Hersh, S., 'Manhunt' *The New Yorker* 23 December 2002.

'How is the Term "Armed Conflict" Defined in International Humanitarian Law?' Opinion Paper, International Committee of the Red Cross, March 2008.

Human Rights First, 'Ending Secret Detentions', June 2004.

—— 'Submission to HRC, 18 January 2006, Re: Follow-Up to Human Rights First's Memorandum to the Human Rights Committee', 18 October 2005.

Human Rights Watch, 'Why They Died: Civilian Casualties in Lebanon during the 2006 War' Vol 19, no 5(E), September 2007.

'The Hunt for Black September' *BBC News*, 24 January 2006.

Ignatius, D., 'A Quiet Deal With Pakistan' *Washington Post*, 4 November 2008.

'Incommunicado, Unacknowledged and Secret Detention Under International Law', Association for the Prevention of Torture, 2006.

'In depth—London attacks' *BBC News online*, available at <http://news.bbc.co.uk/2/hi/in_depth/uk/2005/london_explosions/default.stm>.

'In Qatar, Standing Up to Putin', *Washington Post*, 16 March 2004.

'International Humanitarian Law and the Challenges of Contemporary Armed Conflicts', International Committee of the Red Cross, 2003.

'Interpretive Guidance on the Notion of Direct Participation in Hostilities under International Humanitarian Law' ICRC, 2009.

'Italian cruise ship foils pirates' *BBC News*, 26 April 2009.

'Kidnapped by North Korea' *BBC News*, 5 March, 2003.

Kilcullen, D. and Exum, A., 'Death From Above, Outrage Down Below' *New York Times*, 16 May 2009.

'Killing probes the frontiers of robotics and legality' *The Guardian*, 6 November 2002.

'Lev Davidovich Trotsky' in *Dictionary of Political Biography* (Oxford University Press: Oxford, 2003).

'London bombings: the truth emerges' *The Independent,* 13 August 2005.

'Missile Strike Carried Out with Yemeni Cooperation—Official Says Operation Authorized Under Bush Finding' *Washington Post*, 6 November 2002.

Mueller, J., 'Terrorphobia: Our False Sense of Insecurity' *The American Interest*, vol 3, no 5, May–June 2008.

'NATO frees 20 hostages; pirates seize Belgian ship' *Associated Press*, 18 April 2009.

'Navy May Send Ships to Fight Colombia Drugs' *LA Times*, 23 November 1989.

'Obama Administration Says Goodbye to "War On Terror": US Defence Department Seems to Confirm use of the Bureaucratic Phrase "Overseas Contingency Operations"' *The Guardian*, 25 March 2009.

'Pakistan tries to ease tension after US attack' *Financial Times*, 16 January 2006.

'Pirates can claim UK asylum' *The Sunday Times*, 13 April 2008.

'Pirates halt Somali aid shipments' *BBC News*, 21 May 2007.

'Preventive measures' *Haaretz*, 17 February 2006.

'Questioning Terror Suspects in a Dark and Surreal World' *New York Times*, 9 March 2003.

'The Responsibility to Protect: Report of the International Commission on Intervention and State Sovereignty', International Development Research Centre, 2001.

Roggio, B. and Mayer, A., 'Analysis: A look at US airstrikes in Pakistan through September 2009' *The Long War Journal*, 1 October, 2009.

'Russia "to kill Iraq kidnappers"' *BBC News*, 28 June 2006.

'Scores die in Madrid bomb carnage' *BBC News*, 11 March 2004.

'Scramble for the Congo: Anatomy of an Ugly War' Africa Report no 26, International Crisis Group, 20 December 2000.

'Secretary Rumsfeld Speaks on "21st Century Transformation" of US Armed Forces', remarks as delivered by Secretary of Defense Donald Rumsfeld, National Defense University, Fort McNair, Washington, DC, 31 January 2002.

Security Authorities: Hezbollah and Hamas Networks are being Established in South America' *Haaretz*, 10 February 2004 (translated from original Hebrew).

'Terror cells regroup—and now their target is Europe' *The Observer*, 11 January 2004.

Third Expert Meeting on the Notion of Direct Participation in Hostilities, Geneva, International Committee of the Red Cross and the TMC Asser Institute, 2005.

'Threats and Responses: Hunt for Suspects; Fatal Strike in Yemen Was Based on Rules Set Out by Bush' *New York Times*, 6 November 2002.

'Timeline: Litvinenko death case' *BBC News online*, available at <http://news.bbc.co.uk/1/hi/uk/6179074.stm>.

'Turkish Incursions into Northern Iraq' *Reuters*, 22 February 2008.

'Turkish MPs back attacks in Iraq' *BBC News*, 18 October 2007.

'Under Obama, "War on Terror" Phrase Fading' *Associated Press*, 1 February, 2009.

'US bombs Islamist town in Somalia' *BBC News*, 3 March 2008.

'U.S. Decries Abuse but Defends Interrogations' *Washington Post*, 26 December 2002.

'US justifies Afghan wedding bombing' *BBC News*, 7 September 2002.

'U.S. Navy warships exchange gunfire with suspected pirates off Somali coast' *Seattle Times*, 19 March 2006.

'U.S. Strike Kills Six in Al Qaeda' *Washington Post*, 5 November, 2002.

'"US strike' kills Taleban leader' *BBC News*, 27 October 2008.

'Uzbek rebel 'killed' in Pakistan' 2 October 2009.

'The worst Islamist attack in European history' *The Guardian*, 31 October 2007.

Index

Self defense   IHRC
_____   _____

Nicaragua   Bankovic

ICJ The wall   Al Skeini

DRC v Uganda ~~Congo~~

Caroline.

IHL + IHRL   IHL   ⌒
_____   _____
P CATI 'targeted killings'   ←_____→
 - targets   2 positions   on NIAC
 - conduct.   participation

                                  add more Tadic.

Self defense (ad bellum)   (in bellum) IHL
actors - ~~state~~ / non-state.   reprisals   threshold (armed conflict)
necessity
      threshold (armed attack)   IAC / NIAC
                   reactive.   add
v. reprisals (ad bellum) - punitive. NYRB   legit. target
   - unlawful
   pre-emptive self-defence
   + imminence.

IHRL (law enforcement)   add occupation

ex-judic.   ППППП
                                  = in context   to IAC
                                  of occupation and add occ
necessity
                                        = IAC .   Art. 1 (4)
proporz.

_____   _____
    Self defence   IHL
    UN charter 2 (4) + 51   cleared -

IHRL   + ICRC
_____   SR
ICCPR   2008/me

Brownlee.

x Jurisdiction

Suscedi

Carsese .